Materializing *Six Years*

Materializing *Six Years*

Lucy R. Lippard and the Emergence of Conceptual Art

Edited by
Catherine Morris
Vincent Bonin

Preface by
Lucy R. Lippard

Essays by
Vincent Bonin
Julia Bryan-Wilson
Catherine Morris

Brooklyn Museum
Brooklyn, New York

The MIT Press
Cambridge, Massachusetts,
and London, England

Published on the occasion of the exhibition *Materializing "Six Years": Lucy R. Lippard and the Emergence of Conceptual Art,* September 14, 2012–February 3, 2013, organized by Catherine Morris, Curator of the Elizabeth A. Sackler Center for Feminist Art at the Brooklyn Museum, and the independent scholar Vincent Bonin

This exhibition has been supported by the Elizabeth A. Sackler Foundation.

Copublished by the Brooklyn Museum, 200 Eastern Parkway, Brooklyn, NY 11238-6052 www.brooklynmuseum.org and The MIT Press, 55 Hayward Street, Cambridge, MA 02142

MIT Press books may be purchased at special quantity discounts for business or sales promotional use. For information, please email special_sales@mitpress.mit.edu or write to Special Sales Department, The MIT Press, 55 Hayward Street, Cambridge, MA 02142.

The majority of the photographs of works of art reproduced in this book were provided by the owners or custodians of the work or by the artists, as indicated in the captions. Additional photo acknowledgments, when due, follow the owner's or custodian's name and appear within parentheses.

This publication was organized at the Brooklyn Museum.
Project editor: James Leggio
Photo researcher: Alice Cork

This book was set in Helvetica Neue Pro by The MIT Press.
Designer: Margarita Encomienda
Printed and bound in China.

Library of Congress Cataloging-in-Publication Data

Materializing "Six Years": Lucy R. Lippard and the emergence of conceptual art / edited by Catherine Morris and Vincent Bonin; preface by Lucy R. Lippard; essays by Vincent Bonin, Julia Bryan-Wilson, and Catherine Morris.
p. cm.
Published on the occasion of the exhibition Materializing "Six Years": Lucy R. Lippard and the Emergence of Conceptual Art, September 14, 2012–February 3, 2013, organized by Catherine Morris, Curator of the Elizabeth A. Sackler Center at the Brooklyn Museum, and the independent scholar Vincent Bonin.
Includes bibliographical references.
ISBN 978-0-262-01816-6 (hardcover: alk. paper)
1. Conceptual art—Exhibitions. 2. Lippard, Lucy R.—Exhibitions. 3. Lippard, Lucy R. Six Years—Exhibitions. I. Morris, Catherine, editor of compilation. II. Brooklyn Museum.
N6494.C63M38 2012
709.04'075—dc23
2011053212

10 9 8 7 6 5 4 3 2 1

Contents

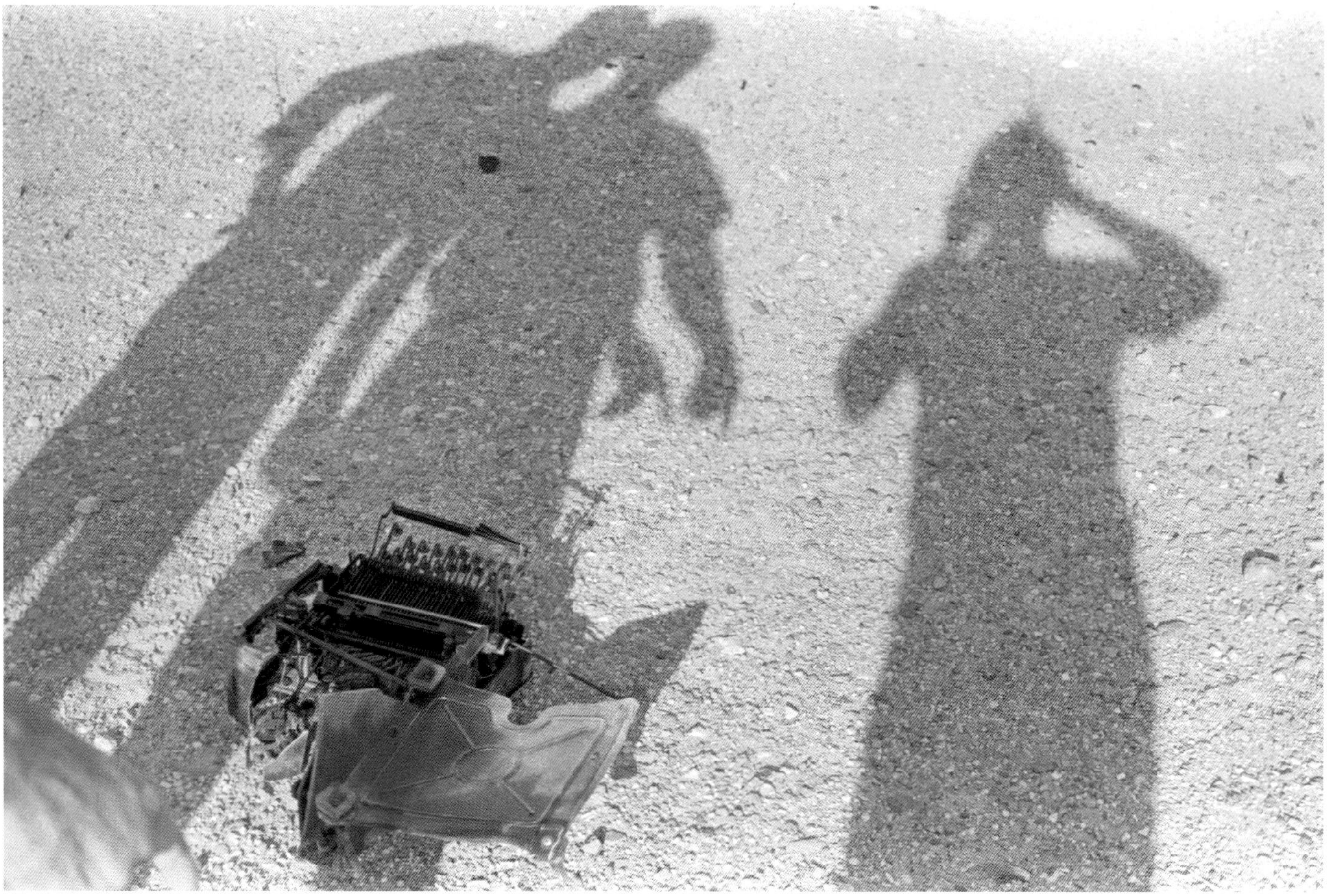

Edward Ruscha with Mason Williams and Patrick Blackwell. Plate from *Royal Road Test*, 1967. See figure 65.

Foreword

In 1971, the Brooklyn Museum hosted a public forum, called "Are Museums Relevant to Women?," at which Lucy R. Lippard, along with artists such as Faith Ringgold and Louise Bourgeois, voiced concern about the failure of arts institutions at that time to support women artists, and demanded that museums do better. It seems particularly fitting, therefore, that the Brooklyn Museum's Elizabeth A. Sackler Center for Feminist Art—a direct institutional response to that challenge—would be the organizing force behind the present project. This exhibition celebrates the historic impact of Lippard's decades of commitment to shaking up business as usual within the art world. At the same time, the exhibition gives us a chance to reflect as well on the Brooklyn Museum's own long-term engagement with questions about the status of women in cultural institutions.

In the years after the 1971 forum, the Museum sponsored the exhibition *Contemporary Women: Consciousness and Content,* in 1977, organized by the feminist painter Joan Semmel, which included a prescient selection of then-emerging artists, several of whom, such as Eleanor Antin, Louise Bourgeois, and Eva Hesse, are featured here. And in 1980, the Museum was one of only a handful of venues willing to exhibit *The Dinner Party*, Judy Chicago's iconic work redressing the exclusion of women from the historical record. *The Dinner Party*, which entered the collection in 2002, has since become the centerpiece for the Elizabeth A. Sackler Center, the first and only permanent gallery space devoted to feminist art within an encyclopedic art museum. The Center's first major international exhibition, *Global Feminisms*, opened in 2007. Now, with this overview of Lippard's unprecedented role in helping to shape the development of contemporary art in the late 1960s and 1970s, we continue to pursue the Center's key goal: to show the myriad ways that women have contributed to visual culture.

Devoting an exhibition to a curator and critic represents an unusual, yet important, step, for it draws attention to the expansive methodology that feminism has brought to the study and practice of art history. This inclusive discourse allows us to explore the ongoing development of feminist thinking, while simultaneously presenting the work of many of the most important male artists of the last fifty years within that ample framework. A broadly contextual approach supports the curators' contention that without Lippard, the careers of most of these artists, regardless of gender, would look very different today. Indeed, without Lippard, much of the current thinking about the dynamic relationship between Conceptual art and political art would not exist.

In realizing this project, we are of course deeply grateful for the generosity of our lenders, in particular Alan Cravitz, who has been informed by the guiding principles of *Six Years* in building his collection of Conceptual art; and the Smithsonian Institution's Archives of American Art, which houses the Lucy R. Lippard Papers, a key resource for historical research and a repository for many items of documentary ephemera presented in the show.

This exhibition has been supported by the Elizabeth A. Sackler Foundation, for which we are most grateful.

The exhibition and its accompanying publication would not have been possible without the support of Dr. Sackler and the dedicated expertise of our two co-curators: Catherine Morris, Curator of the Sackler Center; and Vincent Bonin, an independent scholar. The catalogue has benefited further from the insightful essay contributed by the art historian Julia Bryan-Wilson.

For the ongoing support of the Museum's Trustees, we extend special gratitude to John S. Tamagni, Chairman, and every member of our Board. Without the confidence and active engagement of our Trustees, it would not be possible to initiate and maintain the high level of exhibition and publication programming exemplified by this ambitious project.

Finally, I want most especially to thank Lucy R. Lippard for her generous cooperation throughout the process of organizing this exhibition, and also for writing her personal Preface to the catalogue. On this notable occasion, we all salute her for her enormous, and essential, contributions to the art world over the course of fifty years.

Arnold L. Lehman
Director
Brooklyn Museum

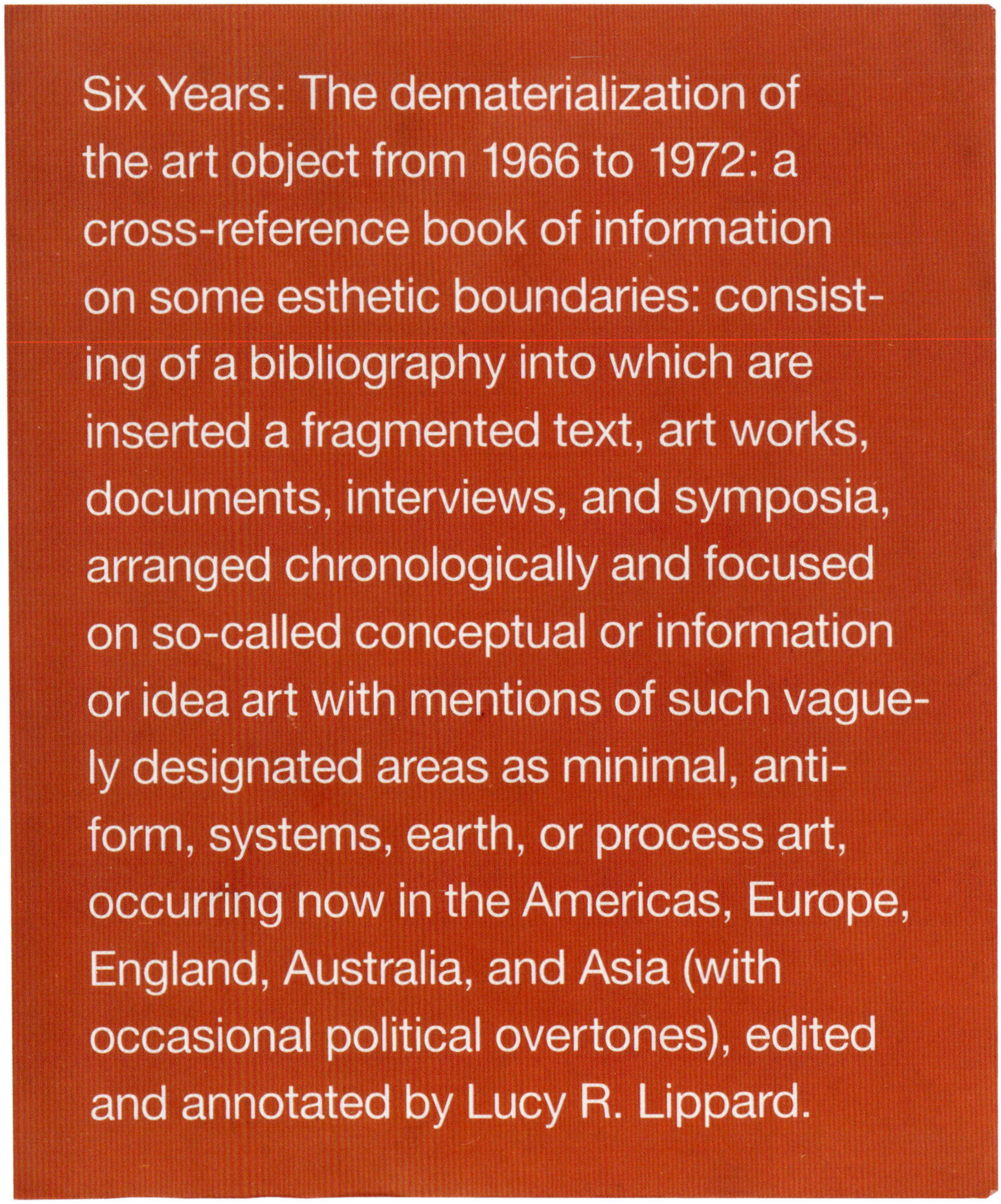
Six Years: The dematerialization of the art object from 1966 to 1972: a cross-reference book of information on some esthetic boundaries: consisting of a bibliography into which are inserted a fragmented text, art works, documents, interviews, and symposia, arranged chronologically and focused on so-called conceptual or information or idea art with mentions of such vaguely designated areas as minimal, anti-form, systems, earth, or process art, occurring now in the Americas, Europe, England, Australia, and Asia (with occasional political overtones), edited and annotated by Lucy R. Lippard.

Front cover of *Six Years: The dematerialization of the art object from 1966 to 1972: a cross-reference book of information on some esthetic boundaries: consisting of a bibliography into which are inserted a fragmented text, art works, documents, interviews, and symposia, arranged chronologically and focused on so-called conceptual or information or idea art with mentions of such vaguely designated areas as minimal, anti-form, systems, earth, or process art, occurring now in the Americas, Europe, England, Australia, and Asia (with occasional political overtones), edited and annotated by Lucy R. Lippard*, 1973. Paperback book, 8¾ × 7½ in. (22.2 × 19.1 cm). New York and London: Praeger Publishers, 1973; second edition, with a new introduction, Berkeley and Los Angeles: University of California Press, 1997. © 1973, renewed 2001, Lucy R. Lippard. (Photo: Brooklyn Museum)

Preface: *Six Years ...* Forty Years Later

Lucy R. Lippard

Six Years (the book) was originally intended to be "everything about everything," to quote the artist Doug Huebler.[1] In the spirit of inclusivity that made life the raw material for art, and ideas as acceptable as forms, its chronological arrangement was "factual," though subjective. The book was in part a criticism of the role of "criticism," with its implications of distance and objectivity—never my strong points. As a former library assistant and closet archivist (or pack rat), I saved everything that came by, and the book was a box in which to put it. The idea of actually *writing* a book on the art that was blowing in the wind was not only daunting but seemed irrelevant. Many of the artworks were already textual and needed no additional explanations. *Six Years* was one of several attempts made during that period to contextualize the art of the times rather than to explicate or theorize it. The context was my own life in an art world full of liberating ideas, where the boundaries between "critic," "curator," and "artist" were blurring.

Having already said so much about this book, this art, and that period (in the original 1973 Preface and Postface and in the long text that introduced the 1997 reprint), the question remains: Why is the work documented here of any interest in 2012? Conceptual or information or idea art and what I called "such vaguely designated areas as minimal, anti-form, systems, earth, or process art" live on, if not necessarily by the same names. Now that ideas in the air are quite literally floating around in cyberspace, those typed sheets and black-and-white snapshots look quaintly obsolete. Though we are yet again engaged in misguided wars in misunderstood places and 1960s slogans are still heard at demonstrations, no mass antiwar movement has emerged. "Socially engaged" art has become acceptable, but "political art" and art (like Hans Haacke's) that names names remains rare within the marketplace. Perhaps disjunctions rather than similarities explain why these six years remain compelling. Or maybe it's cyclical. When I was in my early twenties, my favorite art-historical period was Dada's nose-thumbing at authority—also around forty years earlier.

Anti-establishment fervor in the late 1960s focused in the art world on demythologizing and decommodifying art, on the need to be independent of the greedy sector that owned everything and was promoting the war in Vietnam. These six years also marked the arrival of feminism in the art world. Both movements definitively changed my life, so the project might be considered a kind of professional diary. Conceptual art offered ways of working more closely and more inventively with artists. I also saw it as a way to let artists speak for themselves. The cross-disciplinary DIY (Do It Yourself) movement that has been revitalized today in very different contexts by a much younger global generation was also an integral element of 1960s art. We did it ourselves—bypassing mainstream institutions by having an idea and directly, independently, acting upon it, doing what we could with what was at hand. "Dematerialization" made art-making cheap and easy (though sometimes marred by the lack of spell checks).

I'm often asked why I talk about Minimal and Conceptual art in political terms. Part of the answer is relative. In retrospect, with a few exceptions, the works themselves look timid and disconnected in comparison to the political activism of the times and the activist art of the late 1970s and 1980s, much of which was conceptually aligned. The "occasional political overtones" were just that; "undertones" might have been a more accurate term. Yet in a commercial art world that still idolized Clement Greenberg's arrogant formalism and ignored relationships between art and society, these artists, most of whom were then in their twenties and thirties, sounded like rebels. Conceptual strategies were designed to bypass the paternalistic mainstream, which infantilizes artists by making them dependent on dealers, critics, and curators, sapping their energies with the effort to enter and hang on to the status quo. In this sense, Conceptual art was a kind of adolescence, often involving a countercultural downward mobility. The New York avant-garde in the mid-1960s was deliberately provincial. Minimalists denied their European predecessors such as Constructivism and the Bauhaus, not because they were ignorant of that history, but because they couldn't relate to it. The Oedipal desire to kill off the ancestors in order to arrive at a tabula rasa, or clean slate, led to the denial and suppression of art-historical predecessors. (The palimpsest on that slate becomes obvious in retrospect; history always catches up to rebels.)

In the 1960s, I knew very little about the Paris-based Situationist International; I've since realized that their belief in the power of the idea and their critique of consumerism, capitalism, and spectacle was paralleled, more timidly, by Conceptual art. Similarly, Latin American parallels ("ideological conceptualism"), inspired by political crises unimaginable to comfortably rebellious U.S. artists, were often incompatible with New York abstraction. As Mari Carmen Ramírez has observed, "… these artists developed a series of strategic *inversions* of the North American conceptual model, thereby determining the political character of their art."[2]

Much (but not all) of the art in *Six Years* was dedicated to the subversion of art-world assumptions, a need to challenge authority, to question everything, especially the nature of art itself and the context within which it was made, shown, and distributed. The artists invented ways for art to act as an invisible frame for seeing and thinking rather than as an object of delectation or connoisseurship. Given their opposition to capitalism, their work remained a marginal phenomenon, even after it was grudgingly admitted into the art-historical canon, even after some of its proponents became rich and famous. Its most subversive aspect—institutional critique that happened within the art itself, in its form rather than its content—is among its most important legacies. By the 1970s, an increasing portion of the American middle class had been introduced to museums and galleries, attracted by all the '60s media hoopla around Pop art. So you had this contradictory situation of Conceptual artists trying to move down and out of their towers while their audiences moved up, like escalators passing in the night, or at best meeting in a middle ground controlled by the needs of neither group, but by those of the corporate class.

Conceptual art in the broadest sense was a kind of laboratory for innovations in the rest of the century. An unconscious international energy emerged from the raw materials of friendship, art history, interdisciplinary readings, and a fervor to change the world and the ways artists related to it. Reviewing the second edition of *Six Years*, the artist Liam Gillick chastised me for understating in retrospect the power of the ideas that emerged from 1966 to 1972, when artists, critics, and organizers of the time "articulated a set of thinking and a number of social shifts that were not limited to art and thereby opened up the territory available to us all."[3] He's right, because the imaginative richness and freedom of the era are with me still.

The book *Six Years* has sometimes been seen as a "curatorial" project on a par with the "numbers shows" and their "card catalogues" that I organized from 1969 to 1974 in New York, Seattle, Vancouver, Buenos Aires, and Valencia, California. Now Catherine Morris and Vincent Bonin have actually transformed the book into an exhibition—an ironic reversal of the way Conceptual exhibitions in print (on the Seth Siegelaub model) bypassed bricks and mortar, slick paper, and the official arbiters of aesthetic fashion. With the Brooklyn Museum show, *Six Years* comes full circle.

Notes

1. See Lucy R. Lippard, "Douglas Huebler: Everything about Everything," *Art News*, vol. 71, no. 8 (December 1972), pp. 29–32.
2. Mari Carmen Ramírez, "Blueprint Circuits: Conceptual Art and Politics in Latin America," in Waldo Rasmussen with Fatima Bercht and Elizabeth Ferrer, eds., *Latin American Artists of the Twentieth Century,* exh. cat. (New York: The Museum of Modern Art, 1993), p. 159.
3. Liam Gillick, "Twenty-five Years: The Rematerialisation of the Art World," *Art Monthly*, no. 223 (February 1999), p. 44.

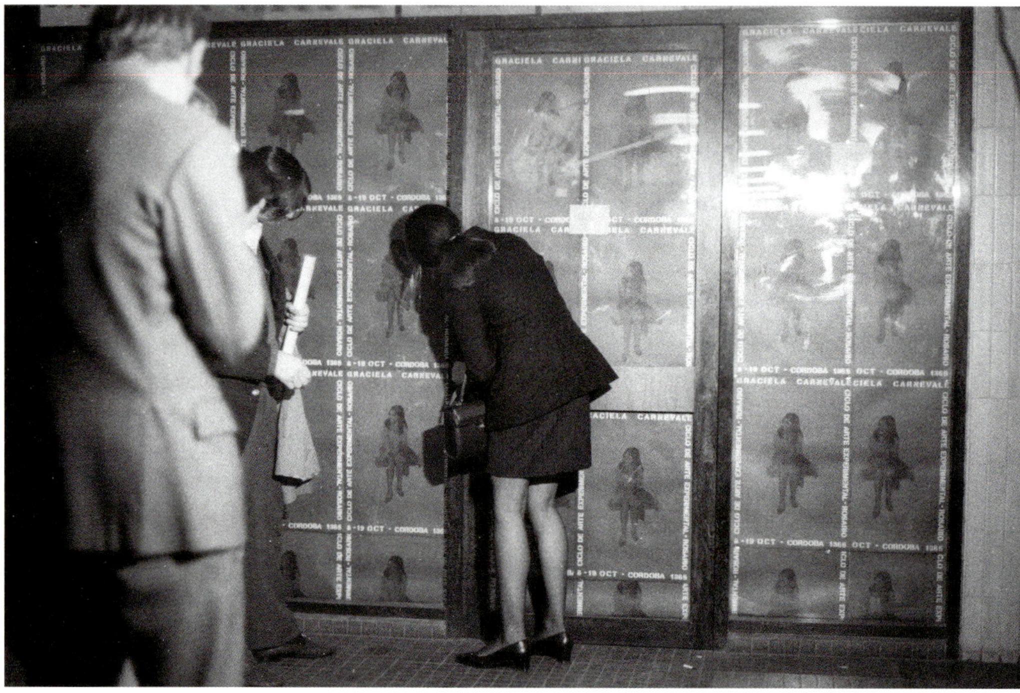

Graciela Carnevale (Argentinean, b. 1942). *Entrapment and Escape (Encierro y escape): Action for the Experimental Art Cycle, Rosario, Argentina,* 1968. Archive Graciela Carnevale, Rosario, Argentina. (Photo: Carlos Militello.) See figure 84.

An Introduction to *Six Years*

Catherine Morris and
Vincent Bonin

The full title of Lucy R. Lippard's influential chronicle of the emergence of the Conceptual art movement is seventy-nine words long and clearly states the breadth of the author's critical ambitions. It reads: *Six Years: The dematerialization of the art object from 1966 to 1972: a cross-reference book of information on some esthetic boundaries: consisting of a bibliography into which are inserted a fragmented text, art works, documents, interviews, and symposia, arranged chronologically and focused on so-called conceptual or information or idea art with mentions of such vaguely designated areas as minimal, anti-form, systems, earth, or process art, occurring now in the Americas, Europe, England, Australia, and Asia (with occasional political overtones).*

Six Years both describes and, in many ways, embodies the type of art-making Lippard set out to identify and catalogue: artwork composed primarily of written instructions, inventories, notations of ideas, and various forms of photographic documentation of things that most people would never have the opportunity to see in person. There was very little that looked even remotely like what was commonly thought of as "art" in 1973, the year the book was published. In a review, the writer and curator Clive Phillpot (who would later serve as director of the library of the Museum of Modern Art) points out that Lippard arranged the conceptual propositions that make up much of her text as an editor would gather and elucidate literary works in an anthology.[1] Organized as an annotated chronology of events, exhibitions, projects, writings, and ideas, both realized and imagined, the book maintains a veneer of objectivity—a sort of haute modernist nod to the authorial voice of impartial rationality—while also enjoying a good-natured rolling around in the chaotic illogic of a group of kindred spirits messing with the art-world status quo.

What this approach pushes to the perimeter, however, is the historical and political context that made so many artists suddenly feel an urgent need to question their role in society and indeed to question the proper limits of authority, in the art world and beyond. Because Lippard offers little editorial commentary per se within the body of the book, however, the chronology it sets out really does have only "occasional political overtones." These references appear infrequently and indirectly, except when highlighted by the artworks or by the artists themselves. More often, they are implied, occurring between the lines in the increasing certainty among the book's protagonists that something needed to be fundamentally altered in their approach not only to art-making, but in the artists' relationship to the political realities of the period in which they lived. In a conversation from 1971 between the artists Douglas Huebler and Donald Burgy that Lippard excerpts in her book, Burgy commented on their thinking about art in 1968:

> One of the important things lies in the fact that both of us were groping for a recognition that during the time we grew to be makers of art and conscious of art we had arrived at a historical state that had isolated art from other things. Artists were supposedly special or different people, who had different views of society. Now it becomes apparent that artists, like anyone else, just

> **arrange the material of the earth, reprocess materials of the earth. We have realized that you cannot successfully isolate art from social or cultural or historical processes, that there is a constant feedback.[2]**

It is these unspecified social, cultural, and historical processes that become the running subtext—or, as Lippard calls it in her Author's Note to the second edition, "the hidden narrative that I thought would be an involuntary secret"—which reveals itself if one reads the book from beginning to end, for its plot, so to speak, filling in the motivations, the constant feedback, and the exchanges in which the artists and authors were engaged throughout this period. That "hidden narrative" becomes a leitmotif taken up, in turn, by the various essays in the present book.

Because the rise of Conceptual art coincided with other era-defining movements—feminism, civil rights, antiwar protest, student activism, environmentalism, and gay rights—the arc of the book, if read from start to finish, as opposed to the "dipping in" approach Lippard imagined most readers would adopt,[3] parallels the political awakening of the author and of many of the artists included. As a result, in addition to the extraordinarily radical rethinking of art-making the book documents, it also hints at how the burgeoning political consciousness of this generation became the impetus for a new art form. In this regard, two structures of authority were being scrutinized by Conceptual art's proponents. First and foremost was the art world itself, where the dominant intellectual force was an entrenched but under-siege formalism. However, what became more apparent and clearly articulated during the period charted in *Six Years* was how much its challenge to traditional aesthetics was tied to a larger questioning of the world order inherited from the World War II generation. In that era, the philosophy of positivism, the idealization of progress, and the self-righteousness and triumphalism of American attitudes and policies, were all increasingly undermined by the ongoing reality of the cold war, by the escalating and seemingly intractable Vietnam conflict—and by the growing awareness of a gap between the rhetoric of liberty and justice for all and the lived experiences of ordinary individuals, both in the United States and among allies in the decades-old fight against communism. It is this implied overarching storyline, imbued with political overtones that retain much of their significance in our own time, that has made *Six Years* a rewarding book to reread, and it is certainly one of the reasons we were interested in reconceiving it as an exhibition.

During the almost twenty-five years it was out of print, *Six Years* circulated among collectors, curators, students, and artists as a rare collectible item, maintaining a significant cult following as the essential reference for the period. Since being reissued in 1997 by the University of California Press, it has become one of the most widely read and quoted references on Conceptual art, providing a wealth of primary material and links to other sources. Its documentary value also stems from the fact that it was written in the immediate aftermath of the events described, and because Lippard was intimately involved in the movement's development, as a critic, writer, curator, and, most important to her, as a friend of and sometime collaborator with many of the artists involved.[4]

Given the book's influential place in contemporary art history, we became intrigued by the challenge of using its structure and content as the template for an exhibition. While it was fairly obvious that our goal could never be to reproduce the entirety of the book in the form of an exhibition, we were interested in reflecting upon, or describing, several aspects of its make-up. Our primary goal was to illustrate, through a discursive display, two intertwined themes that emerge from the book's content. First, we wanted to tell the story of how an attempt by a group of young artists to scrutinize the cultural usefulness of objects, and extricate artworks from the commodity system, morphed into an entirely new and highly influential form of creative practice within a few short years. Second, by examining the development of Lippard's own activities over the course of *Six Years*, we hoped to describe how two fields usually understood as attendant to art-making—criticism and curating—were themselves as radically altered and reconfigured by the development of Conceptual art as was art-making itself. In bringing these two themes together, the exhibition seeks to convey how ideas that emerged purely in reaction to an entrenched set of formal strictures, which up till then had had a stranglehold on art-making, presenting, and reviewing, became an extraordinary set of operational tools for integrating political content into what had been a remarkably apolitical milieu.

In an essay on the impact of Conceptual art, the film scholar Peter Wollen points out how the shift in the art object necessitated new forms of installation and curation, which in turn suggested a new relationship with the world at large:

> Art installations not only made use of verbal language, but themselves became language, like in the way they strung a series of items together to make a significant sequence, as words are combined in a linear fashion to make a sentence. This was not simply a formal shift. It brought with it a new way of referring to the world, through complex forms of narrative, documentation, and metalanguage, far removed from traditional modes of visual representation. Painting and sculpture were not simply problematized but replaced by text, photography, and performance. Artmaking was seen as a cultural and political activity, rather than an aspect of personal creativity.[5]

For Lippard, the roles of art critic and curator seem quickly to have morphed into each other, perhaps growing from an impulse such as Wollen describes, in which she sought to organize objects in an installation, or in a magazine layout, in an unmediated manner, allowing juxtaposition itself to serve as a form of critical dialogue, a dialogue that might previously have been conducted in a piece of analytical writing. As Lippard wrote, concerning how some art "bypasses" criticism, in an essay she co-authored with John Chandler, "Judgment of ideas is less interesting than following the idea through."[6] Using this model, Lippard's critical writing, including *Six Years*, became an experiment in curated concatenation—a gathering of ideas that elucidate by building upon each other, rather than being guided through a singular critical voice. Her writing is the subject of Vincent Bonin's essay in the present volume.

Lippard's personal ambitions made her a good candidate for taking up this experimental process of authorial critique. Wanting to be a writer from an early age, Lippard has said that she chose to study art and art history because, while she was interested in art, her passion was writing and she did not want to put herself in a position of being dictated to on the subject she held most dear.[7] After arriving in New York, and finding work at the Museum of Modern Art as a photo researcher, page, and curatorial assistant, Lippard had the makings of a traditional career laid out for her. She worked on significant publications while on staff at MoMA, and she completed her master's degree because it was understood to be the next appropriate step in a museum career. Even after she left MoMA, taking up a variety of freelance jobs to support herself, she continued to work on projects firmly grounded in the mainstream, albeit the highbrow end, of the art world.[8] The eventual shift in her focus came from her friendships and personal relationships with artists. Lippard has repeatedly given credit to the artists she knew for her introduction to the more avant-garde ideas percolating at the time. The community of people she was close to beginning in the early 1960s included Sol LeWitt, Robert Ryman (her husband at the beginning of this period), Ray Donarski, Robert Mangold, Sylvia Plimack Mangold, Frank Lincoln Viner, Eva Hesse, and Tom Doyle. In this early period, she also got to know the work of Dan Graham, Robert Smithson, Nancy Holt, Hanne Darboven, the Art & Language collective, Hilla and Bernd Becher, Joseph Kosuth, Dorothea Rockburne, Mel Bochner, Carl Andre, Donald Judd, and Robert Morris.

Because Lippard's career trajectory over the period covered by *Six Years* involved the dynamic interaction between her distinct roles as a critic, curator, and activist, we developed the present exhibition to reflect the interrelations among these activities—another leitmotif taken up by each essay in turn. Our exhibition highlights a group of curatorial projects that Lippard completed during these years, taking them as an armature for our own installation. In many ways, Lippard's progressive curatorial endeavors from 1966 to 1974 reflect the refinement and honing of Conceptual art over that time more than *Six Years* does itself, since the book includes citations relating to earthworks, Minimalism, and other proto- or quasi-Conceptual projects.

These endeavors—including *Six Years* as a curatorial project—are the main subject of Catherine Morris's essay in the present volume. They begin with *Eccentric Abstraction* (1966), which can be considered an ideational preface to Conceptual art; Lippard then organized two benefit exhibitions at the Paula Cooper Gallery, in 1968 and 1969, that mixed Minimal, abstract, and Conceptual artists. Ultimately, the most radical and significant of the exhibitions she organized are what have become known as the "numbers" shows. With titles taken from the population figure of the city where each appeared, the numbers shows align closely with an ambition to focus exclusively on the dematerialized aspects of the movement and the potential this provided within a traveling exhibition context. The exhibitions in Seattle (1969), called *557,087*; Vancouver (1970), called *955,000*; Buenos Aires (1970), called *2,972,453*; and Valencia, California (1973), called *c. 7,500*, were often produced from instructions provided to Lippard by the participating artists.

The most lasting legacy of these numbers exhibitions are their catalogues,[9] which are composed of index cards, one for each artist, describing their contribution to the show per their instructions. Additional cards were provided by Lippard with her own writings and pertinent excerpts from other sources. The cards are meant to be reviewed in random order, thereby discarding the typical exhibition catalogue format and replacing the authoritative voice of the curator with a multitude of individuals.

The exhibition *c. 7,500*, though outside *Six Years,* strictly speaking, because it was produced in 1973, nonetheless adds an important endnote to our project. Produced in direct response to the refrain Lippard heard throughout the process of organizing the earlier shows, that "there are no women conceptual artists,"[10] *c. 7,500* set the record straight, and affirmed the longstanding and complex relationship between Conceptual art and the feminist art practices that also emerged during the time Lippard was compiling *Six Years*. Artists cited in the book, such as Agnes Denes, Lee Lozano, Adrian Piper, Martha Rosler, Martha Wilson, and Yoko Ono, among others, played a significant role in politicizing Conceptual practices, particularly in introducing personal content with significant socio-political implications. The chronological order of *Six Years,* however, also plots this as a progression, something that these women came to insist upon, bringing to the fore the conceptual, or constructed, nature of identity—socially enforced yet performative and malleable—as an appropriate subject for advanced art. It also shows the progression of Lippard's own attention to the unequal representation of women's work in the field.

In looking back, it is clear that *Six Years,* as edited in 1973, is very different from what it might have been if edited in 1975, or later; Lippard did not allow herself more hindsight than those she quoted, and there are many early pioneers of feminist performance and video that she might have inserted had *Six Years* been written as a later research project and not as an immediate series of impressions right after the storm. Regardless, the assertions of subjectivity and gender as topics for exploration became their own subtext in the last two years of the book. This challenge to the notion of "pure" Conceptualism not only laid the groundwork for feminist and postmodernist practice, but pointed to the next chapter in Lippard's own life, as a critic overtly engaged in political discourse and attempting to influence both cultural and social change. After working on *c. 7,500*, Lippard devoted most of the next decade to supporting, championing, and theorizing about the impact of feminism and women's experiences on art-making. Lippard herself has acknowledged that she stayed an active participant in the art world much longer than she might otherwise have because of her desire to support the emergent feminist movement in the visual arts.[11] Julia Bryan-Wilson's essay in the present volume offers an illuminating account of Lippard's political activism.

Given Lippard's activism, it is not surprising that throughout our own exhibition planning process, our attention was drawn again and again to that final parenthetical phrase in the book's subtitle—"(with occasional political overtones)"—and over time it seemed to encapsulate the legacy of Lippard's own project and indicate her future direction. It points to Lippard's burgeoning ambition and growing critical clarity regarding the validity of modernism's legacies. During the process of making her book, Lippard came to understand that Conceptual art offered a new structure for art-making and a new method for considering the scope and implications of political content; by the time of its publication, her belief in the political efficacy of this turn had, however, been altered. As her Postface to the book succinctly concludes, "it [is] unlikely that conceptual art will be any better equipped to affect the world any differently, or even as much as, its less ephemeral counterparts."[12] Going forward, she decided that politics should be overt, not through polemical art, but by allowing social, cultural, and historical processes into her personal project, and by making visible the art world's "invisible apron strings to the 'real world's' power structures."[13]

However, this pessimism about art's ability "to affect the world" did not extend to her assessment of Conceptual art's contributions to the field of aesthetics, which she felt had amounted to a new set of criteria by which art could be viewed and revitalized. If Conceptual art effectively—if temporarily—erased the traditional art object from at least part of the discourse about art, in its place it produced a performative field into which all subsequent discussions about contemporary art must enter. Within the discursive milieu that emerged from the Conceptual art movement, objects valued for formal reasons were replaced with instructions, documents, and language, suggesting a sort of philosophical politics, however attenuated, as a prime motivator for making art. The products artists made to convey their ideas were not traditionally aestheticized or intentionally commercialized, and the challenge they attempted to pose to the voracious market system remains an important legacy of the movement. As artists established a new paradigm for themselves and their work, the roles adopted by the various traditional art-world players quickly became more fluid, encouraging morphing and melding, and in some cases appeared to cancel each other out: artists became critics, critics became activists, writers became artists, and anyone could be a curator.

This last point is important because the spaces where art was presented and the means by which it was transmitted were as radically redefined in this moment as the art they were intended to display. The flourishing of these hybrid identities for cultural producers, and alternative spaces and channels for presenting work, may be the most pervasive and institutionally significant contribution of the period—for many historians, marking the definitive break between modern and contemporary art.

Notes

1. Clive Phillpot, "Six Years: The Dematerialization of the Art Object from 1966 to 1972 (...)," *Leonardo,* vol. 8, no. 3 (Summer 1975), p. 261.
2. *Six Years: The dematerialization of the art object from 1966 to 1972: a cross-reference book of information on some esthetic boundaries: consisting of a bibliography into which are inserted a fragmented text, art works, documents, interviews, and symposia, arranged chronologically and focused on so-called conceptual or information or idea art with mentions of such vaguely designated areas as minimal, anti-form, systems, earth, or process art, occurring now in the Americas, Europe, England, Australia, and Asia (with occasional political overtones), edited and annotated by Lucy R. Lippard* (New York and London: Praeger Publishers, 1973; reprinted, with a new introduction, Berkeley and Los Angeles: University of California Press, 1997), p. 251; excerpted from a conversation recorded in Bradford, Massachusetts, October 1971.
3. Lippard noted at least twice that she never thought anyone would read *Six Years* straight through. For example, in the Preface to the first edition of the book she states, "I am probably safe in saying, as I have of some exhibitions I have organized, that no one but me (and my editors) will read the whole book through." See Lippard, *Six Years,* p. 6.
4. Among the many artists Lippard notes as friends, it is Sol LeWitt to whom she dedicated *Six Years*. See her essay "Escape Attempts" (1995), reprinted in *Six Years*, 1997 edition, p. viii.
5. Peter Wollen, "Global Conceptualism and North American Conceptual Art," in *Global Conceptualism: Points of Origin, 1950s–1980s*, exh. cat. (New York: Queens Museum of Art, 1999), p. 80.
6. John Chandler and Lucy R. Lippard, "The Dematerialization of Art," *Art International,* vol. 12, no. 2 (February 1968), p. 35.
7. Lyn Blumenthal and Kate Horsfield, *Lucy Lippard 1974: An Interview,* 1974, color video, 25 min. Distributed by Video Data Bank, Chicago.
8. Lippard, "Escape Attempts," in *Six Years,* p. viii.
9. It should be noted that the Buenos Aires exhibition is more problematic because it was not produced to Lippard's specifications; documentation of the problems with the exhibition and its publication can be found in the Lucy R. Lippard Papers, Archives of American Art, Smithsonian Institution, Washington, D.C.
10. Aside from noting the anecdote in the unpaginated card catalogue for the exhibition, Lippard has recounted this story in various publications. See, for instance, "Escape Attempts," in *Six Years,* p. xi.
11. Blumenthal and Horsfield, *Lucy Lippard 1974.*
12. Lippard, *Six Years,* p. 264.
13. Ibid.

Years as a Curatorial Project

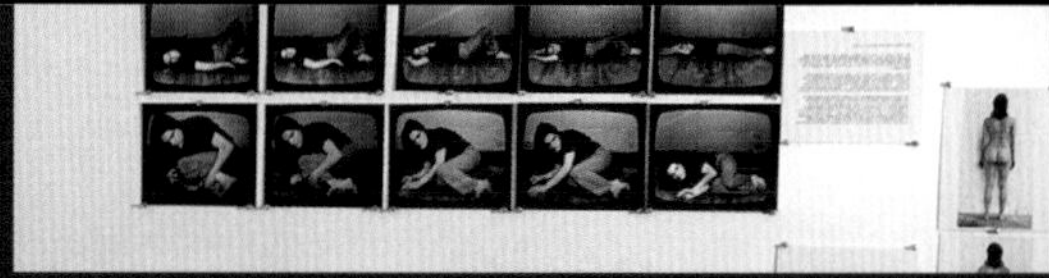

Six Years as a Curatorial Project

Catherine Morris

"... *Six Years* was probably the best show I've ever curated—a show that includes other shows."[1]

Lucy R. Lippard

This project is an experiment in curatorial thinking. It takes Lucy R. Lippard's essential documentary account, *Six Years: The Dematerialization of the Art Object from 1966 to 1972*, and attempts to turn it into an exhibition. Our goal has been to produce a show that reflects the breadth of Lippard's original intentions. Taking its cue from Lippard's assertion that *Six Years* itself had, in fact, been a species of exhibition to begin with, this essay is intended to situate her book within the context of her own curatorial experiments during the period. Indeed, the dynamics of her wide-ranging career during these years suggest how, in a larger sense, the historical nomenclature of the art-world system changed with the emergence of Conceptual art: when the artwork no longer needed to be a physical object, the respective roles of the artist, critic, and curator became interactive and fluid, as the creative and critical parameters open to each of them shifted and overlapped.

Between 1966 and 1973 (the year the book was published),[2] Lippard organized more than a dozen exhibitions, and most of them tie directly into the critical thinking she would examine in *Six Years*. The first of the exhibitions, *Eccentric Abstraction,* was a sort of proto-Conceptual art reconnaissance mission. Two politically motivated fundraising exhibitions at the Paula Cooper Gallery bridged the process of dematerializing exhibitions while also overtly linking Conceptual art to political imperatives. And two "magazine exhibitions" presented in *Studio International* morphed the notion of a curatorial project from an installation of art objects into a representation of ideational experiments. Most important, the development and progressive execution of the four "numbers" shows represented the culmination of Lippard's own experiments in working with Conceptual art in a curatorial framework. The final one of these, *c. 7,500,* announced Lippard's shifting focus, from the seemingly hermetic intellectual issues that occupied the first Conceptual artists, to the work of women artists (see figures 1, 2) who significantly galvanized the movement toward the growing political imperatives of feminism. Ultimately, *Six Years* itself became a creative operation that melded criticism, curatorial methods, and political impulses. In the pages that follow, each of these projects will be discussed in turn.

Conceptual art emerged within a historical moment that championed radicality. The artists from the mid-1960s to the early 1970s who were interested in taking the object out of art-making wanted to make their mark by upsetting the status quo of the art world, and what could be more radical than asserting that the most significant component of the visual arts is not a thing you see, but an idea that makes you see differently? In this dialectical moment, the events chronicled in *Six Years* describe the convergence of ideas that would define the Conceptual art movement, though in 1966 these ideas were not yet distinct, but were intertwined with a variety of reactive and revising art-making strategies being explored by young artists.

In a critical reminiscence, Lippard made clear the personal and biographical context of the book: "The mid-to-late sixties were one of the most exciting times of my life on every

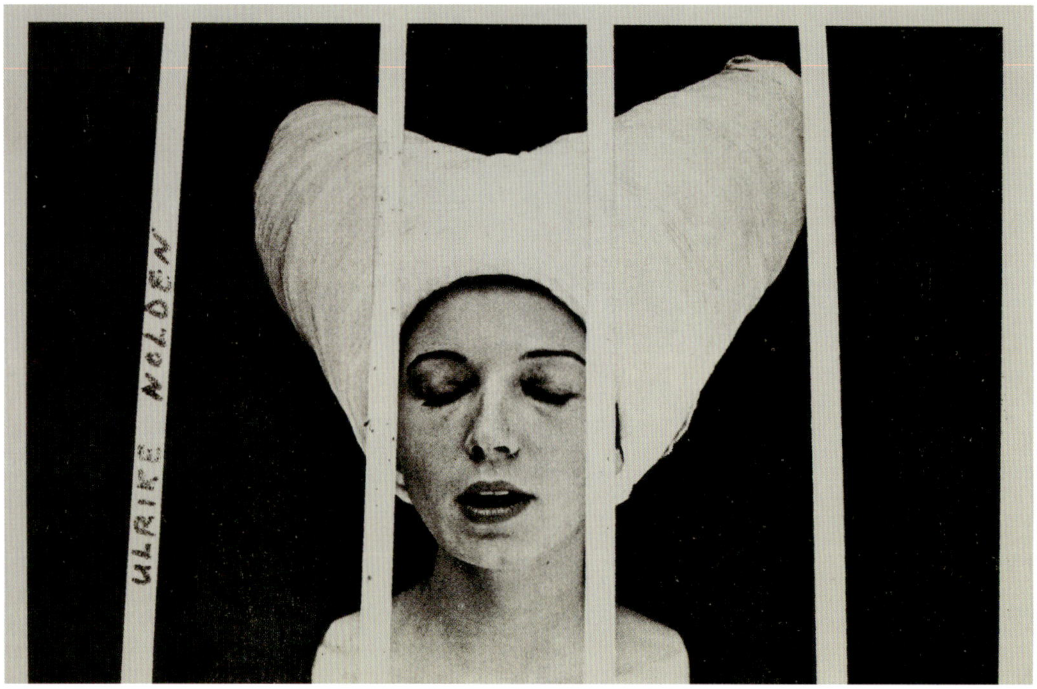

2

FIGURES 1, 2

Ulrike Rosenbach (German, b. 1943). *Haube for a Married Woman* (front and back), 1973. Contribution to the catalogue of *c. 7,500*. Index card, 4 × 6 in. (10.2 × 15.2 cm). Valencia, Calif.: California Institute of the Arts, 1974. Original photograph on card: Sabine Crittall. (Photography of card for reproduction: Michael Tropea)

ULRIKE NOLDEN, BORN 1943, LIVES IN DÜSSELDORF

HAUBE FOR A MARRIED WOMAN : A series of photographs of a married woman wearing a medieval Haube in a modern kitchen. The surroundings and the task remain the same.

The Haube is an obsolete headdress once worn by European women. For centuries it signified something equivalent to a wedding ring. Originally designed to denote possession by the husband, the Haube developed through usage by courtly ladies in the Middle Ages and Renaissance to become a symbol of her self-confidence and equality at her husband's side.

level: I began to make a living from free-lance writing (at almost the exact moment my son was born). I curated my first exhibition, gave my first lectures, published my first two books, began to travel, wrote some fiction, got unmarried, got politicized. Conceptual art was an integral part of the whole process."[3] Of the large community of people Lippard got to know during this period she was closest to Sol LeWitt, and Robert Ryman (whom, as noted, she unmarried in these years). The three had been employed at the Museum of Modern Art: Lippard worked various jobs in the library, LeWitt at the night reception desk, and Ryman as a guard. As a critic whose personal and professional life was largely informed by her relationships with artists—most of whom appear in *Six Years*—Lippard had unique access to the ideas under discussion and the work that was being done in many of the studios in Lower Manhattan.

Perhaps Lippard's strong identification as a writer—a resourceful user of language—rather than as an art critic per se, played a role in her receptivity to these ideas and made her particularly alert to ways of applying Conceptual art methodologies in her own work.[4] During the years that she saw, and gathered documentation about, the events, exhibitions, and projects of her friends and colleagues, her own activities became harder to contain within the traditional parameters of art criticism. The milieu of Conceptual thinking offered its own expansive opportunities for breaking out of strictures and redefining, or undefining, the nature of creativity, including critical writing, curating, and later, political activism.

The shows that Lippard produced, particularly their modes of presentation, reflected her developing facility with the materials and the intellectual implications of Conceptual art. Her curatorial ideas were succinct—all of the shows considered here were group exhibitions devoted to presenting Conceptual art—while the logistics of installation became more challenging: content became less visible and artist participation sometimes included little more than filling out instruction questionnaires she had drafted. At the same time, the curatorial writing she did in relation to the exhibitions also began, in a sense, to dematerialize. That is, instead of describing and providing a historical context for objects, the "catalogues" that accompanied her shows reflected her experimental thinking about narrative content, authorial voice, and the pertinence of critical judgments. The assumed differences between a book, an exhibition, or an article in a periodical were supplanted by inquiries into their similarities, or how they could be operationally linked, thereby permanently altering the existing disciplinary models.

Like much of the groundbreaking work done in this period, *Six Years* was an attempt to identify and elucidate newly developing and often ad hoc approaches to art-making. Diverse production that would later be divided into categories such as Minimalism, Post-Minimalism, Land art, Performance art, and Conceptual art was being made simultaneously in the mid-1960s, and the point of intersection between these varying impulses seemed to be a desire to fundamentally change the conventional relationships between the viewer, the object, and the maker. As a result, the customary material designations of modernity—painting, sculpture, and drawing—were dissected, reduced, and replaced. So while Lippard's book is now mainly understood as a primer on Conceptual art, it is actually a précis of broader impulses, describing a complex state of affairs out of which developed the primary methods of Conceptual art. As Lippard put it, "Conceptual art … was all over the place in style and content, but materially quite specific. Conceptual art, for me, means work in which the idea is paramount and the material form is secondary, lightweight, ephemeral, cheap, unpretentious and/or 'dematerialized.'"[5]

Eccentric Abstraction

In 1966, curators and critics were still trying to sort out what seemed to be related ambitions among a variety of new formal practices. Kynaston McShine, Lippard's friend and colleague, organized the landmark exhibition *Primary Structures* at the Jewish Museum in the spring of 1966, and Lippard's own Fischbach Gallery show *Eccentric Abstraction* took place that fall (figures 3, 4).[6] Opening only five months apart, both exhibitions described emerging approaches to abstraction that rejected traditional sculptural idioms. McShine's exhibition focused on what became known as Minimalism, while Lippard's project presented work that incorporated some of Minimalism's most salient talking points—reductive forms, industrial and commercial materials—but seemed to take those parameters in new directions with the introduction of a more emotive and seemingly derelict content. While the roots of McShine's project dated back at least two years, to conversations he and Lippard had about co-curating an exhibition while they both worked at MoMA, Lippard's more nimble gallery exhibition presented work that was expanding beyond the dialogue that Minimalism had broached. As she described her project in an essay she wrote for a brochure that accompanied the show: "Like the 'primary structure,' eccentric abstraction is usually planar, extremely simple, and large in scale, rejecting figuration, nostalgia and anthropomorphism.... But where formalist art tends to focus on specific formal problems, eccentric abstraction is more allied to the non-formal tradition of opening up new areas in materials, form, color and sensuous experience."[7]

For Lippard, this show was "just another kind of 'criticism.'"[8] The ideas she developed in *Eccentric Abstraction* were published in an essay of the same title in *Art International* that November. The in-depth and varied process of writing about and exhibiting the sculptural work of artists like Alice Adams, Louise Bourgeois, Eva Hesse, Bruce Nauman, and Keith Sonnier, which she described as "nonsculptural," was an important initial step in her recognizing the ways in which the emergent impulses of Conceptual art tended to butt up against the historically vetted fine-art methods artists were still using. And while the work of Hesse and certainly Bourgeois remained firmly committed to the material in a way that denies its easy categorization as Conceptual art, Lippard included them in *Six Years*, pointing to the exploratory nature of the book, but also to how she was grappling with the boundaries of her project, particularly in the first year of the chronology.

The first illustration in *Six Years*, an untitled sculptural object by Bruce Nauman from 1965–66, had been included in *Eccentric Abstraction*. As Lippard wrote in *Art International*, "The majority of Nauman's pieces are carelessly surfaced, somewhat aged, blurred, and repellent, wholly nonsculptural and deceptively inconsequential at first sight."[9] This description illustrates the evolving definition of the dematerialized object as something that lacks formal gravitas, favoring the simultaneity of eerie abjection and inconsequential construction. *Eccentric Abstraction* brought together objects that filter the kinky nature of Surrealist objects through the vulgarity and kitsch of Pop and ended up describing the loss of the monumental (in both formal and ideational terms) on its way to the repudiation of materiality. Eva Hesse's work *Several* (figure 5) is another example of this tendency, which Lippard described as "Energy repressed, or rather imprisoned in a timeless vacuum tinged with anticipation and braced by tension."[10] For these reasons, *Eccentric Abstraction* can be understood as, in many ways, the germ of the idea for her book, and it is certainly the first link between what would become her increasingly interrelated activities as a critic, writer, and curator.

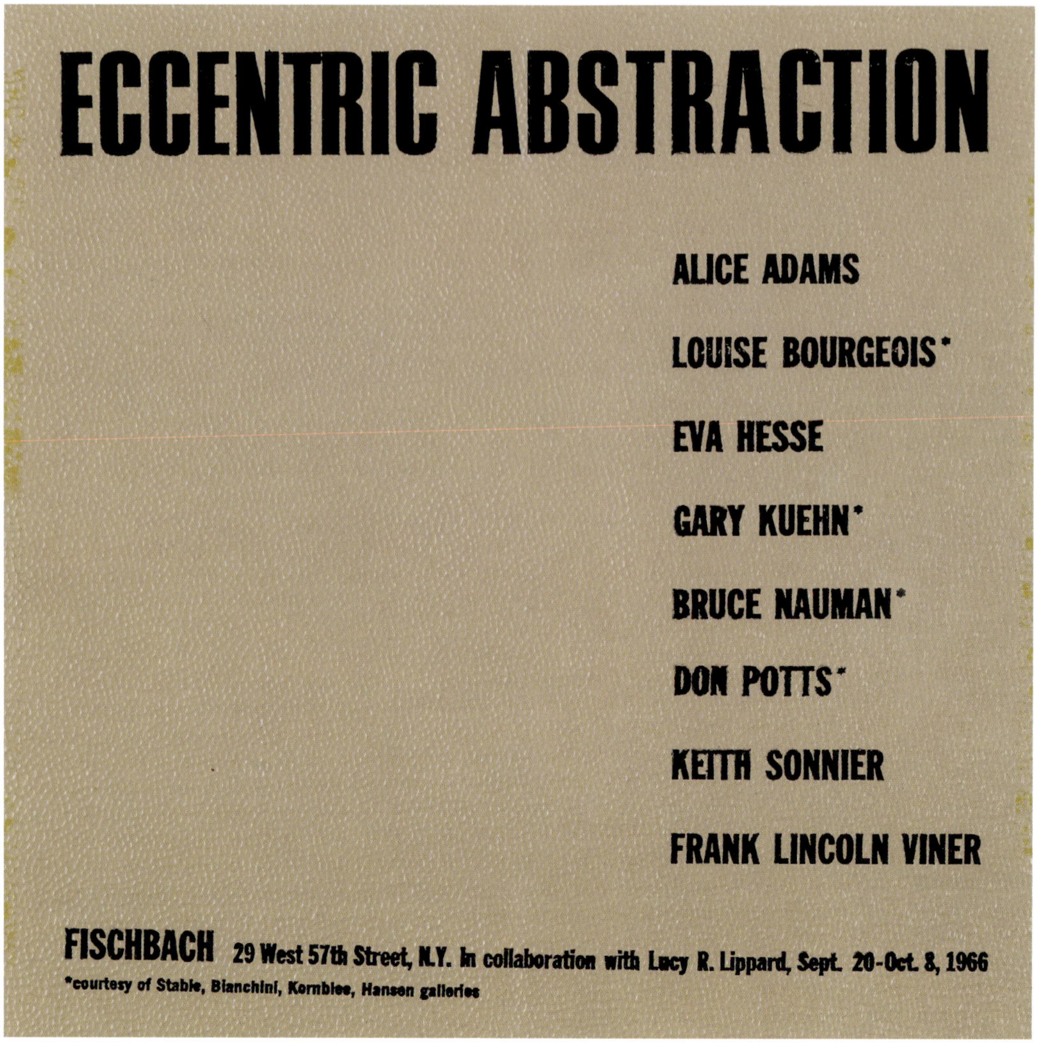

FIGURE 3
Announcement card for *Eccentric Abstraction*, 1966.
Printed text on vinyl, 10¼ × 10¼ in. (26 × 26 cm).
© Fischbach Gallery, New York

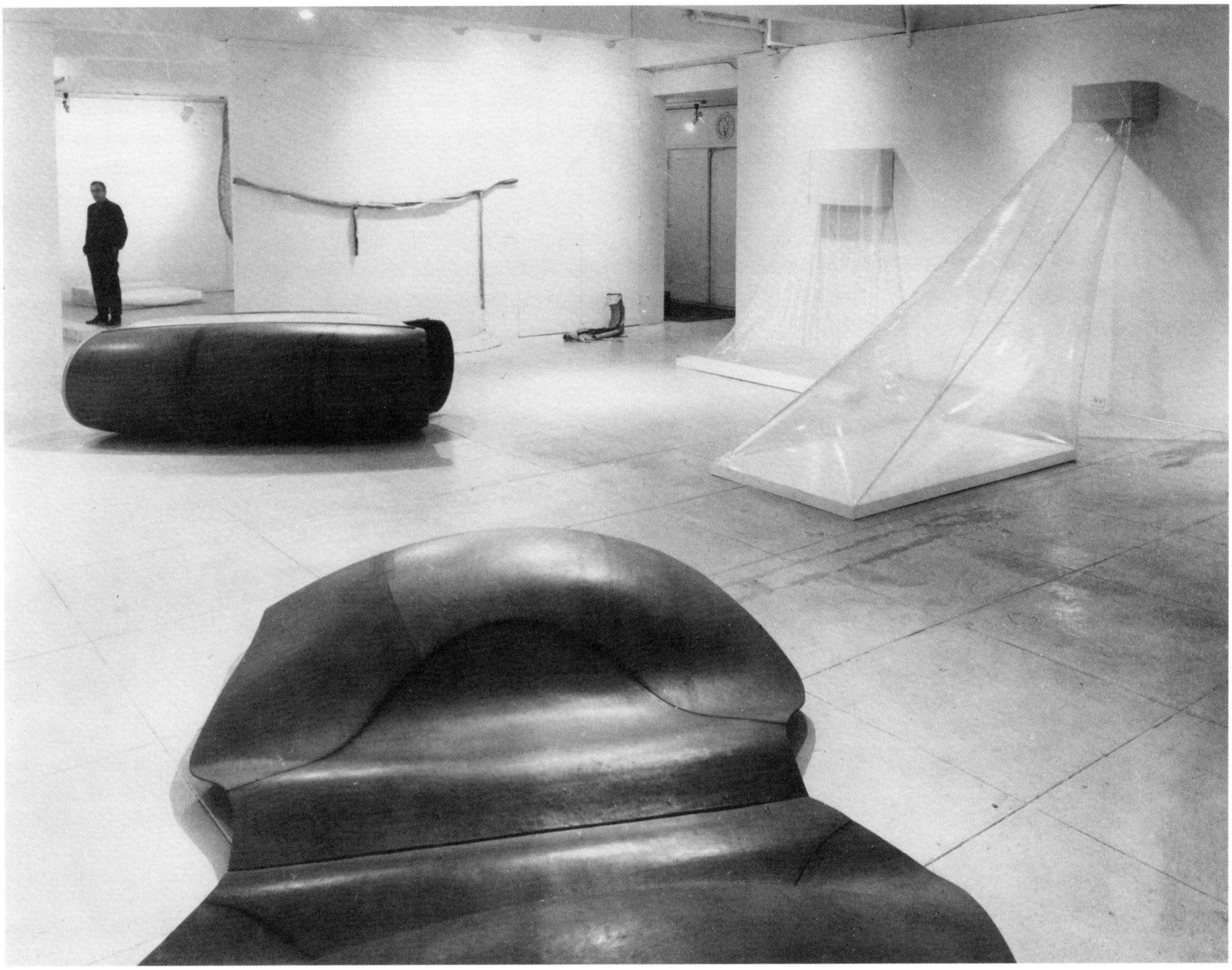

FIGURE 4

Installation view of *Eccentric Abstraction* including works by Don Potts (front and left), Bruce Nauman (back wall), and Keith Sonnier (right); Fischbach Gallery, New York, September 20–October 8, 1966; organized by Lucy R. Lippard. Fischbach Gallery Records, Archives of American Art, Smithsonian Institution, Washington, D.C. (Photo: © Fischbach Gallery, New York)

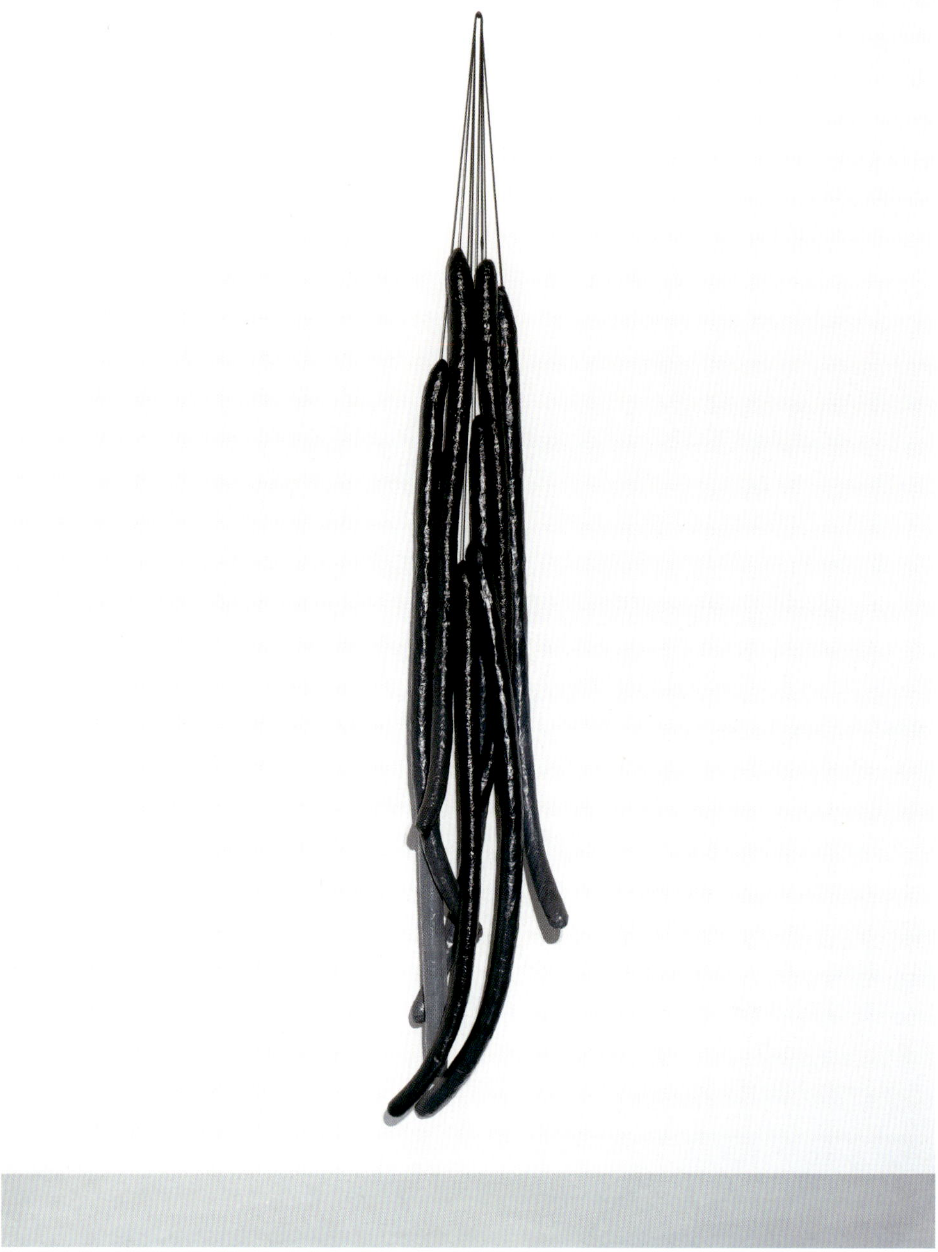

FIGURE 5

Eva Hesse (American, b. Germany, 1936–1970). *Several*, 1965. Acrylic, papier-caché, latex, rubber; 4 units, 88 × 11 × 7 in. (223.5 × 27.9 × 17.8 cm) overall. Collection of Glenstone, Potomac, Md. © The Estate of Eva Hesse, courtesy Hauser & Wirth, Zurich. (Photo: Abby Robinson, New York)

In 1967 Lippard worked with the intellectual historian John Chandler on two articles that codified their ideas about the dematerialization of art objects. The first, a more exploratory rumination on the possible implications for artists of abstract thinking across a variety of intellectual disciplines, was called "Visual Art and the Invisible World" and was published in *Art International* in May 1967. The second, "The Dematerialization of Art," appeared in *Art International* in February 1968, and the cumulative thinking of the two extrapolated the implications of dematerialization for artists, but also for other fields, including critical writing and curating. "The Dematerialization of Art" cogently linked artists' rejection of object-making to two paths: one in which the artist communicates modes of thinking through the most quotidian means possible (written instructions, for instance); and another, in which the artist moves away from commodities and toward performative actions. As the authors wrote (and Lippard later quoted in *Six Years*):

> The studio is again becoming a study. Such a trend appears to be provoking a profound dematerialization of art, especially of art as object, and if it continues to prevail, it may result in the object's becoming wholly obsolete.
>
> The visual arts at the moment seem to hover at a crossroads that may well turn out to be two roads to one place, though they appear to have come from two sources: art as idea and art as action. In the first case, matter is denied, as sensation has been converted into concept; in the second case, matter has been transformed into energy and time-motion.[11]

In a succinct description of the devaluing of the object, Lippard puts into play two ideas that have significant implications for her exhibition work. First, art becomes an idea, often conveyed through the written word (the domain of the writer, whether curator or critic or artist). And second, a performative action—perhaps a curatorial gesture—becomes an activity seen as equal to (rather than in support of) the making of an object.

Politically Motivated Exhibitions

Also in 1967 and 1968, Lippard traveled to Canada, Argentina, and Peru, where she discovered that art communities well outside those known to her and her small group of Manhattan-based peers were engaged in remarkably similar intellectual pursuits. The implications of the apparent zeitgeist she was encountering contributed significantly to Lippard's personal politicization, as she found concrete examples of how dematerialization, by virtue of its inexpensive means of reproduction and ease of dissemination, could actively serve a social or political agenda. Later trips to Europe confirmed her sense that younger artists everywhere (at least those working and being trained within the confines of the Western canon of modernity and its antecedents) were reacting to a sense of constriction and were actively exploring ideas for how to undermine the object and change the parameters of art-making—prioritizing an engaged dialogue over a transfer of commodities.

For Lippard, this was where what she called the "hidden narrative"[12] of *Six Years*—its developing sense of overt political engagement—entered the picture. While there was clearly already an activist impulse in the desire to circumvent, or even undermine, the capitalist nature of the existing art market, that impulse was contained within the terms of a self-referential art-world dialogue, and tended to lack any expansive populist inclination. As the decade of the sixties progressed, however, with it came a growing sense of anguish and outrage over the tragedy of the war in Vietnam, coupled with an intense desire to change the social and cultural landscape of the United States, particularly in regard to the fight for the civil rights of African Americans and other people of color, as well as women and homosexuals. And at this moment in history, some artists began to see the political implications of their dematerialized work in new terms. As Lippard wrote about her trip to Argentina that fall, "I returned belatedly radicalized by contact with artists there, especially the Rosario Group, whose mixture of conceptual and political ideas was a revelation."[13] The work by the Rosario Group that Lippard saw involved a political "exhibition" in conjunction with local labor unions to protest working conditions in Tucumán, a province in northwest Argentina. A direct action such as this, undertaken with organized labor, had no precedent for Lippard in the New York art world, and the influence of the agitprop work she saw would later be felt in the Poster Committee of the Art Workers' Coalition. As she recalled:

> **I was politicized by a trip to Argentina in the fall of 1968, when I talked to artists who felt that it was immoral to make their art in the society that existed there. It becomes clear that today everything, even art, exists in a political situation. I don't mean that art itself has to be seen in political terms or *look* political, but the way artists handle their art, where they make it, the chances they get to make it, how they are going to let it out, and to whom—it's all part of a life style and a political situation.**[14]

As with many others in her circle, working in the "gap" between art and life, a phrase so often quoted from Robert Rauschenberg, was becoming a political act. Lippard recognized that while artists could still choose to make art without overt political content, she felt that artists, critics, and curators had an obligation to engage somehow with the social and political world in which they lived and worked. Folding the political models she discovered in Argentina into her conception of the operational possibilities for Conceptual art would evolve over the following several years—sometimes with feelings of frustration about the lack of direct political engagement in much Conceptual art—and ultimately resulted in her heightened commitment to social issues, particularly feminism, in the 1970s.

Lippard met another important collaborator during this time, the dealer and publisher Seth Siegelaub. His particular strategy for circumventing the gallery and museum system was to refashion his role from a presenter into that of a distributor of information. Rather than attempt to change existing models, he tended simply to ignore them, preferring to focus on methods for direct engagement, and understanding that such methods offered a great deal more interaction with the broadest possible public, on an international level. As Lippard wrote, "Siegelaub's strategy of bypassing the art world with exhibitions that took place outside of galleries and/or New York and/or were united in publications that were art rather than merely *about* art dovetailed with my own notions of a dematerialized art that would be free of art-world commodity status."[15] The most effective of these strategies was to replace exhibitions with publications, and Siegelaub proceeded to make this relatively subtle point repeatedly, through various experimental exhibitions in larger periodicals and through his own stand-alone publications.

When Lippard made her trip to Argentina and Peru, at least one of her goals was to build a support network to produce more populist and accessible exhibitions. Specifically, she was interested in finding ways to capitalize on Conceptual art's easy transportability, sidestepping the cumbersome logistical issues usually so much a part of exhibiting fine art. On her trip, she was working on what she called a "suitcase exhibition" of dematerialized art. Because most of the art was made up of instructions, or diagrams written on cheap paper, or simple photographic documentation, an entire exhibition devoted to the movement could travel in one suitcase, easily transported and installed in each venue by one person; in this case, Lippard envisioned a different artist moving and reinstalling the show from one venue to the next. (As it turned out, this idea was not realized in Argentina in 1968, but the seed of it became the "numbers" shows, the first of which opened at the Seattle Art Museum in September 1969.)

Back in New York in October 1968, a politically invigorated Lippard was invited to co-curate a show of Minimal work, sales from which were to benefit the Student Mobilization Committee (SMC), an antiwar group. The show also happened to be the first held at the Paula Cooper Gallery on Prince Street in SoHo.[16] Organized by Lippard, the painter Robert Huot, and the Socialist Workers Party organizer Ron Wolin, the show (figure 6), called *Art for Peace* in *Six Years,* is noted there not for its political motivations, but solely for the distinction that "Sol LeWitt does his first drawing in pencil on the wall (temporary) at the Paula Cooper Gallery."[17] However, in 1969 Lippard organized another show at Paula Cooper, this one also in support of the growing antiwar mobilization, but this time the benefit was for a new political action group that Lippard was very involved with: the Art Workers' Coalition. This show, called *Number 7*,[18] contained a much stronger Conceptual art presence than had the benefit the year before, illustrating both the growth of the movement and the clarification of Lippard's understanding of the work. For this benefit show, one small room was deliberately crowded with works while another, larger room seemed remarkably empty—though it actually contained nine pieces, including Hans Haacke's *Air Currents* (a small fan), and a *blp*—a lozenge-shaped mark stenciled on the wall—by Richard Artschwager. In many ways, *Number 7* was a developmental counterpoint to *Eccentric Abstraction,* three years earlier. *Number 7* was Lippard's most dematerialized show up to that time and featured a number of Conceptual art methods, notably, devoting a room to work that engaged the idea of emptiness. But just as important as the show's strong Conceptual focus were the political overtones. Both Paula Cooper shows were fundraisers for anti–Vietnam War causes. However, where the *Art for Peace* show featured Minimal work presented in support of a political agenda, in *Number 7,* for the first time, Conceptual art concerns directly overlapped with Lippard's political interests.

The Numbers Shows and Magazine Exhibitions

Given the green light—what she called "the conceptual freedom principle"[19]—to think of her exhibition activities as multivalent and largely self-defining, Lippard tackled the series of presentations that would be her most radical experiment in blurring the boundaries between curating, criticism, and artistic production: the so-called numbers shows. Conceived as group shows, the four exhibitions were not intended to be thematic beyond being Lippard's attempt to present artists working within the dematerialized idiom she had been tracking for several years. From this single common reference point each of the exhibitions offered an exercise in sheer volume and diversity of work that was intended to push viewers into making up their own minds about the validity of this new trend. It seems to have been a priority to present "fragmentation, variety and disparity of intention,"[20] with as little curatorial or critical mediation as possible. In the numbers shows the objective was to present the breadth of Conceptual artists working outside the mainstream, to show at once the simplicity of the notion that art can be primarily about ideas rather than about materials, while also presenting for the first time the truly extraordinary breadth of creative ambitions that came along with that notion. As has

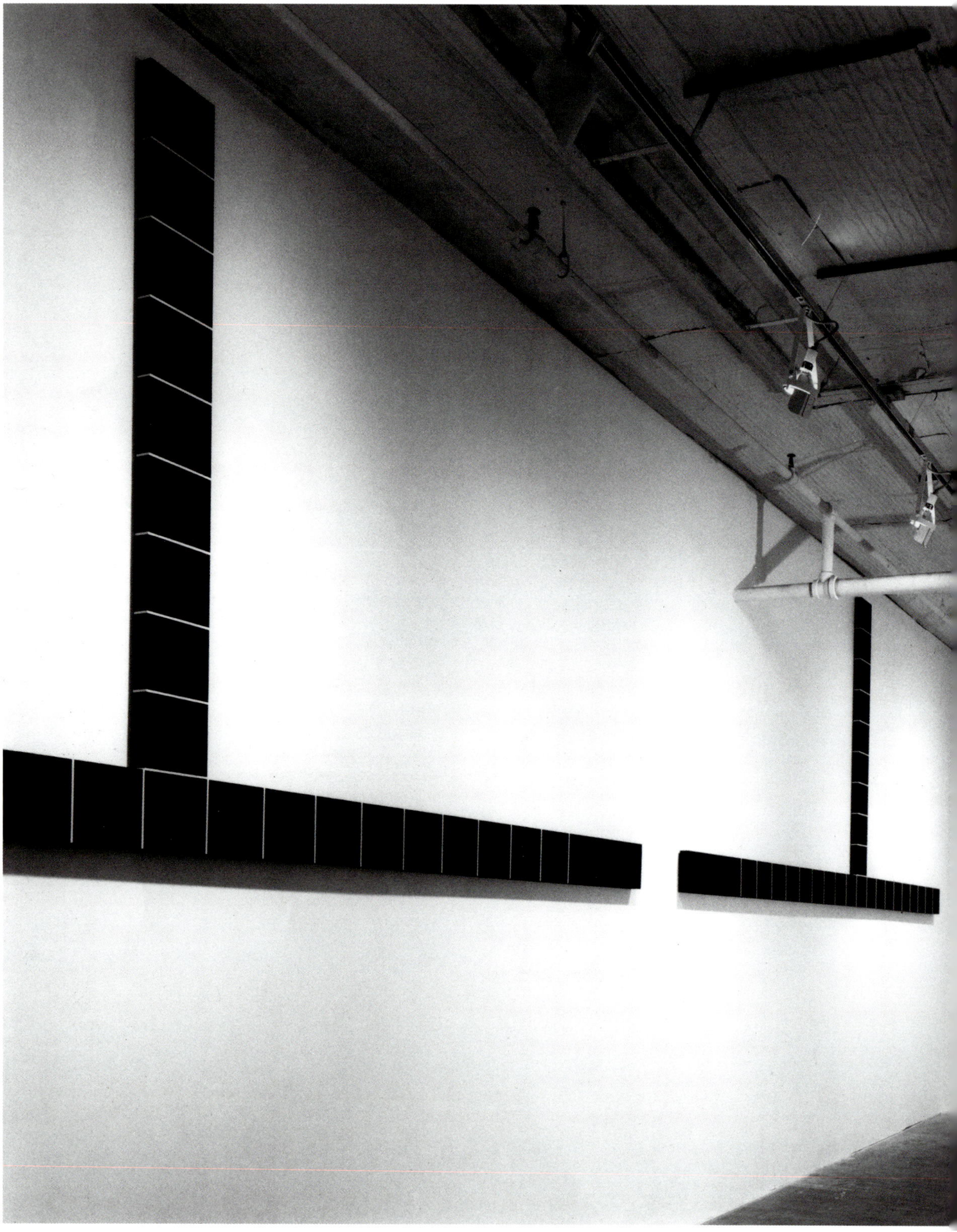

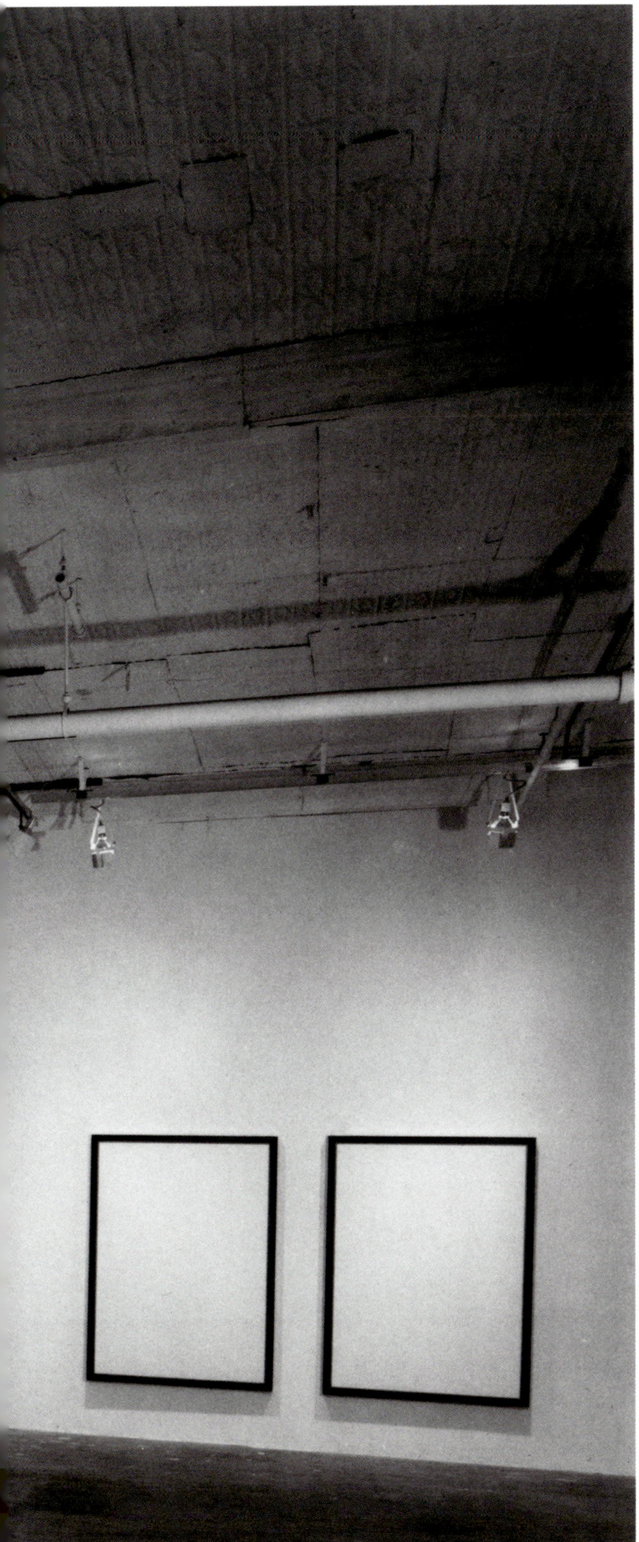

FIGURE 6

Installation view of *Benefit for the Student Mobilization Committee to End the War in Vietnam* including works by Will Insley (left) and Jo Baer (right); Paula Cooper Gallery, New York, October 22–31, 1968; co-organized by Lucy R. Lippard, Robert Huot, and Ron Wolin. © Paula Cooper Gallery, New York. (Photo: James Dee, courtesy Paula Cooper Gallery, New York)

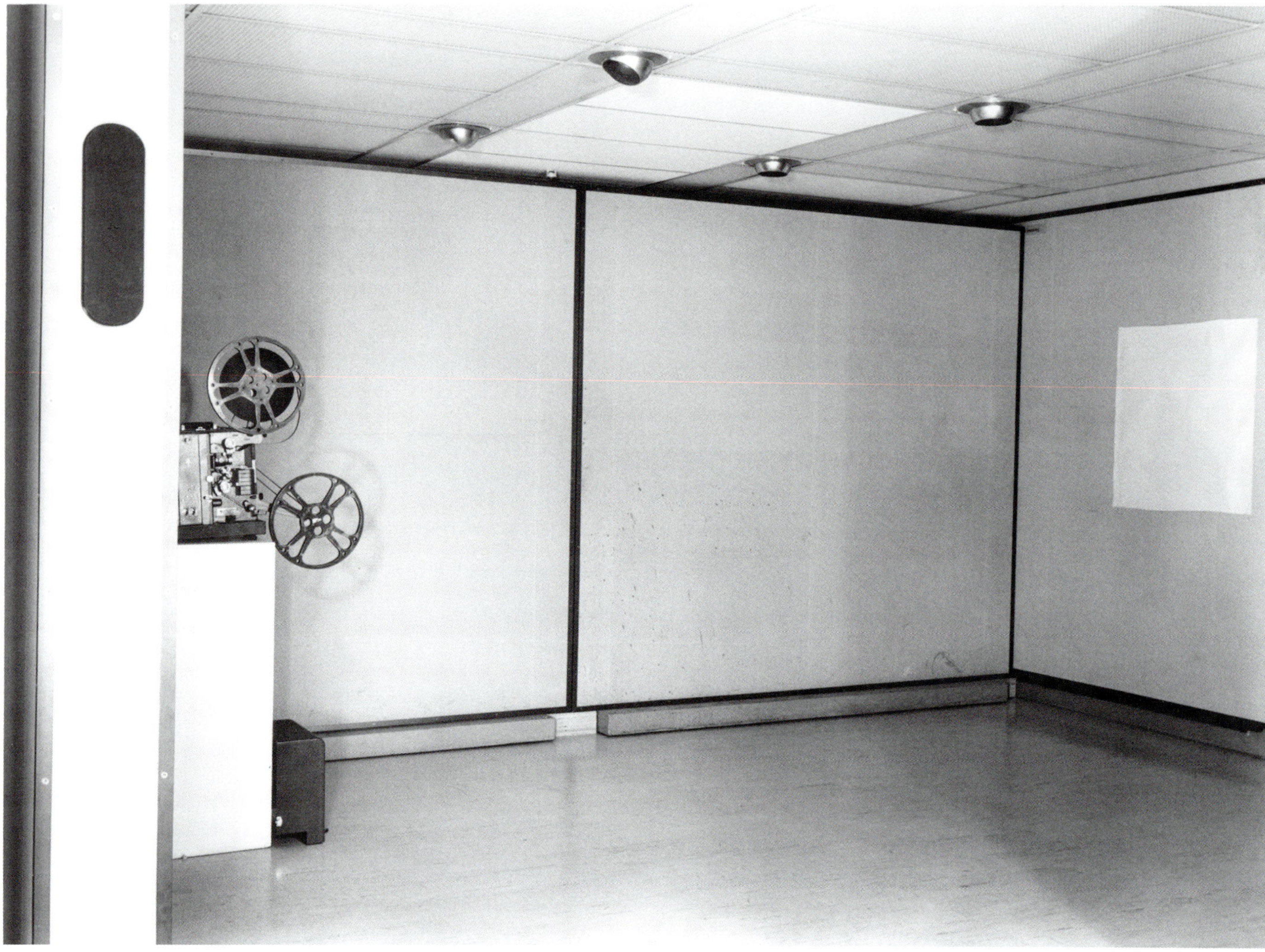

FIGURE 7

Installation view of *557,087* including Richard Artschwager, *blp*, 1969 (front left), and film projector used to show Hanne Darboven, *The Year 68 in 6 Books and 6 Films,* 1969 (right); Seattle Art Museum, September 5–October 5, 1969; organized by Lucy R. Lippard. (Photo: © Seattle Art Museum)

been noted elsewhere, the most lasting legacy of these exhibitions are the unique catalogues made up of index cards, which continue to circulate as a significant prototypical example of non-hierarchical publication design.

The first of the four shows was titled *557,087* (after the population of the venue city). More than seventy artists participated. Sponsored by the Contemporary Art Council of the Seattle Art Museum, it took place September 5–October 5, 1969, at the museum's World's Fair Pavilion Annex (figures 7–9), and at numerous other venues (a map was provided for those interested in attempting to traverse the fifty-mile radius the various installations spanned). Working on a shoestring, and with a very few volunteer helpers, Lippard not only installed, but in many cases made the works herself from instructions provided by the artists (figure 10), and sometimes the results were not what the artists had intended; three pieces were made incorrectly. And not everything got made, some instructions being too expensive or complex for execution within the installation time frame. In much the same vein, the next stop for the show was Vancouver, where it was seen January 13–February 8, 1970, at the Vancouver Art Gallery, the University of British Columbia Art Gallery, and several other venues in the city; it was retitled *955,000* (figure 11). Three artists were added for this stop and the installation was undertaken much as it had been in Seattle. The third numbers show, *2,972,453,* which Lippard called "an unofficial continuation" of the first two presentations, took place in November 1970 in Buenos Aires and included only artists who had not participated in the first two iterations of the project and would seem to be the culmination of her earlier exploratory trip to Argentina to develop a "suitcase" exhibition.

Many came away from the first two numbers shows thinking that Lucy Lippard was not so much a curator as a closet artist.[21] And while that comment may have been intended simply as cutting, it does effectively confirm the very ideas she had been thinking and writing about for three years. What her numbers exhibitions did was to utilize Conceptual art methods to throw a light on the inescapable fact that critics and curators had *always* used artists as their medium. And, to a large degree, she did this simply by laying bare her curatorial method, which was, basically, an organizational exercise in making a Conceptual art project by using Conceptual artworks as her medium. For her, this multi-leveled, convoluted type of activity was a form of appropriation, one with roots in the strategies of Dada,[22] with its strong political connotations. It also seems to have been a test on Lippard's part—an attempt to push the work she had been nurturing out of the nest, so to speak, to see if it would fly.

In 1970 Lippard participated in two exhibition projects organized by, and appearing within the pages of, the influential British periodical *Studio International*, then edited by Peter Townsend. Both curatorial experiments tested the theory that the translation from gallery to publication could be an equally effective means for transmitting information. As she recalled: "One of the things we often speculated about in the late sixties was the role of the art magazine. In an era of proposed projects, photo-text works, and artists' books, the periodical could be the ideal vehicle for art itself rather than merely for reproduction, commentary and promotion."[23] Her first effort in this medium was an adaptation of an exhibition called *Groups* that had been originally installed at the School of Visual Arts Gallery in New York in November 1969. Today, *Groups* would perhaps more accurately be called an installation project rather than an exhibition. The project originated when Lippard—just back in New York from installing *557,087*—sent out a letter to a group of artists asking them to produce photographs of and descriptive texts about groups of people of their own choosing. With these specific instructions, Lippard was

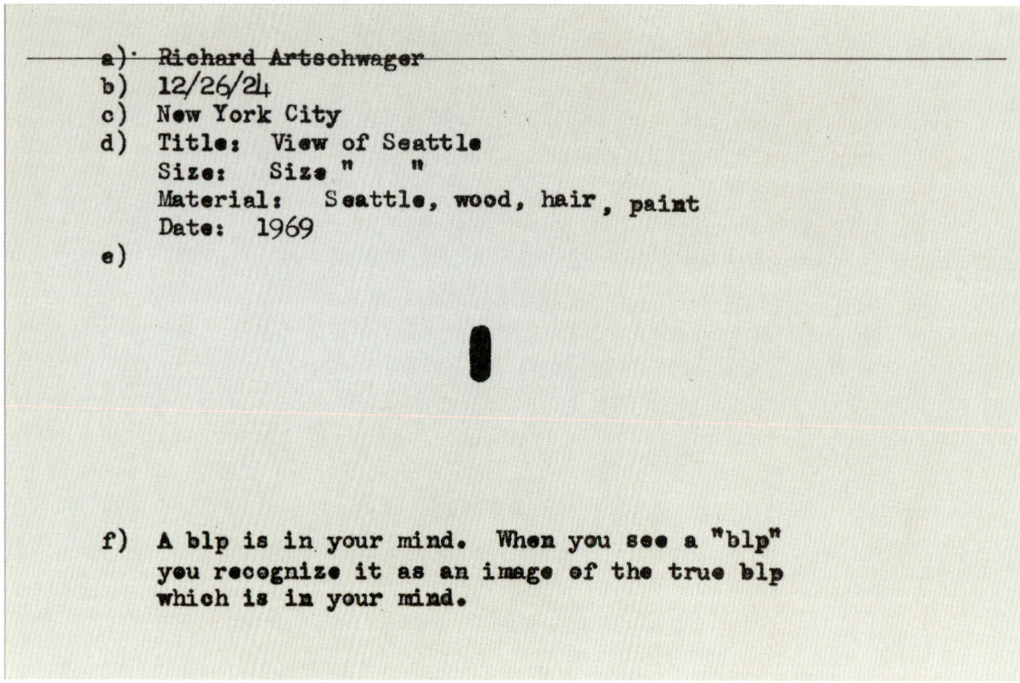

a) ~~Richard Artschwager~~
b) 12/26/24
c) New York City
d) Title: View of Seattle
Size: Size " "
Material: Seattle, wood, hair, paint
Date: 1969
e)

f) A blp is in your mind. When you see a "blp" you recognize it as an image of the true blp which is in your mind.

FIGURE 8

Richard Artschwager (American, b. 1923). *View of Seattle*, 1969. Contribution to the catalogues of *557,087*, 1969, and *955,000*, 1970. Index card, 4 × 6 in. (10.2 × 15.2 cm). Vancouver: Vancouver Art Gallery, 1970. © Richard Artschwager. (Photo: Brooklyn Museum)

FIGURE 9

"Seattle Installation" (enlarged), from the catalogue of *955,000*, 1970. Index card, 6 × 4 in. (15.2 × 10.2 cm). Vancouver: Vancouver Art Gallery, 1970. Catalogue page © Seattle Art Museum. (Photo: Brooklyn Museum)

Seattle installation
1) Sandback, Piper, Castoro, Bochner
2) Hesse, Flanagan, Borofsky

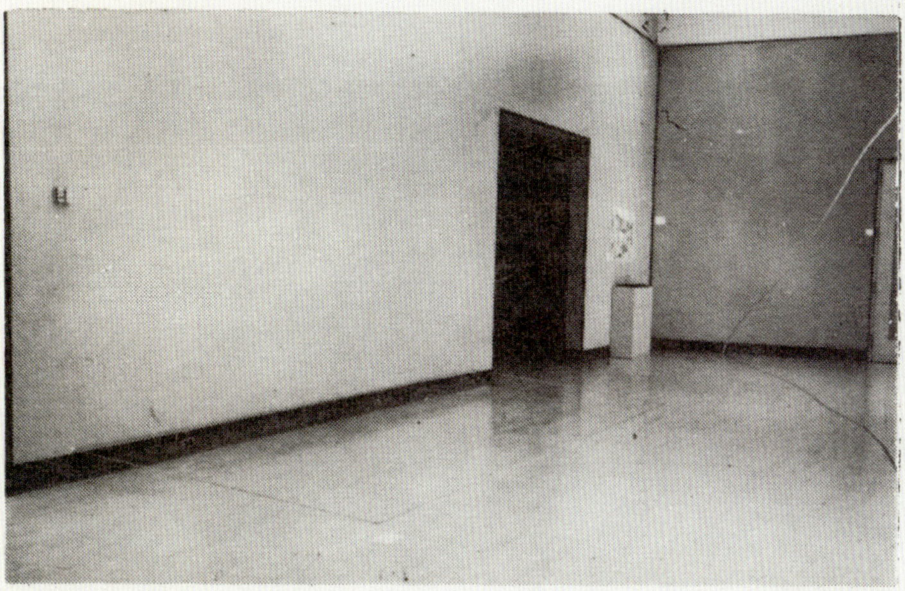

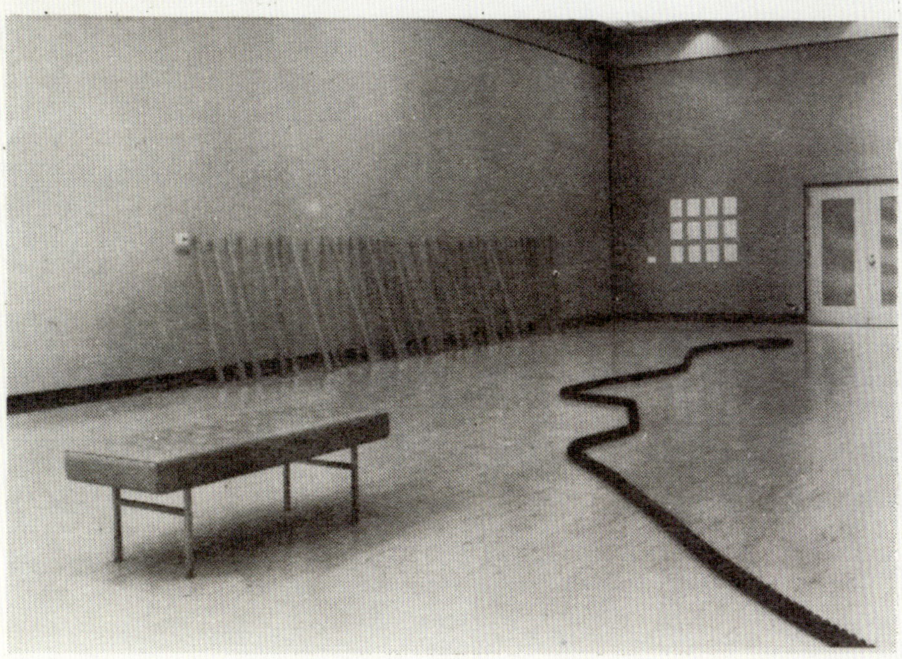

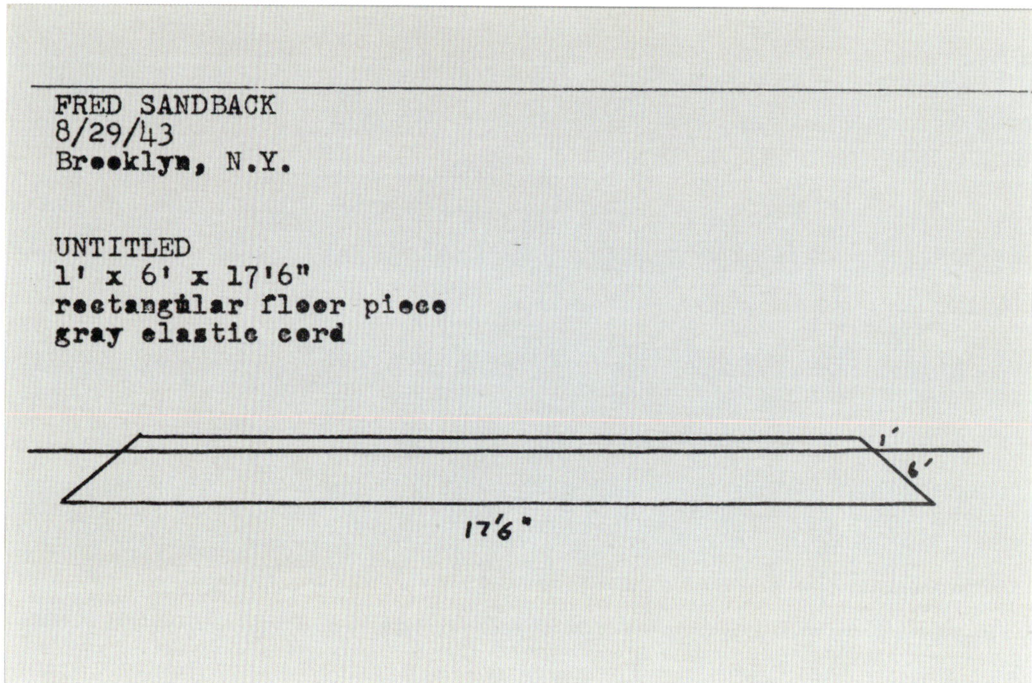
FRED SANDBACK
8/29/43
Brooklyn, N.Y.

UNTITLED
1' x 6' x 17'6"
rectangular floor piece
gray elastic cord

1'
6'
17'6"

FIGURE 10

Fred Sandback (American, b. 1943). *Untitled*, 1969. Contribution to the catalogues of *557,087*, 1969, and *955,000*, 1970. Index card, 4 × 6 in. (10.2 × 15.2 cm). Vancouver: Vancouver Art Gallery; Seattle: Seattle Art Museum, 1970. © 2011 Fred Sandback Archive. (Photo: Brooklyn Museum)

FIGURE 11

Lucy R. Lippard (American, b. 1937). Checklist of artworks for *955,000*, 1969. Typewritten list with handmarked notes, 9½ × 6⅛ in. (24 × 15.5 cm). Lucy R. Lippard Papers, Archives of American Art, Smithsonian Institution, Washington, D.C.

955,000

Acconci V	2 calenders on floor
Andre,C	28 sections of log, Foreshore Park
Arnatt	2 boxes with mirroes, front of gallery
Artschwager	blps
Baldessari	border project I.D. of 3 other pieces in pic ←
? Baldwin,M	5 books, 1 poster on table
Baxter	cn/cp Telex,Xerox Telecopier,B.C.Tel Electrowriter
Beery,G	5' square painting "note - make painting of note"
Bochner	none 46,000 cubic inches blank
Bollinger	large log, Kitsilano Beach
Borofsky,J	12 papers on wall ? more sheets ? ←
Burgy	2 books on table
Buren	stripes
Castoro	reostated room
Curnoe,G	Tape, Victoria Hospital
Darboven	8 books on table
de Maria	tape measure on wall
Dibbets	tape
Dikeakos	file
Ferrer	logs on beach Kits
Flanagan	50' rope on floor
Graham,D	papers, tape on table SUB - in inst shot at U.B.C.
Haacke	plastic tube in ground nr SUB
Hay,A	canvas and dust
Hesse,E	tubes leaning against wall
Huebler,D	Man wanted poster
Huot	room - flat blue
— Kaltenbach	none
Kawara	4 books on table
Kienholz	1 plaque, 1 letter SUB
Kinmont	1 notebook with 9 photos
— Kosuth	telegram
— Koslov	none
Latham	case papers misc.
Le Va	meat cleavers
— LeWitt	drawing
Louw	lathing Stanley Park
— Lunden	large drawing
— McLean	Hoax Piece
Morris	shot gun blast and photo
Nauman	3 reels of films SUB in inst shot of SUB.
N.Y. Graphic Workshop	Camnister Somebody's fragment
	Porter
— Oppenhiem	sepia blue print
Perrault	X all over
Piper,A	2 books on stand, 1 map on wall SUB
Ruppersberg,A	2 pieces stationary, glass, table
Rohm	40' rope on wall SUB
Ryman	20 panels paper on wall
Ruscha	sunset strip book opened on wall
Sandback	elastic cord on wall and and floor
— Sawchuck	3 poles through 3 trees Lynn Valley
— Schum	film Landart
— Sims	paint on trees SFU
Smithson	photos of glue piece SUB
Sonnier	mirrors and fixtures
— Wall,J	clipboard
? Weiner	card on wall
Serra	Gravity piece

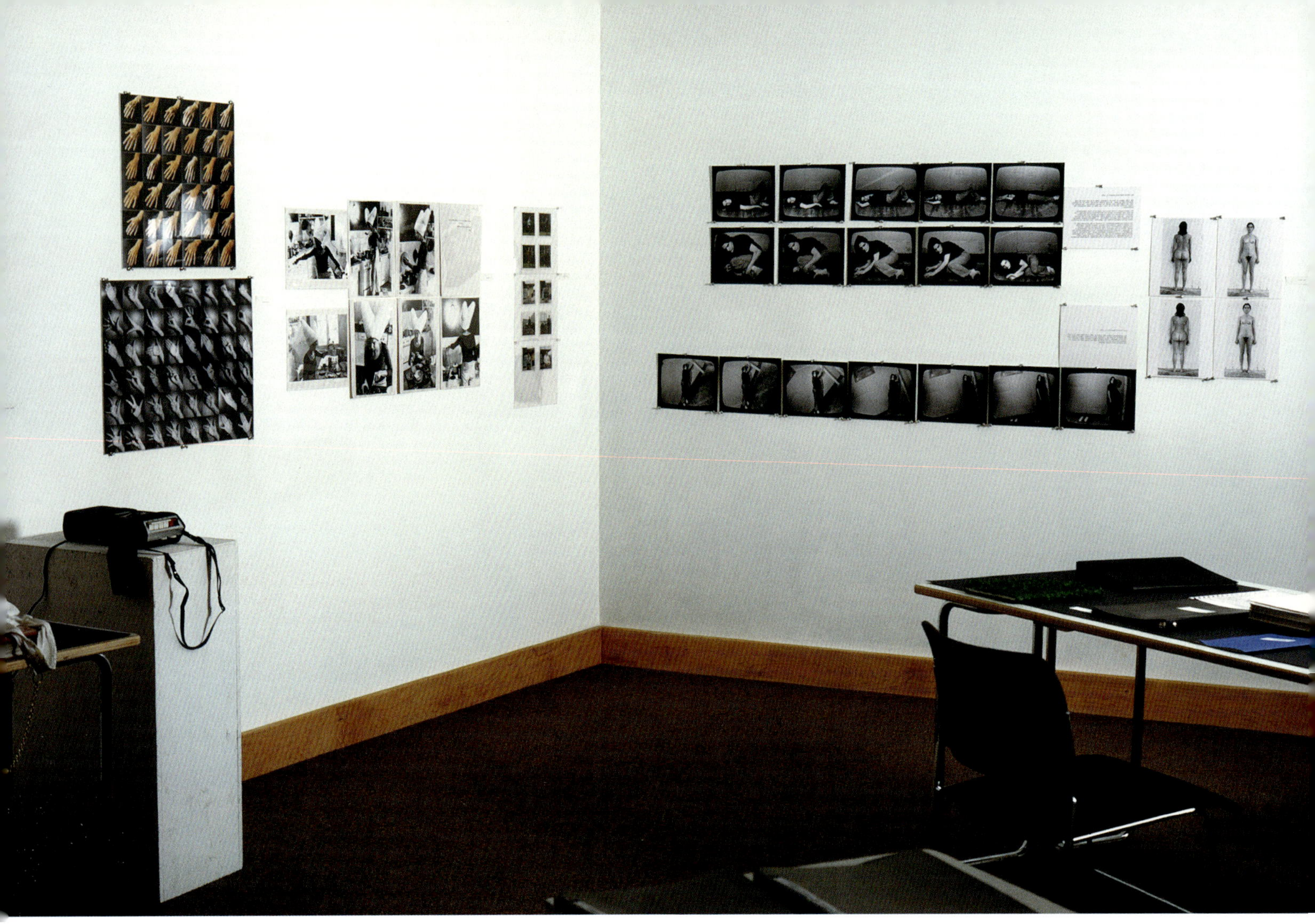

FIGURE 12

Installation view of *c. 7,500* with works by Athena Tacha (far left), Ulrike Rosenbach (second from left), and Rita Meyers (far right); California Institute of the Arts, Valencia, May 1973–February 1974; organized by Lucy R. Lippard. California Institute of the Arts Library Visual Resource Collection, Valencia. (Photo: California Institute of the Arts)

setting a different task than she had for the numbers shows—laying out a more constrictive set of parameters for the artists she invited. The resulting projects were first presented in an exhibition form at the SVA and then reproduced in the magazine. The second project was part of a special issue of *Studio International* (July–August 1970) organized by Seth Siegelaub and called *July/August Exhibition*. In this case, Lippard and her co-contributors inserted "exhibitions" into the pages typically reserved for art criticism, again effecting an experiment in turning the magazine into a portable museum. Lippard instituted a kind of game of telephone, requesting an exchange of ideas between the artists she asked to participate: "I asked each artist to provide a 'situation' within which the next artist was to work, so the works created one cumulative, circular piece."[24] These two projects and the numbers shows share a developmental and investigational approach that was common among Lippard and her peers, who, about three years into it, were constantly thinking about the extended intellectual applications of Conceptual art as it entered a more mature phase.

The fourth and final numbers show, *c. 7,500*, does not fall within the chronological span of *Six Years,* though Lippard was working on it as the book went to press. Originating at the California Institute of the Arts in Valencia, in 1973 (figure 12), this population-number title stuck, and the show continued under the same name to seven additional venues, ending in London.[25] This was an international exhibition of women Conceptual artists,[26] and the desire to do the show grew from Lippard's increasing frustration at hearing, on more than one occasion, that women artists were not significant contributors to the Conceptual art movement. As described in a press release for the show at Smith College (this text appears in various versions edited by Lippard), "it will be difficult to generalize about 'feminine' art with the usual clichés. Some of the participating artists are feminists, some are not. This was not an issue in choosing their work. The show itself, however, was organized in reply to the remark 'There are no women conceptual artists.' (Three years ago one was always hearing that there were no women sculptors). Art has no sex, but artists do."[27]

With the work of the twenty-six artists featured in *c. 7,500* fitting into one packing case (see figures 13–16), and being installed at each venue by a new, local crew, we see confirmed the remarkable tenacity of some of Lippard's earliest notions about how her Conceptual art shows might function: "*c. 7,500* was intended to be inexpensive, easily portable, easily installed, with the art taking precedence over the presentation, due partly to the nature of the work itself and partially in protest against the over elaborate and inflationary exhibition[s] so common to the art world which make it necessary for a society to spend its money subsidizing museums rather than artists."[28] Lippard was still committed to the utility and pragmatism of the model of the suitcase exhibition.

In various writings about the project, some published and some in her notes, Lippard argued that Conceptual art was a method for making art that was particularly well suited to emerging women artists. There have been significant discussions about the place of women in the simultaneously emerging field of video art from this period and they closely parallel the reasons for the success women artists found within the Conceptual art movement. These include: the experimental nature of the medium meant it had not been canonized and institutionalized; as an inexpensive material, it had no immediate market value; and the art-historical and critical discussions about its intentions had not yet had the chance to write the contributions of women out of the picture. As a result of video's arriving on the contemporary art scene at about the

sent to Peter Mori

"C. 7,500"

SHIPPING LIST & NOTES

Package No.	Artist, title, notes....
1.	Nancy Kitchel, "One Hundred Identical Drawings", 99 drawings in plastic bags, 1 drawing without bag, T-pins
2.	Hanne Darboven, "1969 00→00", book, paper cover, torn slightly
	Ulrike Nolden, "The Artist as Married Woman (in her kitchen)", 7 photographs, 1 title card (not needed for installation)
	Christine Möbus, "The Unnecessary Betrothal of Frau Holle with the Shaman", 6 photographs with feathers, installation photo in #15
3.	Jacki Apple notebook, 3 ring binder
	Judith Stein, "Name Change Notebook", 3 ring binder
	Adrian Piper, "Talking to Myself", 3 ring binder, additional copy in #15
4.	N.E. Thing Co., "Act #51", "Act #13", "Act #62", mounted reproductions
	Athena Tacha, "Three Waves", mounted color photos
	Alice Aycock, "Maze", 6 large mounted photos, #1, #2, #3, #4, #6, #8. Text and title cards in #11.
	Jacki Apple, "Transcolor II", 8 cards, 3 with photos, 5 with text, one text card is a duplicate.
5.	Judith Stein, "Anyone to tease a saint seriously.", spiral bound book 4 copies, for sale for $3.00.
	Jennifer Bartlett, "Cleopatra I-IV", large book held together with small pieces of adhesive tape, has tendency to slip apart, needs attention during show.
	Laurie Anderson, "October, 1972", book, first several pages bent, etc.
6.	Christine Kozlov, "1962", "1966", "1967", "1968", "1969", books, paper covers tearing
7.	Mierle Laderman Ukeles, "Maintenance Artwork"- 16 photo holders with dust rag on shredded plastic cord, "Maintenance Art Tasks" - large bound book of photos with dust rag on chain.
	Bernadette Mayer, "Remembering", 3 ring binder

FIGURES 13–15

Lucy R. Lippard (American, b. 1937). Shipping list and notes for the exhibition *c. 7,500*, 1973. Typewritten list with handwritten notes; three sheets, 11 × 8½ in. (27.9 × 21.6 cm) each. Lucy R. Lippard Papers, Archives of American Art, Smithsonian Institution, Washington, D.C.

"C. 7,500" continued

7. (cont.) Eleanor Antin, "Domestic Peace", multi-ring binder

8. Christine Kozlov, "1963", "1964", "1965", "1961", books, paper covers tearing

Doree Dunlap, "People who like my work", "People who don't like my work", 4 sheets of paper to be filled out by viewers.

9. Nancy Kitchel, "The Face My Mother Gave Me", 20 plastic covered pages - 10 photos, 10 text

Laurie Anderson, "Institutional Dream Series", 6 paired photo & text cards, 1 introduction text card plus photo card

10. Rita Myers, "Tilt", "Slow Squeeze", "Body Halves", total of 21 photo cards and 2 text/title cards

11. Martha Wilson, "Red Head" - photo & text in plastic, "Premier"- photo & text in plastic, "Composure" (?) - 1 text & 9 photo cards in plastic. (I'm not sure of the title)

Alice Aycock, 7 text/title cards

12. Patricia Lasch, 4 works -- single page each in plastic, somewhat bent

Athena Tacha, "Ears" (?), color photos on card

Suzanne Kuffler, three works, 3 photos in plastic, 3 text pages

Athena Tacha, "My Mother, A Psychological Portrait", folded paper in plastic case

Mierle Laderman Ukeles, "Maintenance Artworks", 8 mounted cards, covered in plastic, pretty worn

13. Agnes Denes, "Psychograph", 36 sheets

14. Nancy Holt, two photo panels

15. Adrian Piper, extra copy of "Talking to Myself..."

Athena Tacha, "Heredity Study I", book

Renate Altenrath, book with grass mat cover

Judith Stein, additional copy, "Any One to Tease a Saint Seriously."

folder of instructions for several works.... also, empty folder with Christine Möbus' name on outside

16. Athena Tacha, "Feet & Shoes", black & white photos on card

Renee Nahum, 10 color photos in plastic, couples in and out of uniform

Athena Tacha, "Hands", photos on card

Athena Tacha, " Gestures #1, A Study of Finger Motions", photos on card

C. 7,500 continued

16. (cont.) Athena Tacha, "Expressions I, A study of Facial motions", photos on card,

Note: all of Athena Tacha's photos are beginning to show wear, plastic ripping, corners bent, etc.

N.E. Thing Co., two works, with heading "Information", paper one titled "And they had issue", one titled "What is Art?"

Doree Dunlap, two works on single panel, 4 photos & 2 text sheets mounted, puncture approximately in center.

Graphic board/panel, title and text.

17. Mierle Laderman Ukeles, Questionaires and envelopes.

18. Mierle Laderman Ukeles, 3 cassette tapes. (even though the box says "2 tapes."

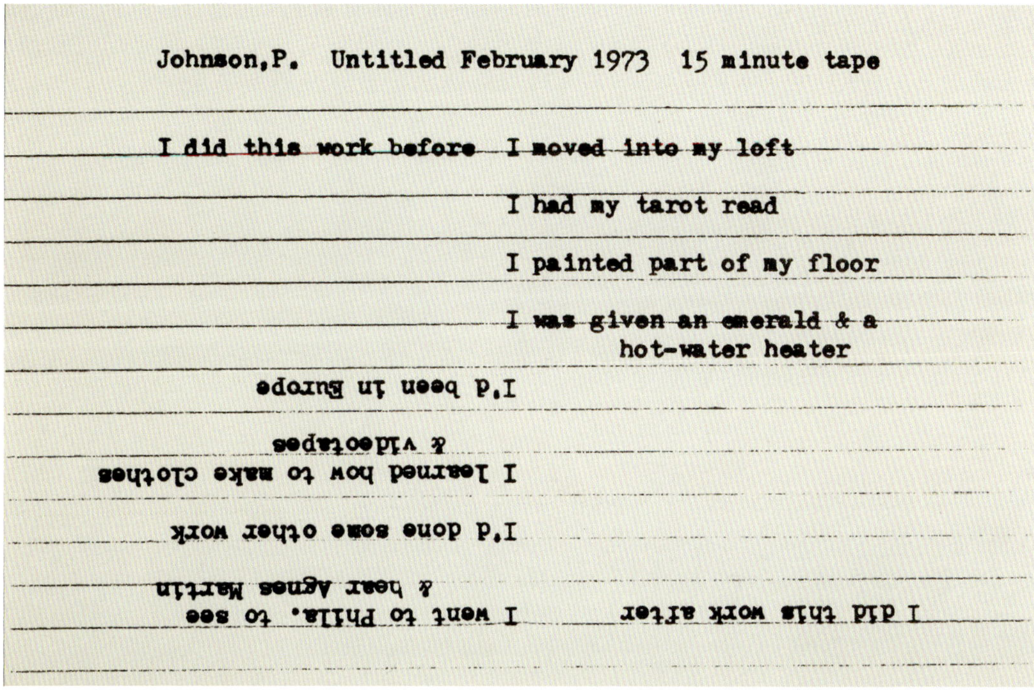
Johnson,P. Untitled February 1973 15 minute tape

I did this work before I moved into my loft

I had my tarot read

I painted part of my floor

I was given an emerald & a hot-water heater

I'd been in Europe

I learned how to make clothes & videotapes

I'd done some other work

I went to Phila. to see & hear Agnes Martin

I did this work after

FIGURE 16

Poppy Johnson (American, b. 1949). *Untitled*, 1973. Contribution to the catalogue of *c. 7,500*. Index card, 4 × 6 in. (10.2 × 15.2 cm). Valencia, Calif.: California Institute of the Arts, 1974. © Poppy Johnson. (Photo: Michael Tropea)

same time as the emergence of the women's movement, female artists were able to participate actively in defining the field.[29] Based on parallel arguments, Lippard suggested the powerful contribution on the part of women Conceptual artists in actively introducing political and social content into the rarified intellectual game-playing of earlier Conceptual art: "The inexpensive, ephemeral, unintimidating character of the Conceptual mediums themselves (video, performance, narrative, text, actions) encouraged women to participate, to move through this crack in the art world's walls. With the public introduction of younger women artists into Conceptual art, a number of new subjects and approaches appeared: narrative, role-playing, guise and disguise, body and beauty issues; a focus on fragmentation, interrelationships, autobiography, performance, daily life, and, of course, on feminist politics."[30]

Although *c. 7,500* opened in California just as *Six Years* was being published, it can perhaps be recast as the clearest realization of the ideas Lippard tracked and attempted to integrate in the book. Despite, or perhaps because of, the time break between the two, a consolidation of her own priorities is more clearly reflected in that 1973 exhibition than in any of her earlier curatorial experiments. Tying her work to the increasing imperative that feminism represented in Lippard's life became the ultimate example of the radical idea the numbers shows represent. In *c. 7,500* Lippard was effectively able to integrate political content with Conceptual art practices. And the merger represented more than the Paula Cooper shows could offer, wherein nonpolitical art had been invested with political significance simply by virtue of its contribution to a cause. Instead, the work of women artists in *c. 7,500* represents a next significant step in the development of Conceptual art itself.

In "Escape Attempts," Lippard is clear about her sense of dissatisfaction in regard to the real-life value of many Conceptual art ideas. "Communication (but not community) and distribution (but not accessibility) were inherent in Conceptual art. Although the forms pointed toward democratic outreach, the content did not. However rebellious the escape attempts, most of the work remained art-referential, and neither economic nor esthetic ties to the art world were fully severed (though at times we liked to think they were hanging by a thread). Contact with a broader audience was vague and undeveloped."[31] For Lippard, as she moved into an activist engagement with feminism, politics, and environmental issues, the hermetic nature of Conceptual art became less compelling, though when talking about Conceptual art in the terms it set up for itself—an art-world dialogue about the uses for art objects and the implications of giving priority to ideas and concepts—she did note, in the closing of "Escape Attempts": "Perhaps most important, Conceptualists indicated that the most exciting 'art' might still be buried in social energies not yet recognized as art."[32] Forty years later, and largely because of the pioneering work of that generation of artists, many social energies are indeed now recognized as art. And while Lippard's active engagement with the politics of feminism in the mid-1970s may have made the work she championed just a few years before seem relatively ineffective and benign in its real ambitions to foster change, nonetheless, the critical foundations and material tools that these artists so effectively marshaled into the realm of the fine arts have had a remarkably long shelf life.

Notes

1. Quoted in Hans Ulrich Obrist, *A Brief History of Curating* (Zurich: JRP/Ringier, 2008), p. 218.
2. It is perhaps helpful to clarify that the six calendar years covered by the publication begin January 1, 1966, and end December 31, 1971; in other words, events from 1972 are not included in the chronology.
3. Lippard, "Escape Attempts," in *Six Years: The dematerialization of the art object from 1966 to 1972: a cross-reference book of information on some esthetic boundaries: consisting of a bibliography into which are inserted a fragmented text, art works, documents, interviews, and symposia, arranged chronologically and focused on so-called conceptual or information or idea art with mentions of such vaguely designated areas as minimal, anti-form, systems, earth, or process art, occurring now in the Americas, Europe, England, Australia, and Asia (with occasional political overtones), edited and annotated by Lucy R. Lippard* (New York and London: Praeger Publishers, 1973; reprinted, with a new introduction, Berkeley and Los Angeles: University of California Press, 1997), p. viii. Lippard originally wrote "Escape Attempts" for the exhibition catalogue *Reconsidering the Object of Art, 1965–1975* (Los Angeles: The Museum of Contemporary Art; Cambridge, Mass.: The MIT Press, 1995). It was subsequently reprinted as a new introduction to the 1997 reissue of *Six Years*.
4. Lippard described the distinction she saw between her ambitions as a writer and her critical work, in a 1974 interview. See Lyn Blumenthal and Kate Horsfield, *Lucy Lippard 1974: An Interview*, 1974, color video, 25 min.
5. Lippard, "Escape Attempts," in *Six Years,* p. vii.
6. *Primary Structures: Younger American and British Sculptors,* The Jewish Museum, New York, April 27–June 12, 1966; *Eccentric Abstraction,* Fischbach Gallery, New York, September 20–October 8, 1966.
7. Lucy R. Lippard, "Eccentric Abstraction," text for *Eccentric Abstraction: Alice Adams, Louise Bourgeois, Eva Hesse, Gary Kuehn, Bruce Nauman, Don Potts, Keith Sonnier, Frank Lincoln Viner,* exh. brochure (New York: Fischbach Gallery, 1966). Also published in *Art International,* vol. 10, no. 9 (November 1966), pp. 34–40; reprinted, slightly cut and rearranged, in Lucy R. Lippard, *Changing: Essays in Art Criticism* (New York: E. P. Dutton, 1971).
8. Lippard, "Escape Attempts," in *Six Years,* p. x.
9. Lippard, "Eccentric Abstraction," *Art International,* p. 38.
10. Ibid., p. 28.
11. John Chandler and Lucy R. Lippard, "The Dematerialization of Art," *Art International*, vol. 12, no. 2 (February 1968), pp. 31–32, as quoted in *Six Years,* pp. 42–43.
12. Lippard, Author's Note to the first edition of *Six Years,* p. 3.
13. Lippard, "Escape Attempts," in *Six Years,* p. ix. In addition to her experiences seeing new art, Lippard also gained first-hand experience with the repressive Argentine government when she and her colleague Jean Clay were pressured to select artists for exhibition for political reasons.
14. Lippard, Preface to *Six Years*, pp. 8–9.
15. Ibid., p. ix.
16. The National Mobilization Committee to End the War in Vietnam was a short-lived coalition of antiwar activists formed in the spring of 1967, after a May meeting, called the Spring Mobilization Conference, held in Washington, D.C. This gathering of antiwar activists convened to consolidate a course of action following a group of successful but more grassroots demonstrations earlier that year, such as draft-card burnings held in San Francisco and New York City. The Student Mobilization Committee (SMC) was founded later and on a similar model. See "National Mobilization Committee to End the War in Vietnam Records, 1966–1969," Swarthmore College Peace Collection, available online at: www.swarthmore.edu/library/peace/DG051-099/dg075nmc.htm
17. Lippard, *Six Years*, p. 57.
18. According to Lippard, "I don't remember why it was [called] *Number 7*, probably because it was her seventh show in that space." Quoted in Obrist, *A Brief History of Curating,* p. 209.
19. Lippard, "Escape Attempts," in *Six Years,* p. x.
20. Lippard, *Six Years*, p. 111.
21. Peter Plagens, "557,087," *Artforum,* vol. 8, no. 3 (November 1969), pp. 64–67.

22. Lippard acknowledges the historical precedent of Dada, while also describing why such earlier movements were not highlighted by Conceptual artists, in "Escape Attempts," in *Six Years*, p. ix.

23. Ibid., p. xviii.

24. Ibid.

25. *c. 7,500*, in Valencia, California, where the show originated at the California Institute of the Arts, before traveling to additional venues: Smith College, Northampton, Massachusetts; Walker Art Center, Minneapolis; Artists in Residence (AIR) Gallery, New York; the Institute of Contemporary Art, Boston; Garage, London; And/Or Gallery, Seattle; and Moore College of Art, Philadelphia.

26. This was not the first show of women artists that Lippard organized. Her *Twenty-six Contemporary Women Artists* opened at the Aldrich Museum of Contemporary Art, Ridgefield, Connecticut, in April 1971 and included Alice Aycock, Adrian Piper, and Christine Kozlov, each of whom also participated in *c. 7,500*.

27. Lucy R. Lippard Papers, Archives of American Art, Smithsonian Institution, Washington, D.C.

28. Card catalogue for the exhibition. Lippard's working notes for this text are in the Lucy R. Lippard Papers, Archives of American Art, Smithsonian Institution, Washington, D.C.

29. An early and important exhibition and publication devoted to presenting the significant contributions of women in the development of video art was Joanne Hanley and Ann-Sargent Wooster's *The First Generation: Women and Video, 1970–1975,* Independent Curators, New York, 1993.

30. Lippard, "Escape Attempts," in *Six Years,* p. xi.

31. Ibid., p. xvi.

32. Ibid., p. xxii.

ABSENCE: 1) withdrawal, nonexistence, nonresi
disappearance, dispersion. 2) emptiness, void
exhaustion, exemption, blank, clean slate, tab
no body, nobody present, nobody on earth, not
nary one, no one, no man, never a one.

Lucy R. Lippard's Writing in and around Conceptual Art, 1969–73

Vincent Bonin

Lucy R. Lippard's Writing in and around Conceptual Art, 1969–73

Vincent Bonin

Lucy R. Lippard broached the concept of dematerialization in 1967, in an article written with John Chandler. They cited in passing John Cage's cryptic suggestion that a "dematerialization of intention" shapes what happens before, during, and after a musical performance.[1] A year later, Chandler and Lippard wrote a second article, in which they noted that the notion could describe the results of a protocol, adopted by certain artists, for conceiving of a work as a proposal or proposition—generally, a set of instructions—with the artist's intentions to be carried out by a third party. In a statement that reads like a kind of manifesto, the two authors observed that this new way of understanding artistic intentionality could also absorb the traditional function of the art critic:

> Idea art has been seen as art about criticism rather than art-as-art or even art about art. On the contrary, the dematerialization of the object might eventually lead to the disintegration of criticism as it is known today. The pedantic or didactic or dogmatic basis insisted on by many of these artists is incorporated in the art. It bypasses criticism as such. Judgment of ideas is less interesting than following the ideas through. In the process, one might discover that something is either a good idea, that is, fertile and open enough to suggest infinite possibilities; or a mediocre idea, that is, exhaustible; or a bad idea, that is, already exhausted, or with so little substance that it can be taken no further. (The same can be applied to style in the formal sense, and style except as an individual trademark tends to disappear in the path of novelty.) If the object becomes obsolete, objective distance becomes obsolete. Sometime in the near future it may be necessary for the writer to be an artist as well as for the artist to be a writer. There will still be scholars and historians of art, but the contemporary critic may have to choose between a creative originality and explanatory historicism.[2]

Lippard chose the first approach (creative originality) in pursuing a series of essays, exhibitions, and hybrid projects realized between 1969 and 1971, of which *Six Years: The Dematerialization of the Art Object from 1966 to 1972* would be the capstone.[3] Though the developments mapped out in *Six Years* started in 1966, it was in 1969 that they truly blossomed and began to be more widely seen. It was also in 1969 that Lippard put into practice the thesis of the article she had co-authored with Chandler in 1968: besides reaffirming "the dematerialization of the art object" and the obsolescence of formalist art criticism, the authors had proposed that the distribution of artworks outside the familiar and well-worn commercial channels might allow artists to circumvent market speculation.

Collaboration as Criticism

A close collaborator of Lippard's at the time, Seth Siegelaub, had comparable aims, as he hoped to bypass the dealer-critic system that set the exchange value of artworks.[4] In his projects, which often took the form of an exhibition that had no existence outside of its publication, such

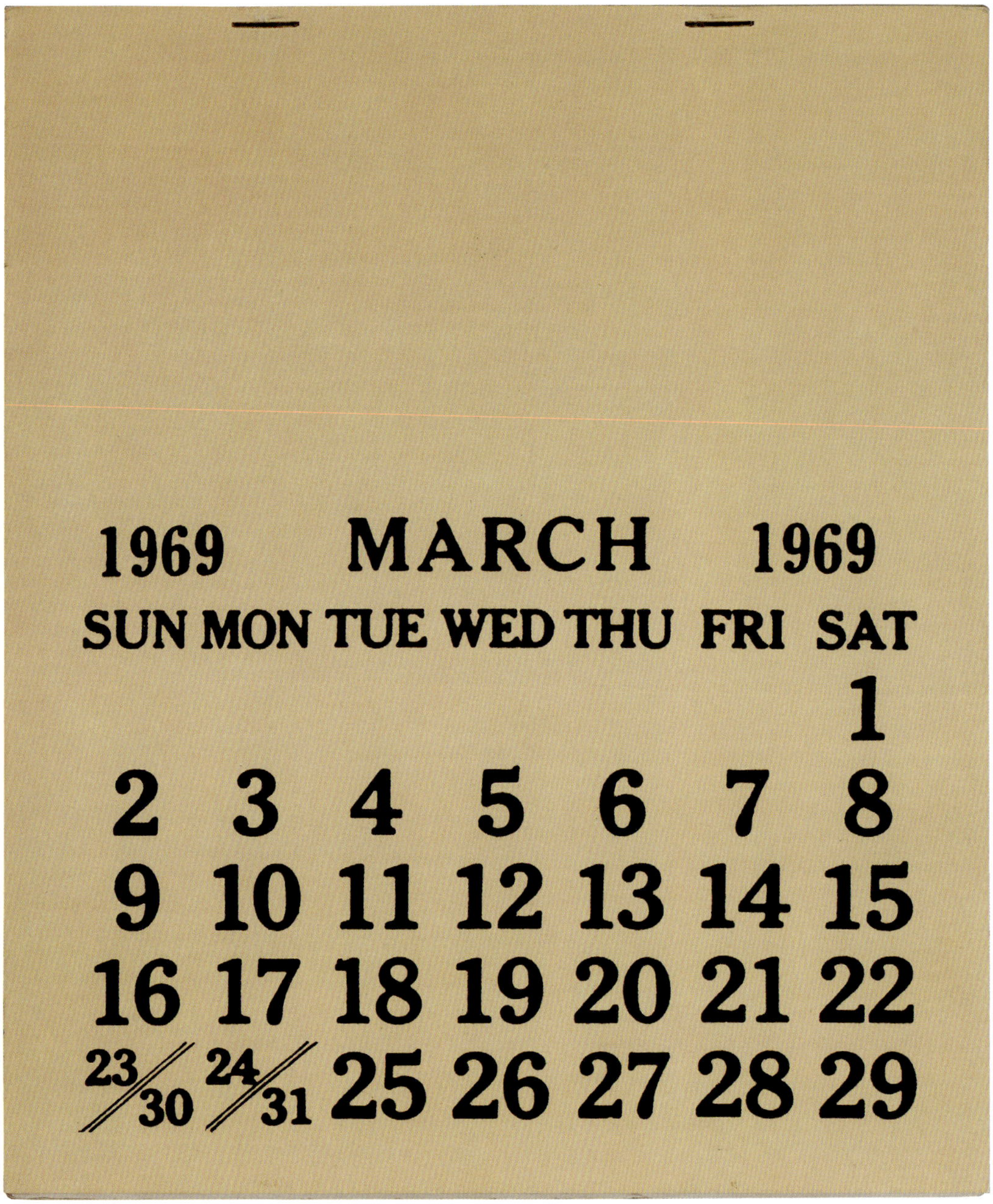

FIGURES 17, 18

Cover and page of catalogue of *One Month (March 1–31, 1969),* 1969. Offset printed, staple-bound catalogue, 8½ × 6⅞ in. (21.5 × 17.5 cm). New York: Seth Siegelaub, 1969. Courtesy The Stichting Egress Foundation, Amsterdam, at the Archives Department of The Museum of Modern Art, New York. (Photos: Michael Tropea)

SETH SIEGELAUB

Dear Mr. _______________,

I am organizing an International Exhibition of the "work" of 31 artists during each of the 31 days in March 1969. The exhibition is titled "One Month."

The invited artists and their dates are:

March			
1	Carl Andre	17	On Kawara
2	Mike Asher	18	Joseph Kosuth
3	Terry Atkinson	19	Christine Kozlov
4	Michael Baldwin	20	Sol LeWitt
5	Robert Barry	21	Richard Long
6	Rick Barthelme	22	Robert Morris
7	Iain Baxter	23	Bruce Nauman
8	James Byars	24	Claes Oldenburg
9	John Chamberlain	25	Dennis Oppenheim
10	Ron Cooper	26	Alan Ruppersberg
11	Barry Flanagan	27	Ed Ruscha
12	Dan Flavin	28	Robert Smithson
13	Alex Hay	29	De Wain Valentine
14	Douglas Huebler	30	Lawrence Weiner
15	Robert Huot	31	Ian Wilson
16	Stephen Kaltenbach		

You have been assigned March __, 1969.

Kindly return to me, as soon as possible, any relevant information regarding the nature of the "work" you intend to contribute to the exhibition on your day.

Your reply should specify one of the following:
1) You want your name listed, with a description of your "work" and/or relevant information.
2) You want your name listed, with no other information.
3) You do not want your name listed at all.

A list of the artists and their "work" will be published, and internationally distributed. (All replies become the property of the publisher.)

Kindly confine your replies to just verbal information.

All replies must be received by February 15th. If you do not reply by that time, your name will not be listed at all.

Thank you for your cooperation.

Sincerely,

SETH SIEGELAUB

21 January 1969

1100 Madison Avenue, New York 10028 (212) 288-5031

conventional mediating tools as the critical prefaces and explanatory texts usually found in exhibition catalogues (i.e., secondary information) disappeared in favor of artists' statements (primary information). In March 1969, Siegelaub organized *One Month* (a.k.a. *The March Show*)—an event made up of a thirty-one-day schedule in which each participant was assigned a particular day (figures 17, 18). Several of Siegelaub's other projects realized during the same year take as their titles the starting and ending dates of an event.[5]

With her "numbers" shows *557,087* (Seattle Art Museum, 1969) and *955,000* (Vancouver Art Gallery, 1970), Lippard, too, isolated raw, quantifiable data (in her case, the current population of each respective city) to create titles.[6] But in highlighting the theoretically maximum possible number of local visitors to each exhibition, she drew attention to human bodies occupying a given space, rather than focusing solely on an event's duration as Siegelaub did.

The publication accompanying these two "numbers" shows did not entirely dismiss the question of temporality, however, but rather invested the format of the catalogue (typically a compendium read after attending an event) with the possibility of being a site of artistic activity in the present moment. The publication consisted of a set of 137 randomly ordered index cards, one by each artist and twenty by Lippard, plus three bibliography cards (figure 19). Some of the cards were printed with instructions to be executed by a technician or Lippard herself. These index cards (also used as labels for some of the exhibited works) suggested a back-and-forth experience between site-specific interventions, discrete sculptural objects, and more rigidly Conceptual projects restricted to text-based descriptions and ad hoc documentation. Contrary to the self-effacing strategies employed by Siegelaub, Lippard retained an authorial voice throughout her curatorial projects realized both in and outside institutional frameworks. For example, some of Lippard's twenty index cards in the *557,087/955,000* catalogue carried theoretical assertions, while others contained discrete commentary on the works in the form of modular thematic blocks (discussing, for instance, Minimalism, the use of photography by artists, Conceptual art, and technology).[7] Another series of cards brought together quotations from authors such as the philosopher Herbert Marcuse, the psychiatrist R. D. Laing, and the art historian George Kubler. Lippard's three bibliographical cards cited articles pertaining to Conceptual or Minimal art exhibitions and texts written by some of the artists participating in *557,087* and *955,000:* Sol LeWitt, Mel Bochner, Robert Smithson, and Robert Morris, among others. In the Prefatory Notes to her collection *Changing: Essays in Art Criticism* (1971), Lippard described her approach to writing as a "fragmentary criticism of cross-references," aligning herself with textual strategies employed by peers at the time. In her view, this approach "seems more specific, more like direct communication, than the traditionally unified methods depending on literary transitions."[8]

Part of the exhibitions' mixed reception had to do with the difficulties of evaluating the degree of freedom Lippard allowed herself in interpreting the participants' instructions. For instance, in a review in *Artforum,* Peter Plagens described her approach as using artists as a "medium," to the end of ultimately transforming herself into an artist. Plagens also likened this new division of labor to "the current practice of a museum's hiring a critic to 'do' a show and the critic then asking the artists to 'do' pieces for the show."[9] Later, Lippard would argue against mixing analytical criticism with Conceptual propositions. That was, perhaps, motivated by a desire to clarify her role, for, as opposed to curators working in an ostensibly comparable way, such as the self-styled "exhibition-maker" Harald Szeemann,[10] she always considered her activities to be first and foremost those of a writer.

SELECTED GENERAL BIBLIOGRAPHY (ARRANGED CHRONOLOGICALLY)

Edward Ruscha, Twenty-Six Gas Stations (1962), Various Small Fires (1964), Some Los Angeles Apartments (1965), Every Building on the Sunset Strip (1966), Thirty-Four Parking Lots (1967), Royal Road Test (1967), Business Cards (1968), Nine Swimming Pools (1968).

Allan Kaprow, Assemblage, Environments and Happenings, Abrams, New York, 1966.

Lucy R. Lippard, "Eccentric Abstraction", Art International, Nov. 1966.

Joseph Kosuth, Christine Kozlov, eds., Non-Anthropomorphic Art by Four Young Artists, Lannis Museum of Normal Art, New York, 1967.

Sol LeWitt, "Paragraphs on Conceptual Art", Artforum, June 1967.

Mel Bochner, "Serial Art, Systems, Solpsism", Arts, Summer 1967.

"Hans Haacke", Robho, Paris, No. 2, Nov. - Dec. 1967.

Robert Smithson, "The Monoments of Passaic", Artforum, Dec. 1967.

Dan Graham, "Carl Andre", Arts, Jan. 1968.

John Chandler, Lucy R. Lippard, "The Dematerialization of Art", Art International, Feb. '68.

Robert Smithson, "A Museum of Language in the Vicinity", Art International, March 1968.

Robert Morris, "Anti-Form", Artforum, April 1968.

Robert Smithson, "A Sedimentation of the Mind: Earth Projects", Artforum, Sept. 1968.

Jack Burnham, "System Esthetics", Artforum, Sept. 1968.

Piero Gilardi, "Primary Energy and the Microemotive Artists, Arts, Sept.-Oct. 1968.

Peter Hutchinson, "Earth in Upheaval: Earthworks and Landscapes, Arts, Nov. 1968.

John Chandler, "The Last Word in Graphic Art", Art International, Nov. 1968.

FIGURE 19

"Selected General Bibliography (Arranged Chronologically)"; from the catalogues of *557,087*, 1969, and *955,000*, 1970. Index card, 4 × 6 in. (10.2 × 15.2 cm). Vancouver: Vancouver Art Gallery; Seattle: Seattle Art Museum, 1970. Catalogue page © Seattle Art Museum. (Photo: Brooklyn Museum)

PLEASE COMPLETE AND RETURN

1

N. E. THING COMPANY LIMITED

Name in Full SCHOOL OF VISUAL ARTS EXHIBITION – GROUPS Date Nov.3/69

Business Address NEW YORK, N.Y. USA.

Information PHOTO – VSI , (GROUP)– October 1, 1969

DESCRIPTION OF PHOTO-VSI

A line of 243 individuals is established. In the nearest right hand corner are GRADE 7 students (the tallest) and the line proceeds in a graduated scale, GRADE 6, GRADE 5, etc. to (the smallest) in GRADE 1 on the end of the line. This accentuates Classical Renassance perspective. Also the individuals make a human wedge 400' by (5'6" to 5'8") at near end by (3'6" to 3'8") at far end by approximately 15 " thick. The black four legged canine in this photo is close to and blending with black in near the centre of the wedge and a little off centre of the picture plane.

* Human wedge– thanks K.James, teachers, and all students, Maplewood School,N.Vancouver, B.C. Canada.

Firm or Company Name N. E. THING COMPANY LIMITED (NETCO)

Company Address 1419 Riverside Drive, North Vancouver, British Columbia, Canada

Cable Address " ANYTHING " Phone (604) 929-3662

List Company Departments THING, RESEARCH, MOVIE, PROJECT, ACT & ART, SERVICE, COP, PRINTING, PHOTOGRAPHY, COMMUNICATIONS, CONSULTING

Describe Company's Business PRODUCERS & CONSULTANT SPECIALISTS IN: Ideas, Planning Sensitivity Information(specialty Visual – V.S.I.), Name Development, Design, Ecology, Communications, Architecture, Aesthetics, Things, Photo-V.S.I., Work, Anything

(over)

(Signed) ....
President, Iain Baxter

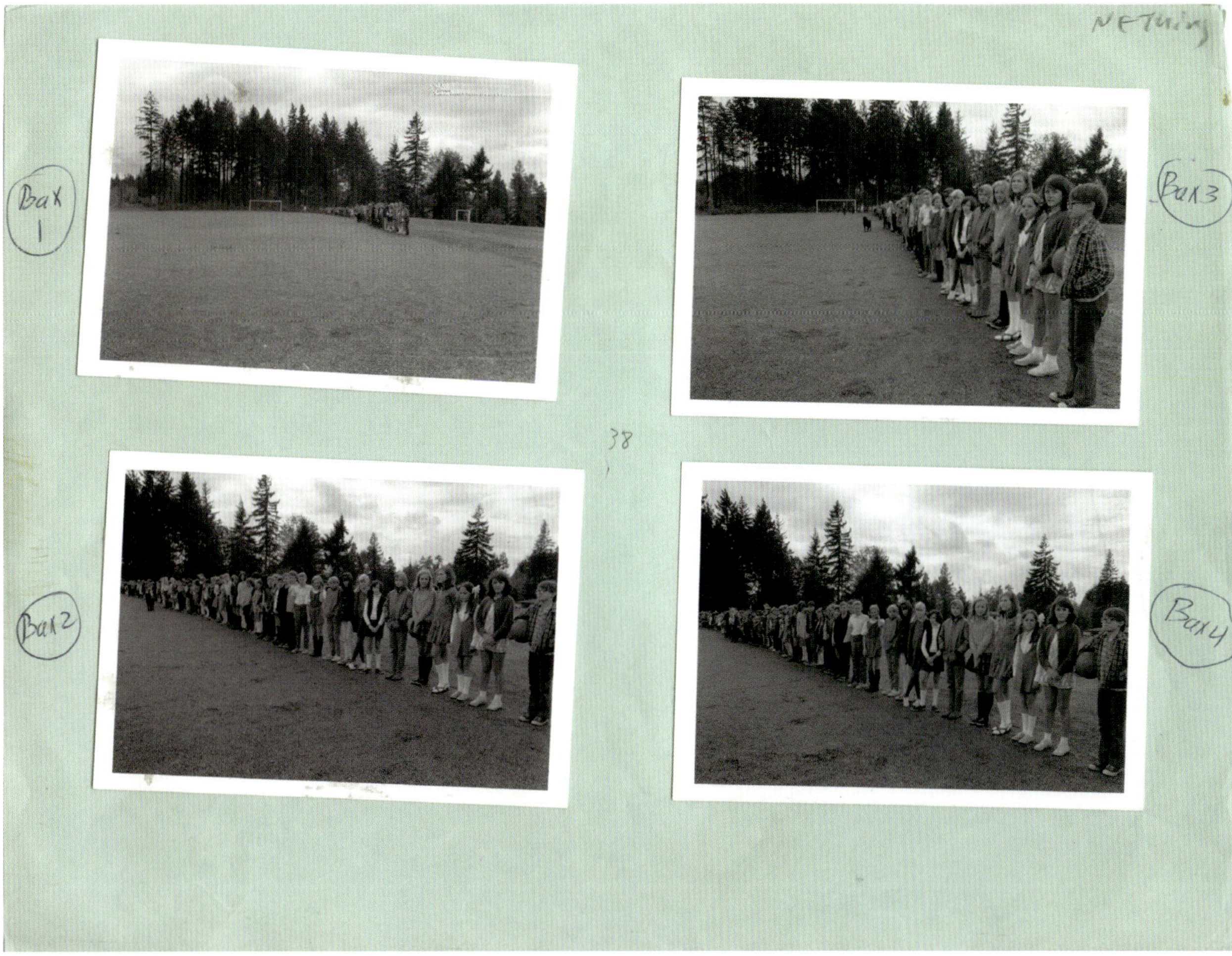

FIGURES 20, 21

N. E. Thing Co. (Iain Baxter& [Canadian, b. England, 1936] and Ingrid Baxter [American, b. 1938]). Contribution to the exhibition *Groups*, as laid out for reproduction in *Studio International* magazine, March 1970. Pasted photographs and pen on paper, 8 × 11 in. (20.3 × 27.9 cm). Studio International Papers, Tate Archive, London. (Photos: © 2011 Tate, London)

With *557,087* and *995,000*, Lippard had solicited written instructions from the participants and took on the responsibility for the works' execution. In subsequent projects she reversed the strategy, asking participating artists to execute *her* instructions, as in the *Groups* exhibition at the School of Visual Arts in November 1969, printed in *Studio International* magazine in March 1970 (figures 20, 21).[11] Thirty artists were invited to photograph a group of five or more people each, in the same place and in similar positions every day for a week.[12] Participants were asked to maintain as neutral a facial expression as possible. The artists then wrote detailed descriptions of the photographs to accompany them. In bringing together contingent artifacts made by individuals under specific constraints, Lippard hoped to keep the images and texts free from any predetermined artistic intentionality. (During the same period, she wrote the first draft of a novel whose content was also restricted to literal descriptions of photographs representing groups of people.)[13]

Around that time, Seth Siegelaub devised a similar project framework. He asked six art critics (David Antin, Germano Celant, Michel Claura, Charles Harrison, Lippard, and Hans Strelow) to fill a forty-eight-page supplement to the summer issue of *Studio International* magazine without writing anything themselves; each critic, individually allotted eight pages, was to choose artists' projects to occupy that amount of space.[14] Lippard's contribution diverged somewhat from the others, because in her section, "each artist was asked to pass on to the next a situation within which to work,"[15] thereby subcontracting out her editorial role to the artists (figure 22).[16]

Toward the end of this phase of her professional life, Lippard added a further complication to the way she viewed her collaborations with peers, as manifested, in part, in the medium of writing. In July 1970, David Lamelas asked a group of artists and critics to send him written reactions to three statements: "1. Use of oral and written language as an Art Form; 2. Language can be considered as an Art Form; 3. Language cannot be considered as an Art Form." The resulting works were shown at the Nigel Greenwood gallery in London and thereafter made available in the breviloquently titled *Publication*.[17] In providing her text, however, Lippard shifted the rules of the exhibition: her contribution was initially a response to a request from Douglas Huebler for her to participate in the collaborative project *Variable Piece #8* by sending him a written statement in exchange for her receiving his *Duration Piece #8, Global*.

FIGURE 22

Lucy R. Lippard (American, b. 1937). Contribution to *July/August Exhibition*, a special issue of *Studio International* magazine, July–August 1970, featuring Frederick Barthelme's contribution in response to a situation defined by N.E. Thing Co.; organized by Seth Siegelaub. Printed magazine, 12 × 9½ in. (30.5 × 24.1 cm). Text © Lucy Lippard; magazine exhibition courtesy The Stichting Egress Foundation, Amsterdam, at the Archives Department of The Museum of Modern Art, New York. (Photo: Brooklyn Museum)

N.E. THING CO. to Frederick Barthelme:
Trans-V.S.I. Situation:
Imaginary transmission of visual sensitivity information.

N.E. THING CO. à Frederick Barthelme:
Situation Trans-V.S.I.;
Transmission imaginaire des informations acquises par sensibilité visuelle ('V.S.I.').

N.E. THING CO. an Frederick Barthelme:
Trans V.S.I. Situation:
Imaginäre Übertragung Visueller Sensibilitäts-Information (V.S.I.).

Classified announcements

(continued from inside back cover)

The rates for advertising in the classified announcements column of Studio International are 25s for the first twenty words (minimum), and 9d for each additional word. Use of box number 2s 6d. These advertisements are prepayable.

Miscellaneous

Compendium 2. Some dates are still available in 1970. If you are interested in exhibiting in a small well situated gallery, send slides or photographs to Brian Hayles, Director. Also enquire about our 'LOOK-IN' slide library. 137 Fulham Road, London S.W.3.

Silk-screen press. 7 ft 4 in. × 5 ft. Vacuum area 3 ft 6 in. × 5 ft 3 in. For sale. Guthrie, Lower Colworth, West Dean, Nr Chichester, Sussex.

Cornwall. Established Pottery, fishing village, £1,000 incl. kilns, etc., S.A.V. Ruth Jones & Palmer, Estate Agents, Falmouth. (Tel.: 313444/5.)

Falmouth, Cornwall. Ideal as artist's home, etc. Large-roomed small mansion, edge of town, 2 acres rich in flowering shrubs. Big hall, 3 large reception, winter garden, big kitchen, etc., 11 bedrooms, 2 bathrooms, stable/garage block, mains. £12,000. Ruth Jones & Palmer, Surveyors, Falmouth. (Tel.: 313444/5.)

Sculptor working marble requires young female model for sittings evenings and week-ends. Tel.: 01-589 6859.

Frederick Barthelme, STUDIO INTERNATIONAL, Vol. 178, No. 913, 1969, page 40.

40

In the text she provided, Lippard rekindled the debate about the ill-defined role of language in art production at the time, and in so doing reaffirmed her identity as a writer and her desire to avoid infringing upon a predetermined zone of artistic competency, saying that "I don't make art." Looking at the literary side of the issue, she contends that a literary work "is worth nothing per se before it is a book," that is, until it is published in book form and thereby gains the potential to reach a readership. And even then, she notes, "Art can be traded and so can books, but if I trade a copy of my book for a painting or a sculpture or even for a print, the receiver of the book will probably feel cheated. My book should be traded, when and if it is printed, for a reproduction of a work of art."[18] For Lippard, therefore, a "fair" exchange with Huebler would seem to be impossible, given the disparity in perceived value between an artwork and a copy of a text. She points out the pretension of certain artists in using language as a tool to disentangle themselves from the diktats of the art market: though the radical nature of some Conceptual propositions did situate them at least at the fringe of what could be considered a work of art at the time, Lippard contends that these practices do not, after all, measure up to the use of language in literary or academic contexts. She goes on to explain that the writer's agency (and not the artist's) better describes her prerogatives as a cultural producer. At the end of the piece's convoluted argument, Lippard brings up the question of authors' rights: returning to the initial transaction undertaken with Huebler, she comes to the circuitous conclusion that in handing over his *Duration Piece* to her, Huebler in return receives ownership of the intellectual property of her written statement—effectively forcing Lamelas into the position of having to ask *him* for permission to publish *her* text.

In 1971, Lippard reiterated a similar scenario, giving Robert Barry the right to take her written work as a critic and exhibit it in a commercial gallery (Yvon Lambert in Paris). For the exhibition titled *ROBERT BARRY presents three shows and a review by LUCY R. LIPPARD* (figure 23), she wrote a "review" (figure 24) to be displayed conjointly with the index cards that constituted the catalogues of the *557,087*, *955,000*, and *2,972,453* numbers shows. Hovering between press release and reflexive commentary, the text once again attempts to disambiguate her professional affiliations, stating that "Ms. Lippard is an American art critic." However, ambiguity reasserted itself when she handed the material over to Barry and it was absorbed into a multilevel presentation carrying his name as well as her own.[19] After a series of speculative questions, at the end of her text she comes to the conclusion that "it doesn't matter what this review says. Its potential is confirmed by its existence rather than by its contents."[20]

FIGURE 23

Robert Barry (American, b. 1936). Installation view of *ROBERT BARRY presents three shows and a review by LUCY R. LIPPARD*, Galerie Yvon Lambert, Paris, April 1971. The Righi Collection and Galerie Yvon Lambert, Paris. © Robert Barry. (Photo: André Morain; Lucy R. Lippard Papers, Archives of American Art, Smithsonian Institution, Washington, D.C.)

FIGURE 24 (FOLLOWING PAGE)

Lucy R. Lippard (American, b. 1937). "Robert Barry at Yvon Lambert." Review contributed to *ROBERT BARRY presents three shows and a review by LUCY R. LIPPARD*, 1971. Typewritten text, 14$\frac{3}{16}$ × 8$\frac{5}{8}$ in. (36 × 22 cm). Lucy R. Lippard Papers, Archives of American Art, Smithsonian Institution, Washington, D.C.

april 2, 1971

ROBERT BARRY AT YVON LAMBERT

Robert Barry's current show at the Yvon Lambert Gallery in Paris is announced by a mailer that reads:"ROBERT BARRY presents three shows and a review by LUCY R. LIPPARD". Ms. Lippard is an American art critic. The show itself consists of this review and of a box of some 150 4 x 6" index cards which constituted the catalogues of three exhibitions organized by Ms. Lippard from 1969-71, each titled according to the population of the city in which it was held: 557,087,Seattle, U.S.A.; 955,000,Vancouver, Canada; 2, 9742,453, Buenos Aires,Argentina (several cards from the latter have been vehemently canceled because instructions were not followed in their printing).

From 1968 Barry has worked in almost invisible nylon cord, invisible but extant radiation, magnetic fields, radio carrier waves, telepathy, repressed knowledge, non-specific qualifications defining undefined conditions. This exhibition is the third in a series of presentation pieces by Barry, the first two involving the work of artists James Umland and Ian Wilson. It is also part of another group, dating from 1969, which comments on the use of gallery space and the international gallery system for an art so dematerialized that it has no fundamental need of either one. The first of this group was a piece that announced: "During the exhibition the gallery will be closed". In January 1971 Lambert showed a Barry piece that read: "Some places to which we can come, and for a while, 'be free to think about what we are going to do' (Marcuse)." "Reads" is the wrong term; Barry does not work with words; he communicates conditions. The newer work indicates an overlap rather than a gap between art and life, in the sense that it attempts to define (again by circling around something) the place of the artist in the world, not socially (though social impact is implied), but as an art-maker rather than as a person. Perhaps the most important of the many questions raised by Barry's work is simply: Does the artist have a place in the world, and, if so, is it changing? Is he/she simply a questioner or is he/she the imposer of conditions upon the esthetic capacity of everyone else, without which the world would be quite a different place?

*

And I have some questions of my own. Is a review which is not published in a journal but constitutes part of an exhibition in itself a fake review? Can it view itself objectively? Or is it valid anyhow because people read it, because it does comment directly upon the show it is part of? Is the writer of such a review an artist even if he/she has made no art? If a writer calls what he/she does "criticism", can anyone else call it art? Is the artist who "presents" a writer's work as a minor part of his piece (the major part being the presentation per se) a critic himself? Is an artist ever not an artist if he/she says he or she is an artist ? Does an artist have to make art? ~~Is good art art that gives sensory pleasure alone? Is good art art that questions? Is good art art that provokes?~~ And finally, it doesn't matter what this review says. Its potential is confirmed by its existence rather than by its contents.

Lucy R. Lippard

42

In her projects realized between 1969 and 1971—at a time when the traditional distinctions between artist, critic, and curator were being undermined—Lippard defined the intrinsic logic of Conceptual art as a process of freely reassigning conventional responsibilities, much as artists were themselves delegating the execution of their works to others, or usurping the role of the critic, or appropriating discourses and methods from various disciplines, and more often than not doing all of these at the same time. Thus, areas of expertise did not overlap, but nevertheless coexisted in a state of notional interchangeability.

Much like artists' projects based on curators' solicitations, Lippard's texts were often the result of a request—in effect, commissioned—and must be interpreted as such, as one factor to be considered while also taking into account the larger context of their writing and publication.

Toward Feminist Critique by Way of Conceptual Art

In the 1960s and 1970s, traditional categories based on skill and competence, which had hitherto framed the evaluation of artworks, broke down considerably. This crisis brought to light a number of diametrically opposed ideological positions among cultural producers. Indeed, it was precisely by embodying the industrial-age divorce between manual and intellectual modes of working that the representatives of Minimalism and Conceptualism privileged creative process over physical product.

During this period, when many artists still regarded subjective intentionality as an irreducible, essential aspect of the work, figures such as Roland Barthes, Jacques Derrida, Michel Foucault, Jacques Lacan, Claude Lévi-Strauss, et al. were busy breaking down the primacy of the Cartesian subject. It is often overlooked that Barthes's influential essay "The Death of the Author" was first published in English, in issues 5 and 6 of *Aspen* magazine in 1967, edited by the Irish-born artist and critic Brian O'Doherty (figures 25, 26). In much the same way as Marcel Duchamp's *Boîte en valise (Box in a Valise)*, that issue of *Aspen* acted as a sort of miniature museum, presenting works by a wide range of notables in the New York avant-garde scene at the time, such as Mel Bochner, John Cage, Merce Cunningham, Dan Graham, and Sol LeWitt.[21]

In "The Death of the Author," Barthes condemned the tyranny of the idea that "the explanation of the work is always sought in the man who has produced it, as if, through the more or less transparent allegory of fiction, it was always finally the voice of one and the same person, the author, which delivered his 'confidence.'"[22] However, Barthes contended that in a linguistic sense, "utterance in its entirety is a void process, which functions perfectly without requiring to be filled by the person of the interlocutors."[23] Barthes went on to suggest that the critic establishes a continuum between the biography of the author and the works to which he appends his signature. When authorial power is undermined, the processes of evaluation and interpretation also see their foundations compromised: "In a multiple writing, indeed, everything is to be distinguished, but nothing deciphered."[24] Occupying a unique place within *Aspen*, "The Death of the Author" affects the way the reader appraises the propositional artworks that surround it. Nonetheless, Barthes's definition of the open text—one that offers itself to multiple interpretations—runs contrary to certain artists' overinvestment in intentionality, and thereby amplifies the paradoxical nature of such an impulse.

FIGURES 25, 26

Aspen, no. 5–6 (Fall–Winter 1967). Magazine in a box, compiled and edited by Brian O'Doherty, with contributions by Robert Morris, Roland Barthes, Dan Graham, and others. Cardboard, printed pages, phonograph records, Super-8 film: box, 8½ × 8½ × 2½ in. (21.6 × 21.6 × 6.4 cm). New York: Roaring Fork Press, 1967. © Brian O'Doherty. (Photos: Michael Tropea)

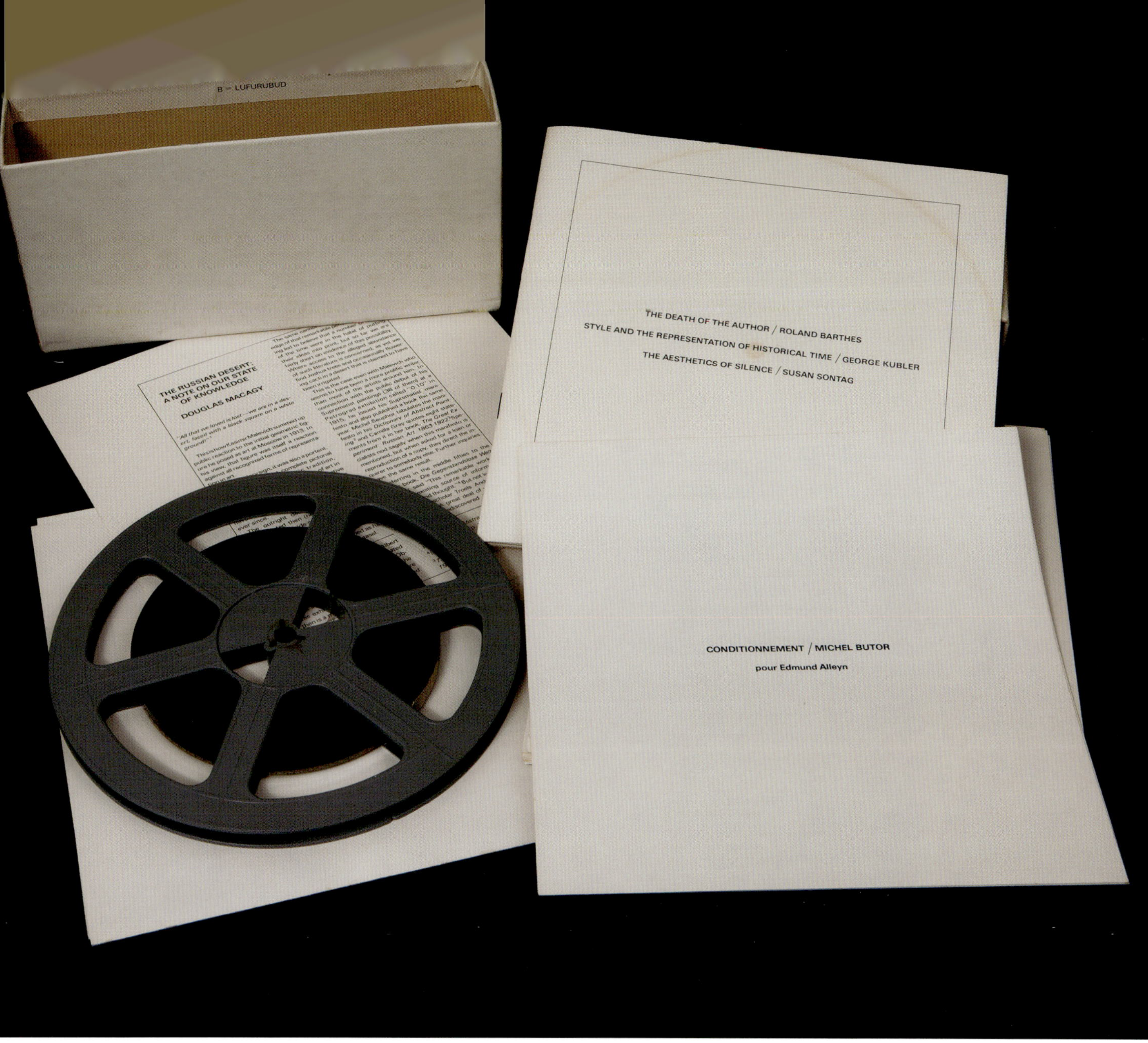
B = LUFURUBUD
THE RUSSIAN DESERT: A NOTE ON OUR STATE OF KNOWLEDGE
DOUGLAS MACAGY
THE DEATH OF THE AUTHOR / ROLAND BARTHES
STYLE AND THE REPRESENTATION OF HISTORICAL TIME / GEORGE KUBLER
THE AESTHETICS OF SILENCE / SUSAN SONTAG
CONDITIONNEMENT / MICHEL BUTOR
pour Edmund Alleyn

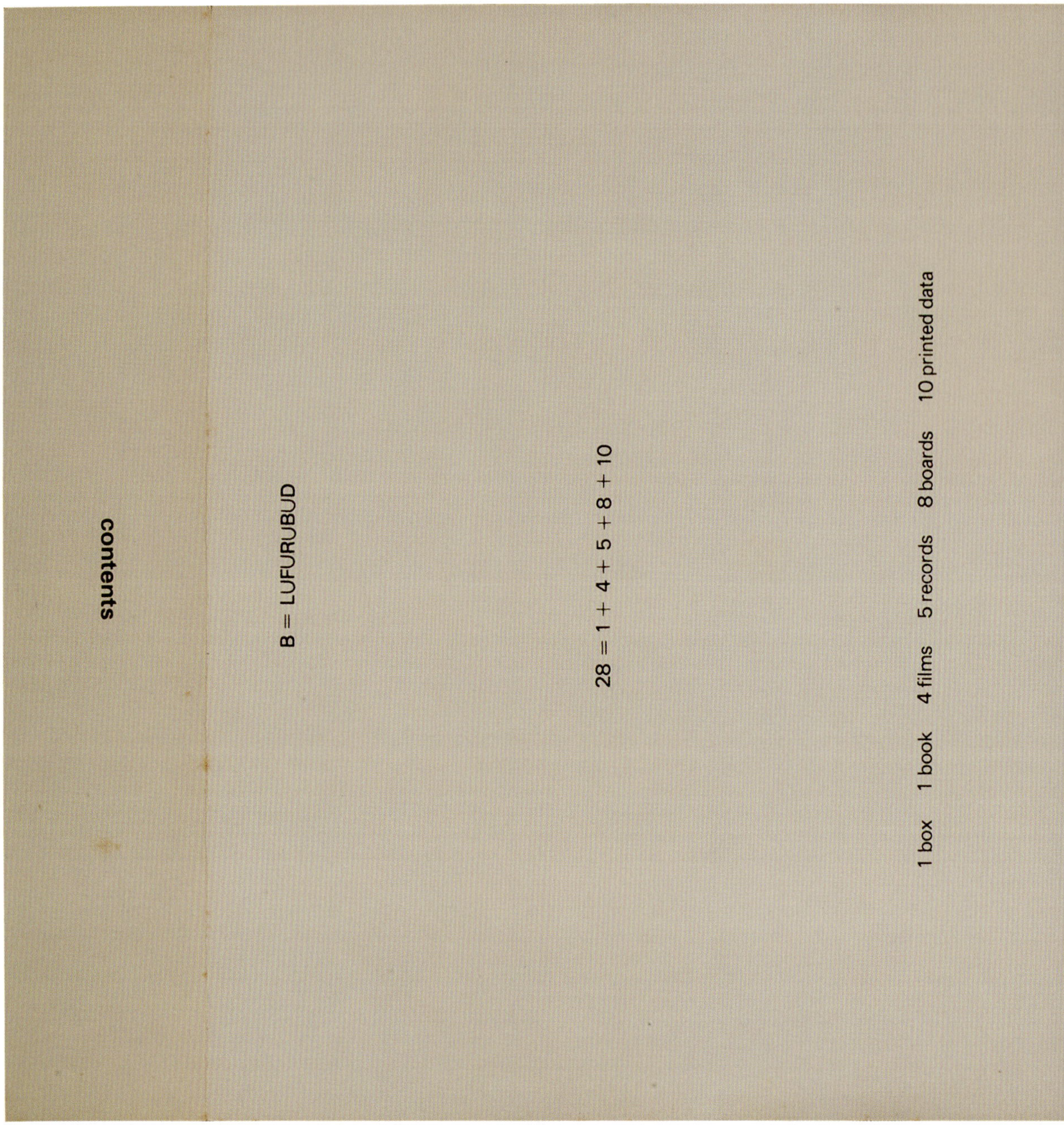
contents
B = LUFURUBUD
28 = 1 + 4 + 5 + 8 + 10
1 box 1 book 4 films 5 records 8 boards 10 printed data

book	essays	The Death of the Author/Roland Barthes/trans. Richard Howard
book		Style and the Representation of Historical Time/George Kubler
book		The Aesthetics of Silence/Susan Sontag
record	fiction	Text for Nothing #8/Samuel Beckett/read by Jack MacGowran
record		Nova Express/ excerpts/William Burroughs/read by the author
record		"Now the shadow of the southwest column" from Jealousy/Alain Robbe-Grillet/read by the author
record	music	Fontana Mix-Feed/John Cage/realized by Max Neuhaus
record		The King of Denmark/Morton Feldman/Max Neuhaus (percussion)
boards	sculpture	The Maze/Tony Smith
film	films	Rhythm 21 (1921)/Hans Richter
film		Lightplay: Black-White-Grey (1932)/Laszlo Moholy-Nagy (excerpt)
film		Site (1964)/Robert Morris/Stan VanDerBeek (excerpt)
film		Linoleum (1967)/Robert Rauschenberg (excerpt)
record	interview	Merce Cunningham
record	documents	The Creative Act (1957)/Marcel Duchamp/read by the author
record		Some texts from A L'Infinitif (1912-20)/Marcel Duchamp/read by the author
record		Four poems from Phantastische Gebete (1916)/Richard Huelsenbeck/read by the author
record		The Realistic Manifesto (1920)/Naum Gabo/Noton Pevsner/read by Gabo
print		The Russian Desert: A Note on Our State of Knowledge/Douglas MacAgy
record		Space, Time and Dance (1952)/Merce Cunningham/read by the author
print	poetry	Conditionnement/Michel Butor/trans. Michael Benedikt
print		Poem, March 1966/Dan Graham
print	data	Serial Project #1/Sol LeWitt
print		Seven Translucent Tiers /Mel Bochner
print		Structural Play #3/Brian O'Doherty
print		Drawings for The Maze/Tony Smith
print		Score for Fontana Mix-Feed/John Cage/Max Neuhaus
print		Score for The King of Denmark/Morton Feldman
print		Translation of Jealousy (recorded excerpt)/Alain Robbe-Grillet/trans. Richard Howard

In a 1981 article reevaluating modernist criticism, Mary Kelly reopened the debate triggered by Barthes by mapping the evolution of artistic subjectivity since the rejection of formalism at the end of the 1960s.[25] She expressed reservations about the more orthodox aspects of Conceptual art, such as those that restrict themselves to authorial intentionality and ignore the artist's, and the spectator's, unconscious drives, noting that many "dematerialized" practices still embraced the author as a sovereign paternal figure who transmits the artwork in a hereditary fashion. For Kelly, however, the methods of systematic inquiry employed by artists should move beyond a given stylistic lineage.

In the mid-1970s, certain women theorists came to define *l'écriture feminine* as being, first of all, a manifestation of a differently sexed voice, based on a primal "oralization" of language.[26] This attention to the oral aspects of discourse allowed the text to approach the act of writing without fully being part of it. Because they examined the specificity of lived, bodily experience, the works of Hélène Cixous, Luce Irigaray, and Julia Kristeva became identified with this sort of biological essentialism. While recognizing the importance of the interpretive framework proposed by these theorists, Kelly contended that it nonetheless reaffirmed the centrality of subjective consciousness. In Kelly's thinking, critique must link the field of signification to sexual difference.

However, by setting the "essentialist" and "deconstructionist" approaches against each other as polar opposites when evaluating feminist art practices, we run the risk of neglecting the possibility of an intermediary moment, one wherein certain Conceptualists, particularly women, were able to counter the didacticism permeating Conceptual art at the time. They instead chose to address ethical questions within this space of political ambivalence. Before the theoretical corpus associated with second-wave feminism was established in the mid-1970s, these artists managed to destabilize the foundations upon which the authoritarian methodologies favored by some of their male counterparts were based. Certain among them would later choose to articulate their message in a clear and direct manner, but the tactics they used at this time did not rely upon the efficacy of manifestos. For these artists, subjectivity was a concept to be problematized rather than forcefully asserted.

In 1966, Joseph Kosuth and Christine Kozlov wrote a text about the painter Ad Reinhardt that prefigured most of the projects subsequently realized, individually or in collaboration, under the auspices of the Museum of Normal Art, a semi-fictional institution without fixed address that the two artists would found the following year.[27] Their collaborative activities, as well as the events and exhibitions organized at the Museum of Normal Art, have never been properly examined, much as the role that Kozlov played in Conceptual art has been largely ignored. Instead of reworking Duchampian strategies or the positivist posturing of analytical philosophy used by most of her contemporaries, her works momentarily suspend communication through a series of sabotage-based gestures. Unlike Lawrence Weiner, whose statements declared the contingent existence of the so-called "dematerialized" artwork, Kozlov's propositions affirm her refusal to realize projects or to hand over their actualization to a third party. For example, she sent text-less telegrams, made lists of concepts rejected over a given period,[28] and exhibited a tape recorder whose mechanism had been modified so as to simultaneously record and erase the surrounding sonic environment over an indefinite time (figure 27). The work of Lee Lozano employed similarly equivocal tactics. Fundamentally anti-didactic, her strikes, boycotts, and

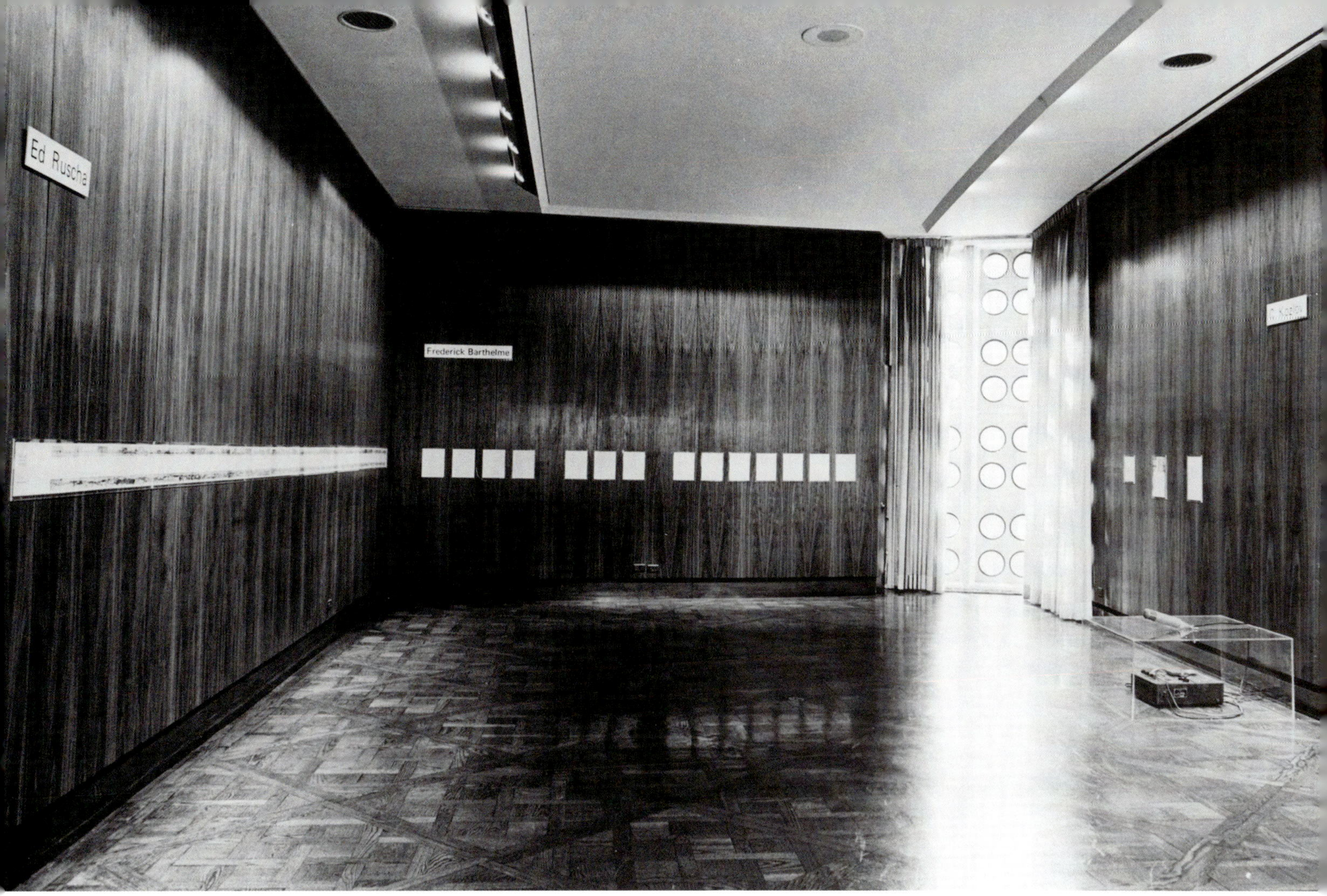

FIGURE 27

Christine Kozlov (American, 1945–2005). Installation view of her *Information: No Theory* (far right), 1969. Tape recorder, Plexiglas case, and microphone, 36 × 24 × 24 in. (91.4 × 61 × 61 cm). The Estate of Christine Kozlov. © Marilyn Thompson. (Photo: Jay Cantor)

36

IF I DO THE NO-GRASS PIECE, WHAT WILL HAPPEN TO THE BOOK-OF-CHANGE PIECE?

GRASS PIECE

25 61

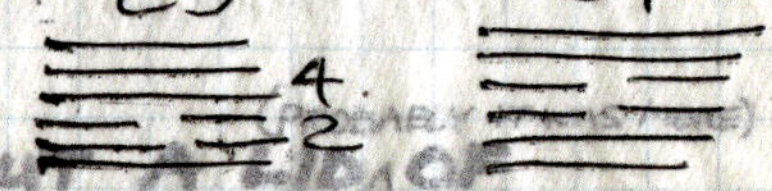

MAKE A GOOD SCORE, ABOUT A LID OF EXCELLENT GRASS. SMOKE IT "UP" AS FAST AS YOU CAN. STAY HIGH ALL DAY, EVERY DAY. SEE WHAT HAPPENS. (APRIL 1, 69)
ONE THING THAT HAPPENS IS THAT IT TAKES MORE AND MORE GRASS TO GET FEELIN GOOD. IMMUNITY BUILDING UP? (APR 17, 69)
THE AMOUNT OF GRASS NEEDED TO GET HIGH HAS STABILIZED ITSELF. TONIGHT I STARTED TO SMOKE THE LAST CONTAINER OF CLEANED SHIT. WHEN THAT IS GONE THERE ARE TWIGS TO SMOKE AND A LOT OF SEEDS WHICH I AM GOING TO EAT. (THIS HAS BEEN A SCINTILLATING PIECE BUT I'D LIKE TO FINISH IT IN A FLASH) DECIDED ON NEXT PIECE: GO WITHOUT GRASS FOR THE SAME AMOUNT OF TIME.

"SEEK THE EXTREMES,
THAT'S WHERE ALL THE
ACTION IS." (APRIL 24, 69)

I GET MORE TIRED EVERY DAY. THIS FEELING WASTED MIGHT BE FROM SMOKING SO MUCH GRASS, OR FROM WORKING SO HARD WHICH I'VE BEEN DOING, OR FROM THE MONOTONOUSNESS OF MY DAYS. (APRIL 29, 69)
I'LL END THE GRASS PIECE WITH A FANFARE: A CAP OF MESCALINE KALTENBACH GAVE ME. (MAY 2, 69)* NOT HIGH ANYMORE, JUST NUMB.
FINISHED GRASS, TWIGS & SEEDS. (MAY 3, 69)

*THIS WAS POSTPONED DUE TO CIRCUMSTANCES BEYOND MY CONTROL. FINALLY TOOK MESCALINE: MAY 11, 69. IT BLANKED OUT, MUST'VE BEEN A DUD PILL, A BAD CAP.

NOTE: ASIDE FROM WHEN I WOKE UP (DOWN) IN THE MORNING THERE WERE TWO OCCASIONS WHEN I WASN'T HIGH DURING THIS PIECE, ABOUT A COUPLE OF HOURS EACH.
THERE'S A SPOT OF YIN IN EVERY YANG & A SPOT OF YANG IN EVERY YIN, AS "THEY" SAY.

FIGURE 28

Lee Lozano (American, 1930–1999). *No Title (Grass Piece)*, 1969. Graphite and ink on paper, 11 × 8½ in. (28 × 21.5 cm). Collection of Alan Cravitz and Shashi Caudill, Chicago. © The Estate of Lee Lozano, courtesy Hauser & Wirth, Zurich

diary pages, distributed to certain well-chosen art-world figures, managed to avoid the hard-line positioning of the manifesto form (figure 28).

Adrian Piper's *The Work Originally Intended for This Space Has Been Withdrawn* suggests a comparable ambivalence toward advocating for a specific political agenda (figure 29). And so, too, does her *Catalysis* series of performances (1970–71): wandering through the city covered in an unpleasantly pungent perfume, or with a towel stuffed in her mouth, she sought ambiguous confrontations between subjects. When Lippard asked her to comment on the experience of these situations designed to exacerbate the already difficult stigmas associated with gender and race, she stated: "As far as the work goes, I feel it is completely apolitical. But I do think that the work is a product of me as an individual, and the fact that I am a woman surely has a lot to do with it."[29]

It is important to note that such approaches are different from the ethics of disengagement, or negative aesthetics, promulgated by Herbert Marcuse and other representatives of the 1960s counterculture. In order to better understand the nature of these artists' ambivalent tactics, we can again refer to Barthes.

In a course of lectures given in 1977–78 at the Collège de France, Barthes expounded the concept of "the Neutral," hoping to free its meaning from the sense of mere stasis with which it is usually associated.[30] The Neutral annuls duality by using a third term that does not, however, lack a certain characteristic intensity. (Barthes adds that this concept designates an asexual state of discourse and an oscillation between passive and active verb function.) The decision *not* to comment on certain circumstances or sets of events can also be a mode of engagement with, and a way of maintaining a grasp on, the real. Barthes constructed the course of lectures around a set of literary and philosophical texts linked, to varying degrees, with the category of the Neutral. The key idea of non-choice dictated the way that content unfolded from one lecture to the next over the thirteen weeks of the series. In effect, he used a randomized system to determine the material for each class from the contents of a general bibliography. This approach did not, however, follow a Cageian model of chance operation, wherein all the elements to be shuffled are assigned an equal status. Instead, Barthes's system attempted to reorganize the carefully selected content through a kind of thesaurus structure, in the hope that this displacement would allow for the possibility of new readings.

FIGURE 29

Adrian Piper (American, b. 1948). *The Work Originally Intended for This Space Has Been Withdrawn*, 1970. Typescript draft of the statement subsequently installed in the exhibition *Conceptual Art and Conceptual Aspects at the New York Cultural Center*, 11 × 8½ in. (27.9 × 21.6 cm). Collection of the Adrian Piper Research Archive Foundation Berlin. © APRA Foundation Berlin. (Photo: Generali Foundation, Vienna)

THE WORK ORIGINALLY INTENDED FOR THIS SPACE HAS BEEN WITHDRAWN.

THE DECISION TO WITHDRAW HAS BEEN TAKEN AS A PROTECTIVE MEASURE AGAINST THE INCREASINGLY PERVASIVE CONDITIONS OF REPRESSION, RACISM, HYPOCRISY, AND MURDER WHICH CHARACTERIZE THIS COUNTRY.

RATHER THAN SUBMIT THE WORK TO THE DEADLY AND CONSTRICTING INFLUENCES OF THESE CONDITIONS, I SUBMIT ITS ABSENCE AS EVIDENCE OF THE INABILITY OF ART/EXPRESSION TO MEANINGFULLY EXIST UNDER CONDITIONS OTHER THAN THOSE OF PEACE, EQUALITY, TRUTH, AND FREEDOM.

ADRIAN PIPER

Lippard's experimental approach was not dissimilar, in that her mode of writing sometimes employed aleatory strategies to de-center the authorial function and thus reevaluate the role of logical argumentation and hermeneutics as the guarantors of aesthetic judgment. In essence, Lippard rejected the conventional definition of the art critic—but, in an act of noteworthy ambivalence, nonetheless decided to place her hybrid writing under the rubric of the very profession that she had declared obsolete. Her aversion to the incestuous and elitist nature of the art world often manifested itself as an anxiety about the role that she necessarily played in it. However, by inserting herself into project frameworks prescribed by various collaborators, she was able to circumvent the obligations to establish criteria of evaluation and to interpret artworks.

"Absentee Information and or Criticism"

The text called "Absentee Information and or Criticism" represents a rupture in Lippard's practice. While beginning to write her novel, Lippard, who at the time was living in Spain, produced this piece as her written contribution to the catalogue of the Museum of Modern Art's 1970 exhibition *Information* (figures 30–33).[31] The exhibition's curator, Kynaston McShine, had initially asked her to contribute an essay, and Lippard had suggested she do an index. However, a postal strike prevented the museum from sending her the necessary materials in time. In their absence, Lippard decided "to substitute some absentee information" for her contribution (and in some sense incorporate that absence of information itself as an ad hoc condition) by compiling a bibliography produced through a series of chance operations. Opening a used copy of *Roget's Thesaurus,* between the pages containing the entry for the word *absence* she found two tickets for a film screening at MoMA. She then used the ticket numbers to generate an equation that would serve as the basis for the piece's instructions, to be carried out by employees of the museum's library. The project was articulated in three parts: Part I was an assemblage of critical quotations about the individual artists included in the exhibition, taken (by random mathematical procedure) from books and periodicals found in MoMA's library. Part II was a group of theoretical and philosophical extracts from about twenty writers, among them Gaston Bachelard, Marcel Duchamp, William James, Joseph Kosuth, On Kawara, and R. D. Laing. Part III put forward several proposals: for example, the pairing of a randomly chosen participating artist with a member of the museum's board of trustees, instructing them to engage in an eight-hour conversation about "art, artist's rights, the relationship of the museum to society at large, or any other subject agreed upon by the two of them." Part III also asked all the American artists in the exhibition to sign a letter addressed to soldiers based in each state in the U.S. urging them to go AWOL in protest against "the unconstitutional war in Vietnam and Cambodia."

FIGURES 30–33

Lucy R. Lippard (American, b. 1937). Pages from "Absentee Information and or Criticism," as published in the catalogue of *Information*, 1970. Printed book, 10 13/16 × 8 3/8 in. (25.9 × 21.3 cm) each page. New York: The Museum of Modern Art, 1970. Catalogue © The Museum of Modern Art, New York; essay text © Lucy Lippard. (Photos: Michael Tropea)

Lucy R. LIPPARD
Lives in New York

$A_1B_2S_{19}E_5N_{14}T_{20}E_5E_5$ $I_9N_{14}F_6O_{15}R_{18}M_{13}A_1T_{20}I_9O_{15}N_{14}$

$A_1N_{14}D_4$ $O_{15}R_{18}$ $C_3R_{18}I_9T_{20}I_9C_3I_9S_{19}M_{13}$*

ABSENCE: 1) withdrawal, nonexistence, nonresidence, nonpresence, nonattendance, disappearance, dispersion. 2) emptiness, void, vacuum, vacuity, vacancy, depletion, exhaustion, exemption, blank, clean slate, tabula rasa. 3) absentee, truant. 4) nobody, no body, nobody present, nobody on earth, not a soul, nary a soul, nobody under the sun, nary one, no one, no man, never a one.
Be absent, absent oneself, go away, stay away, keep away, keep out of the way, slip away, slip off, slip out, hold aloof, vacate. Colloq. hooky, cut, not show up, not show, French Leave, Spanish Pox, make oneself scarce. Slang, go A.W.O.L., jump, skip.
1) absent, away, missing, missing in action, lost, wanting, omitted, nowhere to be found, out of sight, gone, lacking, away from home. Absent Without Official Leave, abroad, overseas, overlooked, overseen, on vacation. Colloq. minus. 2) empty, vacant, void, vacuous, untenanted, unoccupied, uninhabited, uninhibited, tenantless, deserted, abandoned, devoid, forsaken, bare, hollow, blank, clear, dry, free from, drained. Colloq. Godforsaken.
Nowhere, elsewhere, neither here nor there, somewhere else, not here. Dial. nowheres.
Without, wanting, lacking, less minus, sans.
SEE ALSO PRESENCE

*

Games are situations contrived to permit simultaneous participation of many people in some significant pattern of their own corporate lives.
1311819811212 13312218114

PART I

A. For each artist in the exhibition whose name begins with a vowel, proceed as follows: go to the Museum of Modern Art Library and look under the artist's name in the general card catalogue. From the first book or article entered under his last name (whether or not it is his own name), transcribe the 24th sentence (2+9+6+1+6+0=24). If there is nothing under that name, take the first name occurring in the catalogue that begins the same way and has the most beginning letters in common with the artist's name (e.g. for

---

*The following instructions were sent to Kynaston McShine in lieu of an Index to the INFORMATION catalogue, for which the necessary information did not arrive in time. When I realized it would not, I decided to substitute some absentee information arrived at by chance. I opened a paperback edition of Roget's Thesaurus to ABSENCE, hoping to get some ideas. The book had been given to me, second-hand, by a friend in December 1969; I had not opened it until this point (Wednesday, April 15, 1970, 3:30 PM, in Carboneras, Spain). When I did so, I found not only the entry above (now cut and revised) but two red tickets, unused, inscribed as follows: Museum of Modern Art, FILM RESERVATION Wednesday Afternoon 3:00 PM Showing NOT FOR SALE Keller Printing Co. New York; the numbers on them were 296160 and 296159. These tickets determined the initial framework for the following situation/text. Quotations from and debts or references to the works of the following persons are included in it: Art Workers Coalition, Gaston Bachelard, Robert Barry, Frederick Barthelme, D.E. Berlyne, Mel Bochner, John Cage, Marcel Duchamp, Dan Graham, Latvan Greene, Douglas Huebler, William James, On Kawara, Joseph Kosuth, R.D. Laing, Sol LeWitt, Marshall McLuhan, Ad Reinhardt, Saint-Beuve. L.R.L.

74

FIGURE 30

Barthelme: Barthelm, Barthel, Barthe, Barth, Bart, Bar, Ba, B, in that order).

For each artist in the exhibition whose name begins with a consonant, follow the same procedure taking the 32nd sentence (2+9+6+1+5+9=32) of the first book or article occurring in the most recent full volume of the Art Index. If in any case there is no text, or no 24th or 32nd sentence, reproduce in its place the 8th picture or the picture on page 8 or the picture 1/8 of the way through the reference (8=common denominator of 24/32).

B. Make an alphabetical list of these artists, each name followed by the quotation arrived at above, with full bibliographical source in parentheses after it (i.e. author, title of book, publisher, place published, date, page no.; or, in the case of an article: author, title, magazine, vol. no., date, page no.).

ACCONCI, VITO. see: ACCARDI, CARLA.

"Die erste Einzelausstellung in Deutschland findet im September 1966 in der Galerie M.E. Thelen in Essen statt."

(Galerie M.E. Thelen, Essen. Carla Accardi. [Essen, The Gallery, 1966,] p.[3].)

ANDRE, CARL.

"An astronaut who slips out of his capsule in space has lost his environment, any living organism has an environment."

(The Hague, Gemeentemusem. Carl Andre. [The Hague, The Museum, 1969,] p. 5.)

ARMAJANI, SIAH. see: ARMAN.

"Thus, for example, round objects will by their nature make curved marks when dipped in colour and rolled across a surface."

(Jones, Peter. "Arman and the Magic Power of Objects." Art International, v. VII, no. 3, March 25, 1963, p. 41.)

ARNATT, KEITH. see: ARNATT, RAY.

"It is rather like the poet and the sunset."

(Arnatt, Ray. "A View of Opposites." Ark, no. 28, December 1960, p. 31.)

ART & PROJECT. see: ARTARIA, PAUL.

"Ein richtig gebautes Holzhaus ist im Sommer kühl, im Winter wird es rasch warm und hält auch die Wärme."

(Artaria, Paul. Schweizer Holzhäuser aus den Jahren 1920-1940. Basel, B. Wepf, 1942, p. 11.)

ARTSCHWAGER, RICHARD. see: ARUP, OVE.

"In another way his achievement is built on a broad basis: he is not just an engineer, or an architect, or a contractor and constructor, but all three rolled into one."

(Arup, Ove. Foreword to Faber, Colin, Candela/The Shell Builder. New York, Reinhold, [c1968,] p. 7.)

ASKEVOLD, DAVID. see: ASKELAND, JAN.

"I Paris suget han til seg av de maleriske nyvinninger de franske malerne hadde frembragt, i Tyskland synes det derimot først og fremst å vaere de filosofisklitteraere ideene som fanget hans interesse."

(Askeland, Jan. Profiler I. Norsk Grafikk... Oslo, Dreyers Forlag, [1958.] p. 8.)

ATKINSON, TERRY. see: ATKINSON, TRACY.

"A variety of this substance later became the "celluloid" now little used but well-known to our grandfathers in forms as diverse as billiard-balls and shirt collars."

(Atkinson, Tracy. Introduction to Milwaukee, Art Center. A Plastic Presence. Milwaukee, [The Center,] 1969, p. 5.)

BAINBRIDGE, DAVID. see: BAINES, GEORGE GRENFELL.

"As primary and secondary school costs are partly met out of local authority rates, a second interest in maintaining ceiling levels is created, though it does seem that final costs which are known to the local authority are not as well known in the Ministry unless a flagrant breach occurs."

(Baines, George Grenfell. "Cost ceilings - curse or blessing?" Journal of the Royal Institute of British Architects, vol. 76, no. 4, April 1969, p. 160.)

BALDESSARI, JOHN.

See illustration.

(Baldessari, John. "Solving Each Problem". Art News, vol. 67, no. 8, p 7, December 1968.)

BALDWIN, MICHAEL. see: BALDWIN, ARTHUR MERVYN.

"Neben Diversion und Grundlastigkeit, als Prinzipien der New Sculpture, tritt damit die Gesetzmässigkeit der 'Syntax': der Bezug zwischen den formalen Setzungen ist wichtiger als ihre monolithische Einzelpräsenz."

(Kudielka, Robert. "New English sculpture - Abschied vom Objekt." Kunstwerk, v. 22, no. 1-2, Oct.-Nov. 1968, p. 19.)

BARRIO. see: BARRIOS, GREGG.

"A menacing young bitch uses a sharp knife to cut a defenseless victim's jeans."

(Barrios, Gregg. "Naming names: the films of Carl Linder." Film Quarterly, v. 22, no. 1, Fall 1968, p. 42.)

BARRY, ROBERT.

"Also in the show will be a room filled with ultrasonic sound."

(Rose, Arthur. "Four interviews with Barry, Huebler, Kosuth and Weiner." Arts, v. 43, no. 4, February 1969, p. 22.)

BARTHELME, FREDERICK. see: BARTH, BRADI.

See illustration.

(Arts, v. 43, no. 2, November 1968, p. 8.)

BECHER, BERNHARD and HILLA. see: BECHTEL, EDWIN DE TURCK.

" They illustrate."

(Bechtel, Edwin De Turck. "Illustrated books of the sixties: a reminder of a great period in illustration." Print, v. 23, no. 3, May 1969, p. 21.)

BEUYS, JOSEPH.

"Richard Serra se souvient de Pollock, et même de Motherwell; mais où son originalité éclate, non sans quelque afféterie, c'est lorsque, alognant sur un mur neuf harnais de caoutchouc découpés en lanières aux belles inflexions décoratives, il souligne le mouvement de l'un d'entre eux d'une nonchalante arabesque de néon."

(Pierre, José. "Les grandes vacances de l'art moderne." L'Oeil, no. 173, May 1969, p. 13.)

BOCHNER, MEL. see: BOERS, DIETER.

"Die künstlerische Arbeit erweist sich am überzeugendsten dort, wo entgegen aller Irritierung trotzdem eine autonome ästhetische Gestalt gefunden wird."

(Boers, Dieter. "Deutsche Kunst: eine neue Generation II". Kunstwerk, v. 22, no. 9-10, June-July 1969, p. 4.)

75

FIGURE 31

ADDENDA

BRECHT, GEORGE. see BREEZE, CLAUDE.

"Breeze's heartless examination of the conflict between the sexes is forcefully scientific, actual, physical."

(Simmins, Richard, "Claude Breeze: Recent Paintings and Drawings," _Artscanada,_ v. XXVI, no. 128/129, February 1969, p.37.)

D'ALESSIO, CARLOS. see DALEY, WILLIAM.

"These are not cups as such but are _about_ cups: the spirit of cups, cups reincarnated, cups purified by removal of function."

(---, "Exhibitions," _Craft Horizons_, v. XXIX, no. 2, Mar./Apr. 1969, p.43.)

LIPPARD, LUCY.

"Perhaps there is some not merely personal significance in the fact that they all deal with landscape or with implications of an extensive space."

(Lippard, Lucy, "Notes in Review of Canadian Artists '68," _Artscanada,_ v. XXVI, no. 128/129, February 1969, p. 25.)

N.E. THING CO. see: NEUBURG, HANS.

"The world's first great poster museum in the Polish capital bears witness to this fact."

(Neuburg, Hans, "Second International Poster Biennale in Warsaw," _Graphis_, v. 24, no. 137, 1968, p. 242.)

McSHINE, KYNASTON. see MAC TAGGART, WILLIAM.

"These portraits are really the beginning of his emergence from the cave."

(---, "Recent Museum Acquisitions," _The Burlington Magazine,_ v. CXI, no. 790, January 1969, p.32.)

PART II

A. If it is true that the artist possesses the means of anticipating and avoiding the consequences of technological trauma, what then are we to think of the world and bureaucracy of "art appreciation"? Would it not seem suddenly to be a conspiracy to make the artist a frill, a fribble, or a Miltown?

13312218114 171914

...The logic of the photograph is neither verbal nor syntactical, a condition which renders literary culture quite helpless to cope with the photograph....For most people, their own ego image seems to have been typographically conditioned, so that the electric age with its return to inclusive experience threatens their idea of self.

9294

For art as either action or idea, memory, or the absorption of some referent to an art work or an art idea into the observer's consciousness, is instrumental. By memory, I mean less the retentive, the fact-storage faculty, than the associative faculty. From the arts we are learning to make connections, jumps, through cues and clues that come to us in fragments.

1212022114 71855145

It is not so much for you, my friend, who never saw this place, and had you visited it, could not now feel the impressions and colors I feel, that I have gone over it in such detail, for which I must excuse myself. Nor should you try to see it as a result of what I have said; let the image float inside you; pass lightly; the slightest idea of it will suffice for you.

19191420-2521225

79

FIGURE 32

LIPPARD

PART III

A. Match the name of each artist in the exhibition who is or will be in New York or environs with that of a Trustee of the Museum of Modern Art whose last name begins with the same letter (use procedure similar to that in Part I/A, going to the next letter in the alphabet if still incomplete); ask each trustee to spend at least 8 hours talking to that artist about art, artist's rights, the relationship of the museum to society at large, or any other subject agreed upon by the two of them. This should be executed within 6 months of the opening of the exhibition and can be applied to foreign artists if individual travel plans are known far enough in advance.

B. On the first afternoon after the opening of the exhibition (preferably a Wednesday) that this is statistically possible, give the holders of film tickets numbered 296160 and 296159 lifetime free-admission passes to the Museum (valid any day of the week). If the holder is Black, Puerto Rican, Female, or a working artist without a gallery affiliation, give him/her in addition a free xerox copy of any piece or pieces in the INFORMATION exhibition utilizing Roget's Thesaurus; if there aren't any, or if the artist refuses, give a free copy of the catalogue of the Museum's permanent collection.

C. Show no films glorifying war.

Ask the American artists in the exhibition to join those willing on the Museum staff in compiling and signing a letter that states the necessity to go A.W.O.L. from the unconstitutional war in Vietnam and Cambodia; send it to 592,319 (296160+296159) men at armed forces based in each state of the USA. (If this is impossible, to 56 major newspapers.)

D. Purchase one work by those artists in the exhibition whose names appear first, second, fifth, sixth, ninth, nineteenth, and sixtieth (if it goes that far) in the alphabetical list of exhibitors; donate one each to seven (or six) independent museums all over the world which are located in low-income areas, outside of major cities.

E. Xerox and publish as an insert to the catalogue of the INFORMATION exhibition, all available information on any extant proposed reforms concerning artist's rights, such as rental fees, contracts, profit-sharing, artists' control over works sold, shown, etc.

81

FIGURE 33

Part I of the project followed a delegation-based strategy characteristic of Conceptual artworks in which she once more questions the power relations existing between collaborators through the use of a kind of role-playing. In Part III, the script becomes somewhat more explicit, proposing a series of unrealizable performances designed to raise awareness of broader issues, some of them largely beyond the museum context. There, Lippard took the opportunity to denounce a political state of affairs. She temporarily occupied this site of authority, from which she was able to convey the artists' genuine desire to engage in a dialogue with the museum.

The title of the *Information* exhibition, for which "Absentee Information and or Criticism" was produced, presents information itself as one sort of recyclable material among others within the framework of modernist typologies, and in so doing signals the entry of Conceptualism into the art-historical canon. However, at the same time, several artists produced works highlighting political concerns of the era, including the famous antiwar poster *Q. And babies? A. And babies.* (figures 34, 35), which was realized by members of the Art Workers' Coalition.[32]

Independent critics were given a voice during meetings of the Art Workers' Coalition, in which Lippard played a primary role. As the group dynamic became more contentious, several splinter groups formed to address related concerns. In the fall of 1970, Lippard joined with Poppy Johnson, Brenda Miller, and Faith Ringgold to found the Ad Hoc Women Artists Committee.

Lippard's shift toward activism and feminism put into practice, and strengthened, her populist convictions. For a short period of time, she had put faith in the democratic possibilities of Conceptual art. A chronological analysis of her experimental projects, however, demonstrates that by the end of the 1960s she was becoming aware of the limitations of this utopian construct, in the face of the art market's exceptional absorptive capacities and the heterogeneity of artists' approaches. Likewise, in a 1969 interview with Charles Harrison in *Studio International* magazine, Seth Siegelaub, too, seemed already to foresee the possibility of such misappropriation; after twenty-some interventions since 1968, he observed that the aura of his name was beginning to overshadow the intrinsic value of the primary information that he wished to disseminate.[33] His presence as an organizer had become as cumbersome as the critical prefaces and interpretive commentaries that he had aimed to eliminate. Consequently, in the early 1970s he shifted his focus to writing books about Marxism and communication. His withdrawal from the art world was not exceptional: the second half of the decade would see the defection of many of Conceptualism's key players (among them Graciela Carnevale, Lee Lozano, Christine Kozlov, Mel Ramsden, Charlotte Posenenske, and many others). Tired of repeating the same now-sterile formulas, they decided to invest themselves in projects more in step with their political convictions.

It is also at this time that magazine editors who had played key roles in the reform of art criticism were replaced by members of more conservative factions. When Peter Townsend left *Studio International* in 1975, the magazine ceased to privilege the voices of artists, and in so doing definitively left the center of critical debate.[34] The exhaustion of this political project, appended to the discourse of Conceptual art, also coincided with the resurgence of other styles more apt to meet collectors' criteria of salability. So-called "dematerialized" practices were to be pushed aside with the rise of postmodernism, and it would not be until the 1990s that the Conceptualists would see their works reevaluated in an institutional context.

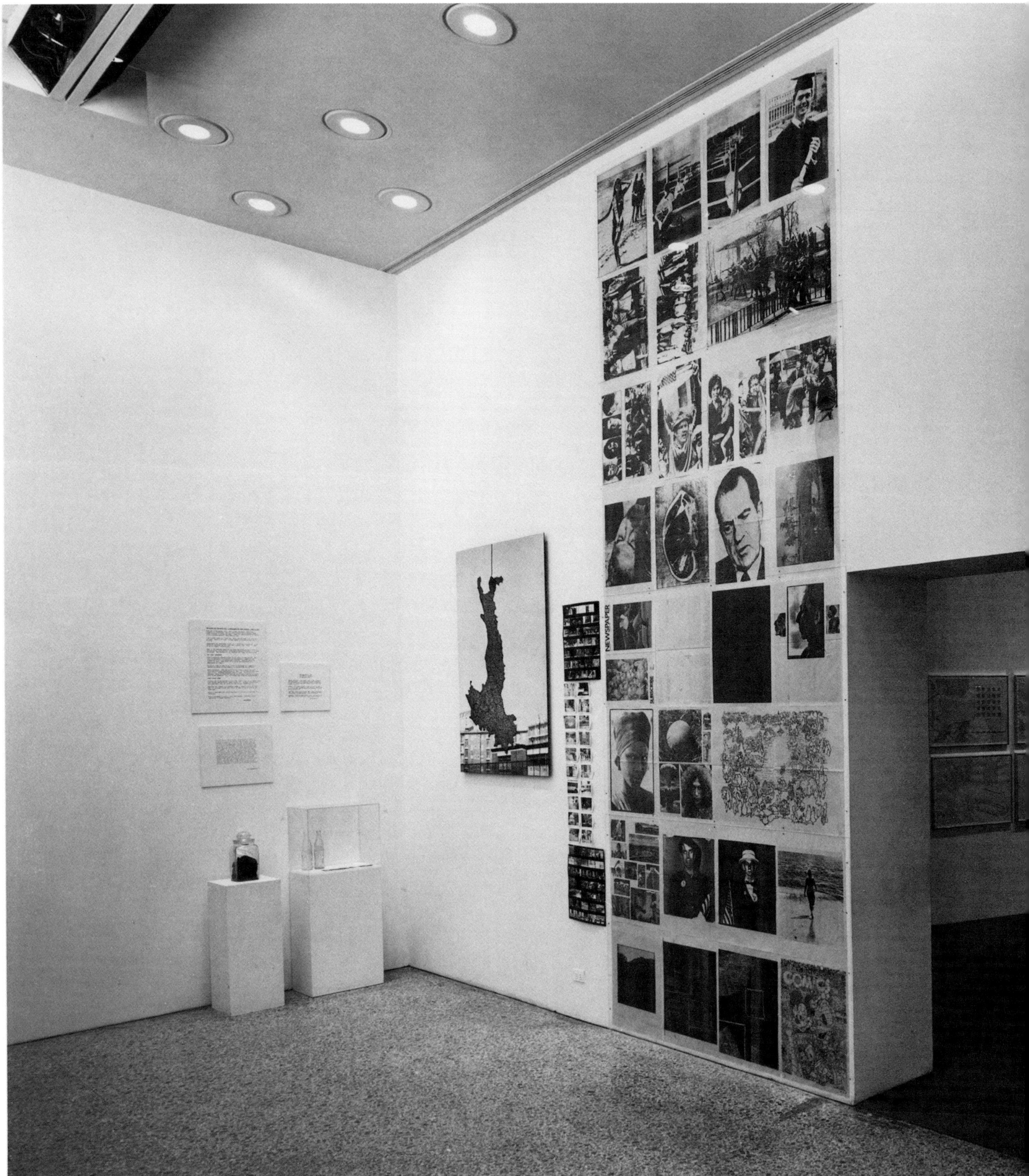
NEWSPAPER

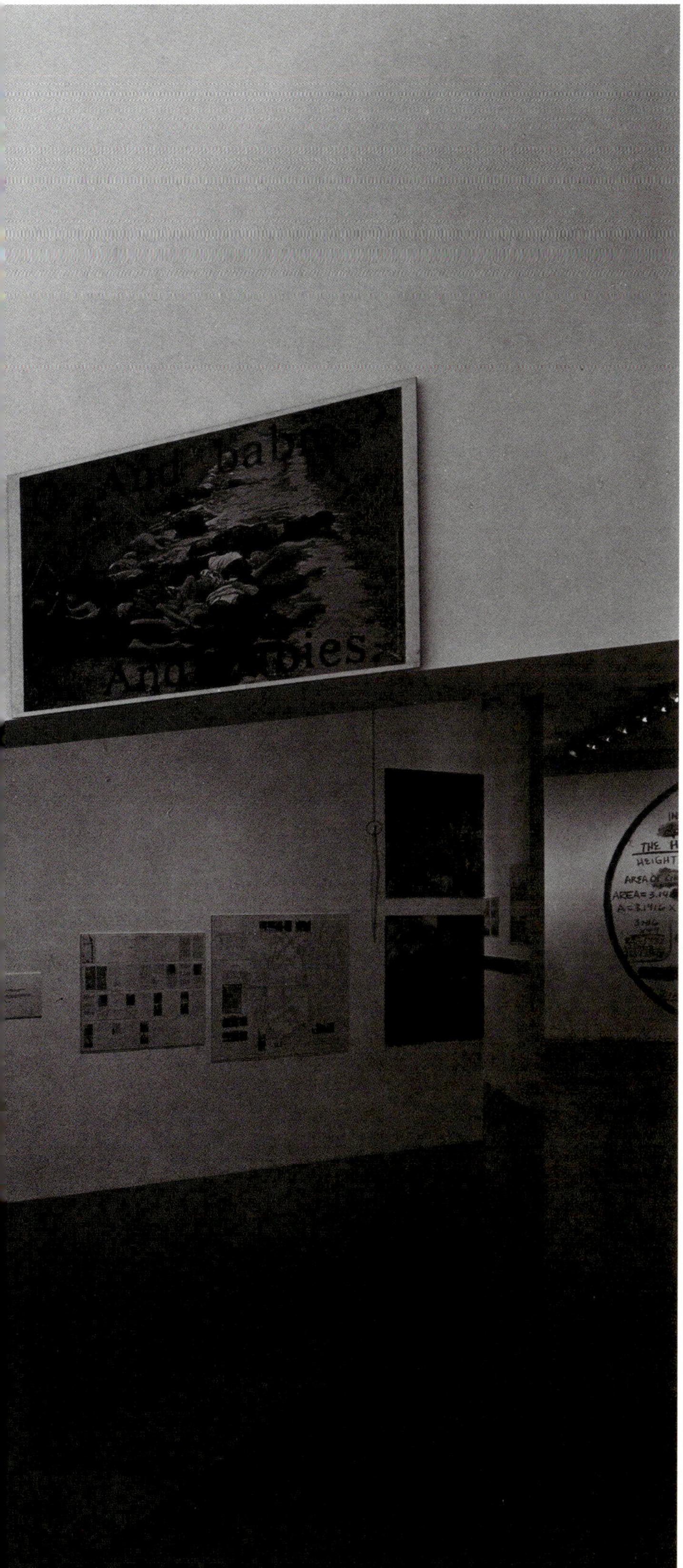

FIGURE 34

Installation view of *Information* including the Artists' Poster Committee of the Art Workers' Coalition, *Q. And babies? A. And babies.*, 1969–70 (above doorway); The Museum of Modern Art, New York, July 2–September 20, 1970; organized by Kynaston L. McShine. The Museum of Modern Art Archives, New York. (Digital image © The Museum of Modern Art/Licensed by SCALA/Art Resource, New York)

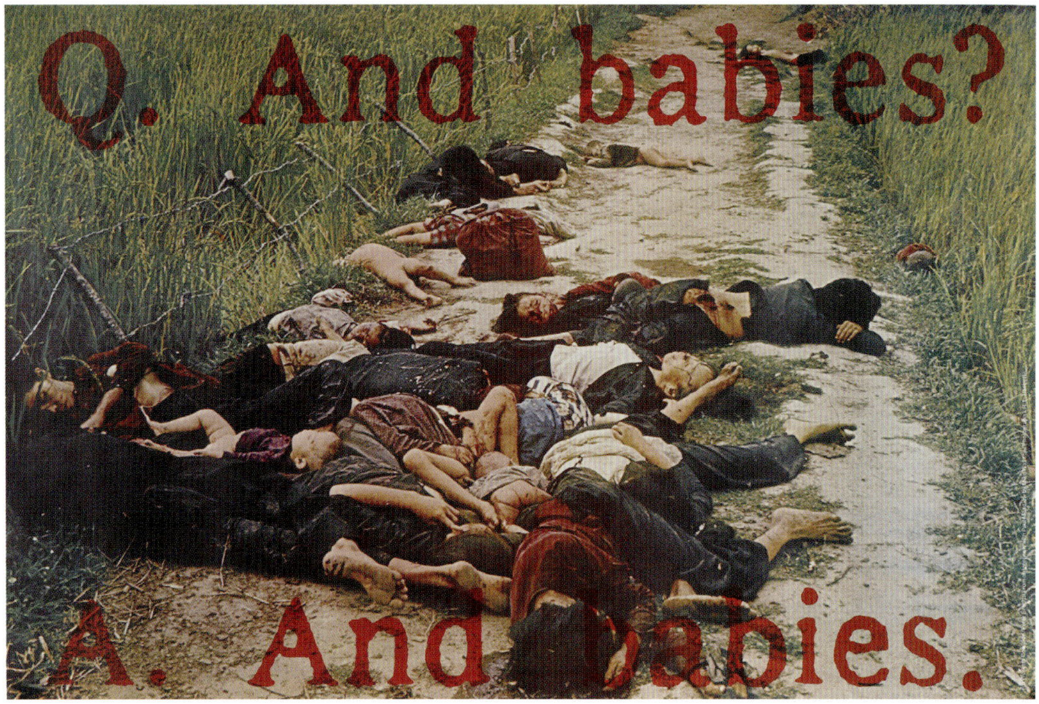

FIGURE 35

Artists' Poster Committee of the Art Workers' Coalition. *Q. And babies? A. And babies.*, 1969–70. Offset poster, 25 × 38 in. (63.5 × 96.5 cm). Private collection. © Artist's Poster Committee of the Art Workers' Coalition: Frazier Dougherty, Jon Hendricks, and Irving Petlin. Original photograph of the My Lai massacre by R. L. Haeberle (b. 1941). (Poster photographed by the Brooklyn Museum)

However, even in the early 1970s, some of the key players from the beginnings of the movement—particularly critics—had already begun this process of recognition and historical objectification.

Situating *Six Years*

In 1971, Lippard signed the publishing contract that set in motion the writing of *Six Years.*[35] During the same year, she published a collection of her essays and exhibition reviews, called *Changing*, tracing her trajectory as a writer from her more formalist period (1965–68) to one characterized by a complex, hybrid use of language (1969–71). Lippard's peers also published several notable books during the early 1970s sharing similar methodology and goals. In *Conceptual Art* (Dutton, 1972), Ursula Meyer brought together a sampling of texts and documents by the key figures in this artistic movement.[36] In 1973, the same publisher released Gregory Battcock's *Idea Art*, which concentrated more heavily on essays by critics (and artist-critics) who had supported Conceptual practices and helped define the theoretical issues surrounding them in publications such as *Artforum* and *Studio International.*[37] *Six Years,* published in 1973, represents, in some sense, a synthesis of these two approaches.

In a review of the book, Clive Phillpot pointed out that Lippard arranged the Conceptual propositions that make up the bulk of her text much as an editor would organize poems or short stories in an anthology.[38] The propositions could be transposed into that new frame of reference without undue loss of meaning, in part because the minutiae of page layout and typography were initially of little concern to the artists. Along with the catalogues produced by Lippard and Siegelaub, in this respect some of the publications that came out of the Fluxus movement can be seen as precursors to Meyer's *Conceptual Art* and Battcock's *Idea Art* as well as to *Six Years* itself. The Flux-Kits, Jackson Mac Low and La Monte Young's *Anthology of Chance Operations,*[39] and George Maciunas's historical charts about the movement all solidified what could be described as the "assembling" impulse of the late 1960s and early 1970s.[40] Given their limited editions, most copies of these publications were quickly bought up and attained the status of collectible art objects.

Battcock, Meyer, and Lippard shared the same goal of making available to a broader readership ideas that had been, until then, the exclusive purview of a few artists, critics, and dealers (who, more often than not, ran in the same social circles). Their anthological surveys were published in editions in the tens of thousands, reviving a project of democratization that the three authors had all advocated a half a decade or so earlier.

The bibliography in the *557,087* catalogue already foreshadowed the structure of *Six Years*; in fact, much of its content can be found in the later book, in recycled form. But with a difference. Between 1969 and 1971, Lippard had followed up her own assertion that formalist criticism was obsolete by designing projects that appropriated the strategies of her peers (the technique of delegation, for example) and that sometimes questioned their political efficacy. *Six Years,* however, was written as a summation of an era. And so she abandoned her former strategies, though without relinquishing the reflexive style that had characterized her earlier projects. But now, fragmentation was to be employed in order to map the diverse actions and attitudes of these various collaborators, who had radically reconfigured the landscape of contemporary art in this short period of time. The gestation period and writing process of the book, during 1971–73, coincided with the awakening of her political consciousness and, thus,

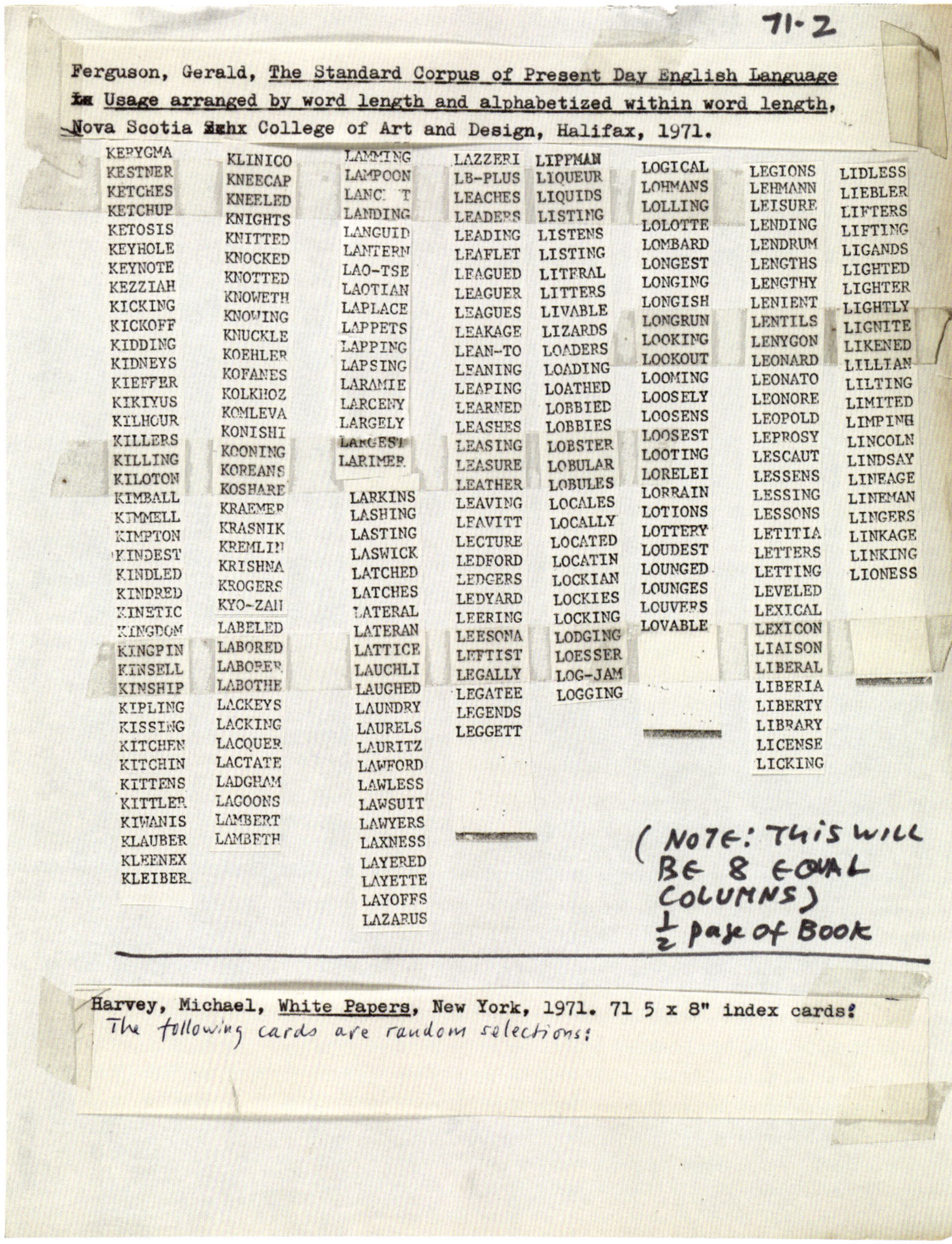

FIGURE 36

Lucy R. Lippard (American, b. 1937). Manuscript of entries subsequently printed on page 209 of *Six Years: The Dematerialization of the Art Object from 1966 to 1972*, c. 1972. Photocopy with cutout words scotch taped on paper, 11 × 8½ in. (27.9 × 21.6 cm). Lucy R. Lippard Papers, Archives of American Art, Smithsonian Institution, Washington, D.C.

her realization that different spheres of activity could no longer be segregated. Consequently, in her authorial/editorial role, she decided to intersperse the book's historical content with her own commentary passages, printed in italics.

Lippard's editorial choices also make themselves felt as the reader becomes aware of the imbalance between sections comprised of simple bibliographical entries and those containing material quoted directly from artists' statements or from transcribed symposia. She often chose to reprint long excerpts of those primary sources, but limited the already published texts (periodicals, exhibition catalogues) to mere listings. Reading through the quoted statements contained in the book helps re-create the sense of a community of speakers and collaborators, perhaps especially so in those instances when the sources are *viva voce* audio recordings, or in others that reveal bits of conversation to which only Lippard was witness.

Though her initial research was wider in scope, the core material in *Six Years* came mostly from Lippard's personal archives. What's more, the original manuscript was twice the length of the text as finally published. The assembly process that Lippard favored was a complex and difficult collaging together of the book's material (figure 36). She accomplished what amounted, in a literal sense, to a daunting cut-and-paste task: taking clippings from the various bulging files accumulated since the mid-sixties, cutting items up as needed, omitting others—assembling, annotating, photocopying, and gluing the scraps of text, over and over, to eventually form a comprehensible whole. While she was working, Lippard says, she expected that "no one would ever read the thing through" to decipher the sequence of events embedded in the chronology. But after the book was published, she was surprised that "a lot of people seemed to be plowing through it, plugging into the hidden narrative that I thought would be an involuntary secret."[41] Nevertheless, the uneasy cohabitation of public and private statements in the book might explain the somewhat mixed initial reception *Six Years* received.

Sharing professional ties and friendships, the figures whose activities are recorded in the book contributed to the creation of a network that saw the light of day largely through collaborative projects or shared professional enterprises. This ad hoc forum brought together various cultural producers united by the goal of ensuring that Conceptual art would align itself with a larger political project, but also develop some sort of economic sustainability.[42] In its final form, *Six Years* represents the distillation of these heterogeneous, and sometimes mutually antagonistic, interactions. Unsurprisingly, some artists initially expressed reluctance when Lippard first asked permission to reprint their documents, the existence of which many had forgotten. In her Preface to the published volume, she acknowledged the problem of going back over positions taken at a certain time and place, now existing solely in the form of irretractable statements.[43]

In his review of *Six Years* for *Artforum* in 1973, Mel Bochner questioned whether the activities of that dialogic community (of which he had been an active member) could later be reduced to such an assemblage of fragments: "The author has assumed a responsibility which cannot be reconciled with the technique of pasting old clippings and announcements together. This 'assemblage' technique is rendered invisible by what Roland Barthes calls 'the terrorism of the printed page.' The device of the invisible narrator is a 19th-century novelistic device for composing historical fiction, in order to manipulate the unaware reader's responses."[44] Despite the fact that she used a personal voice and collated seemingly random material, Lippard managed to generate the illusion of an all-encompassing viewpoint. Bochner points out that the book created for itself a singular power of influence, thanks to its function as the sole venue for the reawakening of many (previously) ephemeral projects. Finally, he further accused Lippard of completely avoiding certain issues: "Her refusal to engage the complex and often contradictory intellectual questions being raised, reduces the intentions of an art attempting a forceful critique of the existing social and aesthetic order into a series of purely self-promotional activities."[45] However, Bochner produces a paradox in policing, after the fact, borders of discursive fields that he himself had originally put into question through his magazine-based interventions.

In 1973, an anonymous individual wrote a text in which Lippard was identified as the only "author-artist" to have questioned the relevance of the methods used by the British collective Art & Language.[46] In an unpublished review of the exhibition *Idea Structures* at the Camden Art Center (1970), Lippard admitted having failed to engage in a dialogue with the group in the 1960s, largely because she found their work somewhat hermetic: "The chaos inherent in their reason fascinates me, but it is also irritating to be unequipped to evaluate their work. I don't know how it is or if it is evaluated by adepts in philosophy as philosophy, but I find it infuriating to have to take them on faith."[47] Her reservations about the importance of Art & Language were in some sense related to the dialogical limits of their work. In the Postface to *Six Years*, she contended that they avoided discussion with an academic community whose protocols of communication served as the template for their artworks: "As yet the 'behavioral artists' have not held particularly rewarding dialogues with their psychologist counterparts, and we have had no feedback on the Art-Language group from the linguistic philosophers they emulate. 'Art use' of elementary knowledge, already accepted and exhausted, oversimplification, and unsophistication in regard to work accomplished in other fields are obvious barriers to such interdisciplinary communication."[48]

The absence of a felicitous middle point between Lippard's hybrid approach and the orthodoxy of Bochner or the Art & Language collective complicates, in hindsight, the reception of Conceptual art as a historical movement, showing not only that it was split into different theoretical factions, but also that it was fundamentally de-centered in its social and political aims. Although the members of the movement did have a shared project—to reveal the inner contradictions of the ideology of medium-specificity, associated with the critic Clement Greenberg—this was not articulated solely through argumentation. And the numerous and varied language-based methods employed by the artists toward this end tended to collide with each other and overlap; *Six Years* effectively made visible this heterogeneity without imposing upon it a structure of value judgments. Indeed, not unlike the rest of Lippard's work, another distinguishing feature of her book is its attempt to eliminate the artificial distinction between the center and the periphery, allowing for the inclusion of South American, Australian, Asian, and Canadian artists, in addition to artists from the U.S., continental Europe, and England.

Since the publication of *Six Years*, the body of knowledge surrounding Conceptual art has grown exponentially, so that it now encompasses even the most obscure of the materials included in Lippard's bibliographical text. Many art historians and curators have in fact taken the content of the book as the starting point for their research. An analysis of the critical fortunes of Conceptualism since the early 1990s demonstrates the extent to which *Six Years* has served as a matrix for the reevaluation of those practices. Artists who were little known ten or twenty years ago are now fully integrated into the canon, thanks to more-inclusive thematic and geographical regroupings.[49] At the end of the day, the oversaturation of discourse surrounding this period may give the impression that the map accurately represents the territory. However, when compiling *Six Years*, Lippard had insisted on its historical incompleteness; and given that the artworks discussed were inextricably entangled with their contexts of production and reception, they remain bound up with the debates they provoked.

Translated from the French by Simon Brown

Notes

1. "… emptiness we took for what it was—a place where anything could happen … More and more we left openings in our space or time … It must be that eventually we will have a music the relationship of which to what takes place before and after ('no' music) is exact, so that one will have the experience that no experience was had, a dematerialization (not of facts) of intentions." John Cage, as quoted in John Chandler and Lucy R. Lippard, "Visible Art and the Invisible World," *Art International*, vol. 11, no. 5 (May 1967), p. 30. The quoted text is from Cage's "Rhythm Etc.," reprinted in *A Year from Monday: New Lectures and Writings by John Cage* (Middletown, Conn.: Wesleyan University Press, 1967, rpt. 1969), pp. 120–32.
2. John Chandler and Lucy R. Lippard, "The Dematerialization of Art," *Art International*, vol. 12, no. 2 (February 1968), pp. 31–32.
3. *Six Years: The dematerialization of the art object from 1966 to 1972: a cross-reference book of information on some esthetic boundaries: consisting of a bibliography into which are inserted a fragmented text, art works, documents, interviews, and symposia, arranged chronologically and focused on so-called conceptual or information or idea art with mentions of such vaguely designated areas as minimal, anti-form, systems, earth, or process art, occurring now in the Americas, Europe, England, Australia, and Asia (with occasional political overtones), edited and annotated by Lucy R. Lippard* (New York and London: Praeger Publishers, 1973; reprinted edition, with a new introduction, Berkeley and Los Angeles: University of California Press, 1997). For the excerpts quoted in this essay, consult the 1997 edition.
4. For a comprehensive account of Seth Siegelaub's role in disseminating Conceptual art, see Alexander Alberro, *Conceptual Art and the Politics of Publicity* (Cambridge, Mass.: The MIT Press, 2003).
5. For example, *January 5–31, 1969: Barry, Huebler, Kosuth, Weiner* and *July–August–September*, *1969*.
6. In 1970, she also organized *2.972.453* at the Centro de Arte y Comunicación in Buenos Aires. The last exhibition of this type, titled *c. 7,500* (referring to the population of Valencia, California, at the time), opened at CalArts, Valencia, in 1973.
7. For a reprint of this fragmented text initially published on several of the cards, see Lucy R. Lippard, "Introduction to *557,087*," in Alexander Alberro and Blake Stimson, eds., *Conceptual Art: A Critical Anthology* (Cambridge, Mass.: The MIT Press, 1999), pp. 178–85.
8. In the same text, she describes the *Six Years* project, then in an embryonic form, in which this strategy of accumulating bibliographical references and quotations would be put to full use; see Lucy R. Lippard, Introduction to her *Changing: Essays in Art Criticism* (New York: E. P. Dutton, 1971), p. 13.
9. Peter Plagens, "557,087," *Artforum*, vol. 8, no. 3 (November 1969), pp. 64–67. Paragraph excerpted in Lippard, *Six Years,* p. 111.
10. On Harald Szeemann's curatorial approach, see Christian Rattemeyer, ed., *Exhibiting the New Art: "Op Losse Schroeven" and "When Attitudes Become Form," 1969* (London: Afterall Books, 2010); and Florience Derieux, ed., *Harald Szeemann: Individual Methodology* (Zurich: JRP/Ringier, 2008).
11. Lucy R. Lippard, "Groups," *Studio International,* vol. 179, no. 920 (March 1970), pp. 93–100.
12. Twenty contributions remained, including projects by Jonathan Borofsky, Douglas Huebler, Stylianos Gianakos, Alex Katz, Leslie Miller, Francis Moyer, N. E. Thing Co., Adrian Piper, Peter Robins, and Lawrence Weiner.

13. Later published under the title *I See/You Mean* (Los Angeles: Chrysalis Books, 1979).

14. Seth Siegelaub, "July/August Exhibition," *Studio International*, vol. 180, no. 924 (July–August 1970), pp. 1–48.

15. Lippard, *Six Years,* p. 179.

16. Robert Barry, Stephen Kaltenbach, Lawrence Weiner, On Kawara, Sol LeWitt, Douglas Huebler, N. E. Thing Co., and Frederick Barthelme contributed pages to Lippard's section.

17. David Lamelas, *Publication* (London: Nigel Greenwood, 1970). The exhibition took place November 23–December 6, 1970. The text is also available in Lippard, *Six Years*, pp. 186–91.

18. Lippard, *Six Years*, p. 187.

19. It is important to mention that her collaborations both with Huebler and Barry were inserted into systems devised by the two artists to create a sequence through which their work could be read: Huebler's series of *Variable Pieces* and Barry's exhibition of "paratextual" materials (mostly invitation cards) stemming from his involvement with the commercial side of the art world.

20. Lippard, *Six Years,* p. 233.

21. Other than Barthes's essay, *Aspen* no. 5–6 contained theoretical articles by George Kubler and Susan Sontag, alongside narrative texts by Samuel Beckett, William Burroughs, and Alain Robbe-Grillet. See *Aspen*, no. 5–6 (Fall–Winter 1967), magazine in a box, compiled by Brian O'Doherty (New York: Roaring Fork Press, 1967).

22. Roland Barthes, "The Death of the Author," trans. Richard Howard, *Aspen*, no. 5–6 (Fall–Winter 1967), unpaginated. Richard Howard's translation is also available online: http://www.ubu.com/aspen/aspen5and6/threeEssays.html#barthes (consulted November 3, 2011, 2:01 p.m.).

23. Ibid.

24. Ibid.

25. Mary Kelly, "Re-viewing Modernist Criticism," *Screen,* vol. 22, no. 3 (1981), pp. 41–61.

26. On *l'écriture féminine,* see Hélène Cixous, *Le rire de la Méduse* (Paris: L'Arc, 1975). English edition, Hélène Cixous, "The Laugh of the Medusa," trans. Keith Cohen and Paula Cohen, *Signs,* vol. 1, no. 4 (1976), pp. 875–93.

27. Joseph Kosuth and Christine Kozlov, "Ad Reinhardt: Evolution into Darkness; The Art of an Informal Formalist—Negativity, Purity, and the Clearness of Ambiguity" (unpublished paper, School of Visual Arts, New York, May 1966).

28. Christine Kozlov, *271 Blank Sheets of Paper Corresponding to 271 Days of Concepts Rejected*, February–October 1968. Exhibited in *Number 7,* organized by Lucy R. Lippard at the Paula Cooper Gallery, New York, in 1969.

29. Lucy R. Lippard, "An Interview with Adrian Piper," *The Drama Review,* vol. 16, no. 1 (March 1972), p. 77.

30. Roland Barthes, *Le Neutre: Cours au collège de France, 1977–1978* (Paris: Seuil, 2002). English edition, Roland Barthes, *The Neutral: Lecture Course at the Collège de France, 1977–1978*, trans. Rosalind E. Krauss and Denis Hollier (New York: Columbia University Press, 2005).

31. Lucy R. Lippard, "Absentee Information and or Criticism," in Kynaston L. McShine, ed., *Information,* exh. cat. (New York: The Museum of Modern Art, 1970), pp. 74–81. Without her being consulted, ultimately the text was put into the section devoted to artists' interventions.

32. On the circumstances of the *Information* exhibition, see Ken Allan, "Understanding Information," in Michael Corris, ed., *Conceptual Art: Theory, Myth and Practice* (Cambridge: Cambridge University Press, 2004), p. 147.

33. See Charles Harrison, "On Exhibitions and the World at Large: Seth Siegelaub in Conversation with Charles Harrison," *Studio International,* vol. 178, no. 917 (September 1969), pp. 202–3.

34. On this shift, see Gwen Allen, *Artists' Magazines: An Alternative Space for Art* (Cambridge, Mass., and London: The MIT Press, 2011), in particular the chapter "This Is Not to Be Looked At: *Artforum* in the 1960s and 1970s," pp. 13–42.

35. "Author's Questionnaire, Praeger Publishers, Inc. (filled out by Lucy R. Lippard, February 12, 1971)," Lucy R. Lippard Papers, Archives of American Art, Smithsonian Institution, Washington, D.C.

36. Ursula Meyer, *Conceptual Art* (New York: E. P. Dutton, 1972).

37. Gregory Battcock, ed., *Idea Art: A Critical Anthology* (New York: E. P. Dutton, 1973). Battcock had published *Minimal Art: A Critical Anthology* in 1968 with the same press.

38. Clive Phillpot, "Six Years: The Dematerialization of the Art Object from 1966 to 1972 (…)," *Leonardo,* vol. 8, no. 3 (Summer 1975), p. 201.

39. Jackson Mac Low and La Monte Young, eds., *An Anthology of Chance Operations* (New York: self-published, 1963).

40. Between 1953 and 1973, Maciunas designed many diagrams and charts that situated Fluxus within a larger historical overview (the European avant-gardes of the turn of the twentieth century, among other contexts). See Astrid Schmidt Burkhardt, ed., *Maciunas' Learning Machines: From Art History to a Chronology of Fluxus* (Detroit: The Gilbert and Lila Silverman Fluxus Collection; Berlin: Vice Versa Verlag, 2003).

41. Lippard, *Six Years*, p. 3.

42. For an analysis of how this network emerged at the end of the 1960s and consolidated itself during the next decade, see Sophie Richard, *Unconcealed: The International Network of Conceptual Artists, 1967–1977: Dealers, Exhibitions and Public Collections* (London: Ridinghouse, 2009).

43. Lippard, *Six Years*, p. 6. Lippard ends the Preface with quotations from an interview with her, done by Ursula Meyer, which she chose not to revise or comment upon in order to compensate for this imbalance.

44. Mel Bochner, "Six Years: The Dematerialization of the Art Object from 1966 to 1972," *Artforum,* vol. 11, no. 10 (June 1973); republished in Mel Bochner, *Solar System and Rest Rooms: Writings and Interviews, 1965–2007* (Cambridge, Mass.: The MIT Press, 2008), p. 106.

45. Ibid., p. 105.

46. Author unknown, "Language into Art" (unpublished manuscript), c. 1973. Art & Language Artist File, Lucy R. Lippard Papers, Archives of American Art, Smithsonian Institution, Washington, D.C.

47. Lippard, *Six Years*, p. 151.

48. Lippard, Postface to *Six Years*, p. 263.

49. Since the publication of *Six Years*, many historians have pursued Lippard's endeavor in order to inscribe the international Conceptual art canon (or extensions of Fluxus) with simultaneously emergent practices from Oceania, Asia, Africa, ex-communist bloc countries, and Latin America. See Luis Camnitzer, Jane Farver, and Rachel Weiss, eds., *Global Conceptualism: Points of Origin, 1950s–1980s*, exh. cat. (New York: Queens Museum of Art, 1999).

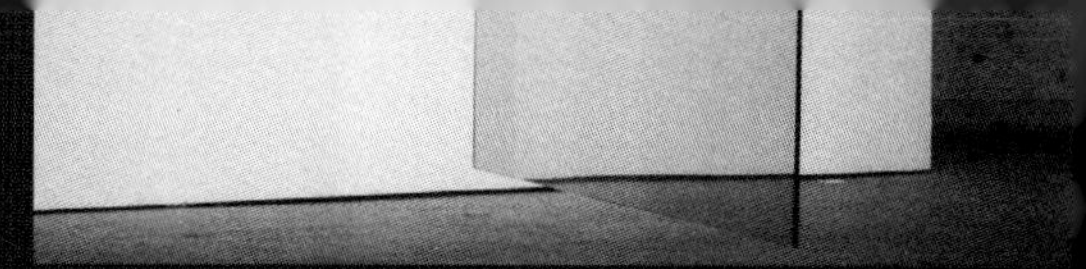

Still Relevant: Lucy R. Lippard, Feminist Activism, and Art Institutions

Julia Bryan-Wilson

Still Relevant: Lucy R. Lippard, Feminist Activism, and Art Institutions

Julia Bryan-Wilson

"Are Museums Relevant to Women?"

On December 12, 1971, twenty-nine speakers took the podium at a forum at the Brooklyn Museum to discuss the question, "Are museums relevant to women?" Co-chaired by the artist and activist Faith Ringgold and the writer Patricia Mainardi, the open meeting provided feminists within New York's art world the opportunity to air grievances about gender discrimination in art institutions. Artists such as Alice Neel and Louise Bourgeois spoke about the need to pressure museums to include more female artists, as well as to dismantle the masculinist standards of quality in which art by women has historically been seen as of lesser value than art by men. In a summary of the event, Mainardi later wrote that the forum's titular inquiry about museums and their "relevance" to women "brought a resounding 'No!' from virtually all the speakers."[1] Art institutions—from bricks-and-mortar buildings themselves to the ideologies they uphold—were castigated for being outdated, sexist, and out of touch with the contemporary realities of feminist politics.

Avowed male allies Jon Hendricks and Jean Toche, founding members of the collective Guerrilla Art Action Group (GAAG), stated: "... the structure of museums is a microcosm of the structure of sexism in our society. It is used to maintain, perpetuate and reinforce the myths, the mental attitudes, and the mechanics of male supremacy."[2] GAAG's statement highlights the palpable discontent regarding museums that was frequently articulated within activist circles of the New York art scene at this time. Museums were viewed as microcosms of all that was wrong with the broader culture, institutions where the massive discrepancies wrought by sexism, racism, and market capitalism could be found in their most potent forms. This notion was asserted in a similar gathering held a few years earlier, in 1969, by the Art Workers' Coalition (AWC) and called "An Open Hearing on the Subject: What Should Be the Program of the Art Workers Regarding Museum Reform and to Establish the Program of an Art Workers' Coalition" (figure 37).[3] While speakers at the AWC event—the prototype for subsequent open hearings—discussed everything from museum deaccessioning policies to the Vietnam War, the Brooklyn Museum meeting was the first of its kind devoted exclusively to women's issues.

The critic and curator Lucy R. Lippard was among the speakers in Brooklyn, and a photograph shows her in mid-gesture (figure 38). A flyer with the heading "Women and Art" was taped to the front of the podium. By 1971, Lippard was already famous for organizing high-profile exhibitions, for writing influential criticism, and for her prominent role within the Art Workers' Coalition, in which she leveled wide-ranging critiques about interlocking systems of art, power, and money. Nevertheless, at the Brooklyn open hearing, she turned to the concrete difficulties she faced not only as an art worker, but specifically as a working mother:

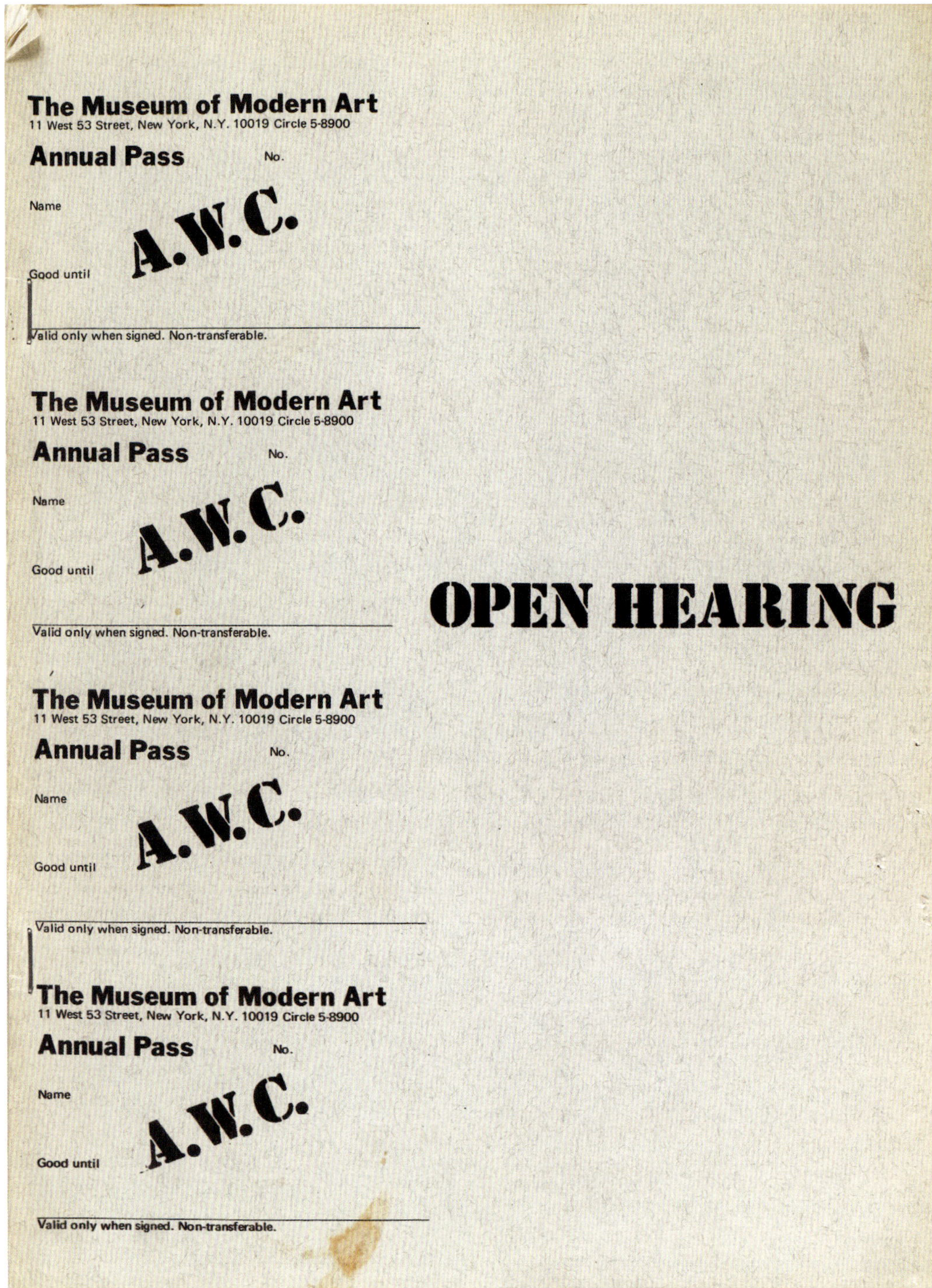

The Museum of Modern Art
11 West 53 Street, New York, N.Y. 10019 Circle 5-8900
Annual Pass No.
Name
A.W.C.
Good until
Valid only when signed. Non-transferable.

The Museum of Modern Art
11 West 53 Street, New York, N.Y. 10019 Circle 5-8900
Annual Pass No.
Name
A.W.C.
Good until
Valid only when signed. Non-transferable.

The Museum of Modern Art
11 West 53 Street, New York, N.Y. 10019 Circle 5-8900
Annual Pass No.
Name
A.W.C.
Good until
Valid only when signed. Non-transferable.

The Museum of Modern Art
11 West 53 Street, New York, N.Y. 10019 Circle 5-8900
Annual Pass No.
Name
A.W.C.
Good until
Valid only when signed. Non-transferable.

OPEN HEARING

Why can't museums have children's art education programs on Saturdays and Sundays where the kids can be left so that women, and couples too for that matter, can look at the work seriously without having to race around after a kid constantly? I haven't been to a museum in peace of mind for about seven years now. They're prejudiced against women in silly ways—like the Guggenheim won't let you take a stroller into the museum. If you've ever dragged a fifty-pound baby up and down the Guggenheim ramp, you know what that's about.[4]

In this speech, Lippard addressed the museum's relevance—or, more precisely, its irrelevance—to women as a matter of practical logistics, citing the lack of daycare, for instance, or advocating for better access for families with young children. These are just some of the matters of daily life that are structured by gender bias and the feminization of child rearing, and as such are connected to larger questions of injustice.

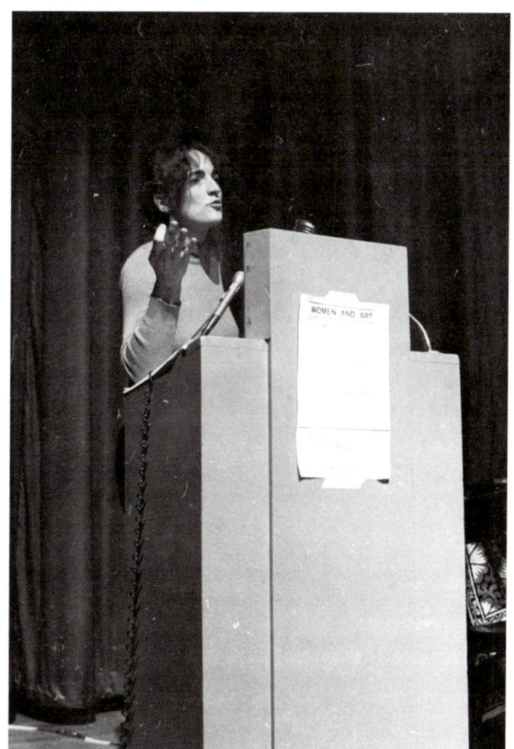

FIGURE 37

Cover of *An Open Hearing on the Subject: What Should Be the Program of the Art Workers Regarding Museum Reform and to Establish the Program of an Art Workers' Coalition*. Staple-bound printed book, 11 × 8½ in. (27.9 × 21.6 cm). New York: Art Workers' Coalition, 1969.

FIGURE 38

Jan van Raay (American, b. 1942). *Lippard at Brooklyn Museum of Art Hearing About Women's Art*, 1971. Black-and-white photograph. Collection of Jan van Raay, Portland, Ore. © Jan van Raay

With this critique, Lippard was not alone; Mainardi reported that one of the most frequently mentioned demands at the open hearing was "provisions for mothers to visit museums" (it was second only to the insistence that institutions purchase and show more art by women).[5] In fact, when a coalition of black women artists presented its list of six demands at the Brooklyn Museum hearing, number one was that museums launch an exhibition of black women's art, and number two was that they "provide day-care centers or children's workshops."[6] Though the call for museums to develop daycare centers might seem to range far afield from debates about the systematic exclusion of women from museum exhibitions, for those at the Brooklyn Museum these requests were all of a piece. They were meant, in part, to increase the accessibility of art institutions to underserved populations. But even more radically, such demands underscored that neither the activity of art viewing nor the architecture in which it occurs (such as the Guggenheim ramp) are gender-neutral. If motherhood and spectating are not in fact distinct realms, Lippard suggested, then why shouldn't the museum address them both on their own terms?

Beyond articulating a vision for an ideal museum, Lippard's speech also indicates the pressures she felt in balancing her many forms of labor—some of which were not fully recognized as work. This dynamic is theorized in the writings of the French materialist feminist Christine Delphy from the early 1970s, which explicate the increasingly politicized notion of "women's work" in public versus private modes of production.[7] Delphy maintains that so-called women's work, such as child care or domestic maintenance, is often "excluded from the realm of value."[8] In what follows, I examine how Lippard understood the shifting "relevance" of her own critical and curatorial practices alongside her roles as a feminist and as an activist.

Institutional Relevance

Lippard had long been sympathetic to leftist causes, but as she has repeatedly said, she became "politicized" during a formative trip to Argentina in 1968, where she met some of the artists, workers, and journalists affiliated with the Grupo de Artistas de Vanguardia (the Rosario Group).[9] The Rosario Group staged the interventionist event *Tucumán Arde* (*Tucumán Is Burning*), which was held at a local union hall and became a model for how to collectively protest current conditions (figure 39). After this trip, and seeing the possibilities for coalitional work in times of severe social crisis, Lippard immersed herself in on-the-street demonstrations, organizing, picketing, and other activities—as well as curating new types of exhibitions that were either explicitly or implicitly in dialogue with these politics. Her initial forays into activism in the late 1960s largely fell under the rubric of the AWC, a loosely organized body founded in 1969 as an artists' rights group that became an important antiwar vehicle until its demise in 1971. In its brief lifespan, it challenged the very institutionalization of art: some of its members wanted to reform, if not dismantle, conventional museums, for-profit galleries, private dealers, art schools, art magazines, and the commodity nature of art itself—in short, to rethink or revolutionize the entire industry of contemporary art.

Lippard was at the forefront of such debates from early on in the formation of the AWC. At the AWC's "Open Hearing" in 1969 she discussed the need for "a new and more flexible system that can adapt itself to the changes taking place today in the art itself."[10] At a time when museums were being excoriated for their board members' complicity with the military-industrial complex, the museums were nonetheless held up as a space of great promise, and as such were

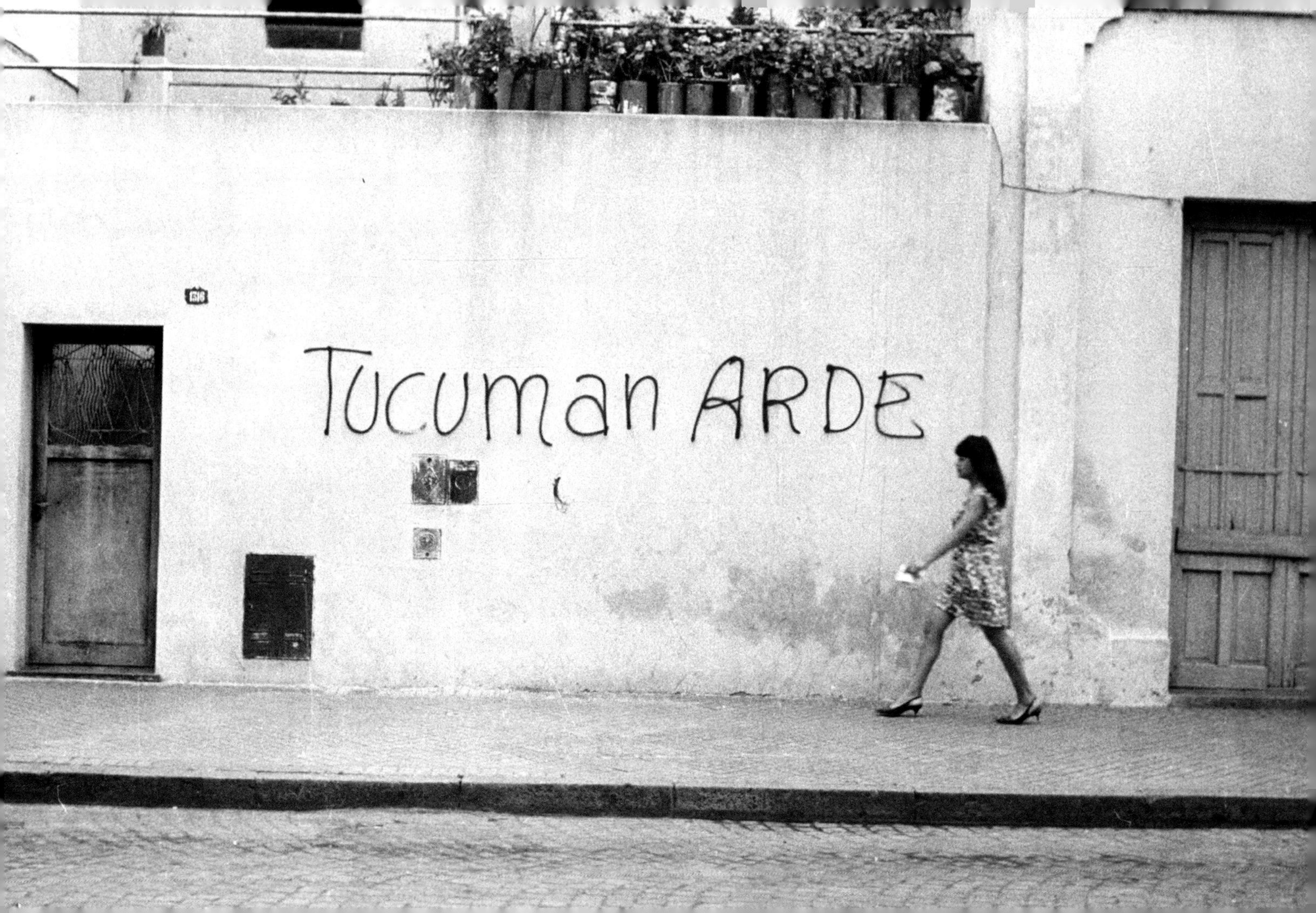
TUCUMAN ARDE

13 DEMANDS

submitted to Mr. Bates Lowry, Director of the Museum of Modern Art,
by a group of artists and critics
on January 28, 1969.

1. The Museum should hold a public hearing during February on the topic "The Museum's Relationship to Artists and to Society", which should conform to the recognized rules of procedure for public hearings.
2. A section of the Museum, under the direction of black artists, should be devoted to showing the accomplishments of black artists.
3. The Museum's activities should be extended into the Black, Spanish and other communities. It should also encourage exhibits with which these groups can identify.
4. A committee of artists with curatorial responsibilities should be set up annually to arrange exhibits.
5. The Museum should be open on two evenings until midnight and admission should be free at all times.
6. Artists should be paid a rental fee for the exhibition of their works.
7. The Museum should recognize an artist's right to refuse showing a work owned by the Museum in any exhibition other than one of the Museum's permanent collection.
8. The Museum should declare its position on copyright legislation and the proposed arts proceeds act. It should also take active steps to inform artists of their legal rights.
9. A registry of artists should be instituted at the Museum. Artists who wish to be registered should supply the Museum with documentation of their work, in the form of photographs, news clippings, etc., and this material should be added to the existing artists' files.
10. The Museum should exhibit experimental works requiring unique environmental conditions at locations outside the Museum.
11. A section of the Museum should be permanently devoted to showing the works of artists without galleries.
12. The Museum should include among its staff persons qualified to handle the installation and maintenance of technological works.
13. The Museum should appoint a responsible person to handle any grievances arising from its dealings with artists.

13

FIGURE 40

Art Workers' Coalition. *13 Demands*, January 28, 1969. Memo submitted to Bates Lowry, director of The Museum of Modern Art, addressing artists' rights at the museum. Typewritten text, 11 x 8½ in. (27.9 x 21.6 cm). Virginia Admiral Papers, Archives of American Art, Smithsonian Institution, Washington, D.C.

places of enormous investment for artists and critics like Lippard. (Such contradiction—and an underlying naïveté—would ultimately make the AWC untenable.) In the late 1960s and early 1970s, the AWC persistently asked much of museums, looking at them as laboratories where collective agitation might cultivate something more socially just. They issued a list of thirteen demands to modern art museums—in particular, New York's Museum of Modern Art, a frequent target of their protests (figure 40). Among the sweeping changes called for, here and in other lists of demands, were provisions related to more artists' input, as well as more equity along lines of class, race, and gender: having a board of trustees comprised one-third of artists, insisting that "admission should be free at all times," "extend[ing] its activities into the Black, Spanish, and all other communities," and "establishing equal representation of the sexes in shows, museum purchases, and on selection committees."

The AWC was also affected by wider anti–Vietnam War sentiment and called for museums to take public stands against the war, including asking MoMA to co-sponsor the production of their protest poster *Q. And babies? A. And babies.* (figure 35). The museum initially agreed to this co-sponsorship, but later backed out, demurring that it preferred to remain "neutral"—though Lippard and others were quick to point out that with Governor Nelson A. Rockefeller (who supported the war in Vietnam) on its board, it could hardly be so.[11]

The Coalition became increasingly disheartened with art institutions and looked to other avenues of display and dissemination that might circumvent traditional museums altogether. What this effort should look like was far from clear, but Lippard embraced process art and Conceptualism as ways to resist the entrenched channels of promotion and commodity exchange. For her, the text-based nature of "dematerialized" art, with its index cards, instructions, advertisements, and blank pages, could defy the logic of the artwork as an object to be bought and sold. In some of her critical writings beginning in 1968, as well as in Conceptual exhibitions she curated, such as *557,087* from 1969, she became an avid proponent of the (to her, inherently) political nature of such artworks.

She also pushed this thesis in curatorial work that was overtly related to her activism, as in the exhibition she co-organized with Robert Huot and Ron Wolin that linked Minimal aesthetics to an antiwar stance. This show, launched at the Paula Cooper Gallery in 1968 as a benefit for the Student Mobilization Committee to End the War in Vietnam, included works by Jo Baer and Carl Andre, along with Sol LeWitt's first wall drawing, which was painted over when the show closed and whose price was based on the number of hours it would take the artist to re-create it (figure 41). This was one model that the New York art left had for art that was deemed "relevant": an exhibition of art where the sales profits are clearly demarcated for an activist cause. Yet Lippard also felt that the formal aesthetics of the works in the show made a "forceful statement for peace," according to the press release (though at least one critic questioned this premise and thought it sounded rather like self-justification).[12]

Along with many in the AWC, such as Hans Haacke, Lippard began to focus on activism within and against museums, actions that to a large degree instigated the development of what came to be called institutional critique. As Lippard's protest actions started to overlap with and reshape her critical and curatorial agendas, she struggled with the contentious issue of relevance, writing in 1970: "… we are all too aware that art itself is 'irrelevant'; when compared to the world of slums, wars, prisons, the art world is a bed of roses. At the same time art is what we do or a focus of what we do."[13] Indeed, the term *relevance* in the late 1960s and early

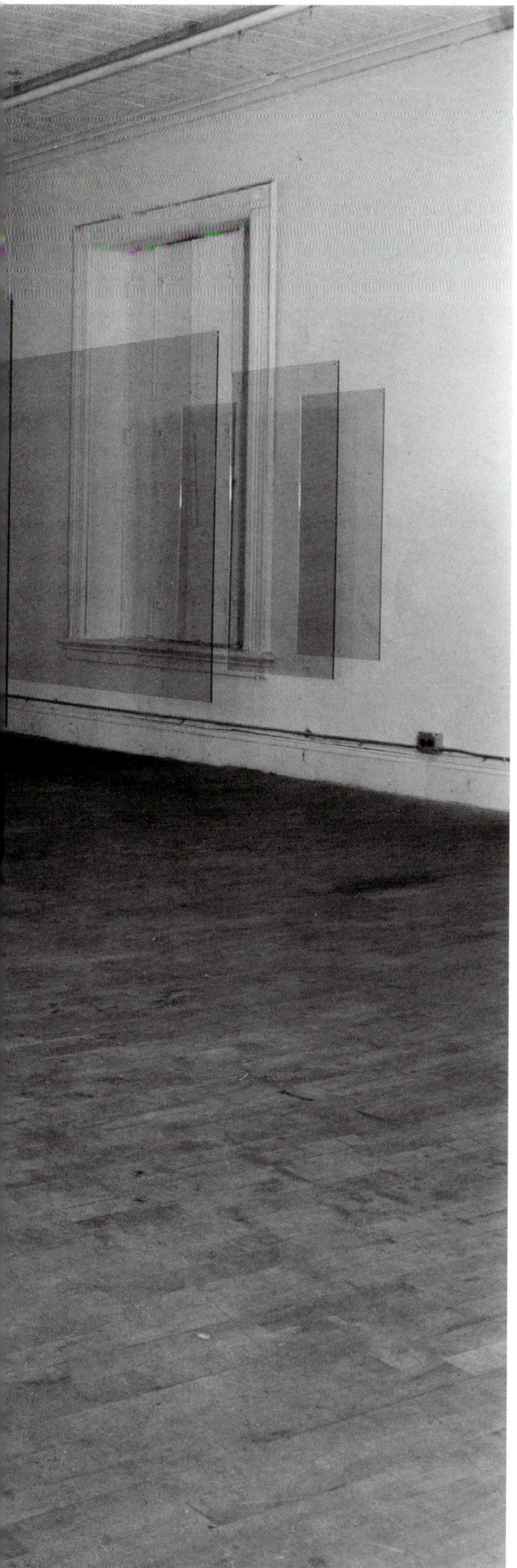

FIGURE 41

Installation view of *Benefit for the Student Mobilization Committee to End the War in Vietnam* including Sol LeWitt's first wall drawing (back wall); Paula Cooper Gallery, New York, October 22–31, 1968; co-organized by Lucy R. Lippard, Robert Huot, and Ron Wolin. © Paula Cooper Gallery, New York. (Photo: James Dee, courtesy Paula Cooper Gallery, New York)

1970s functioned as shorthand for wider anxieties about the waning influence of art in a time of enormous social upheaval.

This emphasis on relevance is further evidenced by other documents from the time, such as Faith Ringgold's statement read at *The People's Flag Show* in 1970: "Theatre, cinema, literature, music, TV, dance, all of the arts and all of life is trying (feebly in most instances), but [as] they begin to know the word *relevance* they begin to politicize, to revolutionize their art, to embrace the people in the street"[14] (emphasis in original). For Ringgold, relevance in art is explicitly linked to revolutionary politics, particularly ones that reach out beyond the usual audiences for art to "the people in the street." Along with GAAG's Hendricks and Toche, Ringgold was arrested for her participation in this exhibition, which included a performance in which GAAG burned an American flag. Ringgold's idea of a "relevant" art that touches the people in the street, however, stands at some distance from Lippard's understanding of the relevance of LeWitt's geometric penciled lines on a wall. The tension between them suggests some of the serious, unresolved paradoxes that haunted the Art Workers' Coalition from the outset and contributed to its collapse: should art strive to be populist, or should it remain autonomous? Should artists make propaganda, should they produce formal experiments, or should they stop making art altogether?

Artists and critics such as Ringgold and Lippard, however differently, worried not only that museums were slipping from their role as vital spaces of cultural exchange into the realm of the unnecessary or frivolous, but that art itself as a form of production might also lack any crucial purpose, demoted to entertainment or decoration. Hilton Kramer dissected the problem in a *New York Times* article titled "Artists and the Problem of 'Relevance,'" in 1969, in which he asserted that despite the current political unrest in the U.S. (arising not least from the bloody war abroad), "artists and art institutions have tended to play a negligible role—if, indeed, any role at all."[15] Kramer saw the organization of the Art Workers' Coalition as an attempt by artists to reassert their potential "place on the cultural scene … [and] ability to function as a cultural force," primarily by rethinking the system by which art is produced and consumed.

Relevance is of course a relative term. Its dictionary definition, "having a direct bearing on the matter at hand," begs the question: what, then, is the matter at hand? One might say that for self-described art workers like Lippard, the word *relevance* meant political relevance, some sort of calibration toward the social unrest of the moment, such as civil rights, feminism, and antiwar agitation. According to this logic, in order to signal its relevance, the museum should not only uphold a mission of public service (thus providing child education classes to benefit working mothers, for example), but also align itself, pointedly, legibly, and even practically, with the concerns of the left. How this might be accomplished was never fully formulated.

Feminist Activism

Starting in 1970—the year that she began to identify herself as a feminist—Lippard's involvement with the women's movement increasingly affected her writing and curating, and even more powerfully altered the course of her career than did her affiliation with the Art Workers' Coalition (where, despite her critical influence, she still struggled to make herself heard as a woman). As mentioned earlier, she claimed Minimalism as political when she co-curated the benefit show for the Student Mobilization Committee in 1968, and the curatorial stance she took in her Conceptual shows also indicated her interest in linking dematerialized art with leftist ideals. However, her inauguration into the women's movement exposed her to new kinds of art, including craft-based work, and led her to champion different kinds of artists, as is chronicled in her collection *From the Center: Feminist Essays on Women's Art* (1976).[16] By embracing women's art that was further marginalized for its use of traditionally "female" techniques, Lippard attacked gendered assumptions about high-art standards (standards that rely upon a debasing of low materials such as handiwork) and raised questions about the radical disparity of opportunities between men and women artists.

Leading the charge to address gender discrimination in the art world was Women Artists in Revolution (WAR), an offshoot of the Art Workers' Coalition that came together in late 1969. Though the AWC's demands had included a measure about women artists, many women who had long felt the sting of sexism felt that this was merely lip service and wanted more concrete results. On December 23, 1969, WAR held a meeting with staff at MoMA to demand non-juried shows and to call for an end to suffocating—and gendered—definitions of what was legitimized as museum-worthy fine art. But such meetings were inevitably frustrating, especially since women had busy lives to lead. As Lippard later said:

> Most of us, especially the women, were working full time trying to make art on the side, trying to raise children, trying to be lovers, and so on, plus all this political activity. So the Modern [MoMA] used to drag us into these long, long talks about everything and just went on and on and on. They were being paid salaries to talk to us and we were tearing our hair, you know, losing time, money, and our minds.[17]

Since talking with museums went nowhere, they started to focus their energies on direct action. The Ad Hoc Women Artists' Committee was formed in 1970 to encompass members from WAR, the AWC, and Women Students and Artists for Black Art Liberation (WSABAL, which consisted, basically, of Ringgold and her daughters Michele and Barbara Wallace). It was organized specifically to lobby the Whitney Painting and Sculpture Annual (the precursor to today's prestigious Biennial), in which women artists were notoriously scarce. Over the course of four months, the Ad Hoc Committee—with Lippard front and center—protested every Saturday, blowing police whistles, wearing red armbands, leaving unused tampons and eggs in the museum stairwells, and picketing outside the front door with signs demanding that the exhibition be 50 percent women artists.[18] They got creative with their tactics, including printing fake tickets for the opening and forging a press release (on smuggled Whitney Museum letterhead) that announced that half of the artists in the exhibition would indeed be women, with a proportional percentage of black, Asian, and Puerto Rican artists. This move was especially ingenious, as it forced the director of the museum, John I. H. Baur, to issue a counterstatement: "URGENT: TO ALL EDITORS. Press release mailed to you, dated 11-9-70, purporting to be from the Whitney Museum of American Art, headlined 'Whitney Sculpture Annual to be 50% Women' is a complete forgery—repeat a forgery. Facts are totally untrue."[19] Though this statement almost comically reasserts the museum's disregard for gender parity, the Ad Hoc Committee's actions did have a measurable impact: the number of women increased from 4.5 percent to 22 percent in one year.

Importantly, these feminist actions were not limited to changing art-world statistics, but branched out into women's issues that spanned a range of concerns. One of WAR's first major organizing initiatives focused on women's reproductive health, and its members made posters and aprons for an abortion-rights demonstration in March 1970.[20] This march, which occurred before the legalization of abortion in 1973, included male members of the Art Workers' Coalition who came out to support the cause (figure 42). In the photograph shown here, WAR member and sculptor Muriel Castanis, with her husband and child, bears a pro-choice sign that reads "Art Workers for Abortion Repeal." This image demonstrates that the loose and often vexed term *art worker* was marshaled at the time as a politically coherent identity, in the same way that one might go to a rally holding a sign, such as "TEACHERS FOR PEACE" or "MOMS AGAINST THE WAR," to indicate a kind of employment or demographic status. One fantasy of such identifications is that, when mobilized en masse, all members of this self-described group can speak with a significant collective voice. Though today the term *art worker* might seem to embody a grave contradiction, given the presumed class and privilege differences between artists and those conventionally understood as "workers," circa 1970 it had real purchase, however unstable and paradoxical. (The term has recently been revived; an organization founded in 2008, Working Artists and the Greater Economy, or WAGE, borrows some of the same terminology as the AWC, though WAGE has not sought to make connections with non-art social movements as the AWC and WAR had.)

The issue of the "relevance" of museums—and art itself—was central to the formation of the AWC, and it continued to percolate throughout diverse feminist actions in the early 1970s. Many at the Brooklyn Museum open hearing in 1971 wondered if museums were "relevant to anyone at all," or if they might already be "obsolete"—and not only for white women.[21] Artists of color increasingly sounded this query; for instance, the question of relevance appeared at a 1971 demonstration organized by the Black Emergency Cultural Coalition at the Whitney Museum of American Art to protest its exhibition *Contemporary Black Artists in America,* curated by Robert Doty, a white man. Among the many signs carried by the protestors is one held by BECC co-founder Benny Andrews's child that reads: "… IS THE WHITNEY RELEVANT????" (figure 43). The answer, presumably, is negative, and next to this question is a hand-drawn image of a black man raising the power-to-the-people fist; it is unclear if the figure is mouthing the words, or stands as a symbolic rebuttal—as if to say *this,* this defiant man, is what is relevant. In the wake of growing consciousness about women's issues, concerns about gender discrimination were also integral to this protest, as is evident in Michele Wallace's holding a stenciled sign demanding "50% Black Women Artists" (figure 44). Others at this rally included Lippard, who appears in a different photograph with the same sign as Wallace.

In accordance with her feminist activism, in the early 1970s Lippard started more aggressively to discuss her antipathy toward the critical policing of what was known in shorthand as "quality," which had become a flashpoint in feminist discussions of art. If women were not represented equally in museums, so the conventional story went, it was because their work was simply not strong enough, simply could not hold its own against art made by men. Linda Nochlin's classic feminist essay from 1971, "Why Have There Been No Great Women Artists?," argues that "greatness," far from denoting innate genius, is a highly constructed, policed, and gendered category. As Nochlin writes, "the total situation of art making, both in terms of the development of the art maker and in the nature and quality of the work of art itself, occur in a social situation, are integral elements of this social structure, and are mediated and determined by specific and definable social institutions, be they art academies, systems of patronage, mythologies of the divine creator, artist as he-man or social outcast."[22] Feminists grew wary of curators

FIGURE 42

Jan van Raay (American, b. 1942). *Art Workers for Abortion Repeal, Muriel Castanis Wearing Sign, with Her Husband and Daughter*, 1971. Black-and white photograph. Collection of Jan van Raay, Portland, Ore. © Jan van Raay

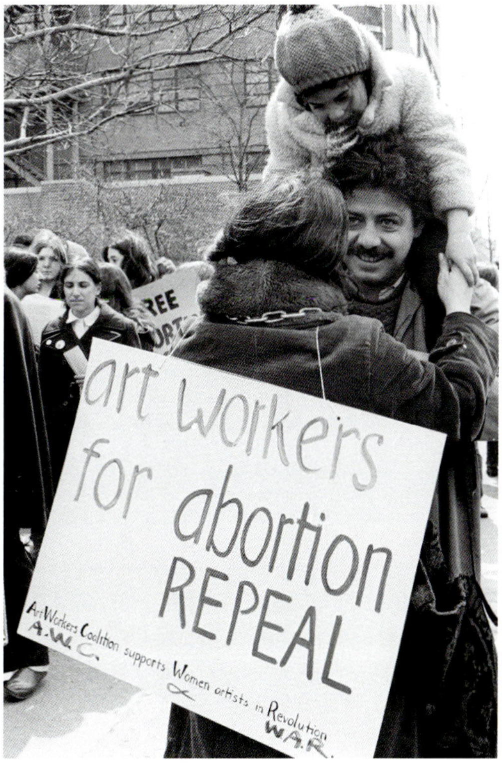

FIGURE 43

Jan van Raay (American, b. 1942). *Black Emergency Cultural Coalition (BECC) Protest at the Whitney Museum*, 1971. Black-and-white photograph. Collection of Jan van Raay, Portland, Ore. © Jan van Raay

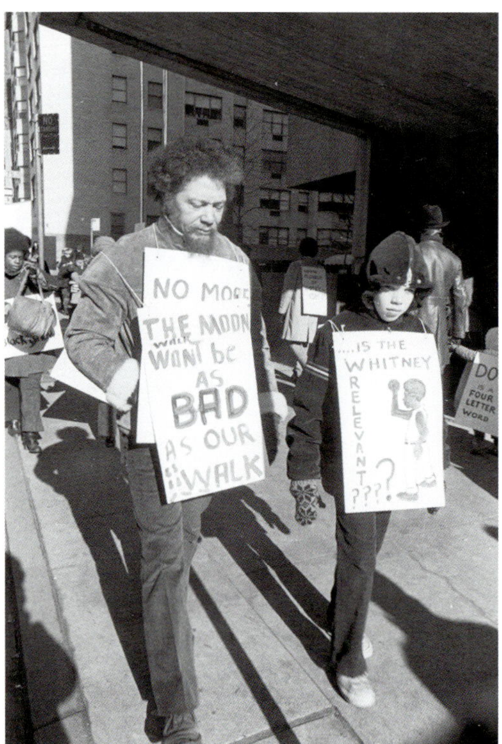

FIGURE 44

Jan van Raay (American, b. 1942). *Michele Wallace Carrying Sign About 50% Black Women Artists*, 1971. Black-and-white photograph. Collection of Jan van Raay, Portland, Ore. © Jan van Raay

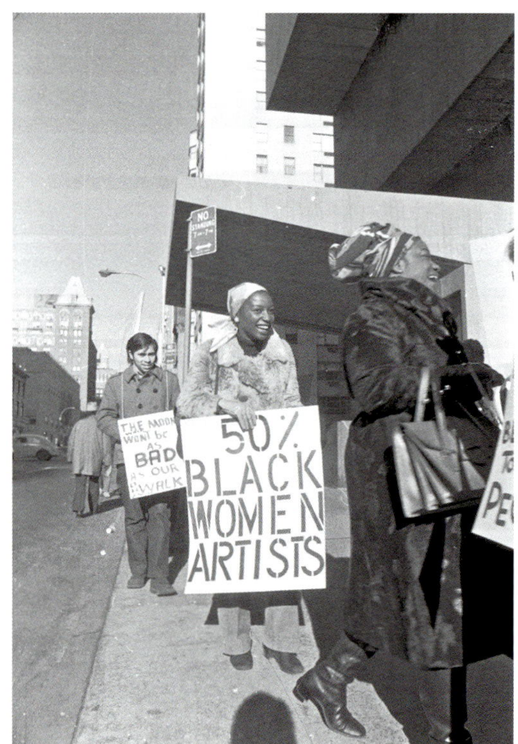

saying that they did not give women solo shows because they were interested only in the "quality" of the work—an ostensibly sex-blind category that invariably favored male artists.

Taste, of course, is never neutral, and the idea of "quality" was, for many feminists, little more than an alibi or an excuse for discrimination, one that encapsulates many levels of gender-biased gate-keeping that shut out women artists, especially as some were beginning to integrate "low" forms such as crafts into their work. Lippard later recognized "the seed of feminism in my revolt against Clement Greenberg's patronization of artists, against the imposition of the taste of one class on everybody."[23] Louise Bourgeois stated it most polemically at a women's protest at the Whitney in 1970: "the question of quality should be suspended for the time being."[24] Lippard began to look at a wide range of women's art—"anything by women, which brought me back towards painting and sculpture."[25] She chose her subjects based on affinities and allegiances, many of which stemmed from her commitment to women artists, writing about untested figures, political propagandists, emerging artists, and other risk takers whose work she felt drawn to for any number of reasons.

Alongside this reorientation of her critical practice toward female artists, Lippard's somewhat belated entry into feminism also shed new light on her curatorial work. Though she had long included women in her exhibitions, she started to see the urgency of putting on all-women shows. In 1971, she organized a show at the Aldrich Museum in Ridgefield, Connecticut, of women who had never had one-person exhibitions in New York; titled *Twenty-Six Contemporary Women Artists*, it was the first of its kind in the area. Lippard has always had a keen eye, and this astonishing show featured many women now considered central to twentieth-century art, including Alice Aycock, Mary Heilmann, Howardena Pindell, Christine Kozlov, Mary Miss, Sylvia Mangold, and Adrian Piper. This was just the beginning of Lippard's groundbreaking decision to create women-only exhibitions, such as her historic show, titled *c. 7,500*, of female Conceptual artists, which originated in Valencia, California.[26]

Six Years in Retrospect

Given the intensity of political action that Lippard was involved in, it is surprising that her major chronicle of exactly this era—*Six Years: The Dematerialization of the Art Object from 1966 to 1972*[27]—appears to record only scant details about the larger turmoil or the connections many were making between activism and art. The book makes no pretense of inclusivity or comprehensiveness, though it offers up a wealth of bibliographical and exhibition information, review snippets, photographic documentation, and interview excerpts. It makes for a lively mix, and Lippard was certainly far too modest when she said, in the Preface to the first edition, that "I am probably safe in saying, as I have of some exhibitions I have organized, that no one but me (and my editors) will read the whole book through."[28]

In fact, *Six Years* is a peculiar document on several fronts (for instance, it is unexpected to read in the acknowledgments that Carl Andre compiled the index), not least with regard to the "occasional political overtones" mentioned in the book's extended subtitle: as Lippard notes, they are more like "undertones."[29] This is not to say that mentions of contemporary political events don't exist (they do). For the record, and to be overly mechanistic, the first reference to war occurs in the book's eighth entry: a speech given in 1966 by Yoko Ono (who is also the first woman to make an appearance) that mentions "the time of the Second World War, when we had no food to eat."[30] The important organization Students for a Democratic Society is summoned

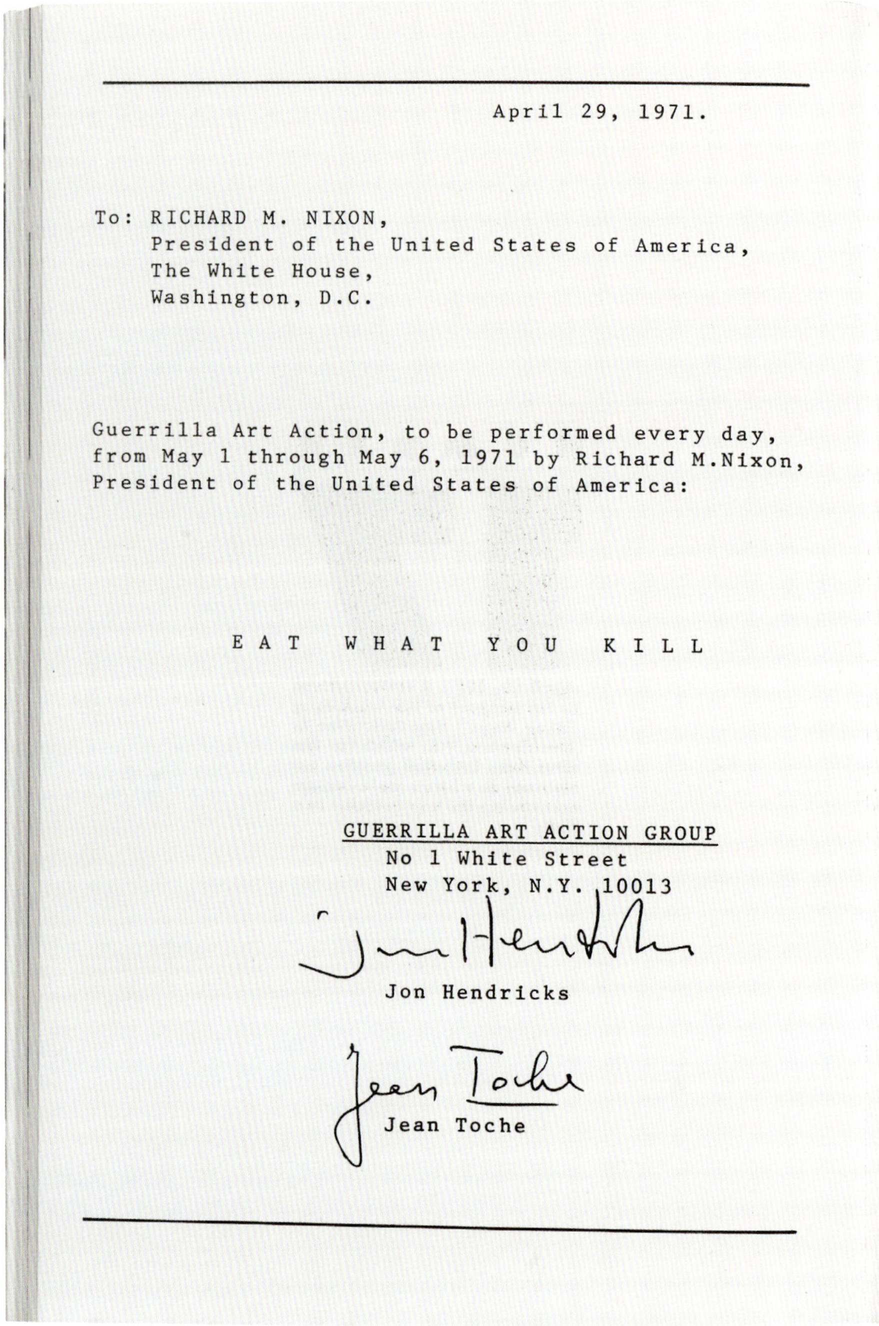

April 29, 1971.

To: RICHARD M. NIXON,
President of the United States of America,
The White House,
Washington, D.C.

Guerrilla Art Action, to be performed every day, from May 1 through May 6, 1971 by Richard M.Nixon, President of the United States of America:

E A T   W H A T   Y O U   K I L L

GUERRILLA ART ACTION GROUP
No 1 White Street
New York, N.Y. 10013

Jon Hendricks

Jean Toche

FIGURE 45

Guerrilla Art Action Group (Jon Hendricks [American, b. 1939] and Jean Toche [American, b. Belgium 1932]). *Send Letters to Nixon, Agnew, Hoover, Mitchell, Laird, Kissinger … April 29, New York (Eat What You Kill)*, 1971. Typewritten letter, 11 × 8½ in. (27.9 × 21.6 cm). Collection of Alan Cravitz, Chicago

early on by Joseph Beuys, who dismisses it completely: “A rabbit running from one ‘Fat Corner’ [a sculpture by Beuys] to the next can do more for mankind than the SDS, which deals with Marxist thoughts without understanding them.”[31] Arrogantly trumpeting his version of criticality, Beuys voices none of the anxieties about relevance seen in Lippard’s writings.

The Vietnam War appears first on page 24, in an entry about the French artists Buren, Mosset, Parmentier, and Toroni, who issued the following declaration on June 2, 1967: “Inasmuch as to paint is a function of estheticism, flowers, women, eroticism, the daily environment, art, dada, psychoanalysis, the war in Vietnam, WE ARE NOT PAINTERS.” The term *peace* shows up once, in relation to LeWitt’s wall drawing at the *Art for Peace* benefit show,[32] and the Art Workers’ Coalition appears only in a passage about its protest of the cancellation of Hans Haacke’s solo show at the Guggenheim in 1971.[33] Finally, *Six Years* includes a description of GAAG’s 1971 missive to President Nixon: “EAT WHAT YOU KILL” (figure 45), an example of letter writing as a form of Conceptual art.[34]

Still, there is no mention of the AWC or its activities in 1969 or 1970, though some of them arguably had a direct bearing on the formation of Conceptualism and institutional critique, and likewise, there is nothing on organizations such as Women Artists in Revolution, the Ad Hoc Committee, or the Black Emergency Cultural Coalition (there is a striking paucity of African American work in the book). Though Lippard was immersed in feminist activities during the time she was editing *Six Years* from her massive storehouse of material, very little of that registers within its pages, even though actions like the forged Whitney press release could certainly count as Conceptually based art, as much as GAAG’s letters to Nixon do. However, it is misleading to try to chronicle all the literal appearances of ostensibly “political” actions within *Six Years*, for Lippard’s underlying premise was that Conceptualism itself formed part of a nascent alternative network that could, conceivably, remake the art world. In her view, the very act of, say, sending letters as art—regardless of content—was potentially political.

Though the book has come to seem indispensible, the early reviews of *Six Years* were decidedly mixed, with some dismissing Lippard’s intellectual labor as an act of rote compiling. Not so: she made major organizational and editorial decisions, and wrote short passages that function as connective tissue and interject her own theories and opinions. In a few cases, she took out the more polemical material—for instance, among the many draft pages of *Six Years* in Lippard’s papers at the Archives of American Art is one with a passage by Haacke crossed out (figure 46). This passage, in a letter written by Haacke in 1968 to Jack Burnham, speaks directly to the thorny issue, again, of “relevance”: “The murder of Martin Luther King pressed into focus something that I had known for a long time but never realized so bitterly and helplessly—namely, what we are doing: the production and the talk about sculpture has nothing to do with the urgent problems of our society.... All the shows of Angry Arts will not prevent a single Napalm bomb from being dropped. We must face the fact that art is unsuited as a political tool.” It is impossible to reconstruct why Lippard excised this negative assessment, though perhaps it may have seemed too jarring, within the generally more optimistic tone of the book as a whole. In addition, Haacke appears to have changed his mind not long after, given his turn toward institutional critique and overtly critical art circa 1970 (in concert with his activism in the AWC); she might not have wanted to represent outdated views.

Much has been made about the failures of this moment and the collapse of its utopian dreams, including by Lippard herself. In the Postface to *Six Years,* she admits: “Hopes that

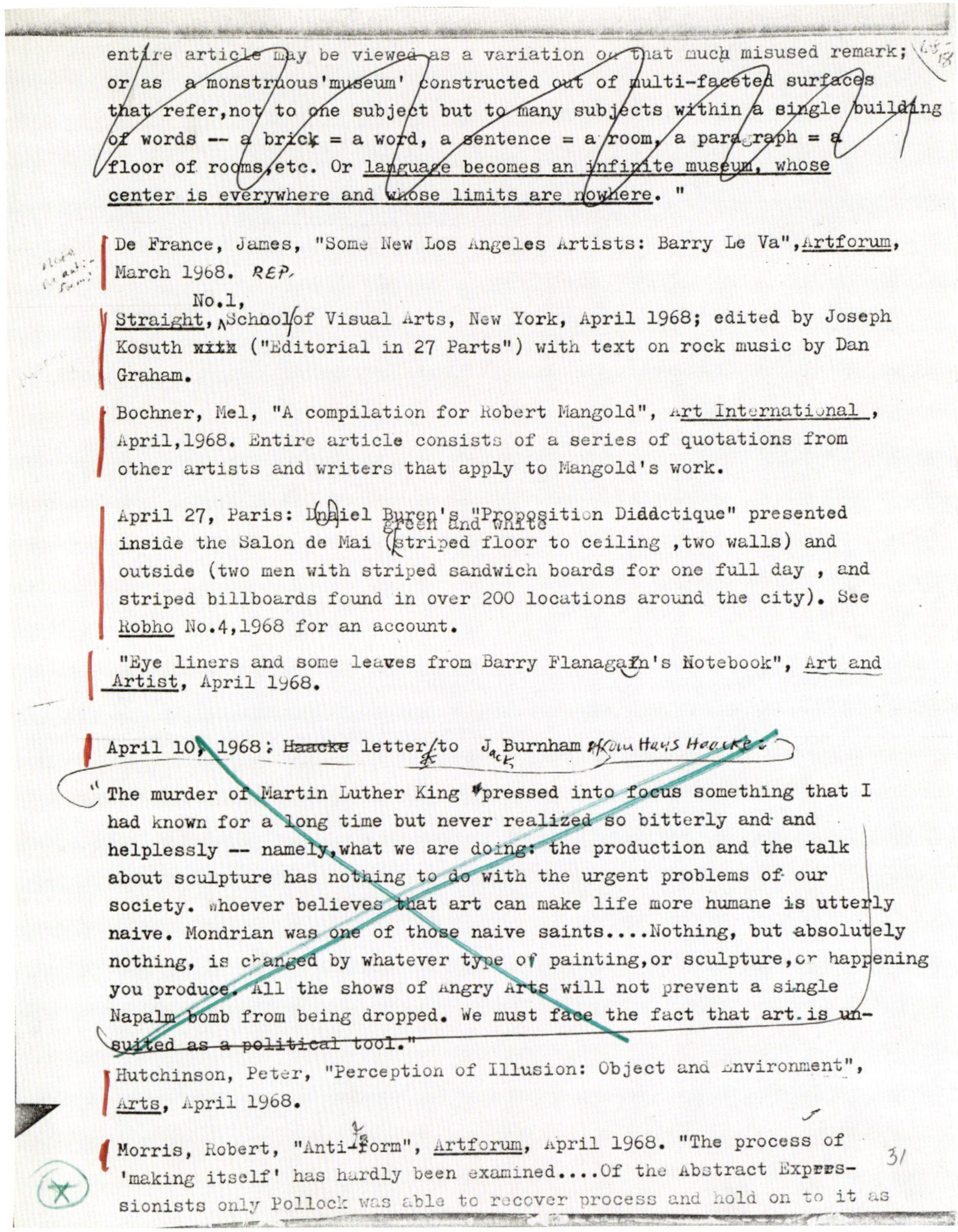

entire article may be viewed as a variation on that much misused remark; or as a monstrous 'museum' constructed out of multi-faceted surfaces that refer, not to one subject but to many subjects within a single building of words -- a brick = a word, a sentence = a room, a paragraph = a floor of rooms, etc. Or language becomes an infinite museum, whose center is everywhere and whose limits are nowhere. "

De France, James, "Some New Los Angeles Artists: Barry Le Va", Artforum, March 1968. REP.

Straight, No.1, School of Visual Arts, New York, April 1968; edited by Joseph Kosuth ~~with~~ ("Editorial in 27 Parts") with text on rock music by Dan Graham.

Bochner, Mel, "A compilation for Robert Mangold", Art International, April, 1968. Entire article consists of a series of quotations from other artists and writers that apply to Mangold's work.

April 27, Paris: Daniel Buren's "Proposition Didactique" presented inside the Salon de Mai (green and white striped floor to ceiling, two walls) and outside (two men with striped sandwich boards for one full day, and striped billboards found in over 200 locations around the city). See Robho No.4, 1968 for an account.

"Eye liners and some leaves from Barry Flanagan's Notebook", Art and Artist, April 1968.

April 10, 1968: ~~Haacke~~ letter to Jack Burnham from Hans Haacke:

"The murder of Martin Luther King pressed into focus something that I had known for a long time but never realized so bitterly and and helplessly -- namely, what we are doing: the production and the talk about sculpture has nothing to do with the urgent problems of our society. Whoever believes that art can make life more humane is utterly naive. Mondrian was one of those naive saints....Nothing, but absolutely nothing, is changed by whatever type of painting, or sculpture, or happening you produce. All the shows of Angry Arts will not prevent a single Napalm bomb from being dropped. We must face the fact that art is unsuited as a political tool."

Hutchinson, Peter, "Perception of Illusion: Object and Environment", Arts, April 1968.

Morris, Robert, "Anti-form", Artforum, April 1968. "The process of 'making itself' has hardly been examined....Of the Abstract Expressionists only Pollock was able to recover process and hold on to it as

31

FIGURE 46

Lucy R. Lippard (American, b. 1937). Manuscript of entries subsequently printed on page 45 of *Six Years: The Dematerialization of the Art Object from 1966 to 1972*, c. 1972. Photocopy with handwritten ink markings, 11 × 8½ in. (27.9 × 21.6 cm). Lucy R. Lippard Papers, Archives of American Art, Smithsonian Institution, Washington, D.C.

‘conceptual art’ would be able to avoid the general commercialization, the destructively ‘progressive’ approach of modernism were for the most part unfounded.”[35] In an article on entrenched class bias in the art world published in 1977 in the feminist art magazine *Heresies* (Lippard was a co-founder of the collective), she elaborated:

> Conceptual Art’s democratic efforts and physical vehicles were canceled out by its neutral, elitist content and its patronizing approach. From around 1967 to 1971, many of us involved in Conceptual Art saw that content as pretty revolutionary and thought of ourselves as rebels against the cool, hostile artifacts of the prevailing formalist and Minimalist art. But we were so totally enveloped in the middle-class approach to everything we did and saw, we couldn’t perceive how that pseudo-academic narrative piece or that art-world-oriented action in the streets were deprived of any revolutionary content by the fact that it was usually incomprehensible and alienating to the people “out there,” no matter how fashionably downwardly mobile it might be in the art world.[36]

It is a hallmark of Lippard’s brilliance that she is able to admit when she might have been wrong. Her willingness to be flexible, to be self-critical, and to change course are part of what makes her writing so necessary. She has faced brutal critiques and dismissals—many of them overtly sexist—yet she consistently pursues what is important to her. Lippard was a pioneer in many respects, but one of her most significant contributions to postwar art is her self-aware, self-reflective critical writing. She was at the forefront of Conceptualism and feminism (and, later, activist art and environmental issues), to be sure, but she has also redefined what we think of as an engaged curator and critic: someone unafraid to be skeptical and anti-institutional, someone with strongly held beliefs, motivated not by market demands but by a deep passion for art and an unparalleled respect for artists. Along with her productive refusals and protests, Lippard also modeled acceptance and embrace—she championed the artists she respected, she advocated for causes, and she argued *for* as much as she agitated *against*.

That is to say, the greatest lesson Lippard offers is that criticism, as well as activism, might draw on love as well as anger. The most frequently reprinted poster made by the Art Workers’ Coalition is the one of massacred villagers in Vietnam (figure 35); but there is also one, much less widely shown, that quotes Che Guevera: “Let me say, at the risk of seeming ridiculous, that the true revolutionary is guided by great feelings of love” (figure 47). Lippard has consistently risked “seeming ridiculous,” and in so doing has made room for an activist brand of writing and curating that has changed the face of the art institution as we know it.

In 2010, a panel was held at the Brooklyn Museum’s Elizabeth A. Sackler Center for Feminist Art on the topic “Invisibility to Visibility: Are Museums Opening Up to Women?” This question asks if museums are becoming more welcoming to women as artists and as spectators, and appears to echo the Brooklyn open hearing “Are Museums Relevant to Women?” held almost thirty years prior. But the 1971 query had a different tone than one of number counting: it asked, do museums *matter* to women, to their art as well as to their lives and their politics? Are they meaningful places for critical dialogue; are they responsive to current debates; are they vibrant spaces for culture? In the early 1970s, feminists answered no—and in response, they started their own alternative organizations and pushed museums to address issues of discrimination. The persistence of gender inequality today (and the depressing need to keep asking if museums are “opening up to women”) demonstrates that in some respects, art institutions have not come very far since 1971.

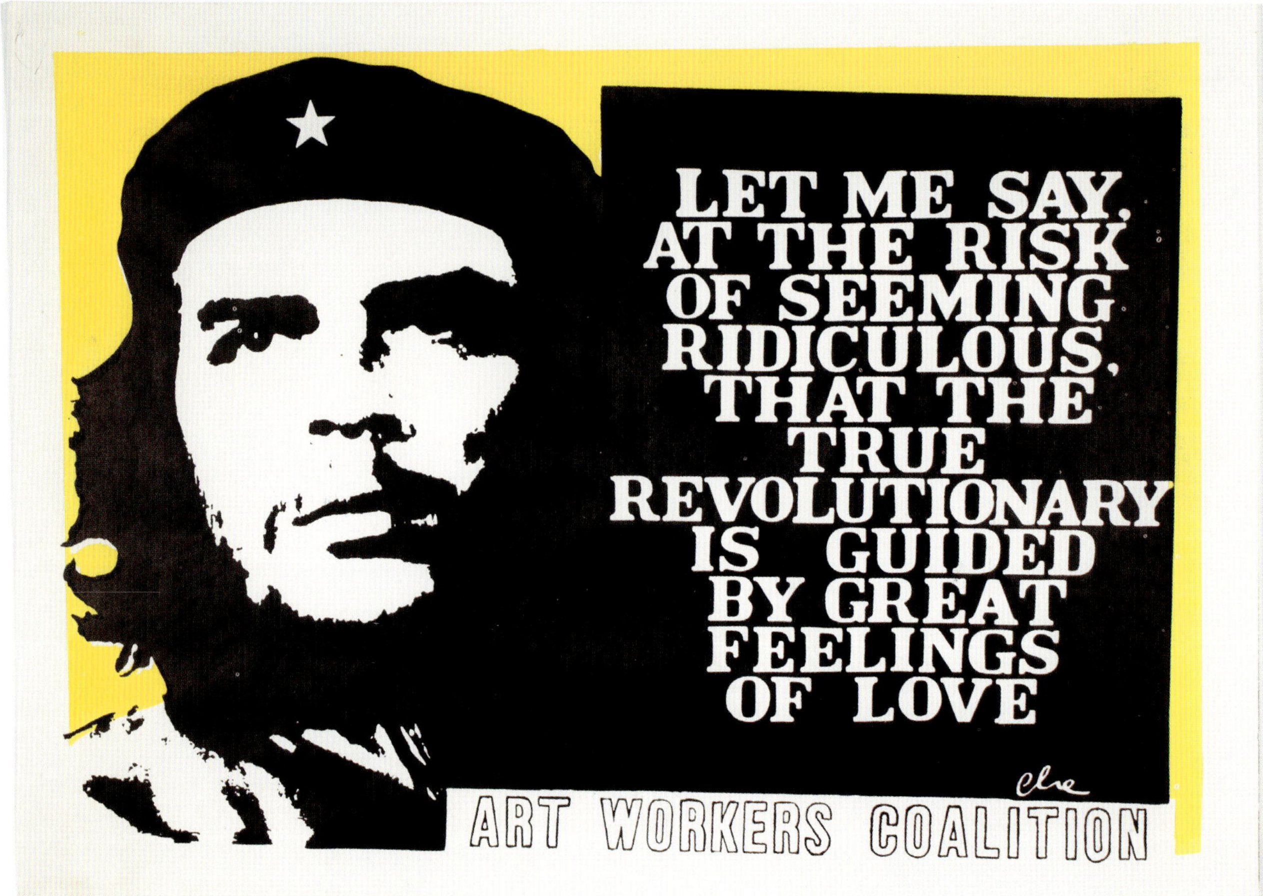

FIGURE 47

Artists' Poster Committee of the Art Workers' Coalition. *Let Me Say, at the Risk of Seeming Ridiculous, That the True Revolutionary Is Guided by Great Feelings of Love*, c. 1971. Offset poster, 15½ × 21 13/16 in. (39.4 × 53.8 cm). International Center of Photography, New York; Gift of the Artists' Poster Committee with funds provided by the ICP Acquisitions Committee, 2002. Designed by Ursula Meyer. © Art Workers' Coalition. (Photo: International Center of Photography, New York)

At the same time, however, the very existence of the Sackler Center, which opened in 2007, signals a shift, a shift that Lippard herself helped instigate as she insisted upon the centrality of feminism within art, and of the centrality of art within feminism. That an exhibition on *Six Years* and Lippard's influence is being launched at the very place where she loudly enumerated the many ways museums discriminate against women indicates more than simply coming full circle. Lippard's unique blend of activist and critical commitments has proven to be not just relevant, but essential.

Notes

1. Pat Mainardi, "Open Hearing at Brooklyn Museum," *The Feminist Art Journal,* vol. 1, no. 1 (Spring 1972), p. 6.
2. Jon Hendricks and Jean Toche, "Open Hearing at the Brooklyn Museum: 'Are Museums Relevant to Women?,' Guerrilla Art Action Group Testimony," no. 28 (December 12, 1971); reprinted in *GAAG: The Guerrilla Art Action Group, 1969–1976: A Selection* (New York: Printed Matter, 1978), unpaginated.
3. For more on this hearing, and for an examination of shifting notions of artistic labor in this time, see my *Art Workers: Radical Practice in the Vietnam War Era* (Berkeley: University of California Press, 2009).
4. Quoted in Mainardi, "Open Hearing at Brooklyn Museum," p. 6. Alongside full-length statements by Ann Sutherland Harris and Cindy Nemser, Mainardi's summary included other brief excerpts from speeches delivered at the open hearing.
5. Ibid.
6. Kay Brown, "'Where We At': Black Women Artists," *The Feminist Art Journal,* vol. 1, no. 1 (Spring 1972), p. 25.
7. Christine Delphy's writings were collected in English in her *Close to Home: A Materialist Analysis of Women's Oppression*, ed. and trans. Diana Leonard (Amherst, Mass.: University of Massachusetts Press, 1984).
8. Christine Delphy, "The Main Enemy" (1970), reprinted in *Close to Home*, p. 60.
9. See, for example, *Get the Message?: A Decade of Art for Social Change* (New York: E. P. Dutton, 1984), p. 2.
10. AWC, *An Open Hearing* (New York: Art Workers' Coalition, 1969).
11. For more on this incident, see Francis Frascina, *Art, Politics, and Dissent: Aspects of the Art Left in Sixties America* (Manchester: Manchester University Press; New York: St. Martin's Press, 1999).
12. Gregory Battcock, "Art: Reviewing the Above Statement," *Free Press Critique,* no. 31 (October 1968), p. B1.
13. Lucy R. Lippard, "The Dilemma," *Arts Magazine,* vol. 45, no. 2 (November 1970), p. 28.
14. Faith Ringgold, "Black Women Art Is Political," typewritten speech delivered at the opening of *The People's Flag Show*, Judson Memorial Church, New York (December 9, 1970); Judson Memorial Church Archives, Fales Library and Special Collections, New York University.
15. Hilton Kramer, "Artists and the Problem of 'Relevance,'" *New York Times,* May 4, 1969, p. D23.
16. Lucy R. Lippard, *From the Center: Feminist Essays on Women's Art* (New York: E. P. Dutton, 1976).
17. Ibid, p. 4.
18. See Therese Schwartz, "50%—No Joke," *New York Element,* vol. 2, no. 3 (November—December 1970); reprinted in Jacqueline Skiles and Janet McDevitt, eds., *A Documentary Herstory of Women Artists in Revolution* (New York: Women Artists in Revolution, 1971), p. 29.
19. John I. H. Baur, press release, November 11, 1970, Whitney Museum of American Art Archives.

20. Jullette Gordon, "The History of Our WAR from the Beginnings to Today or Life under Fire in the Art World Dear Workers," *Manhattan Tribune,* May 2, 1970; reprinted in *A Documentary Herstory of Women Artists in Revolution*, p. 4.

21. Mainardi, "Open Hearing at Brooklyn Museum," p. 6.

22. Linda Nochlin, "Why Have There Been No Great Women Artists?," *Art News* (January 1971); reprinted in her *Women, Art, and Power and Other Essays* (New York: Harper & Row, 1988), p. 158.

23. Lucy R. Lippard, "Changing since *Changing*," in her *From the Center,* p. 3.

24. Quoted in Grace Glueck, "Women Artists Demonstrate at the Whitney," *New York Times,* December 12, 1970, p. 19.

25. Lucy R. Lippard, videotaped interview by Lyn Blumenthal and Kate Horsfield (1979) for "On Art and Artists: Video Data Bank," unedited transcript, p. 8; Lucy R. Lippard Papers, Archives of American Art, Smithsonian Institution, Washington, D.C.

26. For more on this show, see Cornelia Butler's study of *c. 7,500*, in Pablo Lafuente, ed., *From Conceptualism to Feminism: Lucy Lippard's Numbers Shows, 1969–74* (London: Afterall Books, forthcoming in 2012).

27. *Six Years: The dematerialization of the art object from 1966 to 1972: a cross-reference book of information on some esthetic boundaries: consisting of a bibliography into which are inserted a fragmented text, art works, documents, interviews, and symposia, arranged chronologically and focused on so-called conceptual or information or idea art with mentions of such vaguely designated areas as minimal, anti-form, systems, earth, or process art, occurring now in the Americas, Europe, England, Australia, and Asia (with occasional political overtones), edited and annotated by Lucy R. Lippard* (New York: Praeger Publishers, 1973; reprinted, with a new introduction, Berkeley and Los Angeles: University of California Press, 1997).

28. Ibid., p. 6.

29. Lucy R. Lippard, "Preface: *Six Years* … Forty Years Later," in the present volume.

30. Yoko Ono, "To the Wesleyan People (who attended the meeting): a footnote to my lecture of January 13th, 1966" (January 23, 1966); excerpts printed in Lippard, *Six Years,* p. 13.

31. Quoted in Lippard, *Six Years*, p. 19.

32. Ibid., p. 57.

33. Ibid., pp. 227–29.

34. Ibid., pp. 235–36.

35. Ibid., p. 263.

36. Lucy R. Lippard, "The Pink Glass Swan: Upward and Downward Mobility in the Art World," *Heresies*, no. 1 (January 1977); reprinted in Lippard, *The Pink Glass Swan: Selected Essays on Feminist Art* (New York: The New Press, 1995), pp. 121–22.

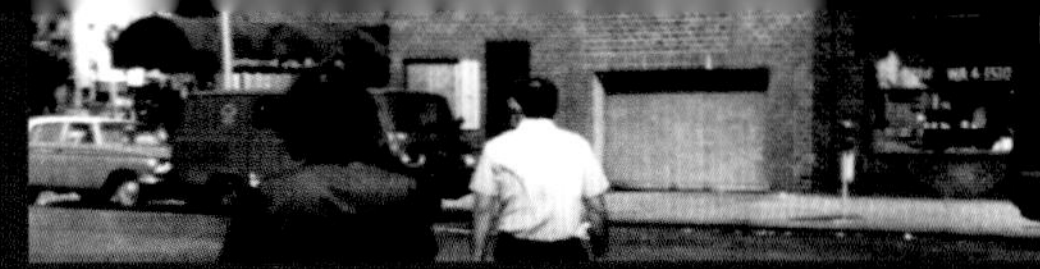

Illustrations and Commentary

The illustrations here represent a selective overview of significant works and events mentioned in Lucy R. Lippard's *Six Years*. (A complete checklist of the present exhibition is available on the Brooklyn Museum's website: www.brooklynmuseum.org.) The illustrations are organized by year, following the structure of *Six Years*. Within each year, books are listed first, then events (those without a specific starting month preceding the general month-by-month breakdown). Certain works of art not specifically cited in *Six Years* are included if they appeared in important exhibitions listed in the book. Related ephemera, works of art, and documentation have been grouped together when they pertain to the same specific event, publication, or exhibition. Certain works therefore appear under the year they were exhibited rather than the year they were made.

In the captions, dimensions are given in the order height by width, followed in the case of sculpture by depth, first in inches and then in centimeters. The dimensions of bound publications refer to page size, with height first. Unless otherwise indicated, drawings, prints, and posters, and documents in handwritten or typewritten form, are on paper. All documentary photographs are digitally reproduced from archival sources, so no dimensions or print details are specified for them. Mass-produced materials such as catalogues and periodicals are not attributed to a particular collection. Information on exhibition dates, venues, and organizers appears in the captions of installation views. Sources of photographs are given within parentheses.

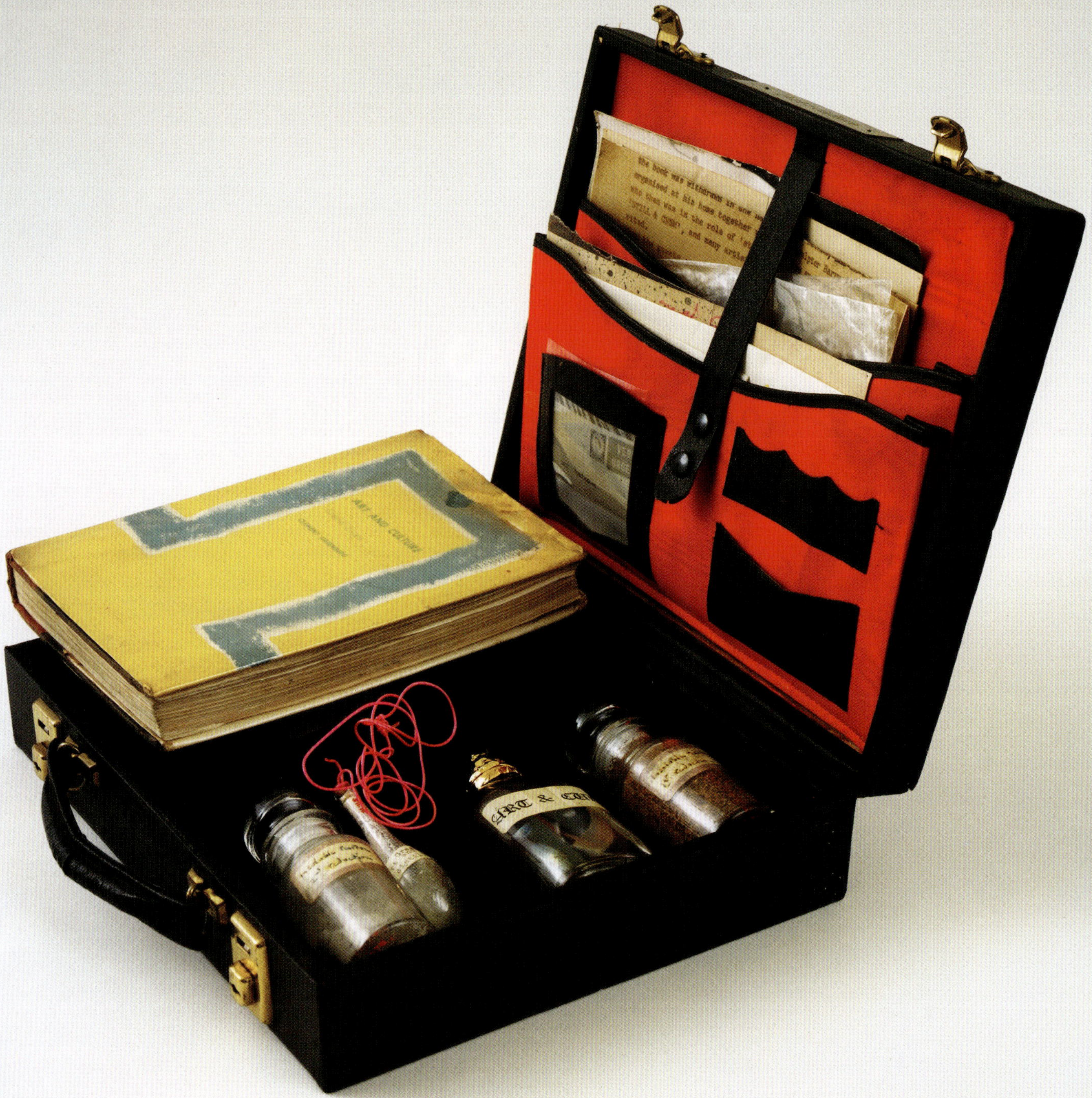
ART AND CULTURE

1966

Perhaps no work expressed the dissatisfaction with the status quo of the 1960s art market as directly as John Latham's *Art and Culture*. This work gathers together the relics of an action that began when Latham checked the critic Clement Greenberg's seminal book of the same name out of the library of the St. Martins School of Art, where he was teaching. He and his friend Barry Flanagan then threw a party at which everyone was invited to chew its pages into a pulp. After introducing yeast, an "Alien Culture," into the masticated results, Latham held onto the brew until he received an urgent overdue notice from the library almost a year later. Presented in a suitcase are the cover of the book, the distilled pages in vials, the library notice, and the letter he subsequently received after his thwarted attempt to return the "book," informing him he would not be rehired the following year.

FIGURE 48

John Latham (British, b. Zambia, 1921–2006). *Art and Culture*, 1966–69. Leather case containing book, letters, photostats, and labeled vials filled with powders and liquids: case, 3⅛ × 11⅛ × 10 in. (7.9 × 28.2 × 25.3 cm). The Museum of Modern Art, New York; Blanchette Hooker Rockefeller Fund. © 2011 John Latham. (Digital image: © The Museum of Modern Art/Licensed by SCALA/Art Resource, NY)

FIGURES 49–56: In the early 1960s, as the influence of Abstract Expressionism waned, the New York art scene was dominated by the emerging movements of Pop art and Minimalism. When Lucy R. Lippard organized the landmark exhibition *Eccentric Abstraction*, at the Fischbach Gallery in 1966, she brought together tendencies that blurred the rigid contours that defined these very different movements. At the same time, the show also contributed to a shift in thinking about what a work of art might actually look like, and what criteria could be used to evaluate it. Using industrial or commonly found materials to construct irregular rather than strictly geometric forms, sculptural work by Alice Adams, Louise Bourgeois (figure 51), Eva Hesse (figure 52), Bruce Nauman, Don Potts, Keith Sonnier, and Frank Lincoln Viner blurred divisions between emotive and rational abstraction, as well as between a strict formalism and referentiality. Nancy Holt's *Eccentric Abstraction* crossword puzzle (figures 53–56) is a humorous nod to the significant impact Lippard's show had on many artists living in downtown Manhattan.

FIGURE 49

Installation view of *Eccentric Abstraction* including works by Keith Sonnier (left, on floor), Louise Bourgeois (left wall), Frank Lincoln Viner (back), Don Potts (front and right, on floor), and Eva Hesse (right wall); Fischbach Gallery, New York, September 20–October 8, 1966; organized by Lucy R. Lippard. Fischbach Gallery Records, Archives of American Art, Smithsonian Institution, Washington, D.C. (Photo: © Fischbach Gallery, New York)

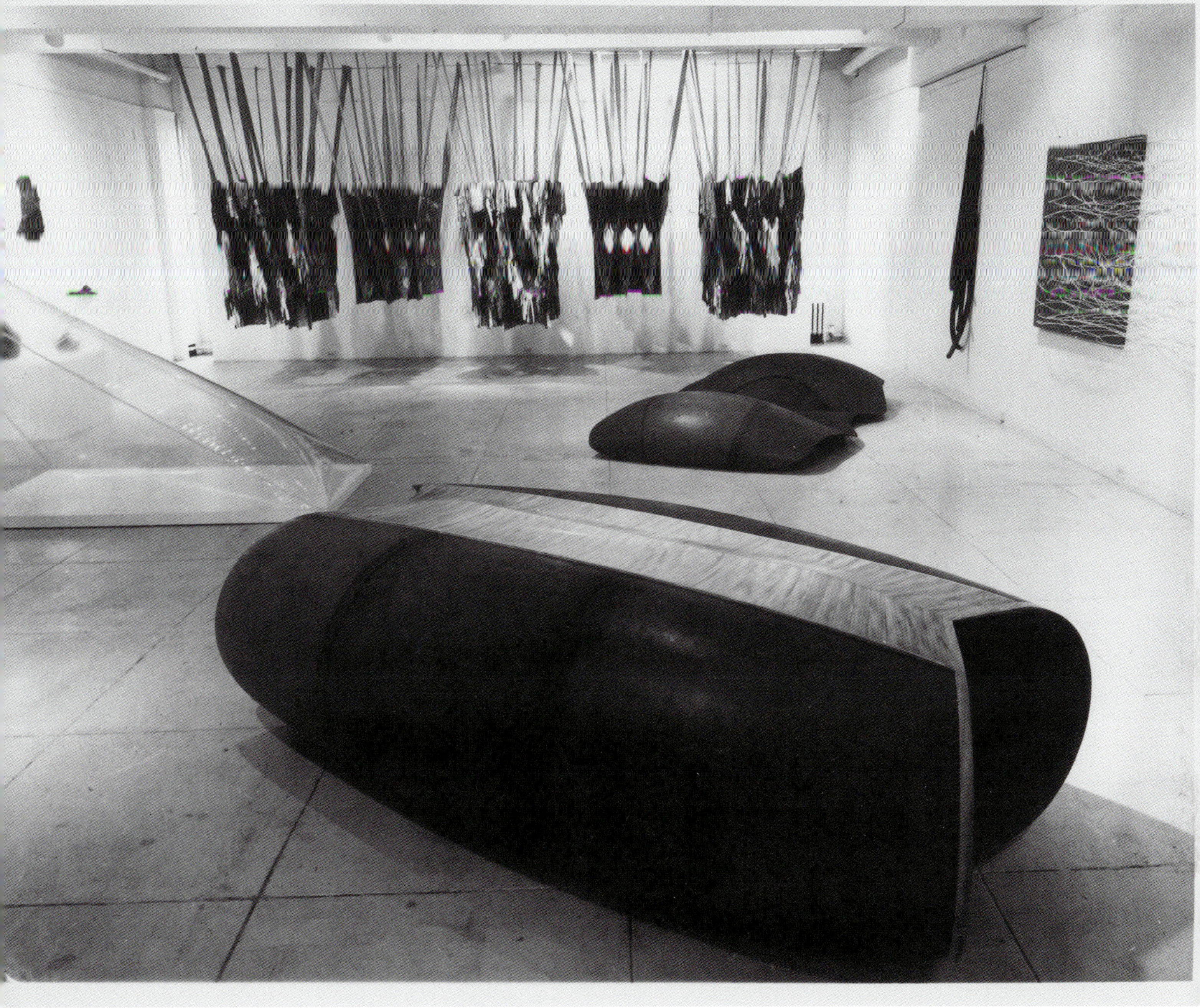

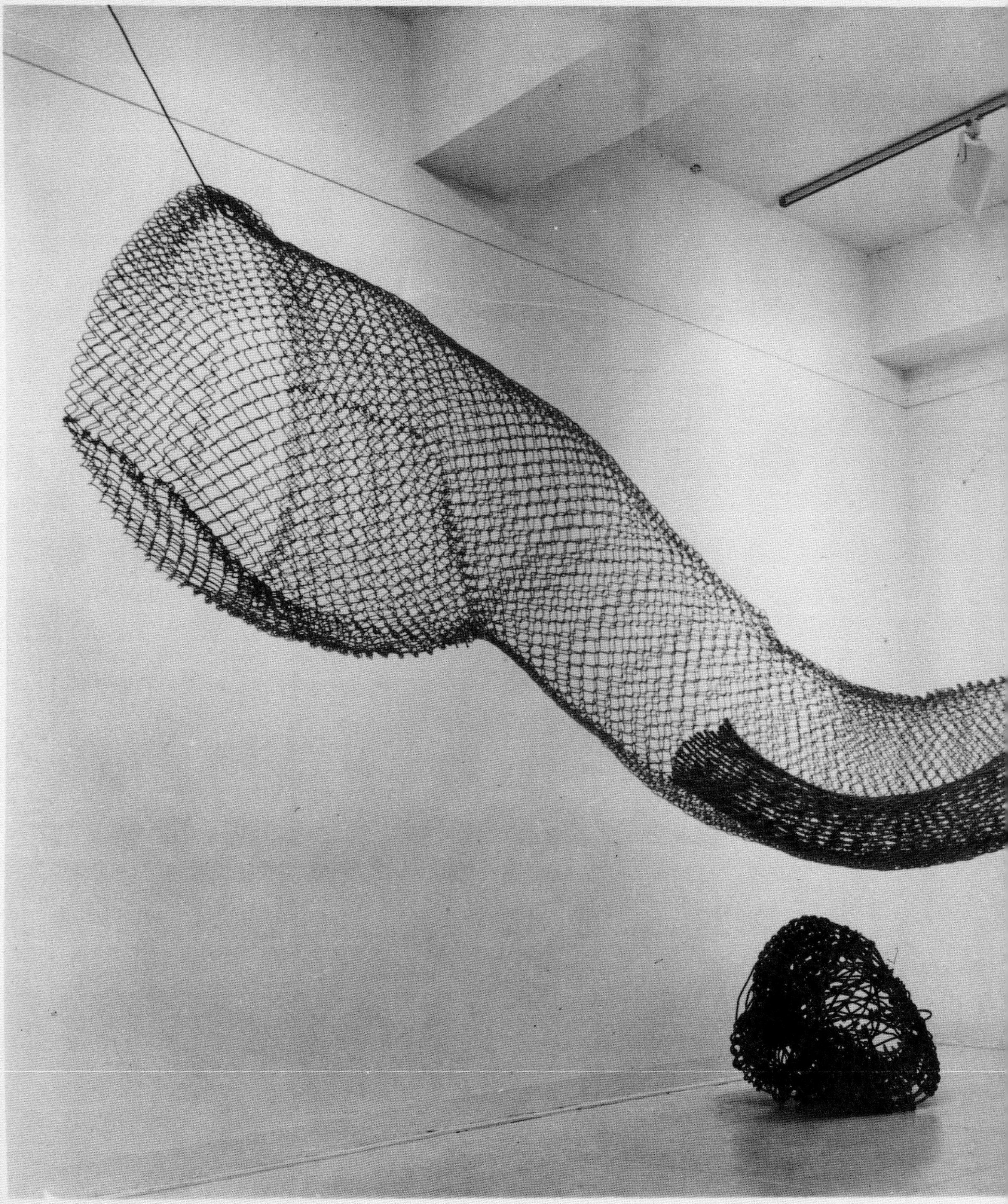

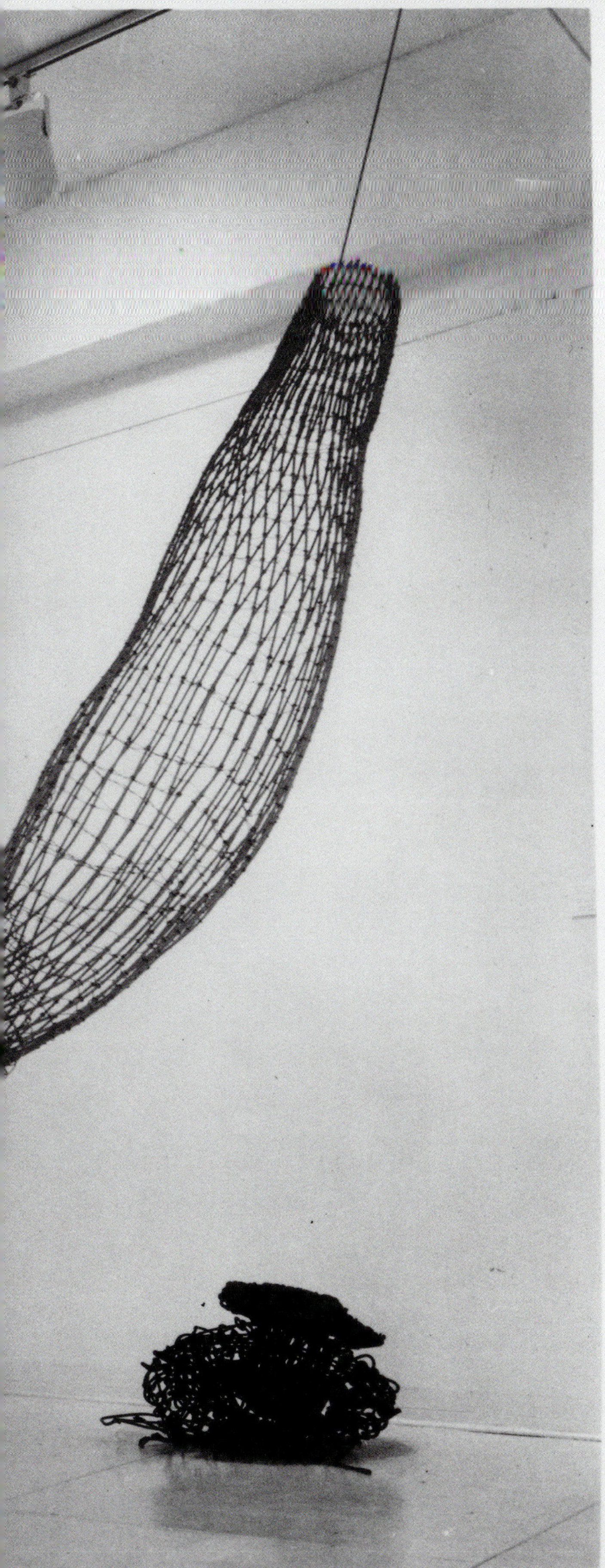

FIGURE 50

Installation view of *Eccentric Abstraction* including Alice Adams, *Big Aluminum,* 1965; Fischbach Gallery, New York, September 20–October 8, 1966; organized by Lucy R. Lippard. Fischbach Gallery Records, Archives of American Art, Smithsonian Institution, Washington, D.C. (Photo: © Fischbach Gallery, New York)

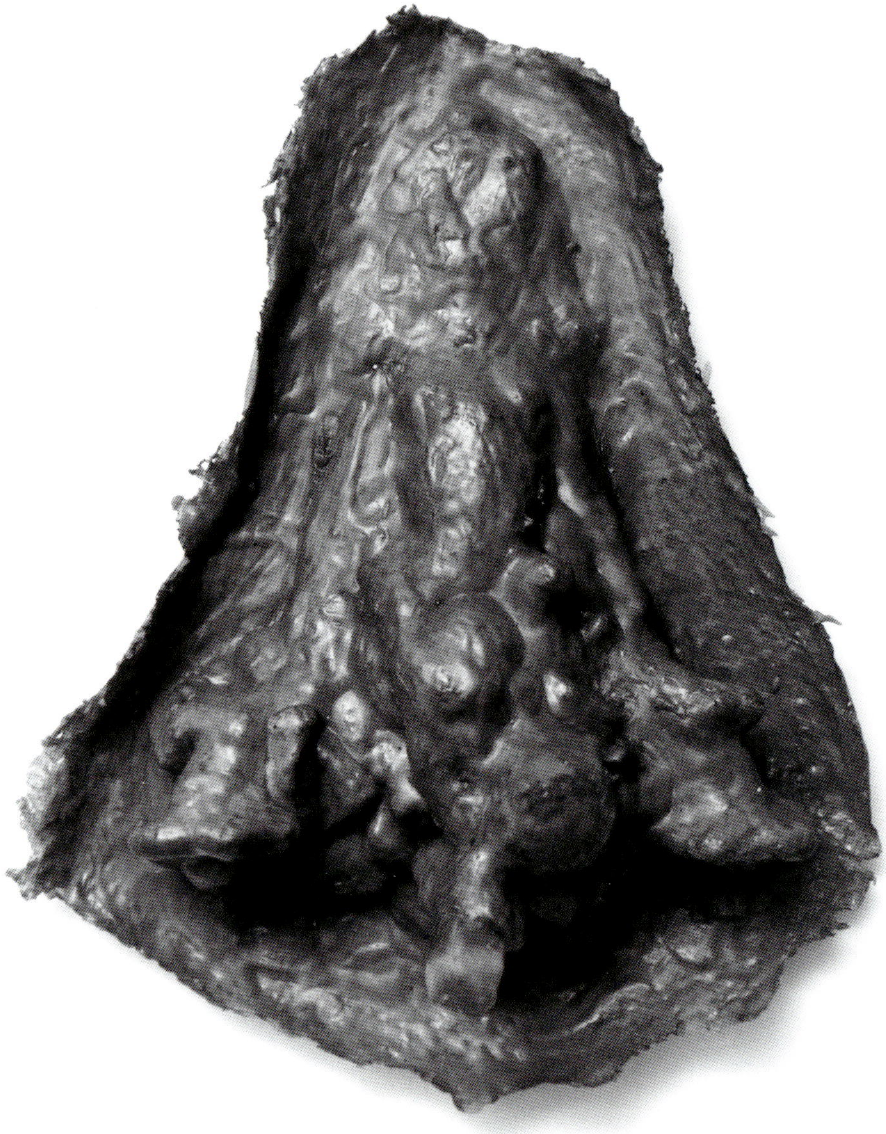

FIGURE 51

Louise Bourgeois (American, b. France, 1911–2010). *Portrait*, 1963. Latex, 15⅜ x 12⅜ x 4⅛ in. (39 x 31.5 x 10.5 cm). The Museum of Modern Art, New York; Gift of Arthur Drexler. © 2012 Louise Bourgeois Trust/ Licensed by VAGA, New York. (Photo: Peter Moore)

FIGURE 52

Eva Hesse (American, b. Germany, 1936–1970). *Ingeminate,* 1965. Enamel, cord, papier-caché, latex, rubber hose, 188 in. (478 cm) long × 4½ in. (11.5 cm) diameter; installation dimensions variable. Daros Collection, Switzerland. © The Estate of Eva Hesse, courtesy Hauser & Wirth, Zurich. (Photo: Abby Robinson, New York)

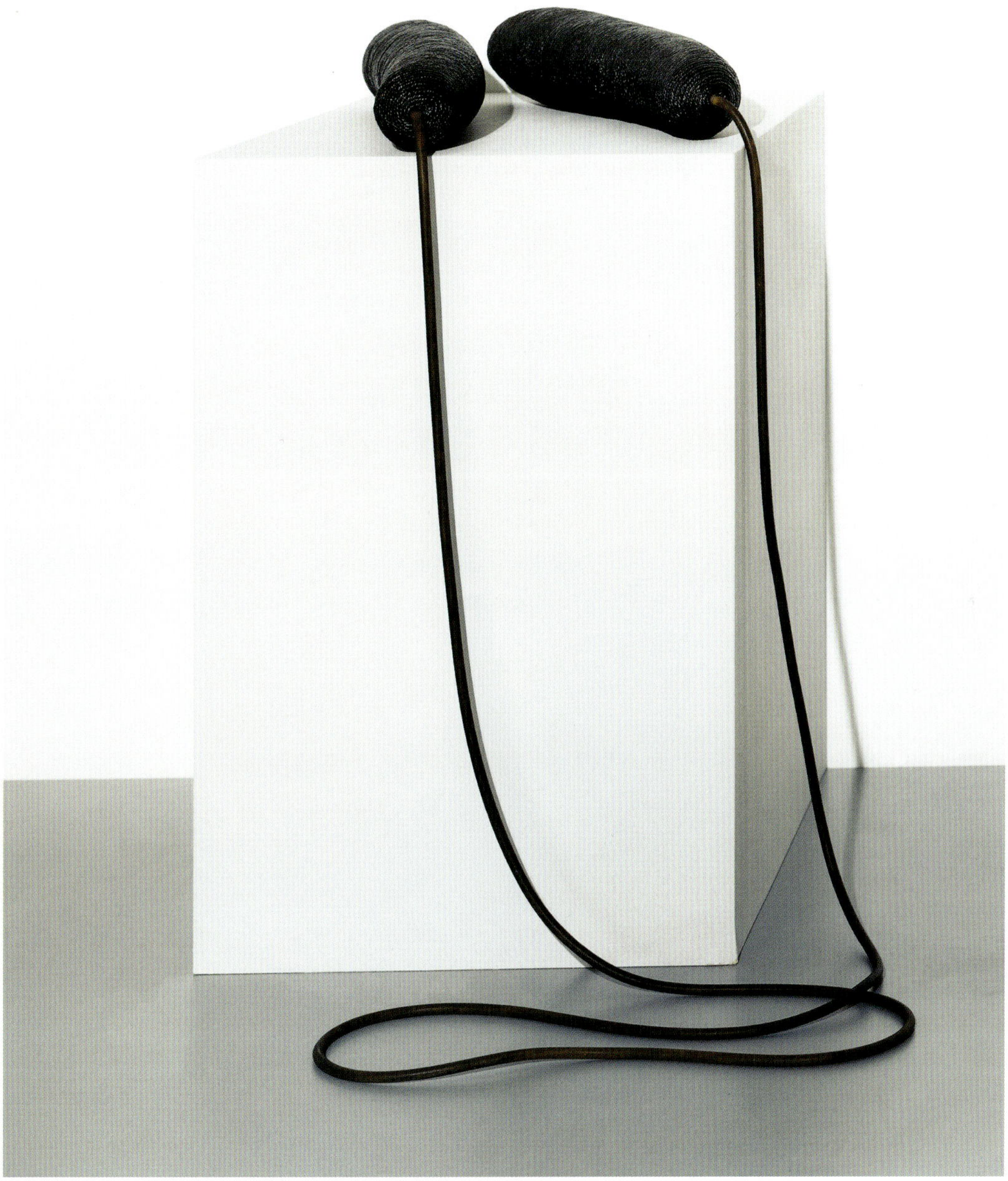

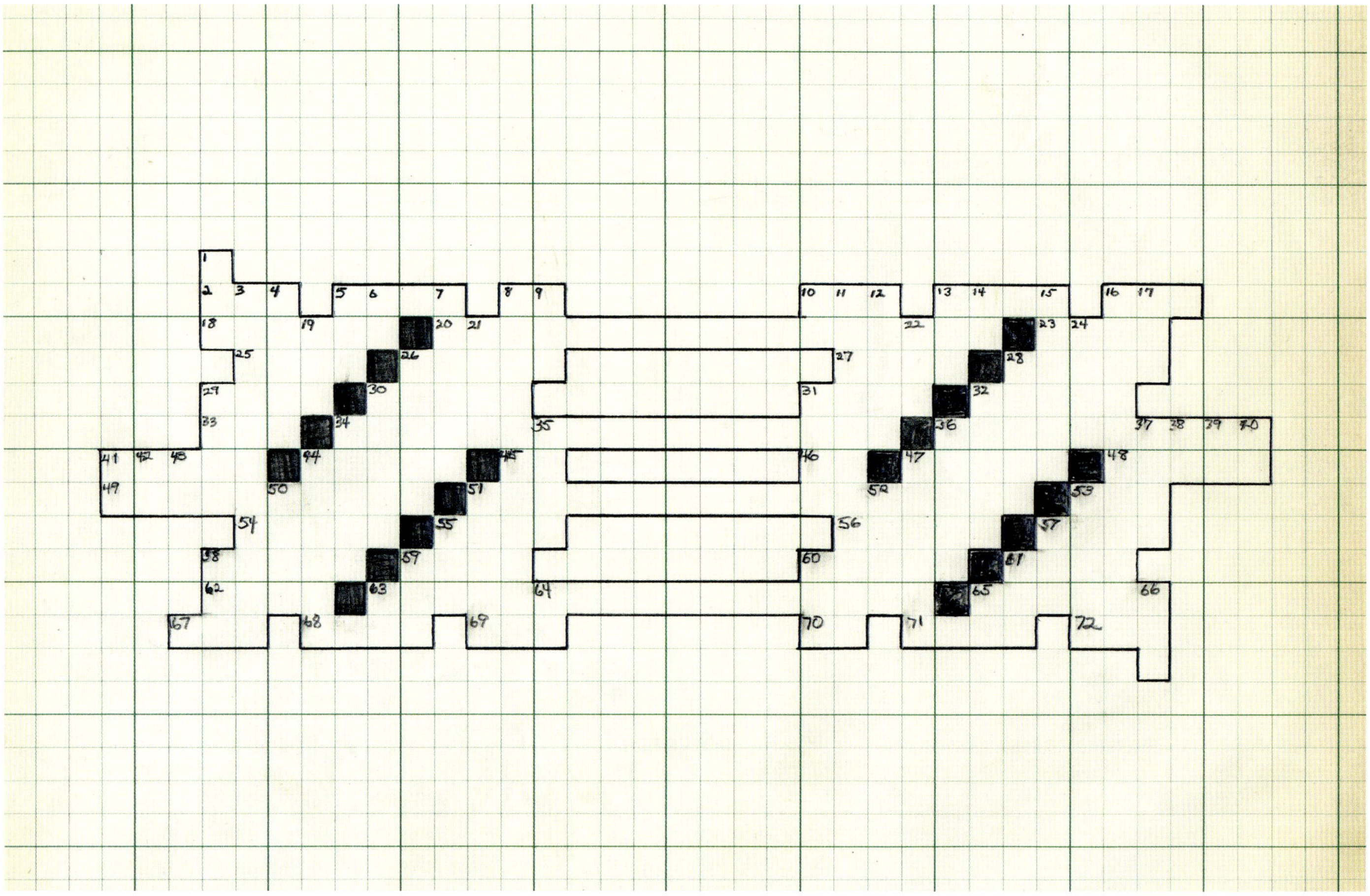

FIGURES 53–56

Nancy Holt (American, b. 1938). *Crossword Work*, 1966. Pencil and ink on four pages: two sheets, 8½ × 10¾ in. (21.6 × 27.3 cm) each; and two sheets, 11 × 8½ in. (27.9 × 21.6 cm) each. Collection of Nancy Holt. © Nancy Holt

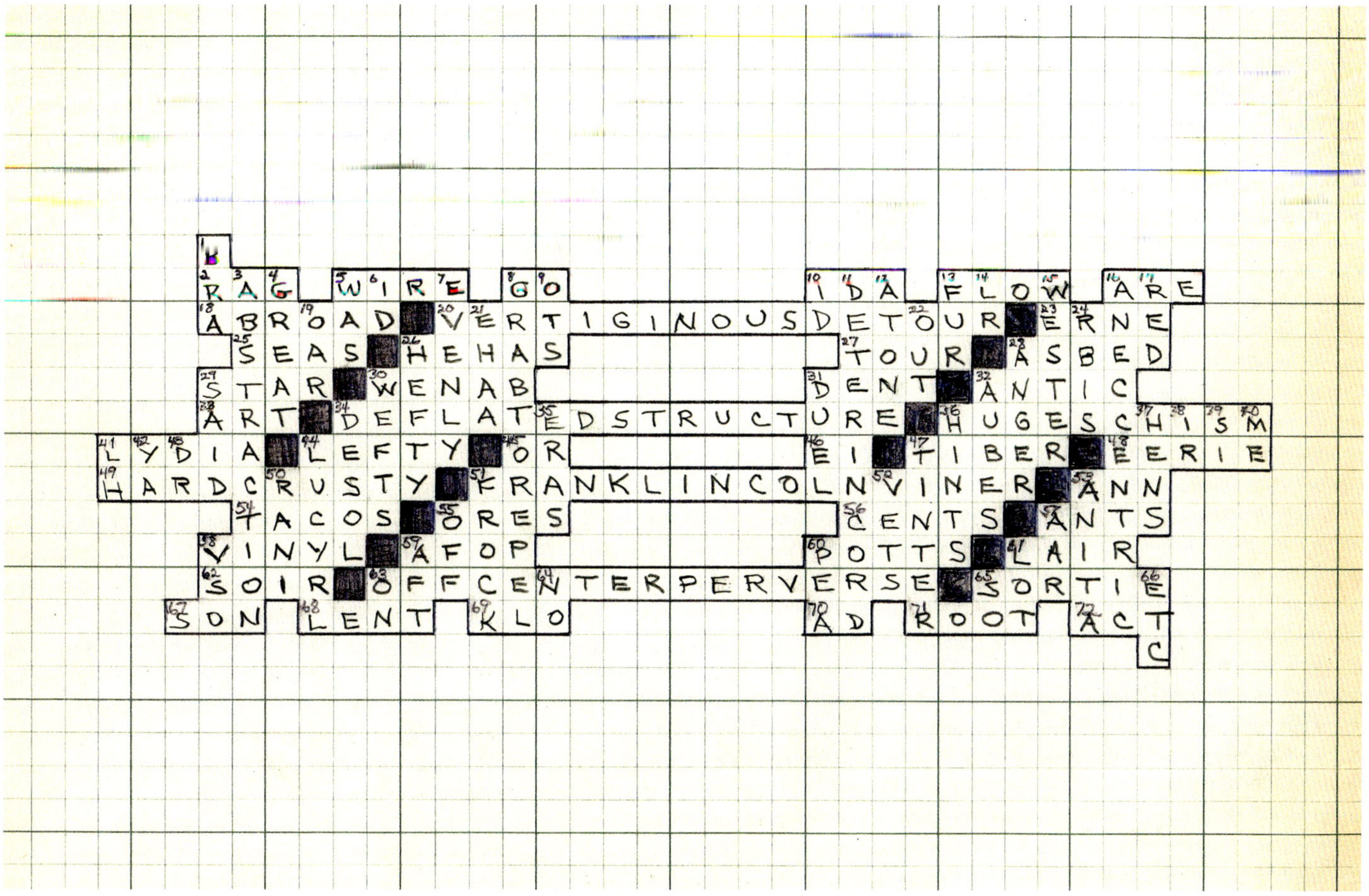

ACROSS

2. What a Nauman work sometimes appears to be. (Also a material in Hesse's work)
5. Material used in works by Adams and Hesse.
8. Something these "inactive" works lack.
10. Lupino.
13. What Kuehn's "precise rectangular structures melt into".*
16. Exist
18. To or in foreign countries.
20. Title of a Hesse work (two words).
23. Sea eagle.
25. Bodies of water.
26. ____ ____ given himself up.
27. Sightseeing trip.
28. When fatigued, nothing seems as good ____ ____.
29. A conventionalized flat figure having 5 or 6 symmetrical projecting points.
30. If ____ ____ the thief now, we will run a risk.
31. Slight hollow in a surface.
32. Grotesque, ludicrous act.
33. What the EA show consists of.
34. Title of a Sonnier work.
36. Frequent result of contraversy. (two words)
41. Woman's name.
44. What some baseball pitchers are.
45. Conjunction.
46. Abbreviation for the islands southeast of Asia.
47. A river in Rome.
48. Description of the EA show. (one word)
49. Two adjectives to describe Hesse's surfaces.
51. Full Name of an AE show artist.
53. Sheridan.
54. Mexican food.
55. Unwrought metals.
56. Monitary units.
57. Type of insect. (plural)
58. Material used in an "expandable wallpiece (which) combines garish pattern and disciplined form".
59. A vain, affected man (two words)
60. Artist in EA show who makes "luxury items" which "invites touch but repels emotion".
61. Title of a Bourgeois work. (also means animal resting place)
62. Evening (French)
63. Two words meaning "eccentric" used by Lucy Lippard.
65. Sudden attach, raid.
67. Offspring.
68. Period of penance.
69. Knowledge Loss Objective (abbr.)
70. Reinhardt
71. Source, origin
72. Deed

---

*All quotes are from a review of the EA show written by Lucy R. Lippard.

DOWN

1. Lady's undergarment
3. Type of art included in this show.
4. Common opinion of EA show.
5. Existed.
6. Psychic source of instinctive energy.
7. Uniformly.
8. The two ways "body ego" can be experienced, in condensed form (three words).
9. Old Testaments (abbr.)
10. Same as 6 Down.
11. The effect of Hesse's "Several" is to ____ ____ ____ the bulbous forms.
12. To make amends.
13. Material used by Potts.
14. Initials of the artist who finds George Washington a worthy subject.
15. First two syllables of the last name of an EA show artist (with "nor", meaning north in New England dialect, a storm).
16. Kind of person who makes EA (two words).
17. Title of an Adams work (also a color).
19. Wooden pole for a boat.
21. First and last initials of two EA artists.
22. Away from.
24. What all New York Mets are striving for (abbr.).
26. Weighty, heavy.
28. Indignation, rage.
29. Uttered.
30. Yarns carried back and forth across the warp.
31. Contest between two people.
32. River in Northern France (possessive).
34. Of, sun (Spanish). 35. Periods of time.
36. Clues.
37. Kind of domestic fowl (plural).
38. To go (French).
39. Yes (Spanish).
40. Pronoun.
41. Initials of a U.S. Black poet and author.
42. Yes (German).
43. Doctor (abbr.).
44. EA show collaborator (first name, last two initials).
47. A person who colors things, especially paper.
50. Title of the wife of an Indian rajah.
51. Kind of white that Kuehn sometimes uses.
52. Article of clothing.
53. Woman's name.
55. Ex-servicemen.
57. River in Switzerland.
58. Very Strange Oddity (Abbr.)
59. Near the ship's stern.
60. A legume.
61. Fortune, fate.
63. In a position above, but in contact with. 64. Negative
65. As a result.
66. And so forth (Latin, abbr.)

FIGURES 57, 58: Robert Morris's *Steam Cloud*, conceived of in 1966 and reiterated numerous times, is a sculpture composed of evaporation. It signaled his move away from the solid, assertive "objectness" of Minimalism toward work that dissipates, incorporating atmospheric, environmental, and temporal factors into its morphing existence.

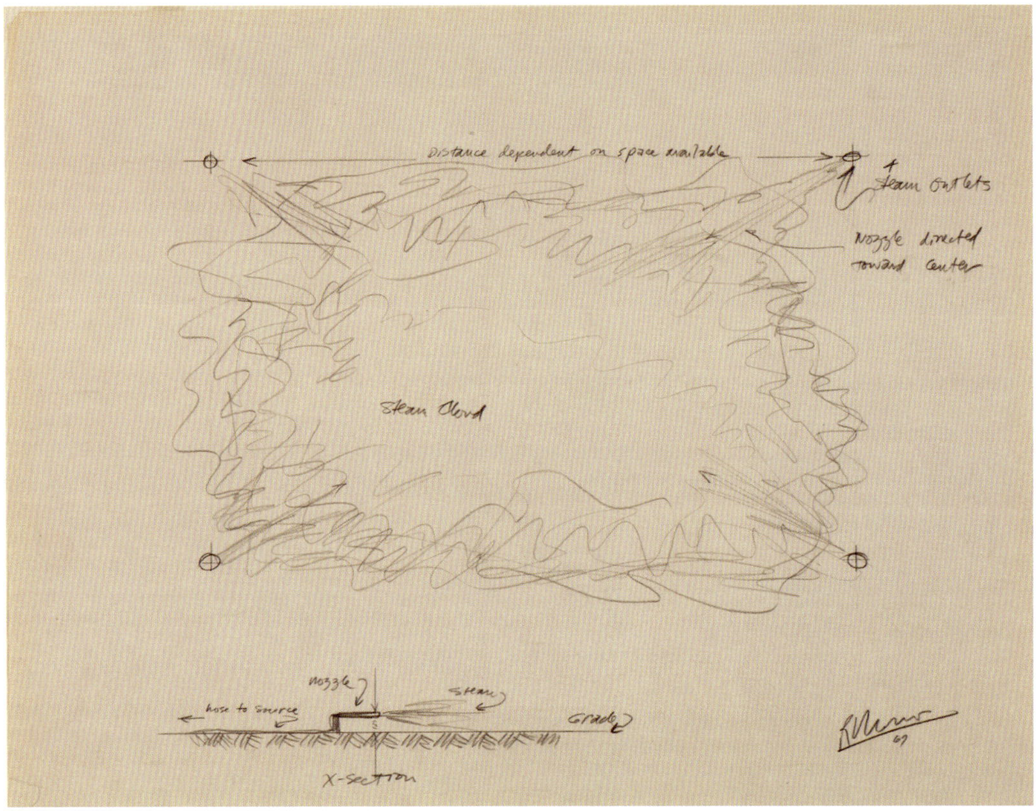

FIGURE 57

Robert Morris (American, b. 1931). Drawing for *Steam Cloud*, 1969. Pencil on paper, $17\frac{15}{16} \times 22\frac{15}{16}$ in. (45.6 × 58.3 cm). The Corcoran Gallery of Art, Washington, D.C.; Museum Purchase. © Robert Morris/Artists Rights Society (ARS), New York. (Photo: The Corcoran Gallery of Art, Washington, D.C.)

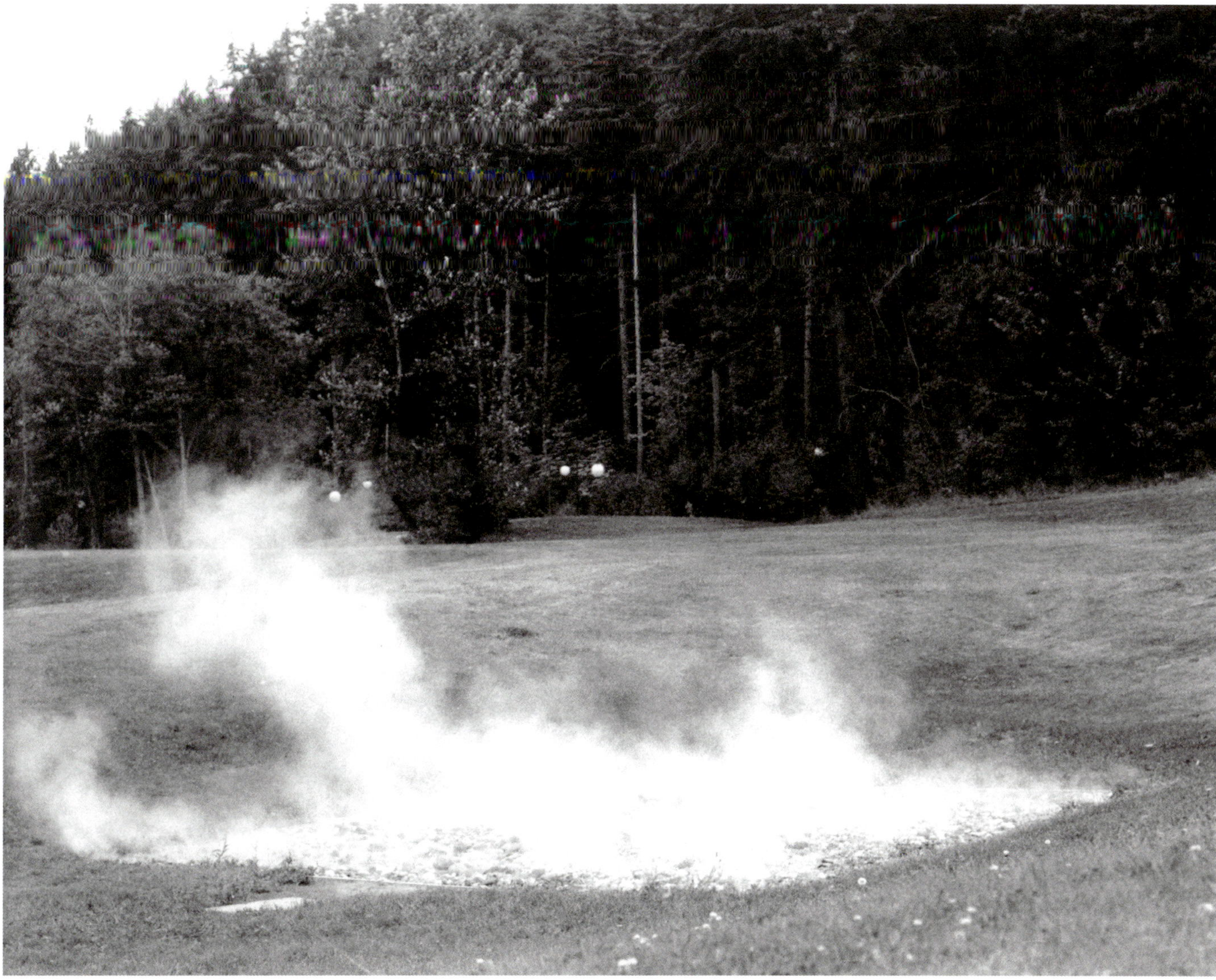

FIGURE 58

Robert Morris (American, b. 1931). *STEAM*, 1967; photograph of refabrication at Western Washington University, Bellingham, 1974. Steam, multiple steam outlets under a bed of stones, outlined with wood, dimensions variable. Sonnabend Gallery, New York. © Robert Morris/Artists Rights Society (ARS), New York. (Photo: Sonnabend Gallery, New York)

FIGURES 59–63: *Working Drawings and Other Visible Things on Paper Not Necessarily Meant to Be Viewed as Art*, curated by the artist Mel Bochner in 1966 at the School of Visual Arts, is generally considered the first public exhibition of Conceptual art. The entire exhibition was presented as a collection of pieces of paper, submitted by artists, that were Xeroxed and gathered together in binders that the visitor could leaf through. Along with the provocative title, the ironic placement of these binders on sculptural plinths begged the question of how these documents were meant to be viewed in relation to Art.

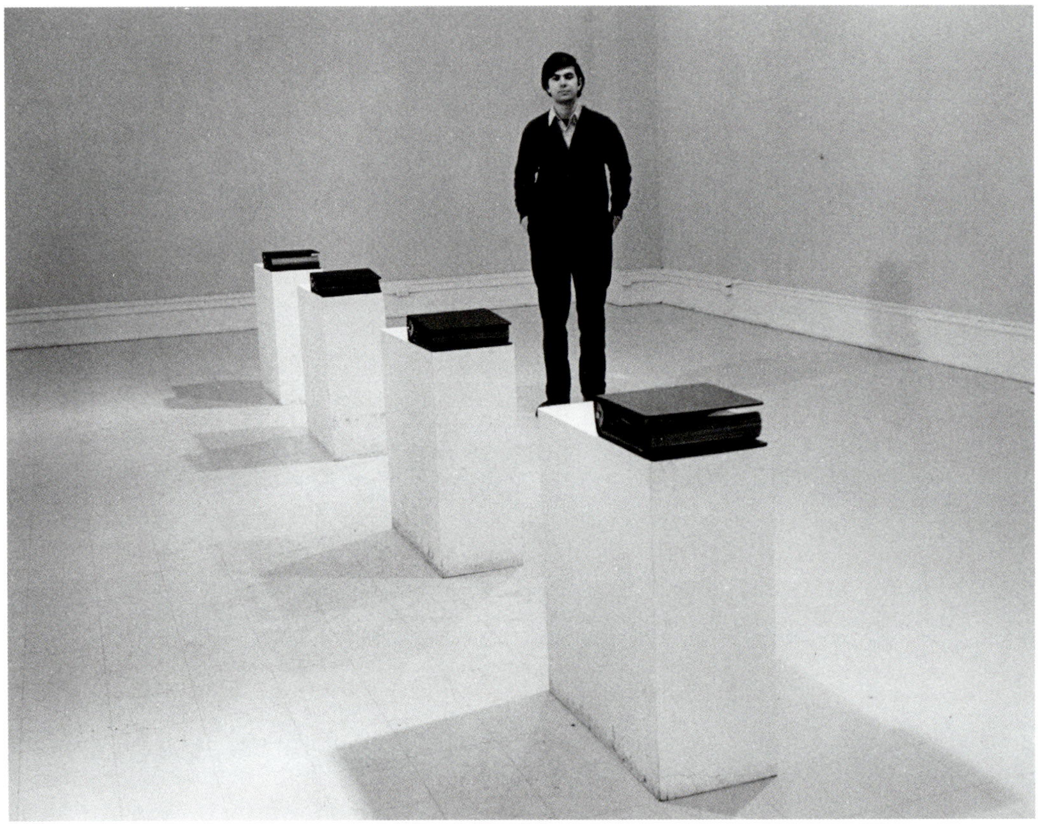

FIGURE 59

Installation view of *Working Drawings and Other Visible Things on Paper Not Necessarily Meant to Be Viewed as Art* with curator Mel Bochner. School of Visual Arts, New York, December 2–23, 1966; organized by Mel Bochner. Four identical loose-leaf notebooks with 100 Xeroxed copies of studio notes, working drawings, and diagrams collected and Xeroxed by the artist, displayed on four sculpture stands.
© Mel Bochner. (Photo: Mel Bochner)

FIGURES 60–63

Mel Bochner (American, b. 1940). Four contributions to *Working Drawings and Other Visible Things on Paper Not Necessarily Meant to Be Viewed as Art*: Xeroxes of (figure 60) *Scientific American Diagram,* (figure 61) Dan Flavin drawing, (figure 62) Eva Hesse drawing, and (figure 63) Donald Judd fabrication bill, all 1966. Xerox copies, 11 × 8½ in. (27.9 × 21.6 cm) each.
© Mel Bochner. (Photos: Mel Bochner)

```
[illegible]((
(PEOPLE IS THE PLURAL OF PERSON)
(FEET IS THE PLURAL OF FOOT)
(YARDS IS THE PLURAL OF YARD)
(FATHOMS IS THE PLURAL OF FATHOM)
(INCHES IS THE PLURAL OF INCH)
(SPANS IS THE PLURAL OF SPAN)
[illegible]
(THREE NUMBERS ALWAYS MEANS THE FIRST NUMBER AND THE SECOND
NUMBER AND THE THIRD NUMBER)
(FIRST TWO NUMBERS ALWAYS MEANS
THE FIRST NUMBER AND THE SECOND NUMBER)
(MORE THAN ALWAYS MEANS PLUS)
(THESE ALWAYS MEANS THE)
(TWO NUMBERS SOMETIMES MEANS ONE NUMBER AND THE
     OTHER NUMBER)
(TWO NUMBERS SOMETIMES MEANS ONE OF THE
       NUMBERS AND THE OTHER NUMBER)
(HAS IS A VERB)
(GETS IS A VERB)
(HAVE IS A VERB)
(LESS THAN ALWAYS MEANS LESSTHAN)
(LESSTHAN IS AN OPERATOR OF LEVEL 2)
(PERCENT IS AN OPERATOR OF LEVEL 2)
(PERCENT LESS THAN ALWAYS MEANS PERLESS)
(PERLESS IS AN OPERATOR OF LEVEL 2)
(PLUS IS AN OPERATOR OF LEVEL  2)
(SUM IS AN OPERATOR)
(TIMES IS AN OPERATOR OF LEVEL 1)
(SQUARE IS AN OPERATOR OF LEVEL 1)
(DIVBY IS AN OPERATOR OF LEVEL 1)
(OF IS AN OPERATOR)
(DIFFERENCE IS AN OPERATOR)
(SQUARED IS AN OPERATOR)
(MINUS IS AN OPERATOR OF LEVEL 2)
(PER IS AN OPERATOR)
(SQUARED IS AN OPERATOR)
(YEARS OLDER THAN ALWAYS MEANS PLUS)
(YEARS YOUNGER THAN ALWAYS MEANS LESS THAN)
(IS EQUAL TO ALWAYS MEANS IS)
(PLUSS IS AN OPERATOR)
(MINUSS IS AN OPERATOR)
(HOW OLD ALWAYS MEANS WHAT)
(THE PERIMETER OF $1 RECTANGLE SOMETIMES MEANS
TWICE THE SUM OF THE LENGTH AND  WIDTH OF THE RECTANGLE)
(GALLONS IS THE PLURAL OF GALLON)
(HOURS IS THE PLURAL OF HOUR)
(MARY IS A PERSON)
(ANN IS A PERSON)
(BILL IS A PERSON)
(A FATHER IS A PERSON)
(AN UNCLE IS A PERSON)
(POUNDS IS THE PLURAL OF POUND)
(WEIGHS IS A VERB)
))
REMEMBER ((
(DISTANCE EQUALS SPEED TIMES TIME)
(DISTANCE EQUALS GAS CONSUMPTION TIMES
NUMBER OF GALLONS OF GAS USED)
(1 FOOT EQUALS 12 INCHES)
(1 YARD EQUALS 3 FEET)
))
```

FIGURE 60

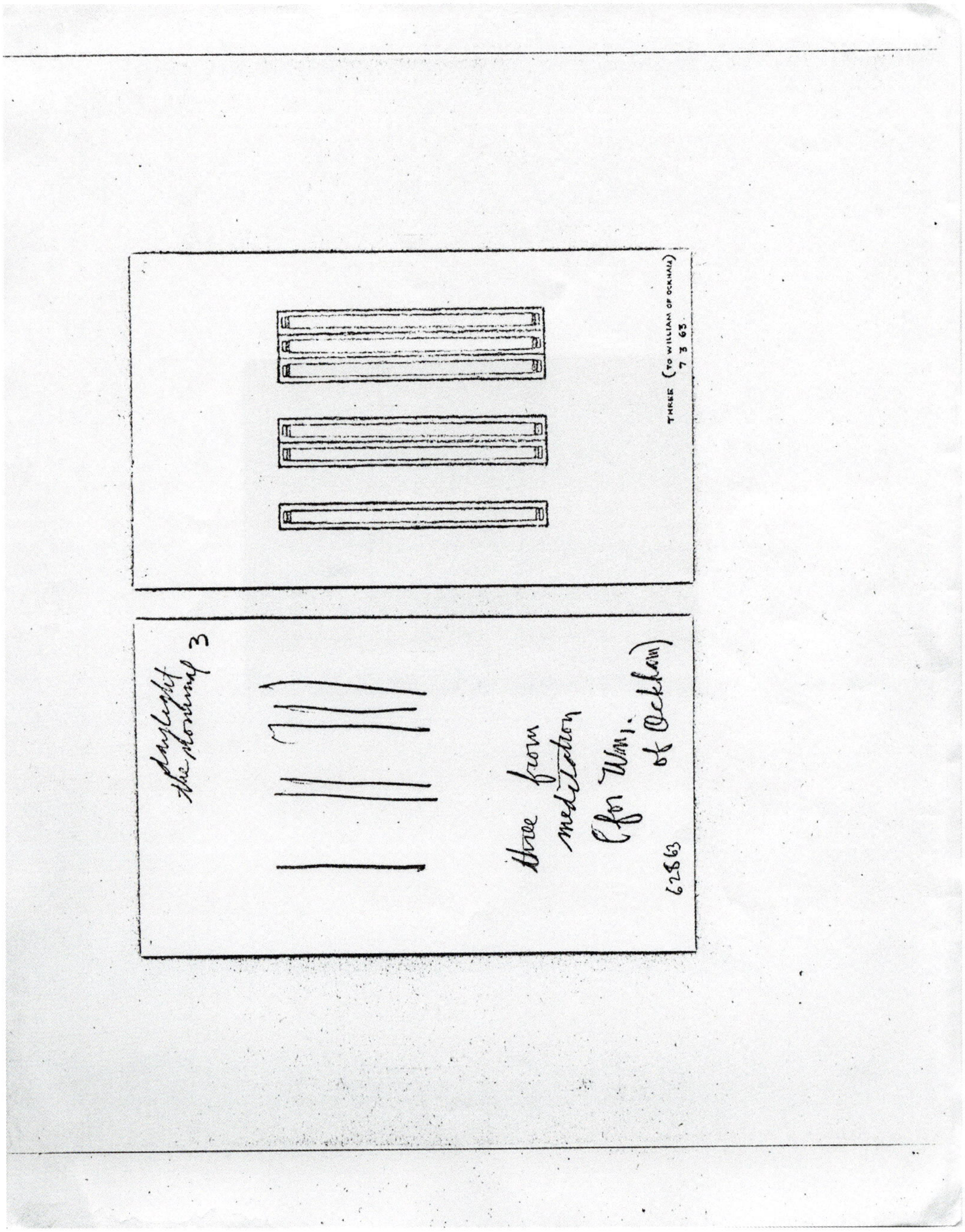
THREE (TO WILLIAM OF OCKHAM)
7 3 63
three from meditation
(for Wm. of Ockham)
6 28 63

FIGURE 61

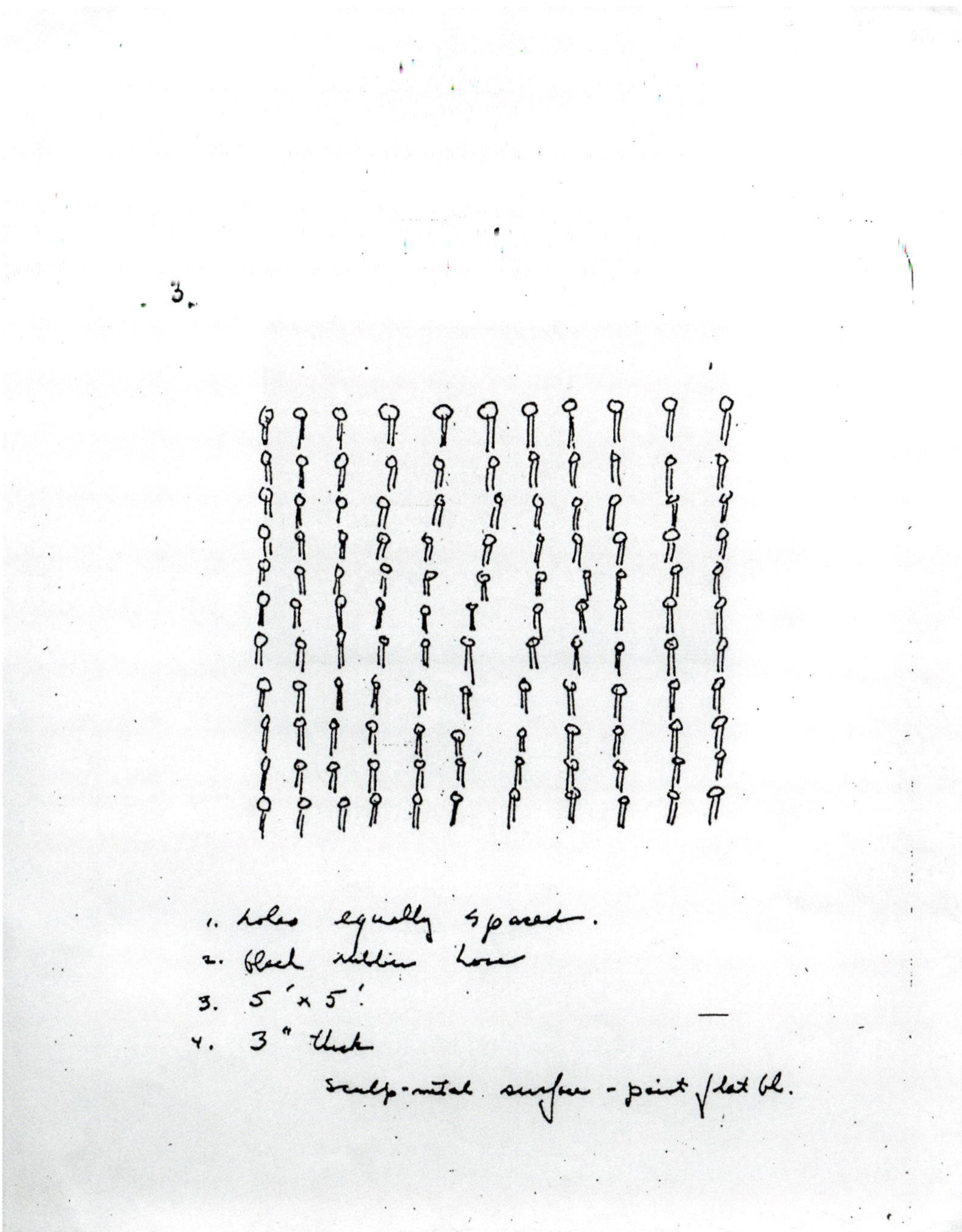
3.
1. holes equally spaced.
2. black rubber hose
3. 5' x 5'
4. 3" thick
sculp-metal surface - paint flat bl.

FIGURE 62

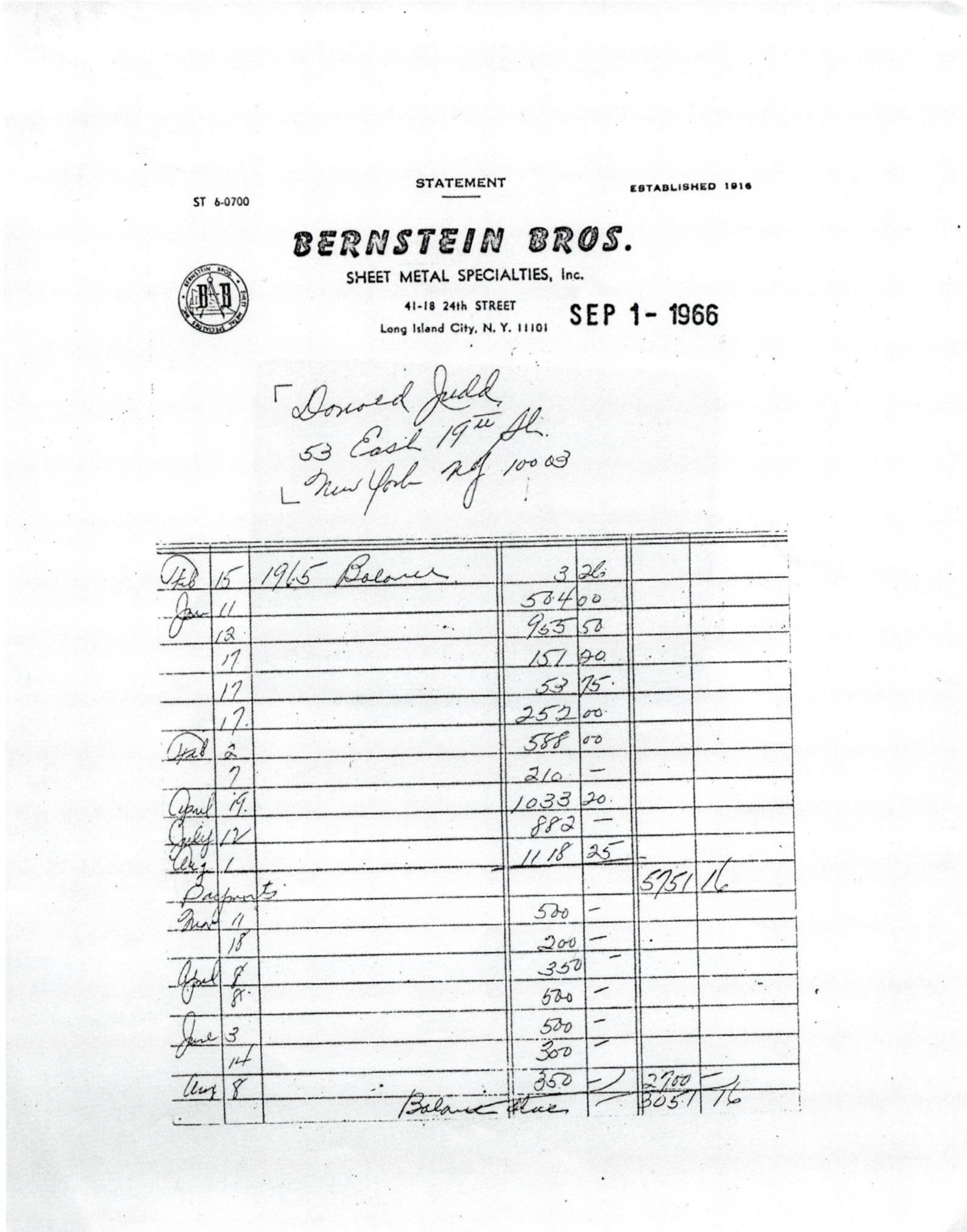

STATEMENT

ESTABLISHED 1916

ST 6-0700

BERNSTEIN BROS.

SHEET METAL SPECIALTIES, Inc.

41-18 24th STREET
Long Island City, N. Y. 11101

SEP 1 - 1966

Donald Judd
53 East 19th St.
New York NY 10003

Feb	15	1965 Balance	3	26		
Jan	11		584	00		
	12		955	50		
	17		151	90		
	17		53	75		
	17		252	00		
Feb	2		588	00		
	7		210	—		
April	19		1033	20		
July	12		882	—		
Aug	1		1118	25	5751	16
Payments						
Nov	11		500	—		
	18		200	—		
April	8		350	—		
	8		500	—		
June	3		500	—		
	14		300	—		
Aug	8		350	—	2700	—
		Balance due			3051	16

FIGURE 63

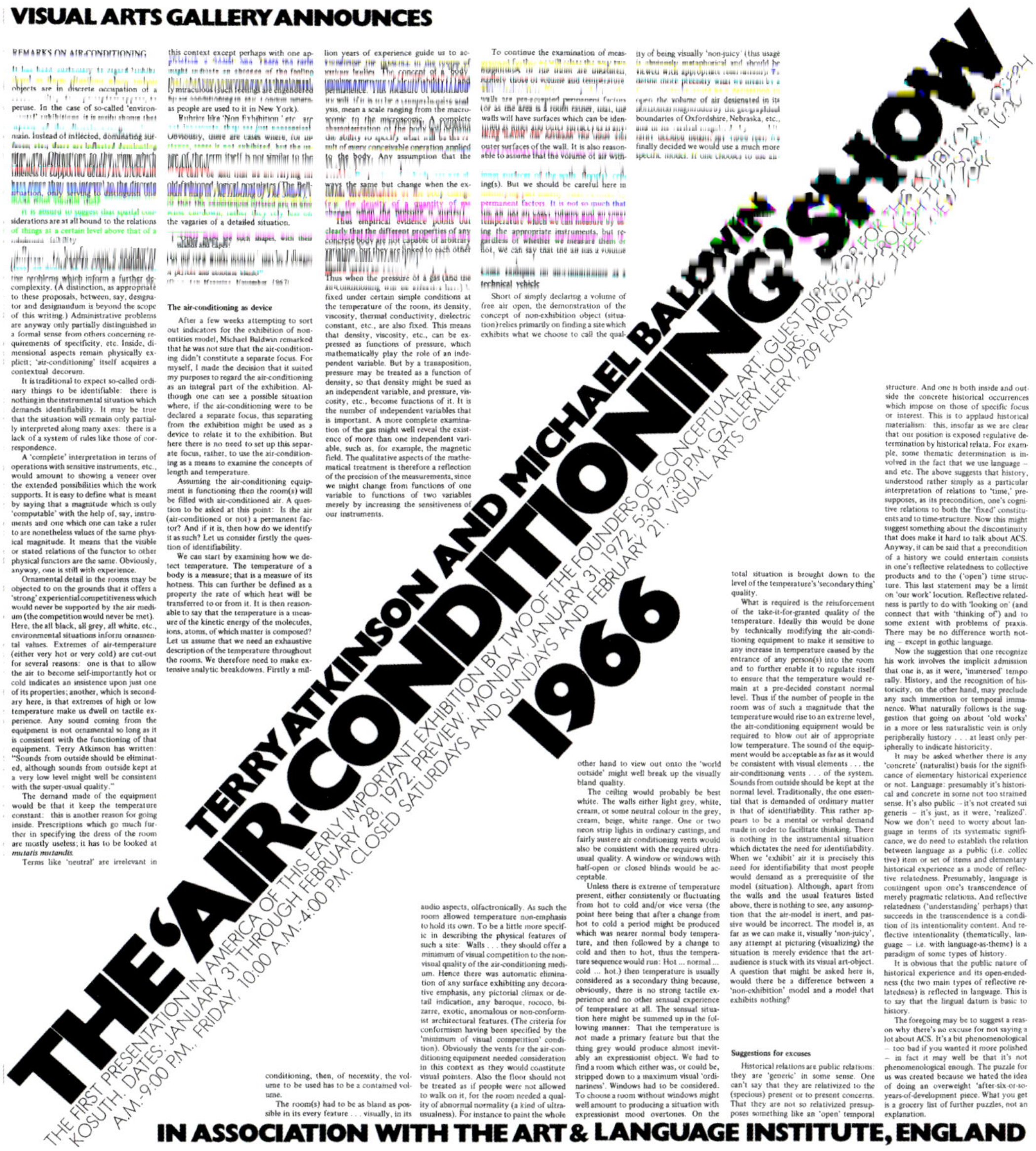

FIGURE 64

Art & Language (Terry Atkinson [British, b. 1939] and Michael Baldwin [British, b. 1945]). Poster for *The Air-Conditioning Show 1966;* concept realized in 1972. Lithograph, 18⅞ × 16⅞ in. (48 × 43 cm). Museu d'Art Contemporani de Barcelona, Deposit Philippe Meaille, Barcelona. © Art & Language, courtesy Lisson Gallery, London

In a literal dematerialization of not just the art object but the art exhibition, in 1966 the U.K.-based collective Art & Language conceived of an exhibition during which the gallery would be left empty, save for an air-conditioner programmed to balance the temperature inside the space with that of the outside environment. Part of the text had been published in *Arts Magazine* in November 1967. The poster was designed and published in conjunction with the concept's realization in 1972 at the Visual Arts Gallery in New York as *The Air-Conditioning Show*. Announcements for the exhibition were of a similar graphic form.

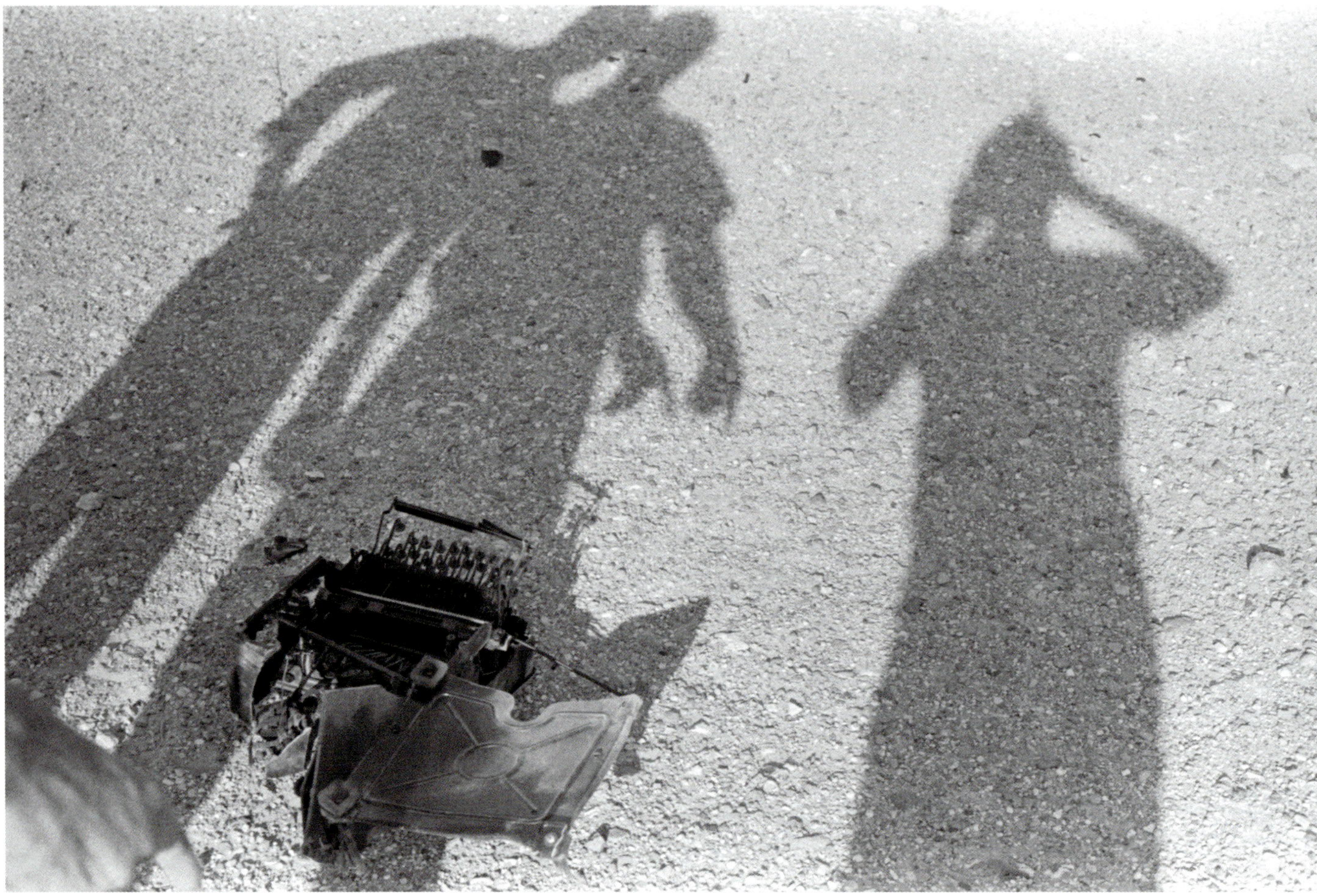

FIGURE 65

Edward Ruscha (American, b. 1937) with Mason Williams and Patrick Blackwell. Plate from *Royal Road Test.* Softcover book, spiral-bound, offset printing on 80-lb. white Prentice Gloss Text paper, 9 7/16 × 6½ in. (24 × 16.5 cm). New York: G. Wittenborn, 1967. © Ed Ruscha collaboration with Mason Williams and Patrick Blackwell. Courtesy Gagosian Gallery, New York. (Photo: Patrick Blackwell)

On the West Coast, Ed Ruscha, along with Mason Williams and Patrick Blackwell, experimented with literal and metaphorical notions of destruction in their *Royal Road Test,* in which the three artists documented the destruction of a vintage Royal typewriter thrown out the window of a 1963 Buick Le Sabre going 90 miles an hour down a road 122 miles southwest of Las Vegas. The resulting photographs were published without commentary as an artist's book.

NON-ANTHROPOMORPHIC ART
BY FOUR YOUNG ARTISTS:
JOSEPH KOSUTH
CHRISTINE KOZLOV
MICHAEL RINALDI
ERNEST ROSSI
AT THE LANNIS GALLERY ON
315 E 12TH ST NEAR 2ND AVE
OPENING FEB 19, 12 TO 12

FOUR STATEMENTS

FIGURE 66

Cover of catalogue of *Non-Anthropomorphic Art by Four Young Artists: Joseph Kosuth, Christine Kozlov, Michael Rinaldi, Ernest Rossi*, 1967. Printed book, 8¼ x 7 in. (21.0 x 17.8 cm). New York: Lannis Gallery, 1967. © 2011 Joseph Kosuth/Artists Rights Society (ARS), New York. (Photo: Brooklyn Museum)

Before converting the Lannis Gallery into the Museum of Normal Art, Joseph Kosuth played with normal expectations for catalogues by reproducing short texts written by these four artists describing their work, instead of reproducing images of the work.

FIGURE 67

Robert Ryman (American, b. 1930). *Adelphi*, 1967. Oil on unstretched linen canvas, installed with staples, waxed paper, masking tape: canvas, 102 × 102 in. (259 × 259 cm); overall with waxed paper, approx. 112 × 112 in. (284.5 × 284.5 cm). Museum für Moderne Kunst, Frankfurt am Main. © 2011 Robert Ryman/ Artists Rights Society (ARS), New York. (Photo: Demel und Wittmar, Essen, courtesy Museum für Moderne Kunst, Frankfurt am Main)

Unlike most artists discussed in *Six Years,* Robert Ryman continued to explore the viability of painting as a medium, but in its most reductive form. In 1967, he started to tape or staple works like *Adelphi* straight onto the wall, and at his first one-person show in New York, he exhibited his *Standard Series:* thirteen works made up of white brushstrokes on thin sheets of steel, hung flush with the white gallery walls so as to be almost invisible.

FIGURES 68–70: Joseph Kosuth and Christine Kozlov, who were collaborators during this period, conceived of the Museum of Normal Art, a semi-fictional institution without a fixed address, which the two artists used as a forum for presenting work that interested them while also mocking the institutionalization of avant-garde art.

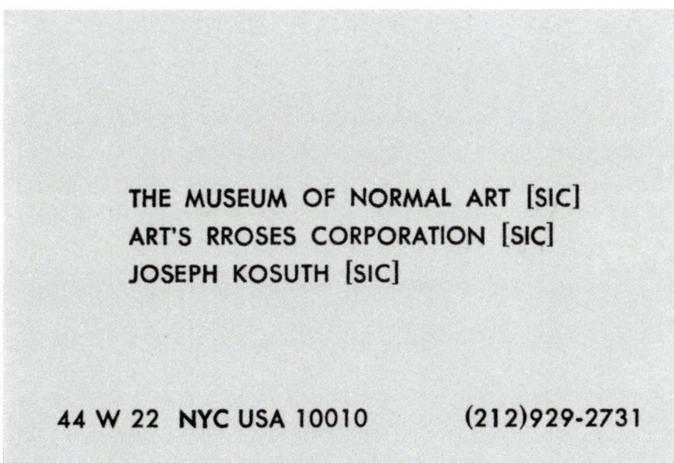

FIGURE 68

Joseph Kosuth (American, b. 1945). Business card for The Museum of Normal Art, 1968. Printed card, 2½ × 3½ in. (6.4 × 8.9 cm). Courtesy Joseph Kosuth. © 2011 Joseph Kosuth/Artists Rights Society (ARS), New York. (Photo: Brooklyn Museum)

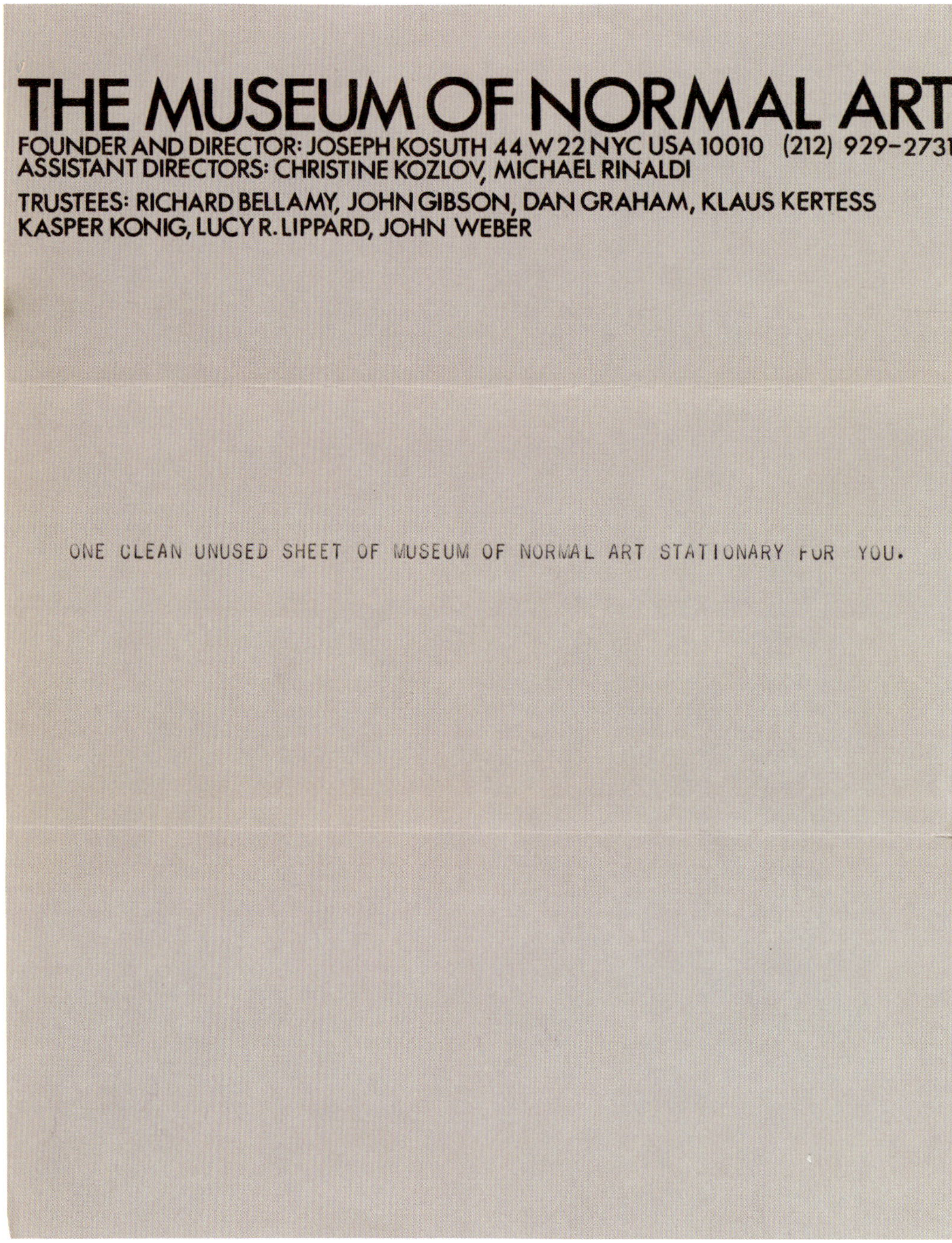

THE MUSEUM OF NORMAL ART
FOUNDER AND DIRECTOR: JOSEPH KOSUTH 44 W 22 NYC USA 10010 (212) 929-2731
ASSISTANT DIRECTORS: CHRISTINE KOZLOV, MICHAEL RINALDI
TRUSTEES: RICHARD BELLAMY, JOHN GIBSON, DAN GRAHAM, KLAUS KERTESS
KASPER KONIG, LUCY R. LIPPARD, JOHN WEBER

ONE CLEAN UNUSED SHEET OF MUSEUM OF NORMAL ART STATIONARY FOR YOU.

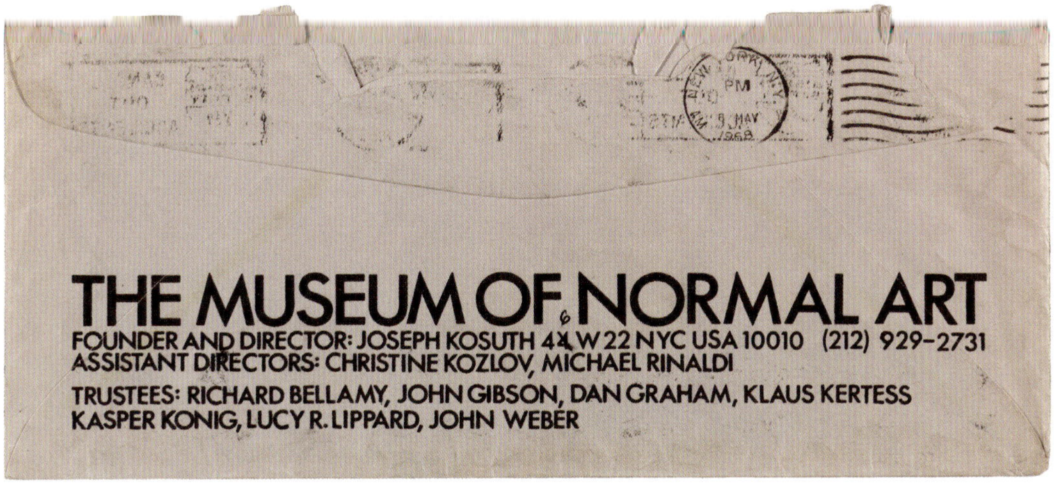

FIGURES 69, 70

Joseph Kosuth (American, b. 1945). Envelope and sheet of The Museum of Normal Art letterhead stationery sent to Lucy R. Lippard and John Chandler, 1968. Typewritten text and stamps on printed stationery: sheet, 11 × 8½ in. (27.9 × 21.6 cm); envelope, 4⅛ × 9½ in. (10.5 × 24.1 cm). Lucy R. Lippard Papers, Archives of American Art, Smithsonian Institution, Washington, D.C. © 2011 Joseph Kosuth/Artists Rights Society (ARS), New York

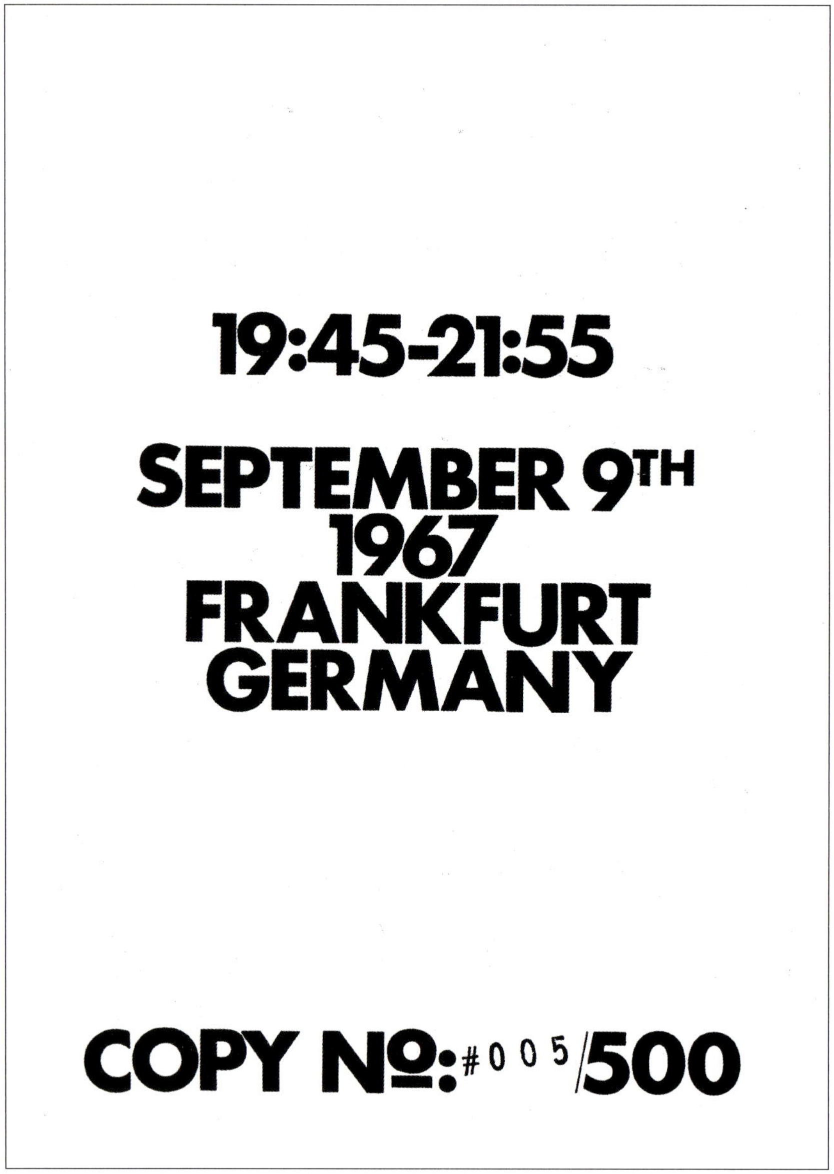

FIGURES 71, 72

Cover and title page of catalogue *19:45–21:55, September 9th, 1967, Frankfurt, Germany*. Printed book, 11 × 8 in. (27.9 × 20.3 cm). Frankfurt: Paul Maenz, 1967. © Paul Maenz. (Photo: Archiv Paul Maenz, Berlin)

On September 9, 1967, Paul Maenz produced this exhibition, which, as its title indicates, existed for slightly more than two hours, between 7:45 and 9:55 p.m., and was more a series of events than a display of objects. The ephemeral nature of this project makes the small sentence at the top of the title page, which translates as "All this will one day be yours, sweetheart," pointedly ironic.

Dies alles Herzchen wird einmal Dir gehören

PARTICIPATING:

JAN DIBBETS
BARRY FLANAGAN
BERNHARD HÖKE
JOHN JOHNSON
RICHARD LONG
KONRAD LUEG
CH. POSENENSKE
PETER ROEHR

Arranged by Paul Maenz

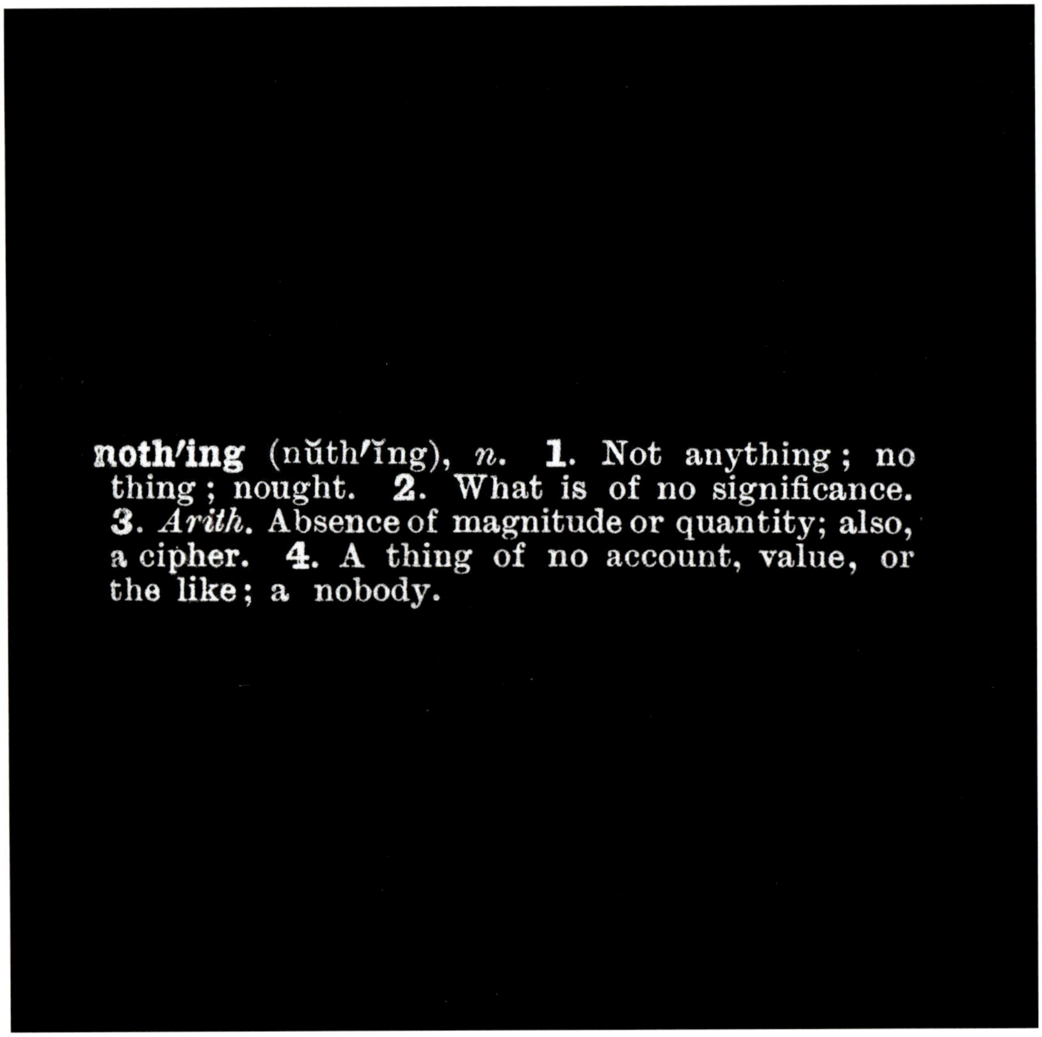
noth'ing (nŭth'ĭng), *n.* **1.** Not anything; no thing; nought. **2.** What is of no significance. **3.** *Arith.* Absence of magnitude or quantity; also, a cipher. **4.** A thing of no account, value, or the like; a nobody.

FIGURE 73

Joseph Kosuth (American, b. 1945). *Titled (Art as Idea as Idea), [Nothing]*, 1967. Negative photostat, 48 × 48 in. (121.9 × 121.9 cm). Sean Kelly Gallery, New York. Courtesy Joseph Kosuth and Sean Kelly Gallery. © 2011 Joseph Kosuth/Artists Rights Society (ARS), New York

This work succinctly challenges generally accepted presumptions about the stability of authorial, aesthetic, and linguistic meaning. Kosuth's *A.A.I.A.I.* series—composed of photostat enlargements of dictionary definitions, in this case, the word *nothing*—investigates how meaning is produced within representational systems by interjecting one system (language) into another (visual art). As such, his work appears to participate in the philosophical discussion instigated by Roland Barthes's important essay "The Death of the Author," published the same year in *Aspen* (figures 25, 26), which suggested that a work's meaning is constructed in a dialogue between the artist/author and a viewer/reader.

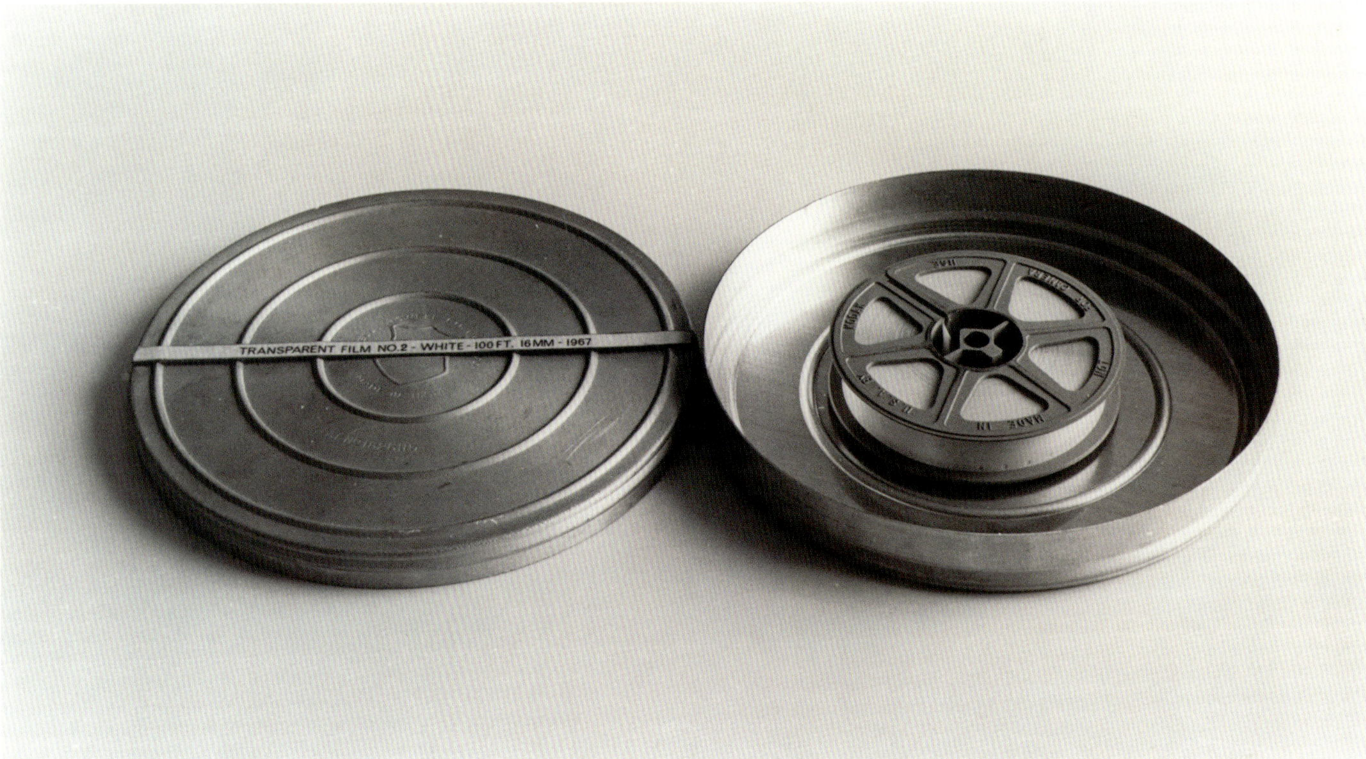

FIGURE 74

Christine Kozlov (American, 1945–2005). *No title, transparent film #2*, 1967. 16mm film leader, film reel, and canister: canister, 7 in. (17.8 cm) diameter. The Estate of Christine Kozlov. © Marilyn Thompson. (Photo: Jay Cantor)

Kozlov's work often raises questions about how experience and interpretation are structured by conventions. In this case, she questions assumptions about how materials can be used by displaying a reel of white film leader—that is, film with no actual content or information aside from its existence as an object—together with its canister. Instead of using film to record images and sound, this piece suggests alternate criteria, whether sculptural or philosophical, for its assessment.

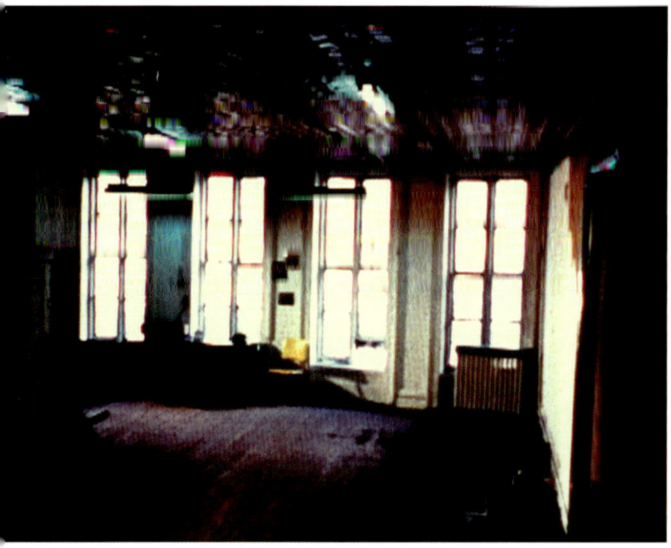

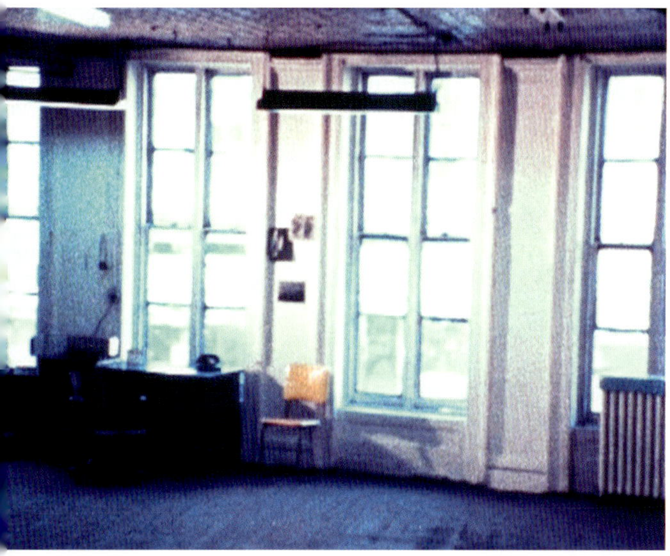

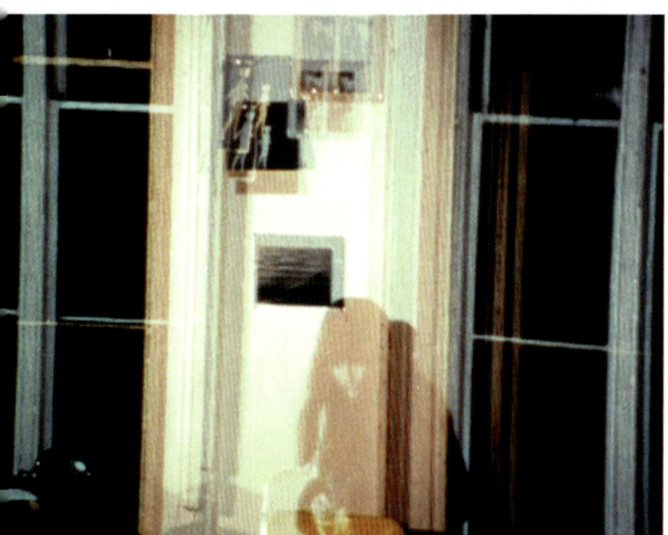

FIGURES 75–79: Michael Snow demonstrated his interest in mediating visual perception through various technical means, exaggerating basic camera properties, such as an extended zoom, in structuralist films such as *Wavelength* (1967), and using prisms and mirrors in sculptural work, including *First to Last* (1967).

FIGURES 75–77

Michael Snow (Canadian, b. 1929). Stills from *Wavelength*, 1967. 16mm color film with sound, 45 min. Canadian Filmmakers Distribution Centre, Toronto. © Michael Snow. (Photo: Canadian Filmmakers Distribution Centre [CFMDC], Toronto)

FIGURES 78, 79

Michael Snow (Canadian, b. 1929). *First to Last* (two views), 1967. Painted plywood, aluminum, glass, 82⅛ × 82⅛ × 5⅞ in. (208.5 × 208.5 × 15 cm). Art Gallery of Ontario. © Michael Snow

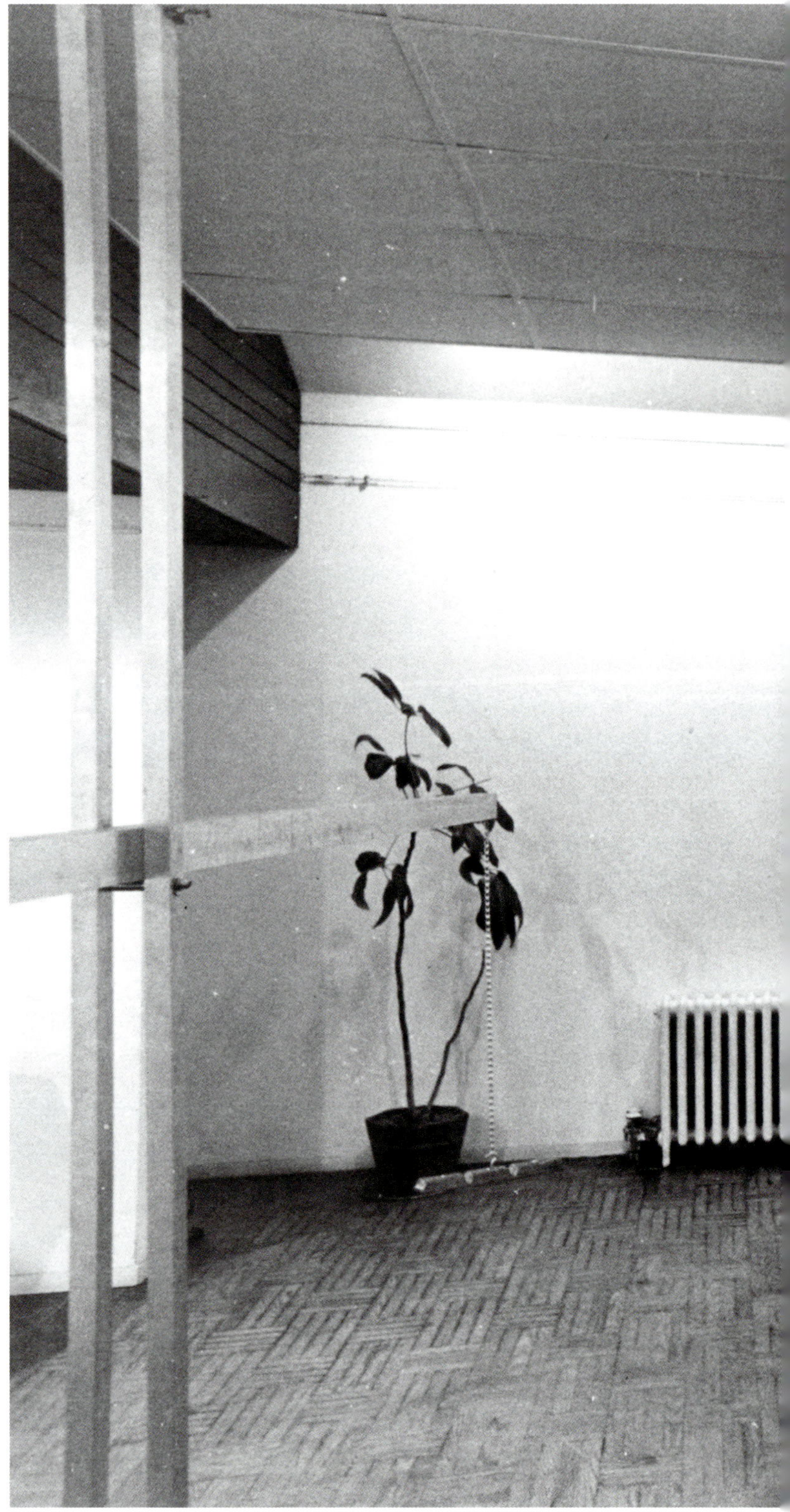

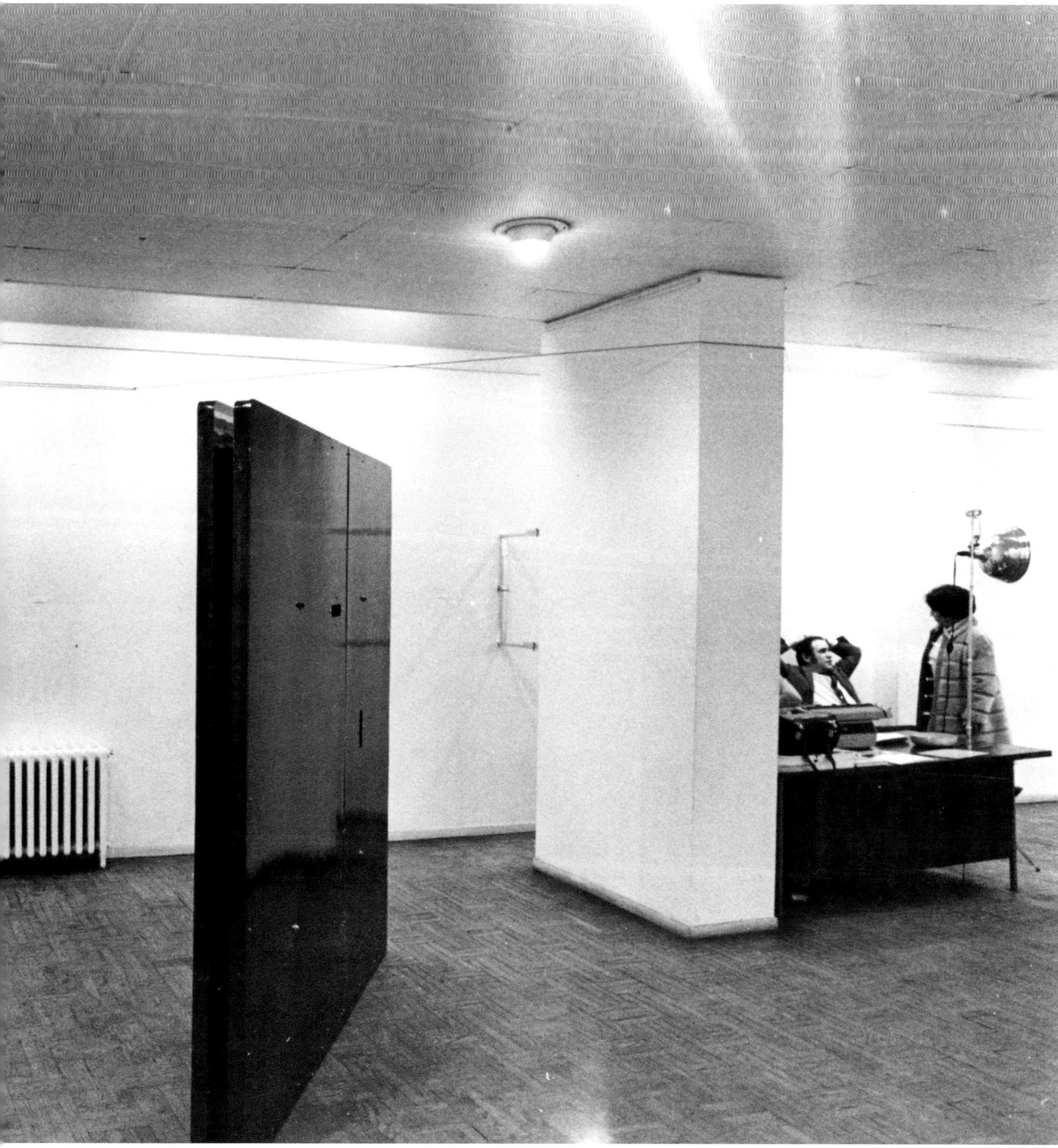

Illustrations and Commentary

Illustrations and Commentary

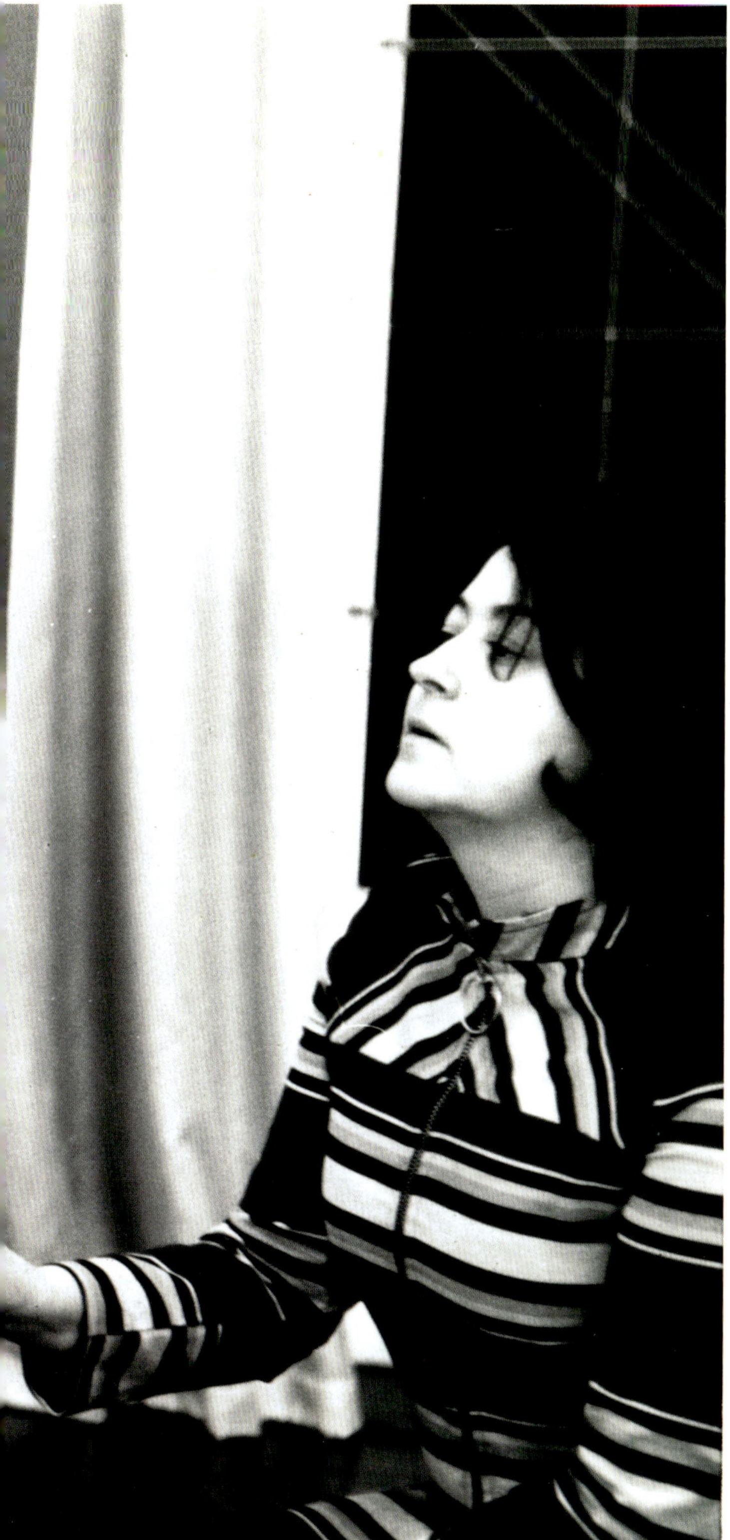

FIGURES 80–82: Founded in 1965 by the expatriate Latin American artists Luis Camnitzer, José Guillermo Castillo, and Liliana Porter, the New York Graphic Workshop produced editions and organized mail art exhibitions. The Workshop's goal was to remove fine-art printmaking from its rarified preoccupation with technique and aesthetics, focusing instead on alternative technical possibilities and printmaking's original use as a medium for repetition and the populist dissemination of information.

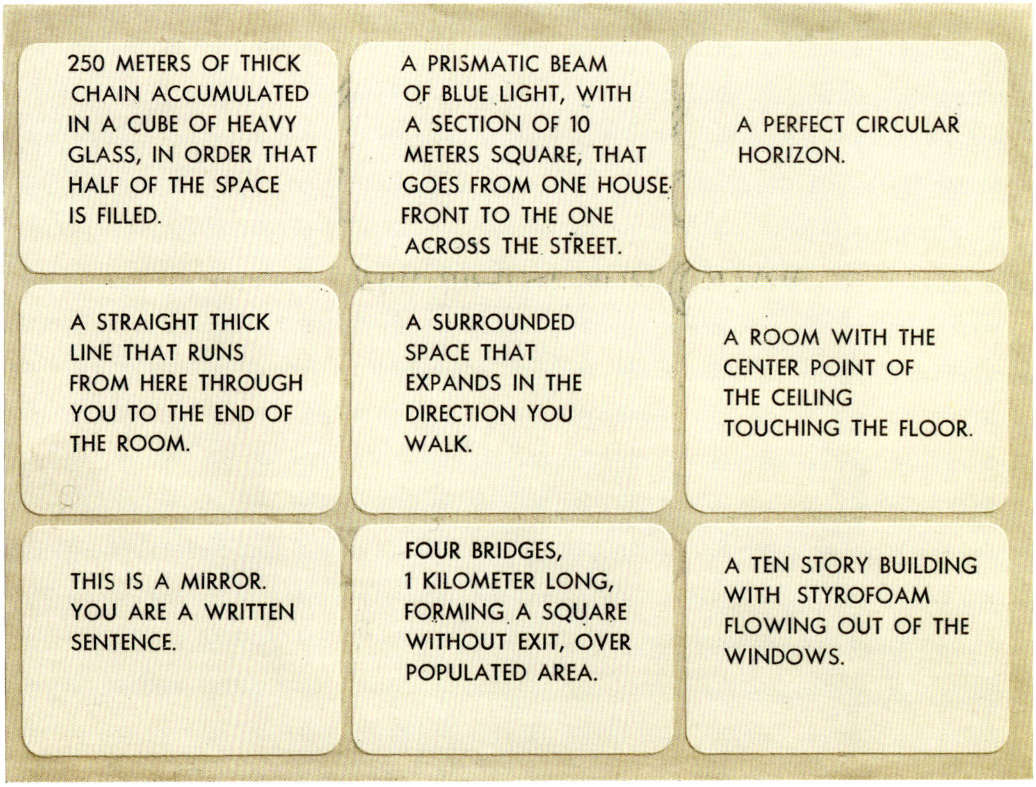

FIGURES 80, 81

Luis Camnitzer (Uruguayan, b. Germany, 1937) and New York Graphic Workshop. *Sentences* [labels for New York Graphic Workshop's *Mail Exhibition #1*], 1968 (front and back). Offset printed adhesive labels, 4 × 5½ in. (10.8 × 14.2 cm) each. Daros Latinamerica Collection, Zurich. © Luis Camnitzer. (Photo: Peter Schälchli, Zurich)

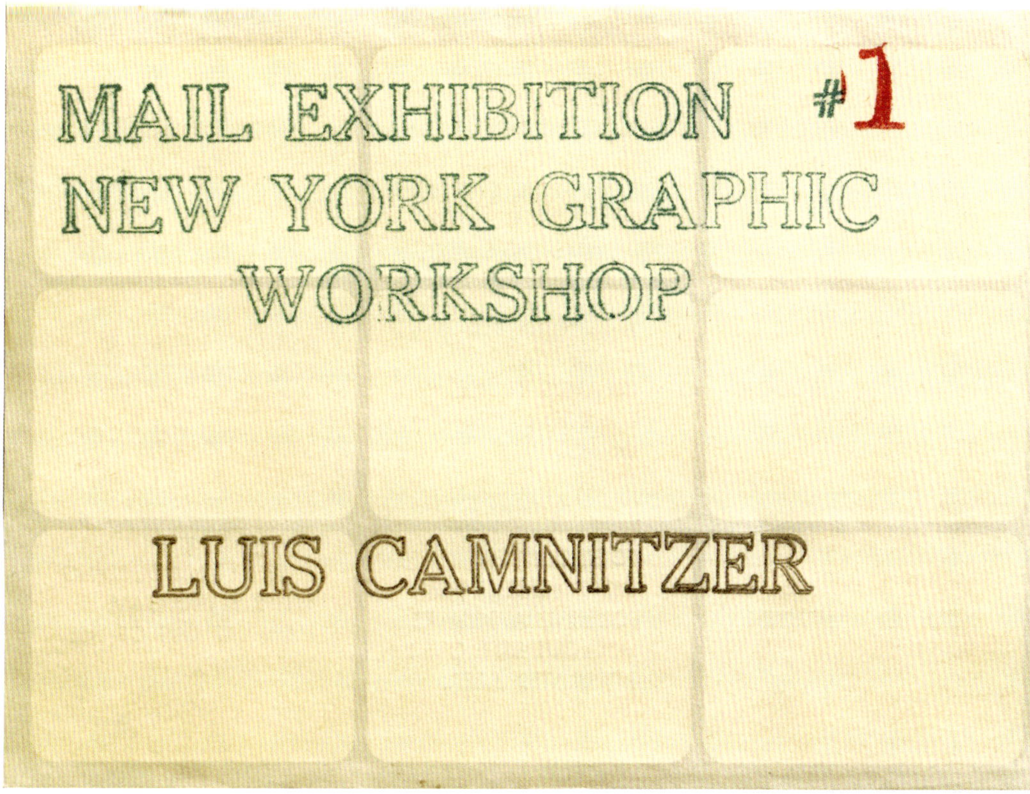
MAIL EXHIBITION #1
NEW YORK GRAPHIC
WORKSHOP
LUIS CAMNITZER

FIGURE 82

Luis Camnitzer (Uruguayan, b. Germany, 1937) and New York Graphic Workshop. *Content: Exhibition No. 1, Luis Camnitzer (Contenido: Exhibición No. 1, Luis Camnitzer)*, 1968. Offset printed letterhead: card, 5½ × 4 in. (13.7 × 10.7 cm); envelope, 5 × 6 in. (12.5 × 15.5 cm). Daros Latinamerica Collection, Zurich. © Luis Camnitzer. (Photo: Peter Schälchli, Zurich)

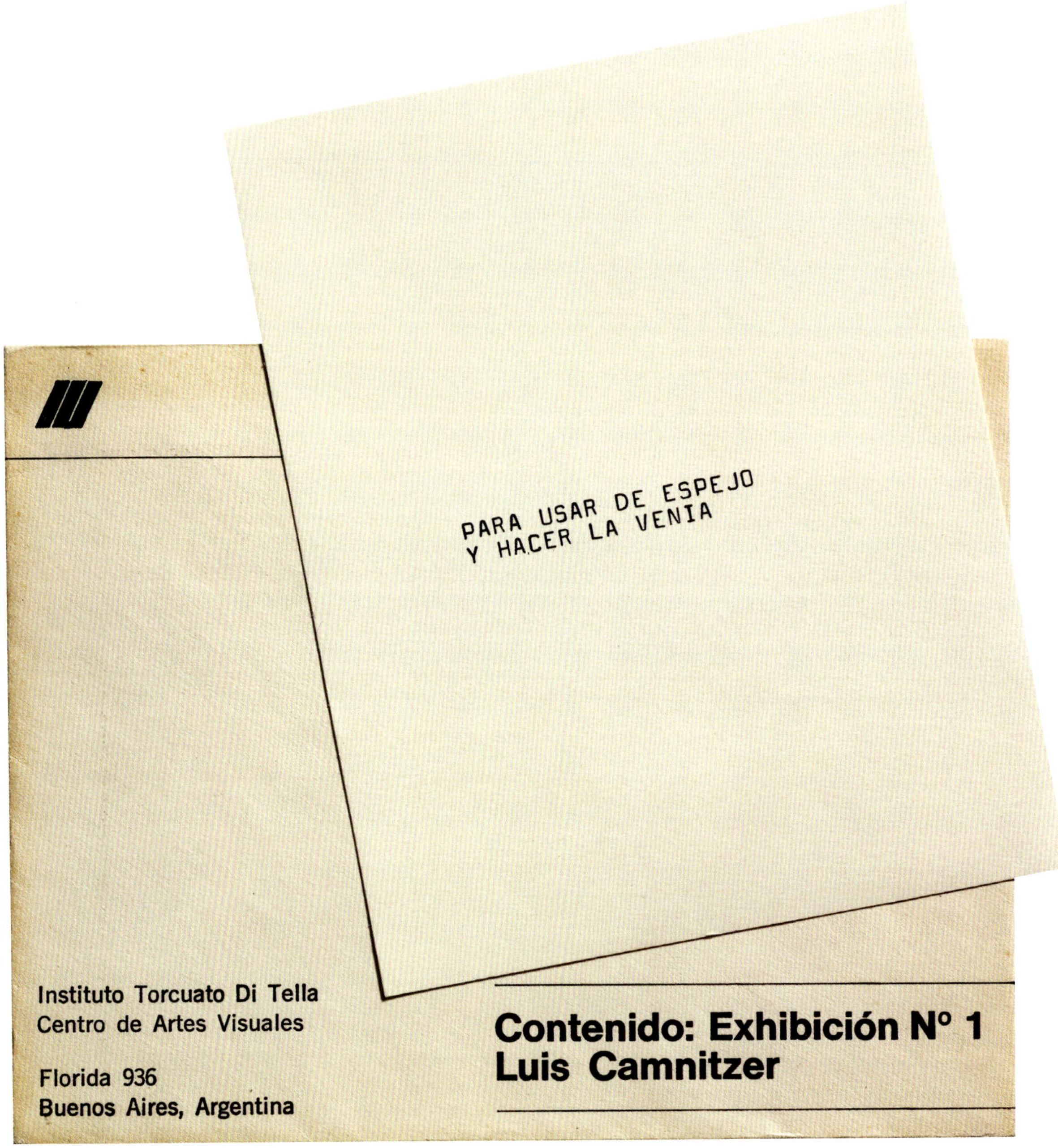

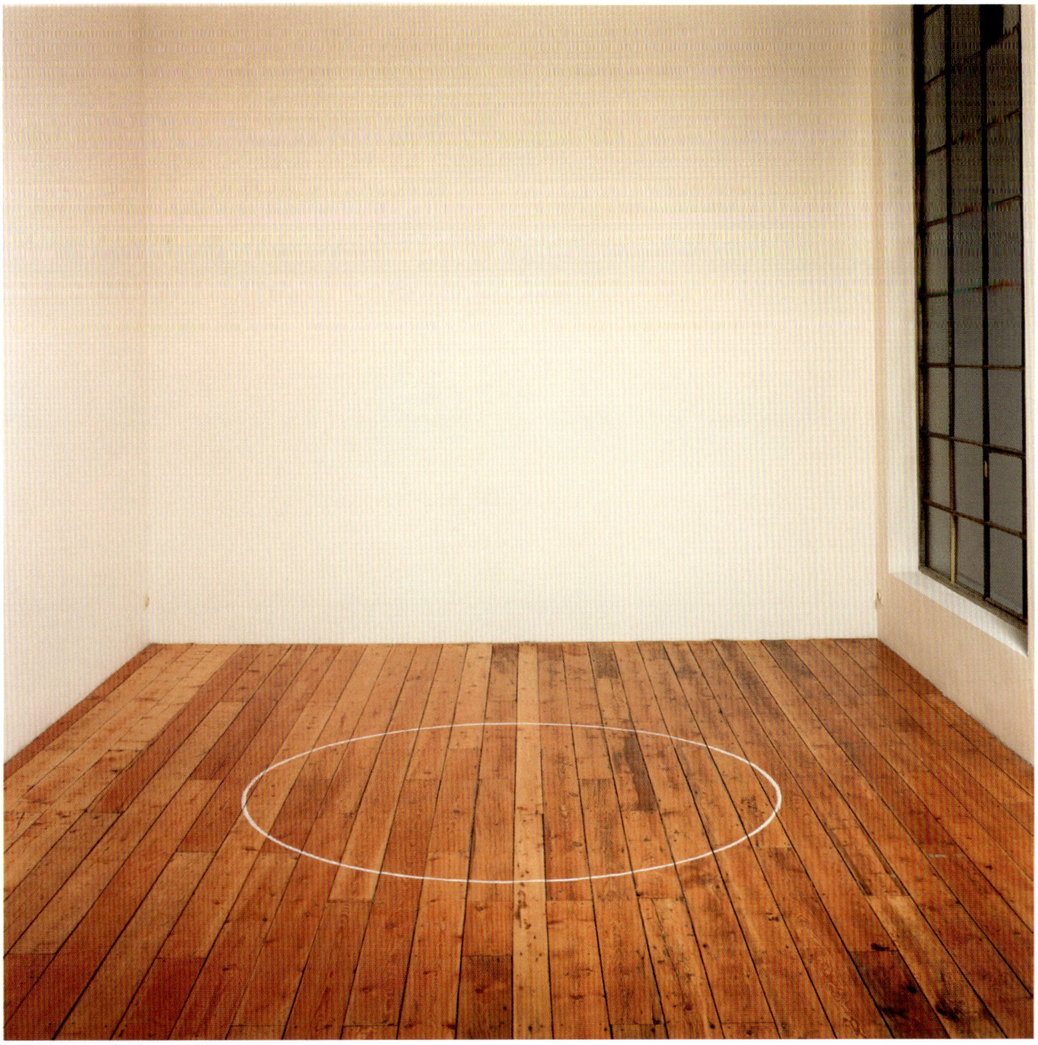

FIGURE 83

Ian Wilson (British, b. 1940). *Circle on Floor (Chalk Circle)*, 1968. Originally installed at Bykerk Gallery, New York, May 25–June 22, 1968; refabrication photographed at Galerie Jan Mot, Brussels, 1998. Chinagraph, chalk on wood floor, 72 in. (182.9 cm) diameter. © Ian Wilson. Courtesy Jan Mot, Brussels. (Photo: Philippe De Gobert)

Honing sculpture to its most ephemeral state and seeking to empty it of content, Wilson's *Circle on Floor (Chalk Circle)* temporarily, and ineffectively, marks out the space where a traditional sculpture might be placed.

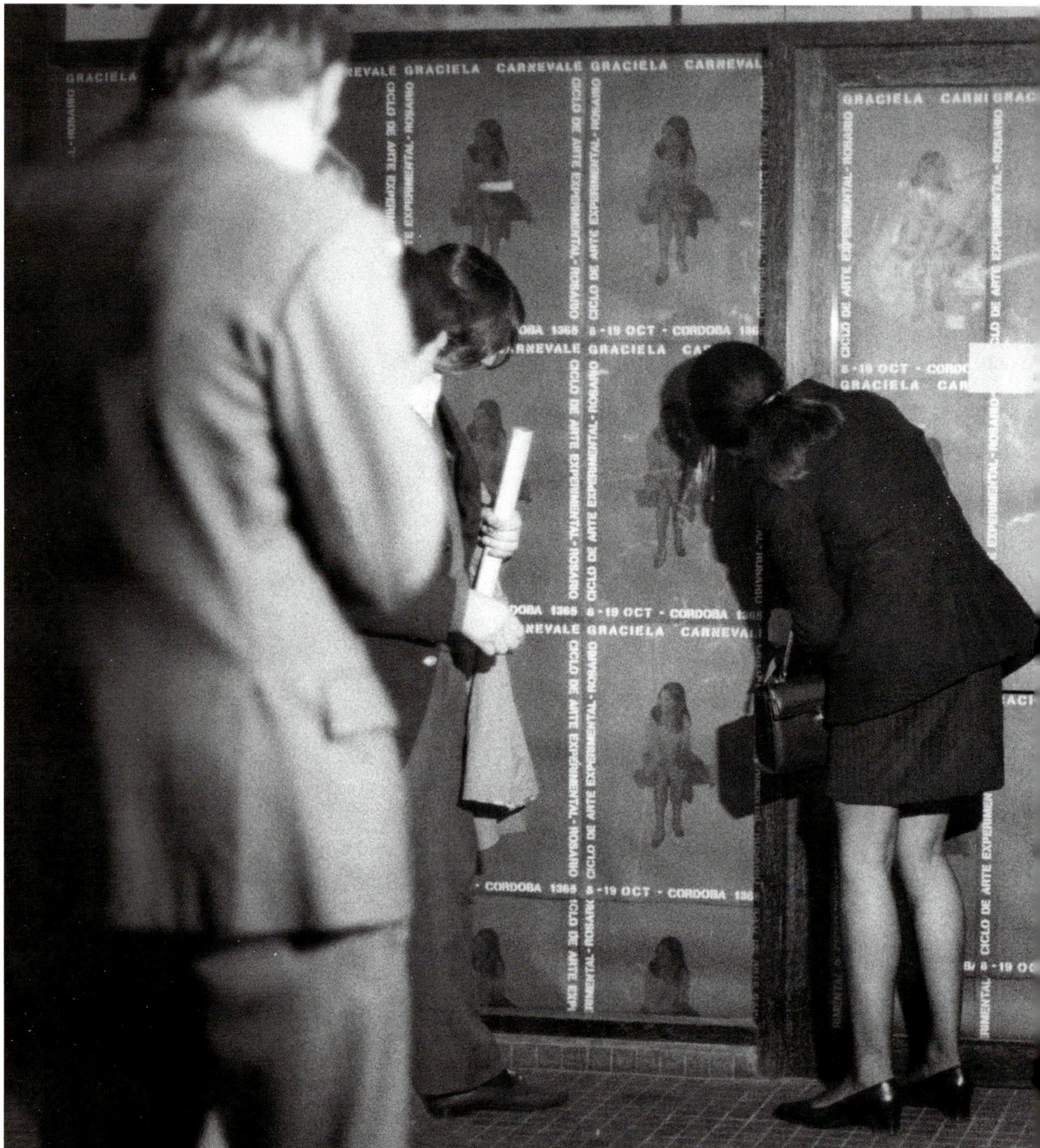
GRACIELA CARNEVALE
CICLO DE ARTE EXPERIMENTAL · ROSARIO
8 - 19 OCT · CORDOBA

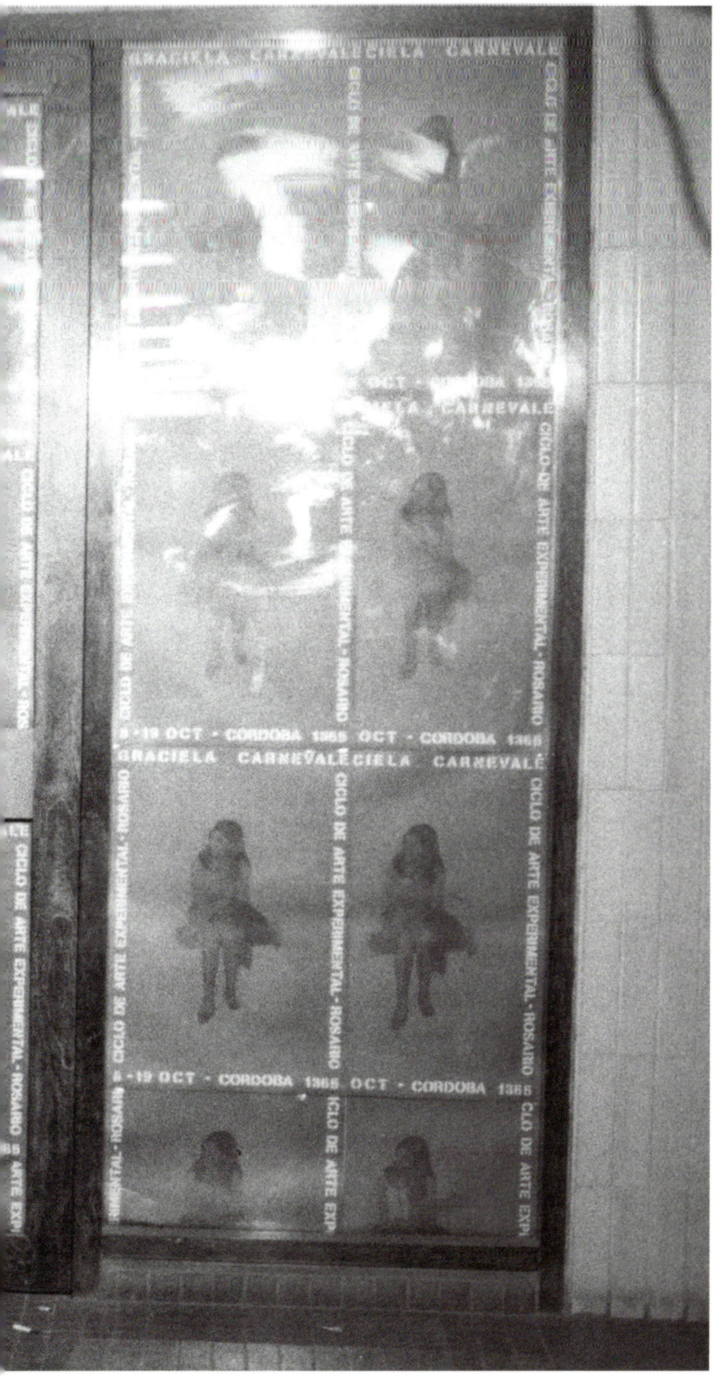

FIGURE 84

Graciela Carnevale (Argentinean, b. 1942). *Entrapment and Escape (Encierro y escape): Action for the Experimental Art Cycle, Rosario, Argentina*, 1968. Archive Graciela Carnevale, Rosario, Argentina. © Graciela Carnevale. (Photo: Carlos Militello)

In 1968, Lippard traveled to Argentina, where she was strongly influenced by artists working within the environment of a governmental dictatorship. In this context, she met artists who were making use of dematerialized strategies for subversive political reasons—their rationales often being as much about issues of personal safety as they were about questions of aesthetics. As her contribution to the *Experimental Art Cycle*, a series of artist actions organized by the avant-garde Rosario Group, Carnevale locked unsuspecting opening attendees into an art gallery to see how long it would take them to realize their predicament and break the front window to escape. The inferences of social control and revolutionary self-liberation were intentionally metaphoric, and the work, as a performative event and an ideological challenge, operated outside the purview of government control or intervention.

FIGURES 85–88

Charlotte Posenenske (German, 1930–1985). Documentation of the sculpture *Square Tubes, Sheet Steel, Series D (Vierkantrohre aus Stahlblech Serie D),* 1967. Reproduced in *Art & Project Bulletin*, no. 1, 1968. Printed single sheet, 11¾ × 16½ in. (29.7 × 42 cm), folded in two. © Archive Art & Project, RKD, the Hague, and Charlotte Posenenske. (Photo: Estate Charlotte Posenenske)

In Amsterdam, Art & Project Gallery began publishing a bulletin that was both a vehicle for information and a venue for artists to realize projects or pieces; the German sculptor Posenenske was the featured artist in the first issue. All of the bulletins, which were published between 1968 and 1971, are mentioned in *Six Years*.

art & project

bulletin

1

architectural research

amsterdam 9
richard wagnerstraat 8
(020) 720425

drukwerk
printed matter

charlotte posenenske
605 offenbach-m
schlosz-strasse 66
w.duitsland

art & project tracht u vertrouwd te maken met de ideeën van kunstenaars, architecten en technici om gezamenlijk een zinnige oplossing te vinden voor de vorm van uw woon- en werkruimte.
art & project nodigt u uit zijn tentoonstellingen te bezoeken om deze samenwerking tussen u en de ideeën van kunstenaars, architecten en technici tot stand te brengen.

open: vrijdag 12-22 / zaterdag 12-18 / zondag 12-18 / woensdag 20-22 uur.

art & project plans to bring you together with the ideas of artists, architects and technicians to discover an intelligent form for your living and working space.
art & project invites you to participate in its exhibitions which will explore ways in which art, architecture and technology can combine with your own ideas.

open: friday 12-22 / saturday 12-18 / sunday 12-18 / wednesday 20-22 h.

FIGURE 85

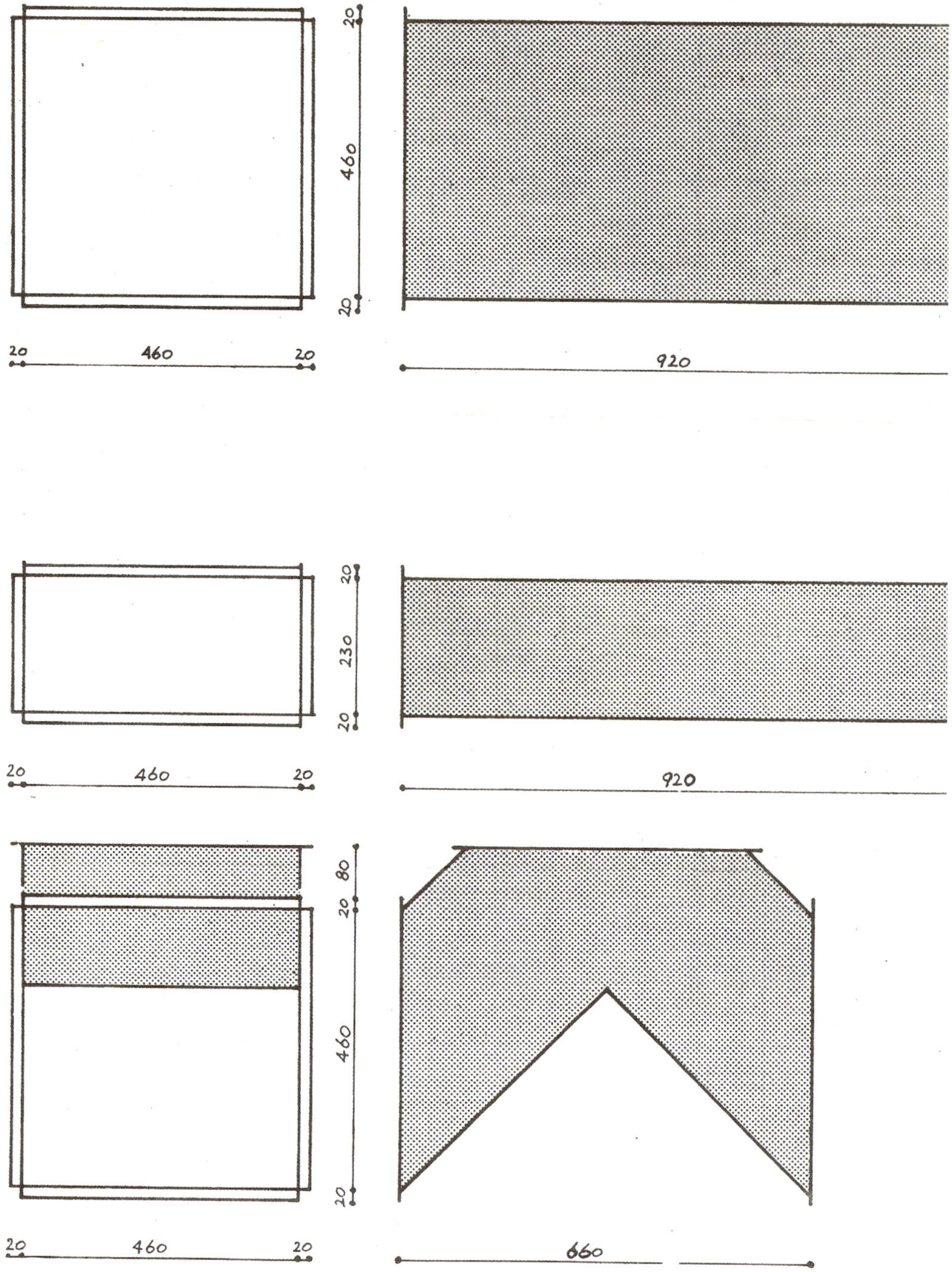
20
460
20
20
460
20
920
20
230
20
20
460
20
920
80
20
460
20
20
460
20
660

FIGURE 86

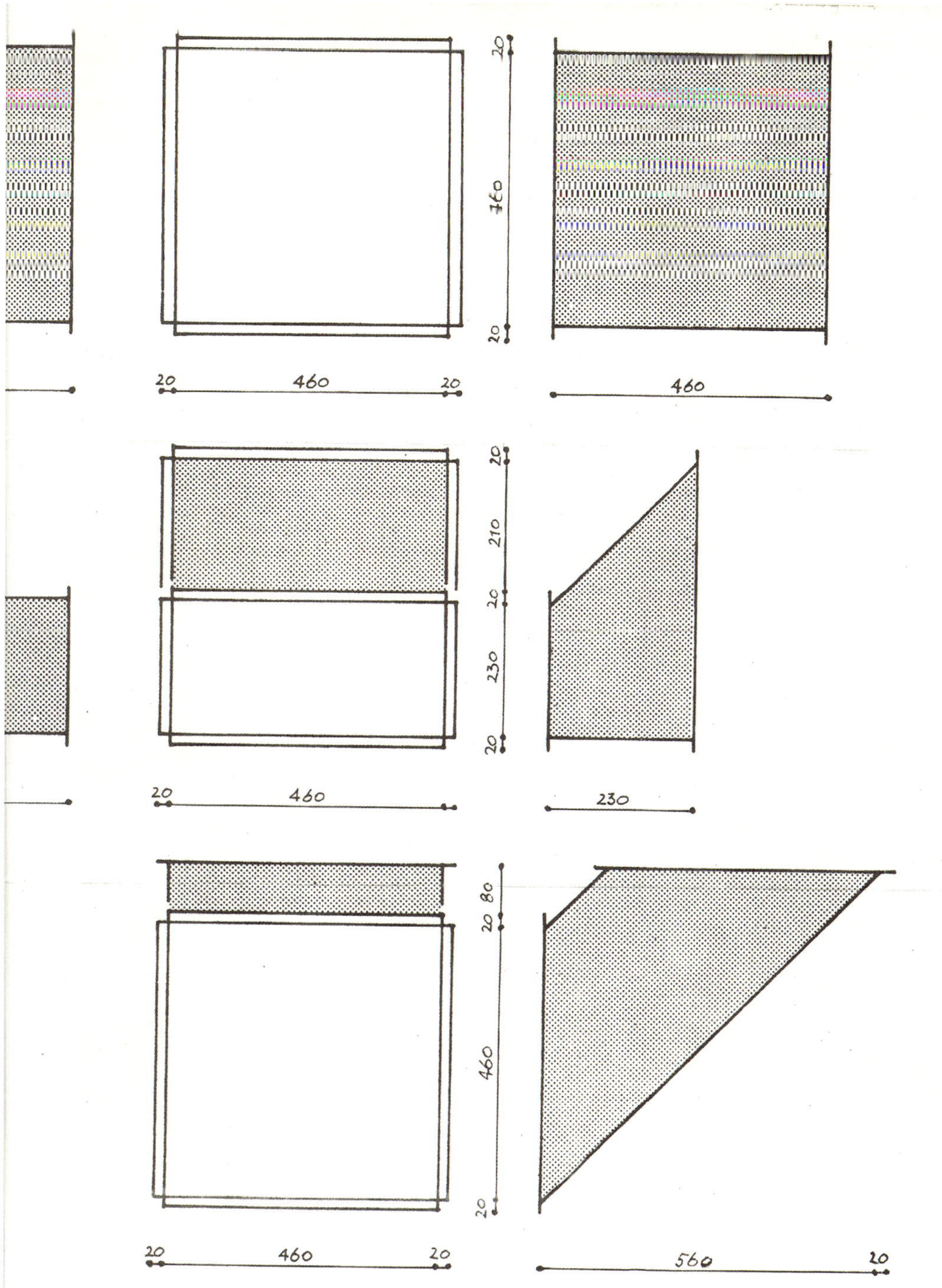
20
760
20
20
460
20
460
20
210
20
230
20
20
460
230
20 80
460
20
20
460
20
560
20

FIGURE 87

20.9 - 16.10.1968

posenenske

auf der zeichnung sehen sie 6 elemente der serie D.
alle teile sind hohlformen, und die masse sind aufeinander abgestimmt.
es gibt ein quadratrohr (46x46 cm), das 92 cm lang ist,
ein quadratrohr, das halb so lang ist,
ein rohr mit rechteckigem querschnitt (die hälfte des langen quadratrohrs),
ein winkelstück,
ein T-stück
und ein übergangsstück.
sie können diese elemente zu kombinationen zusammenschrauben. mit den winkelstücken und T-stücken verändern sie die richtung und machen abzweigungen, mit den übergangsstücken verändern sie den querschnitt.
das material ist galvanisiertes stahlblech, 0,5 mm stark.
die elemente sind reproduzierbar, und die auflage ist unbegrenzt.
sie sind nach zeichnungen von charlotte posenenske im juni 1967 in einer werkstatt hergestellt worden. der preis beträgt hfl. 260,- pro element.

diese elemente und ihre kombinationen sollten kunst sein. plastik, bei der man eine gewisse entscheidungsfreiheit hat, wie sie aussehen soll. allerdings innerhalb eines begrenzten vorgegebenen systems.
man kann das aussehen von räumen damit verändern, die teile sind ähnlich wie bauelemente. von diesen unterscheidet sie der fehlende gebrauchswert und der anspruch, kunst zu sein. ausser diesem anspruch ist alles an ihnen kontrollierbar.

charlotte posenenske

1930 geboren in wiesbaden
1951-52 schilderopleiding in stuttgart
1952-55 decors in lübeck en darmstadt
woont in offenbach am main

tentoonstellingen:
1959 kassel - galerie weiss
1961 frankfurt - galerie loehr
1966 frankfurt - galerie loehr
1967 wiesbaden - städtisches museum
hannover - galerie h
frankfurt - 'dies alles, herzchen, wird einmal dir gehören'
schwenningen - kleine galerie
düsseldorf - galerie fischer
1968 frankfurt - galerie loehr
berlijn - galerie block
neurenberg - kunsthalle
amsterdam - art & project

publikaties:
1967 aujourd'hui jrg.10 no.57-58, blz.161 (+ afb.)
kultermann, u. - neue dimensionen der plastik. tübingen, blz.132 (+ afb.), 226
edition et 'deutschlandreport'
1968 art international jrg.12 no.2, blz.71-72 (+ afb.)
art international jrg.12 no.5, blz.50 (+ afb.)
egoist jrg.4 no.14, blz.39 (+ afb.)

FIGURE 88

FIGURE 89

Daniel Buren (French, b. 1938). *Photo-souvenir: Papiers collés blanc et vert*; work in situ. Installed at Galleria Apollinaire, Milan, October 1968. Paper, glue, dimensions variable. Detail © D.B.-ADAGP Paris. (Photo: Zarini)

As part of the group BMPT (Daniel Buren, Olivier Mosset, Michel Parmentier, and Niele Toroni), who were committed to reducing their individual painting styles to a single, repeatable motif, Daniel Buren adopted stripes, alternating between white and a color, as his sole imagery. By installing the same pattern in a variety of art and non-art spaces, Buren focused on the significance of context in interpretive understanding. Questioning the primacy of the gallery as the ideal venue for art, Buren barred entry to his first gallery exhibition by sealing the front door with one of his signature green and white pasted paper works, forcing the art and the viewer to remain on the street, where their interaction would be less predictable.

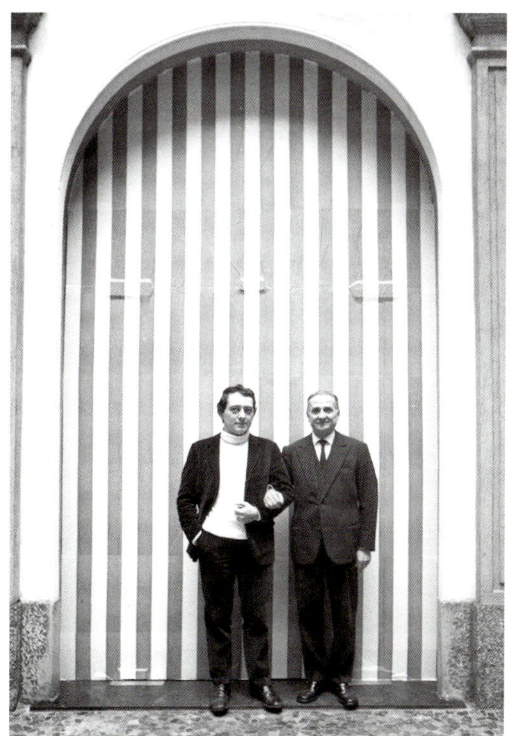

FIGURES 90, 91: As artists were challenging museums and collectors with their disruption of every remotely standard definition of art, they also began engaging with larger social and political issues, galvanized by the groundswell of opposition to the Vietnam War. One pragmatic approach to joining art and politics was taken by Lippard when she co-organized the exhibition *Benefit for the Student Mobilization Committee to End the War in Vietnam* at the newly opened Paula Cooper Gallery in SoHo. Thanks to Lippard's combination of curatorial activity and activism, sales of Minimalist-inspired works like Jo Baer's *Untitled* (1967) could lend support to the growing antiwar movement in spite of their lack of overt political content.

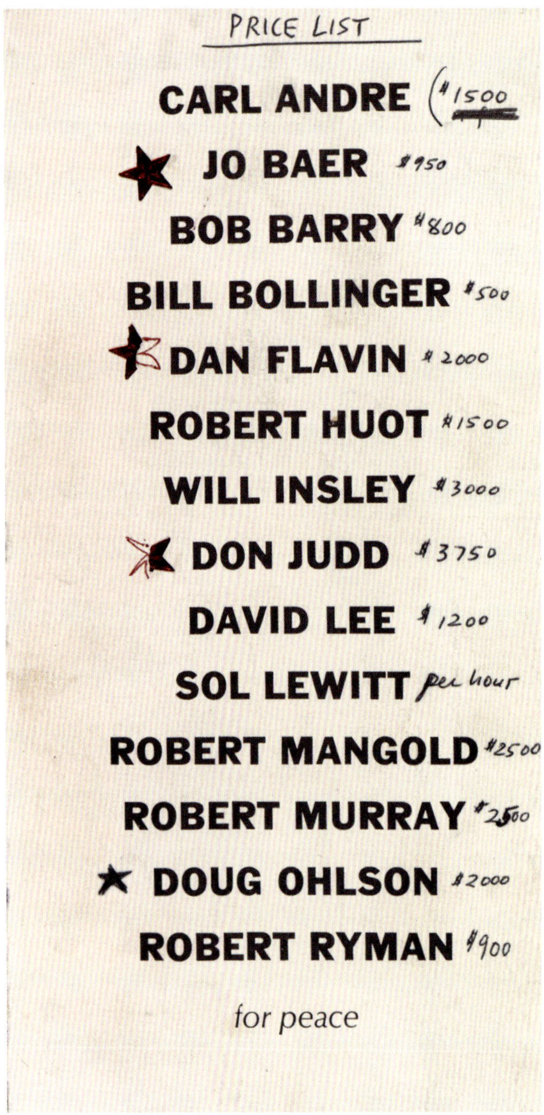
PRICE LIST

CARL ANDRE $1500
JO BAER $950
BOB BARRY $800
BILL BOLLINGER $500
DAN FLAVIN $2000
ROBERT HUOT $1500
WILL INSLEY $3000
DON JUDD $3750
DAVID LEE $1200
SOL LEWITT per hour
ROBERT MANGOLD $2500
ROBERT MURRAY $2500
DOUG OHLSON $2000
ROBERT RYMAN $900

for peace

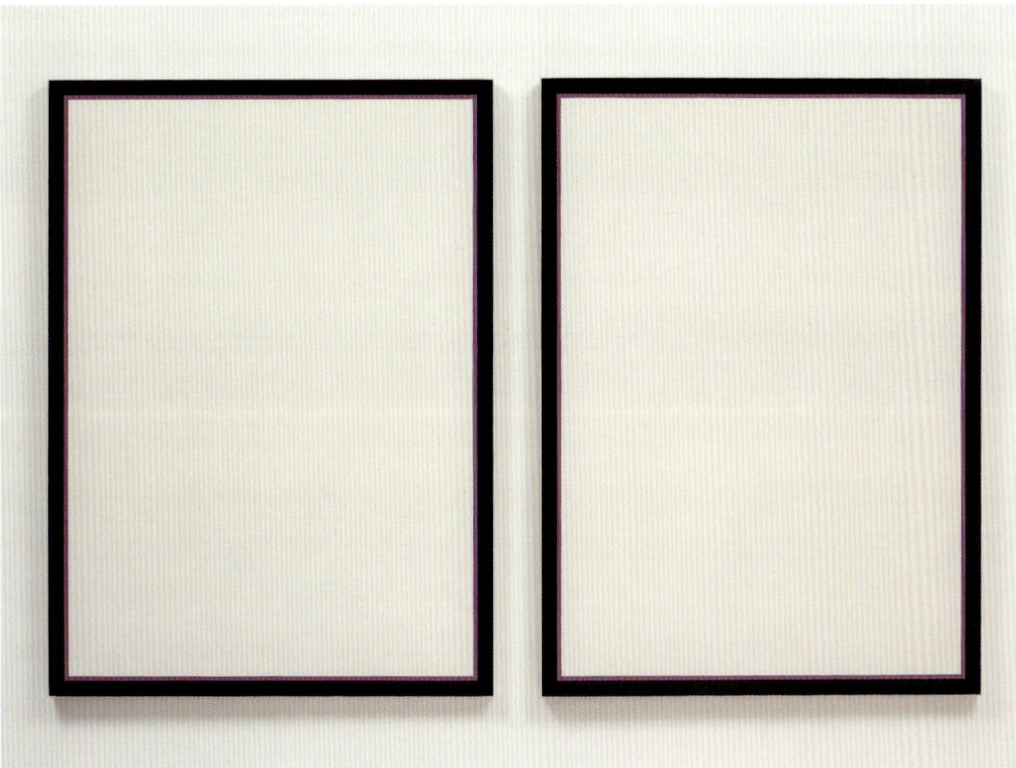

FIGURE 90

Price list for *Benefit for the Student Mobilization Committee to End the War in Vietnam*, 1968. Printed sheet with handmarked notes, approx. 7 × 4 in. (17.8 × 10.2 cm). Lucy R. Lippard Papers, Archives of American Art, Smithsonian Institution, Washington, D.C.

FIGURE 91

Jo Baer (American, b. 1929). *Untitled*, 1967. Oil on canvas: two panels, 60 × 43 in. (152.4 × 109.2 cm) each. The Museum of Contemporary Art, Los Angeles; Gift of Lannan Foundation. © Jo Baer

FIGURE 92

Installation view of *Tucumán Arde (Tucumán Is Burning)* at CGTA (Workers General Confederation of Argentina) Trade Offices, Rosario, Argentina, 1968; organized by the Rosario Group. Archivo Graciela Carnevale, Rosario, Argentina, © Grupo de Artistas de Vanguardia. (Photo: Grupo de Artistas de Vanguardia)

As a continuation of their activities linking avant-garde art practices with political activism, the Rosario Group worked with Argentina's main trade union to organize this participatory exhibition. Seeking to use art as a means for real social change, the group employed a variety of artistic and educational strategies to bring attention to the living conditions of workers in the Tucumán province.

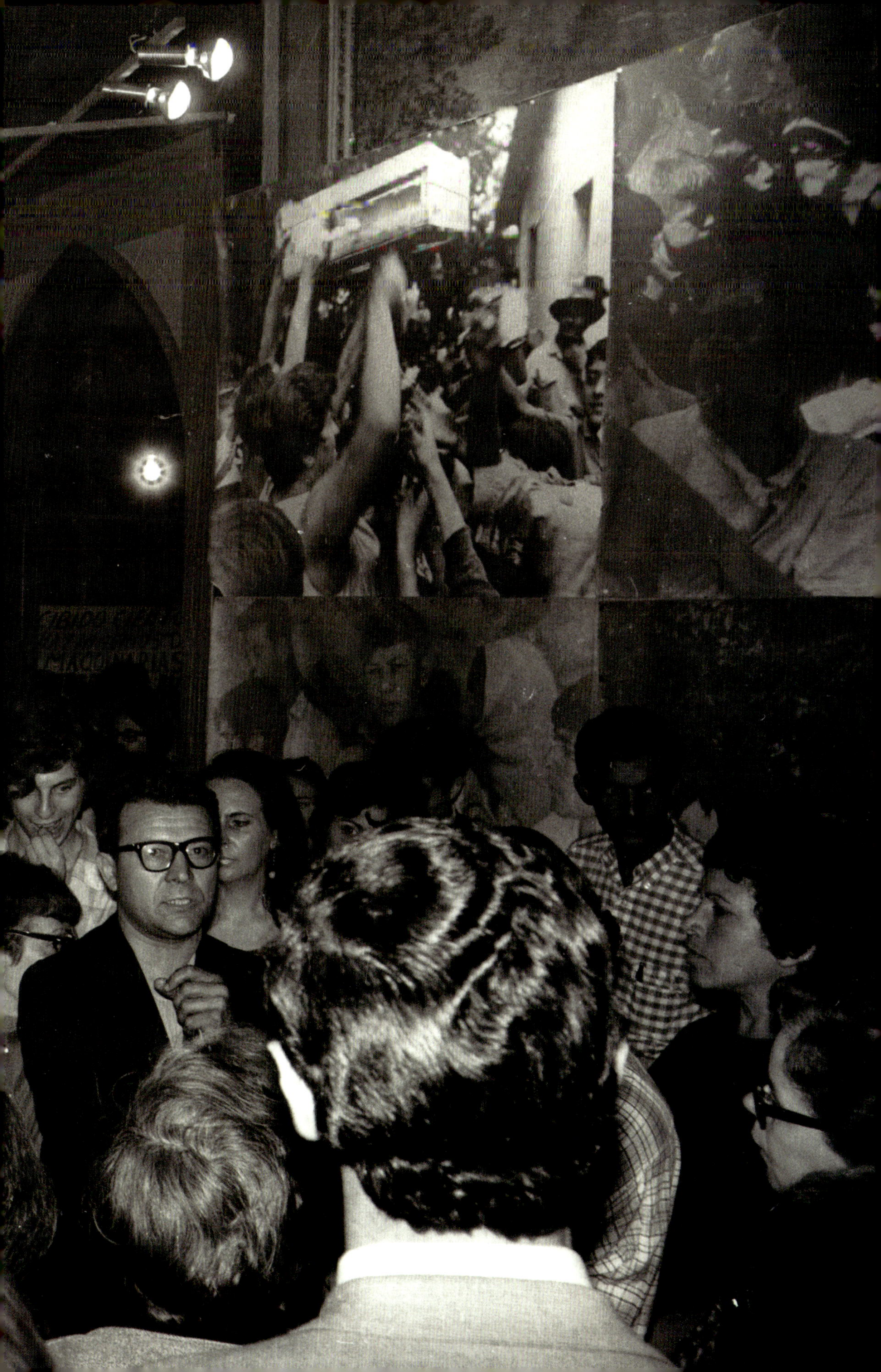

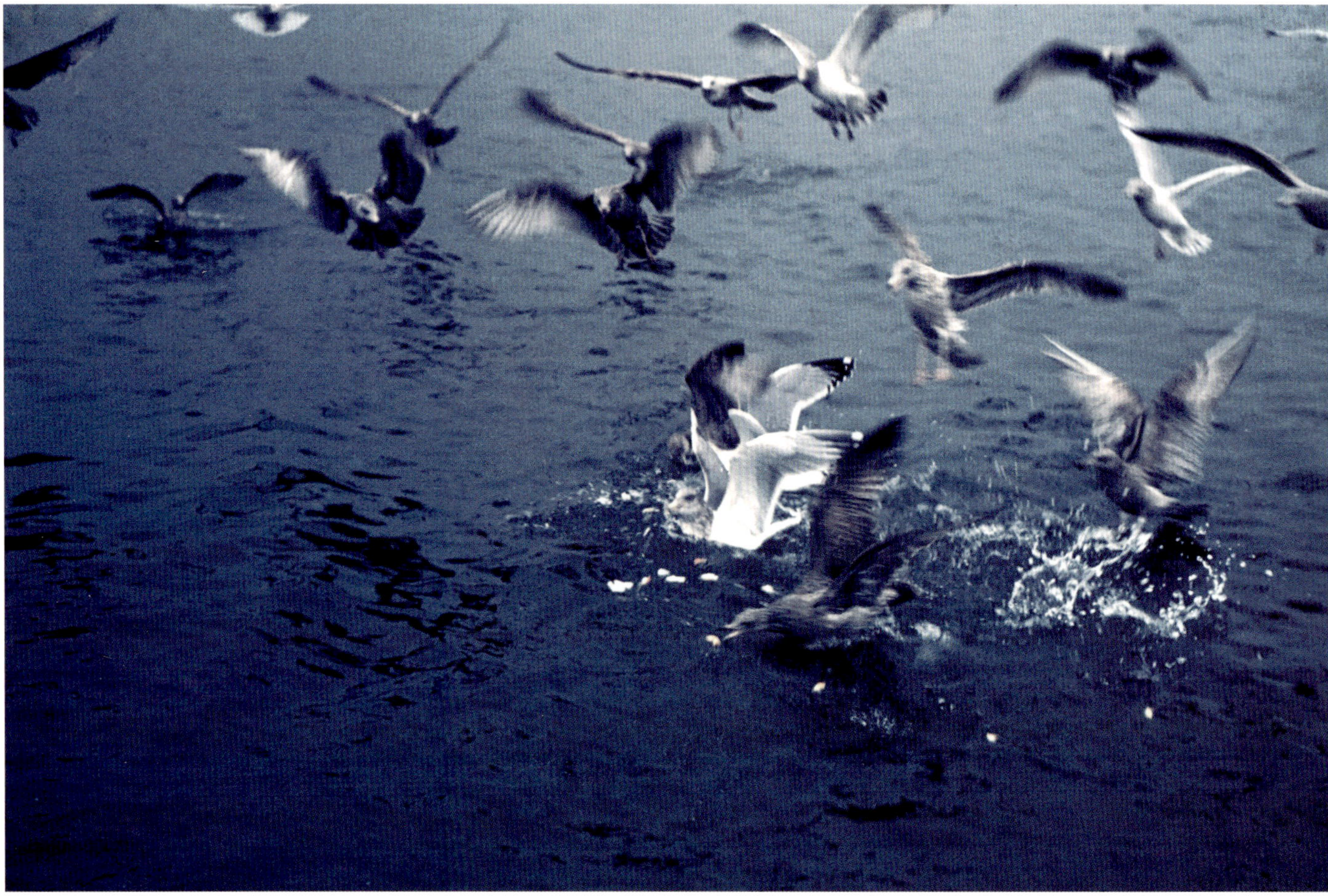

FIGURE 93

Hans Haacke (American, b. Germany, 1936). *Live Airborne System, November 30, 1968*, planned 1965, executed 1968: seagulls, breadcrumbs; Coney Island, New York. © Hans Haacke/Artists Rights Society (ARS). Courtesy Paula Cooper Gallery, New York. (Photo: Hans Haacke)

As artists became politicized by the Vietnam War, they also began scrutinizing the relationships between art institutions and larger economic and political power structures. Museum funders such as trustees, governmental agencies, and charitable foundations became clear targets. Conceptual art tended to address this issue, however, not with work that was stridently political, but rather with projects that emphasize art's non-autonomous status and its interconnectedness with and dependence upon existing social and philosophical structures. Photo-documentation of Haacke's *Live Airborne System* captures the artist's intervention in an ecological system, throwing crumbs to seagulls off a pier in Brooklyn. The system becomes the medium, and the forms produced by the artist's interactions with it become the sculptural object.

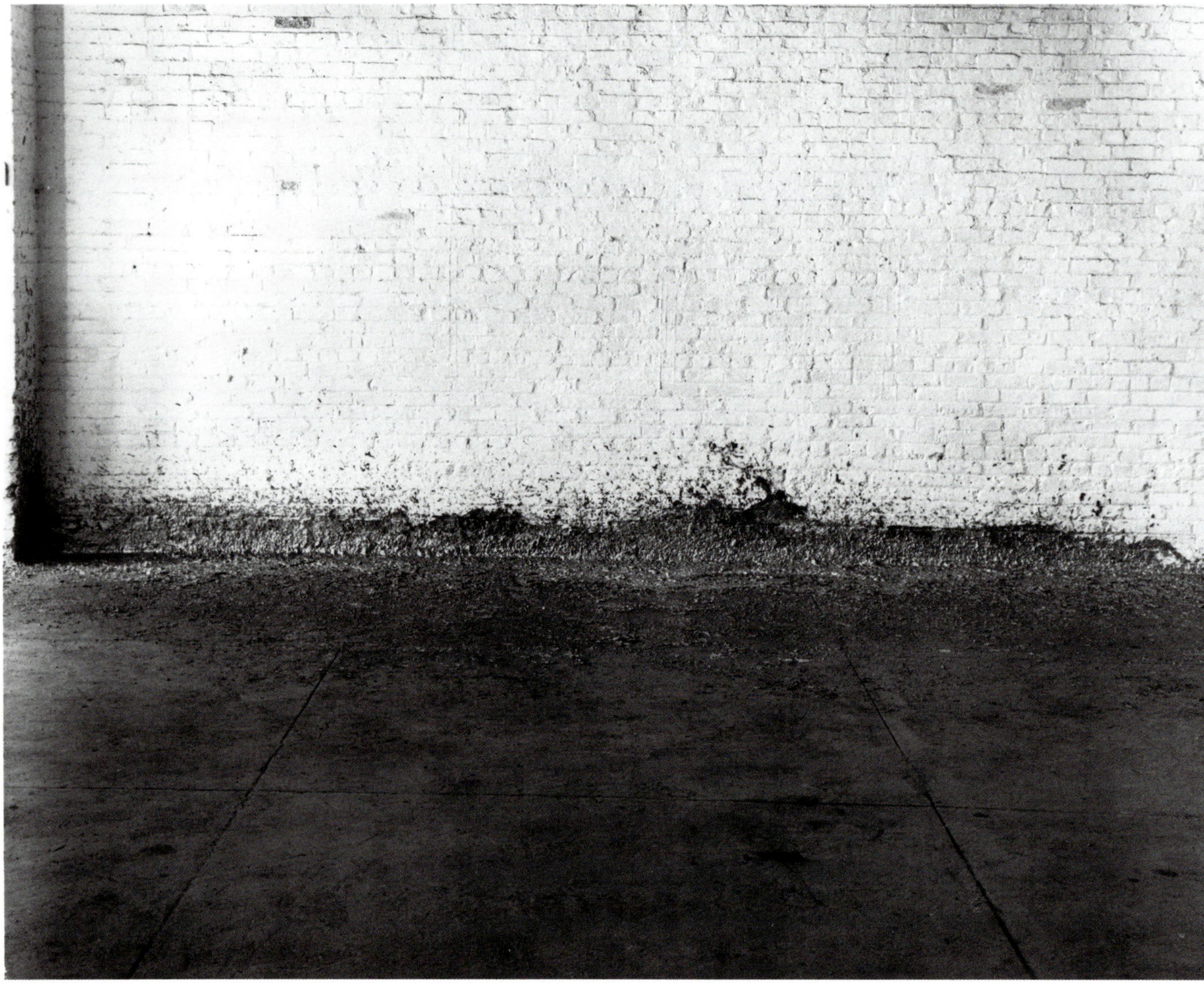

FIGURE 94

Richard Serra (American, b. 1938). *Splashing*, 1968. © 2011 Richard Serra/Artists Rights Society (ARS), New York. (Photo: Richard Serra Studios, New York)

When the sculptor Richard Serra splashed molten lead into the corner where the floor meets the wall he reconfigured salient aspects of both Abstract Expressionism (the gesture of throwing his chosen material is reminiscent of Jackson Pollock's famous technique and the movement's other moniker, action painting) and Minimalism (turning the metal commonly used in solidly hulking Minimal sculpture into a fluid material). He thereby irreverently highlighted the temporality, theatricality, and, perhaps, obsolescence of both.

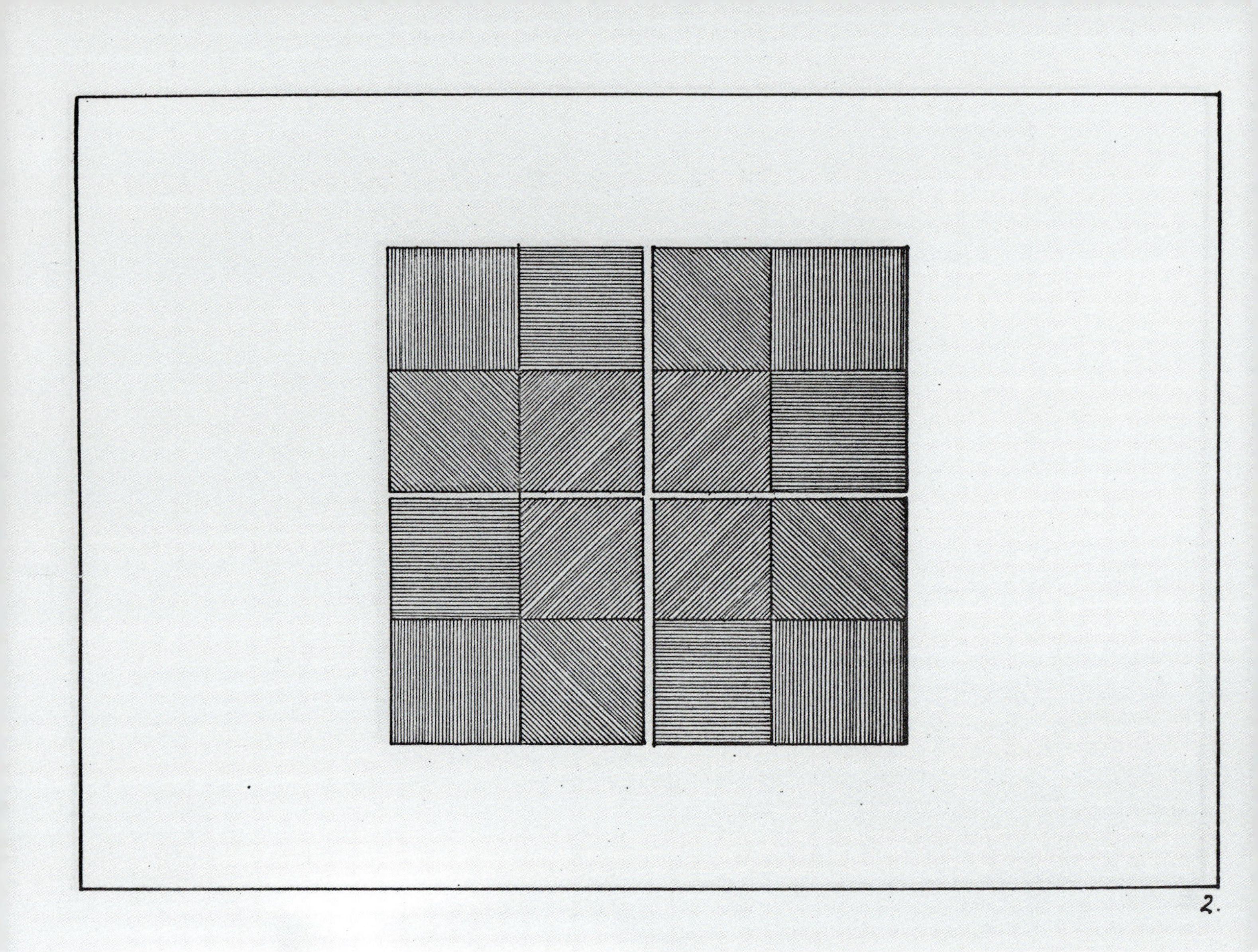

FIGURES 95, 96

Sol LeWitt (American, 1928–2007). Contribution to *Carl Andre, Robert Barry, Douglas Huebler, Joseph Kosuth, Sol LeWitt, Robert Morris, Lawrence Weiner (The Xerox Book)*. Printed book, 8½ × 11 in. (21.6 × 27.9 cm). New York: Siegelaub/Wendler, 1968.

Throughout this period, Seth Siegelaub, an important Lippard collaborator and similarly crucial behind-the-scenes figure in the development of Conceptual art, was conceiving of new forms for his role as a dealer and gallerist. With projects like *The Xerox Book*, in which each of the seven invited artists was given twenty-five pages to produce work, Siegelaub rejected the necessity of a physical gallery and became a dealer through printed matter alone.

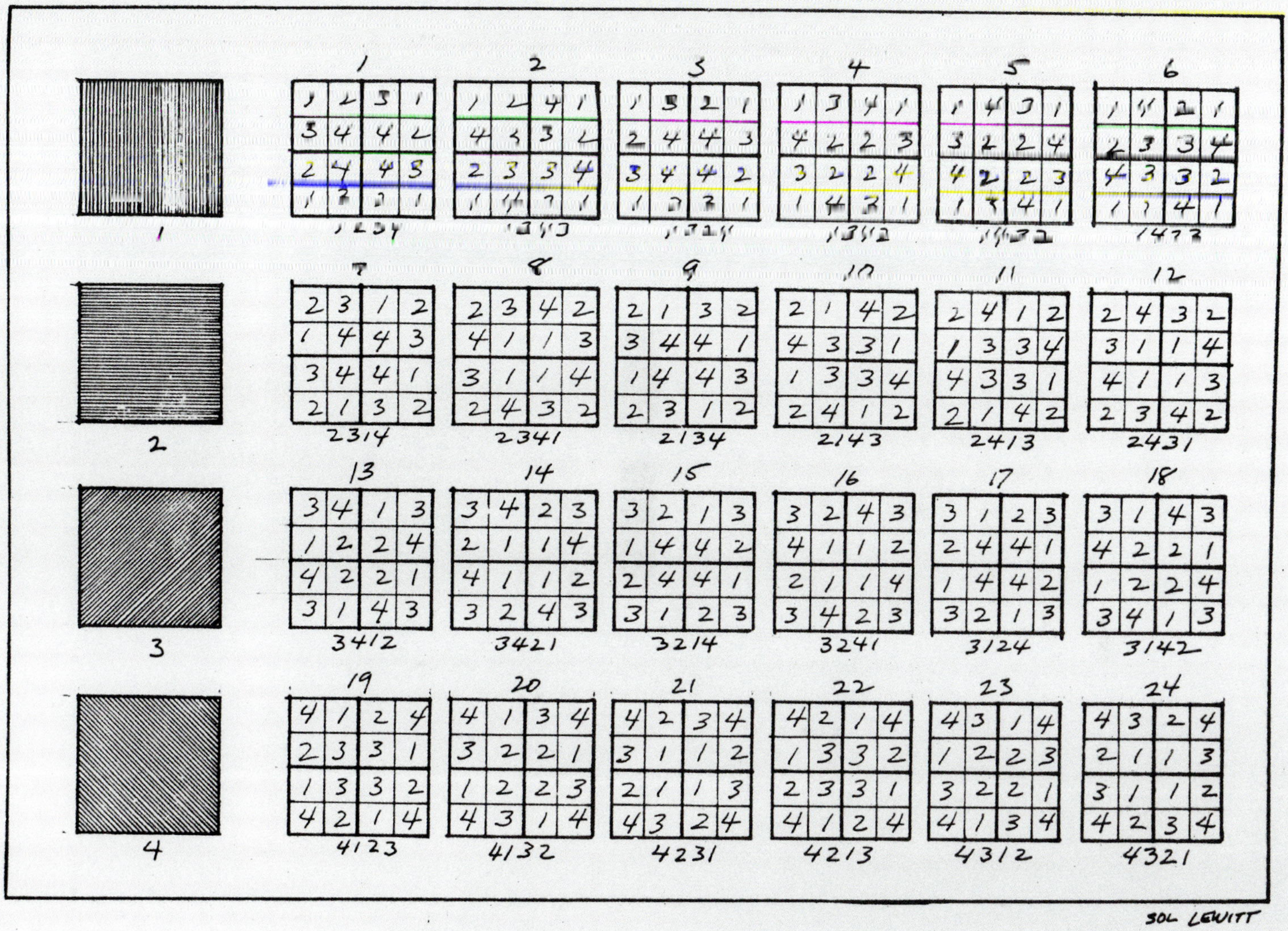

FIGURES 97–99: Nineteen sixty-nine was the watershed year for the Conceptual art movement. Work that three years earlier would have been dismissed as intellectual tinkering or creative gamesmanship had become part of an accepted dialogue within the field. Its effects were felt within museums and institutions as its methods were adopted by more artists and professionals in the field. The traditional means for presenting work continued to seem ineffective, and artists and exhibition organizers further scrutinized, manipulated, and rethought how to disseminate their work. Siegelaub, who briefly became one of the most active gallerists supporting Conceptual artists, functioned as a publisher, distributor, and promoter, proclaiming his "show," *January 5–31, 1969*, to be the first exhibition to exist solely in the form of a catalogue. As he wrote in the press release, "The exhibition consists of (the ideas communicated in) the catalog; the physical presence (of the work) is supplementary to the catalog." Even so, artworks were present in the gallery, either visually undetectable, such as Robert Barry's ultrasonic waves, which "filled" the space; or partially represented, as in Kosuth's project, which placed ads in major newspapers, sample copies of which were tacked to the wall though the actual work remained in circulation.

FIGURE 97

Publicity photograph of the artists in *January 5–31, 1969: Barry, Huebler, Kosuth, Weiner,* held at The McLendon Building, 44 East 52nd Street, New York; organized by Seth Siegelaub. Seth Siegelaub Papers, The Museum of Modern Art Archives, New York. (Digital image: © The Museum of Modern Art/Licensed by SCALA/Art Resource, NY)

FIGURE 98

Installation view of *January 5–31, 1969: Barry, Huebler, Kosuth, Weiner,* including Joseph Kosuth, *The Second Investigation,* 1968–69 (right wall). Seth Siegelaub Papers, The Museum of Modern Art Archives, New York. (Digital image: © The Museum of Modern Art/Licensed by SCALA/Art Resource, NY)

1969

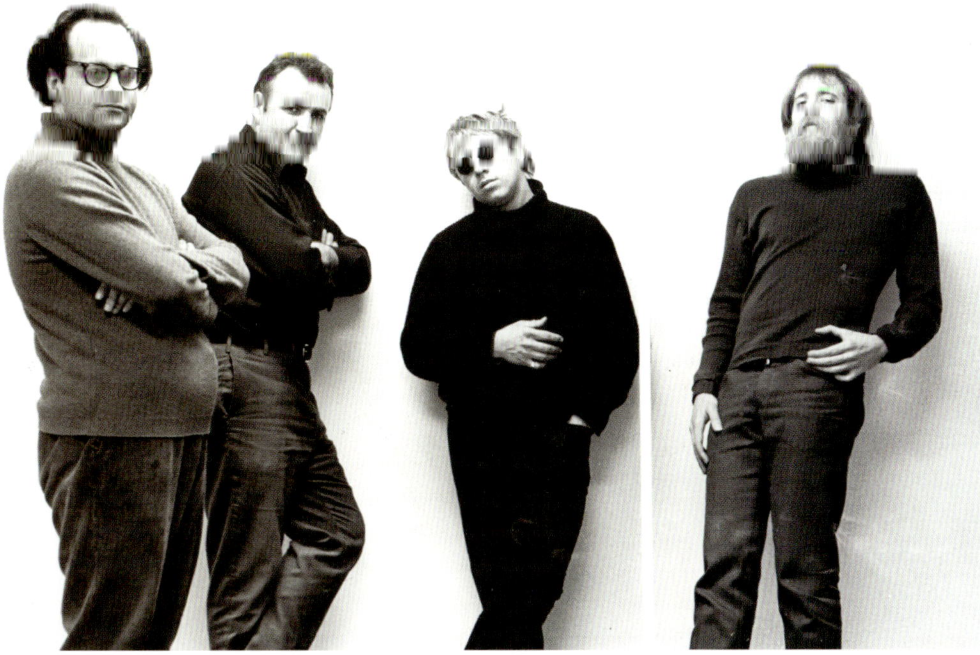

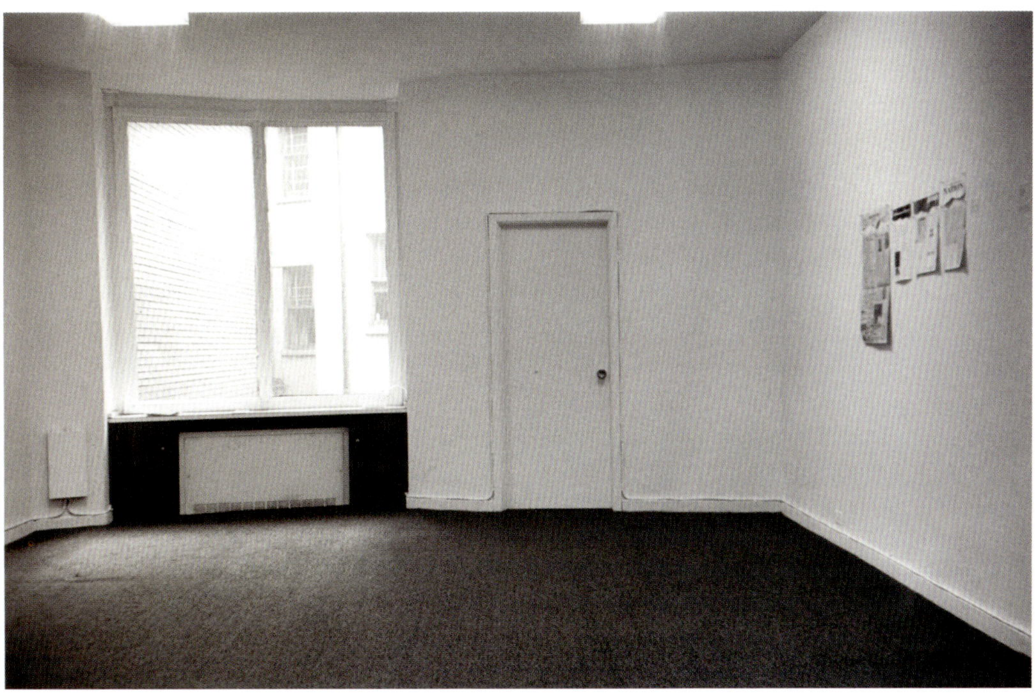

FIGURE 99

Installation view of *January 5–31, 1969: Barry, Huebler, Kosuth, Weiner*, with temporary receptionist Adrian Piper. Seth Siegelaub Papers, The Museum of Modern Art Archives, New York. (Digital image: © The Museum of Modern Art/Licensed by SCALA/Art Resource, NY)

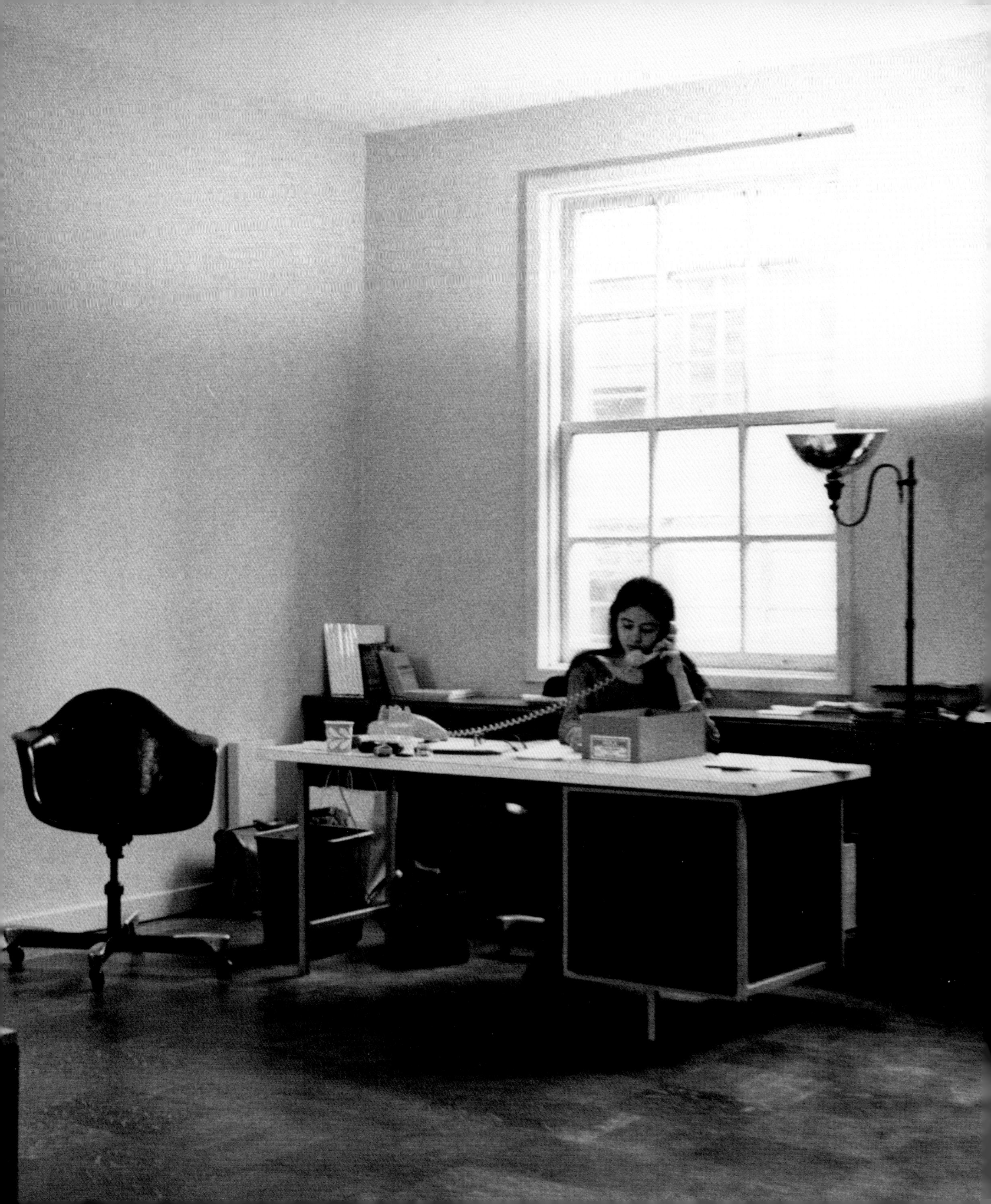

("QUOTE"): SOUND OF "DAISY" FADING IN BACKGROUND FOLLOWED BY SOUND OF "ALSO SPRACH ZARATHUSTRA" (R. STRAUSS) FOLLOWED BY SOUND OF "THE BLUE DANUBE" (J. STRAUSS) – SOUNDTRACK, <u>2001</u> (S. KUBRICK)

<u>GENERAL STRIKE PIECE</u> (STARTED FEB. 8, 69)*

GRADUALLY BUT DETERMINEDLY AVOID BEING PRESENT AT OFFICIAL OR PUBLIC "UPTOWN" FUNCTIONS OR GATHERINGS† RELATED TO THE "ART WORLD" IN ORDER TO PURSUE INVESTIGATION OF <u>TOTAL PERSONAL & PUBLIC REVOLUTION</u>.♀ EXHIBIT IN PUBLIC ONLY <u>PIECES</u> WHICH FURTHER SHARING OF IDEAS & INFORMATION RELATED TO <u>TOTAL PERSONAL & PUBLIC REVOLUTION</u>.§

IN PROCESS AT LEAST THROUGH SUMMER, '69.⊕

* WITHDRAWAL FROM 3-~~MAN~~ ARTIST SHOW COMPILED BY RICHARD BELLAMY, GOLDOWSKY GALLERY, 1078 MADISON AVE.

† DATE OF LAST VISIT TO UPTOWN GALLERIES FOR PERUSAL OF ART – FEB. 13 OR 14, 69
" " " " " A MUSEUM – MARCH 24, 69
" " " " " UPTOWN GALLERY OPENING – MARCH 15, 69
" " " " " A BAR – APRIL 5, 69
" " " ATTENDANCE AT A CONCERT – APRIL 18, 69
" " " " " " FILM SHOWING – APRIL 4, 69
" " " " " AN "EVENT" – APRIL 18, 69
" " " " " A BIG PARTY – MARCH 15, 69

♀ TERMS OF <u>TOTAL PERSONAL & PUBLIC REVOLUTION</u> SET FORTH IN BRIEF STATEMENT READ AT OPEN PUBLIC HEARING, <u>ART WORKERS COALITION</u>, SCHOOL OF VISUAL ARTS, APRIL 10, 69. FURTHER PARTICIPATION IN <u>ART WORKERS COALITION</u> OR ANY OTHER GROUP DECLINED AS PART OF <u>GENERAL STRIKE PIECE</u>. THIS INCLUDES <u>ARTISTS AGAINST THE EXPRESSWAY</u> GROUP & OTHERS.

§ FIRST <u>PIECE</u> EXHIBITED AT ART/PEACE EVENT, N.Y. SHAKESPEARE FESTIVAL, PUBLIC THEATER, MARCH 5, 69. <u>GRASS PIECE</u> & <u>NO-GRASS PIECE</u> EXHIBITED IN NUMBER 7 SHOW COMPILED BY LUCY LIPPARD, PAULA COOPER, MAY 18, 69. <u>INVESTMENT PIECE</u> & <u>CASH PIECE</u> EXHIBITED IN LANGUAGE III SHOW, DWAN GALLERY, MAY 24, 69.

⊕ ENDED FALL '69 WHEN SCHIZ SYMPTOMS BEGAN TO APPEAR (<u>ME</u> IN HERE VS. <u>THEM</u> OUT THERE). I STILL REGRET MISSING SOME ART EVENTS THAT TOOK PLACE DURING SPRING '69, & APPEAR TO HAVE ALIENIATED A FEW HUMANS BECAUSE OF MY WITHDRAWAL AT THIS TIME. (<u>JAN 21, 71</u>)

LEE LOZANO, JUNE 12, 69

PUBLISHED IN <u>0 TO 9</u>, NO. 6, JULY, 69, VITO ACCONCI & BERNADETTE MAYER, EDITORS (CARBON COPY)

FIGURE 100

Lee Lozano (American, 1930–1999). *General Strike Piece*, 1969. Xerography, 11 × 8½ in. (27.9 × 21.6 cm). The Wadsworth Atheneum Museum, Hartford.

In the late 1960s, Lee Lozano began writing "pieces" that turned decisions from her personal life into artworks, such as *No Title (Grass Piece)* (figure 28), in which she instructed herself to smoke as much marijuana as possible over a set period of time, or *General Strike Piece*, in which she determined to withdraw permanently from the art world

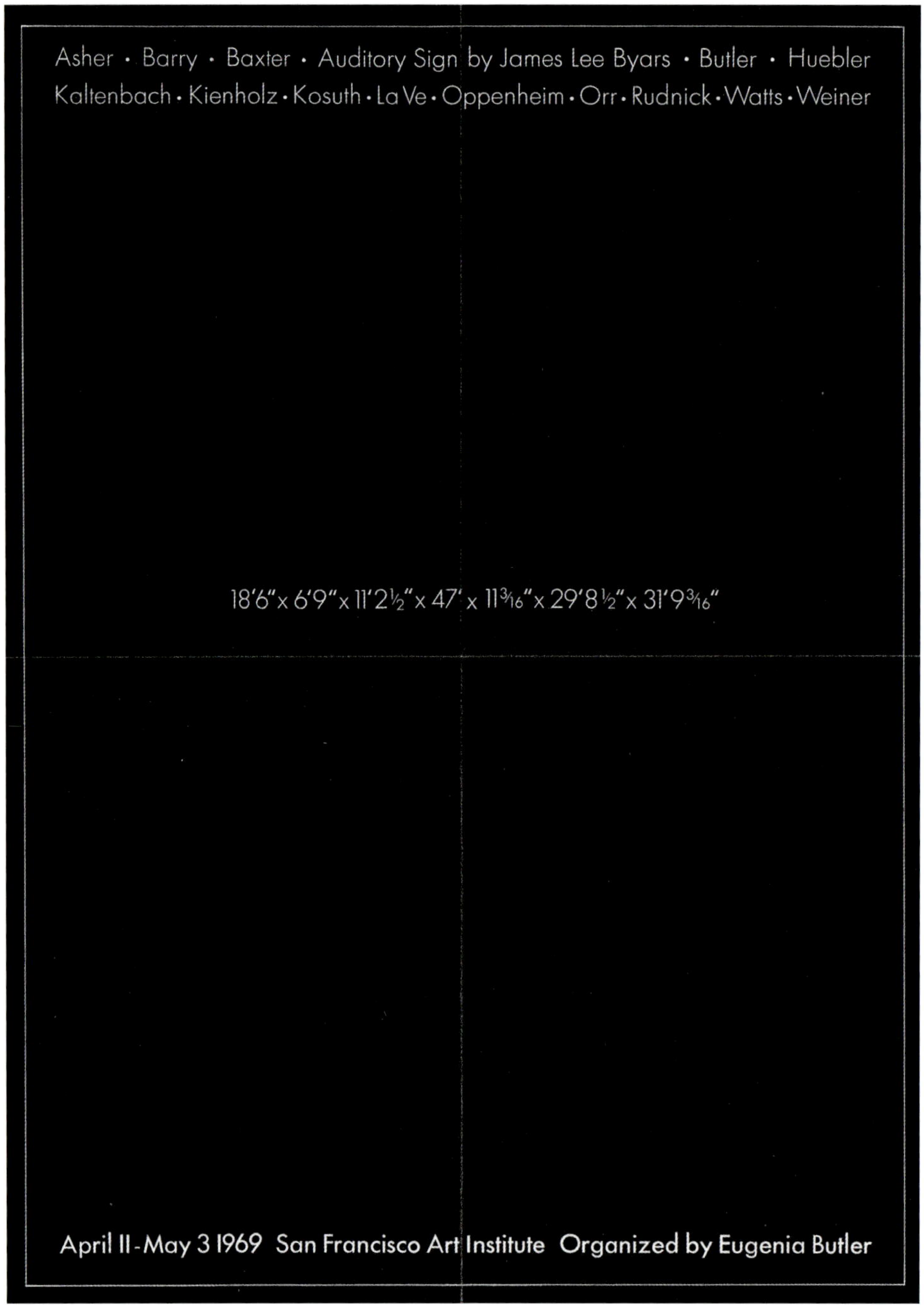

FIGURE 101

Poster for *18′6″ × 6′9″ × 11′2½″ × 47′ × 11³⁄₁₆″ × 29′8½″ × 31′9³⁄₁₆″*, 1969. Offset lithograph, 20 × 14 in. (50.8 × 35.6 cm). San Francisco Art Institute Archives. (Photo: San Francisco Art Institute)

As one of the few people willing to show this kind of work on the West Coast, Eugenia Butler, an artist herself, also became an important champion of Conceptual art as a curator and gallerist. Her exhibition at the San Francisco Art Institute was an early opportunity for Los Angeles–based artists like Michael Asher to be seen alongside their New York colleagues.

FIGURES 102, 103: Reviving the model used a year earlier to benefit the Student Mobilization Committee to End the War in Vietnam, Lippard organized the exhibition *Number 7* at the Paula Cooper Gallery, this time as a fundraiser for the Art Workers' Coalition (AWC), a group with which Lippard was closely involved. The AWC sought to galvanize artists, politicized by larger national and international issues, to address power inequities within the art world itself. *Number 7* was a more dematerialized exhibition than the first fundraiser, as Castoro's contribution indicates.

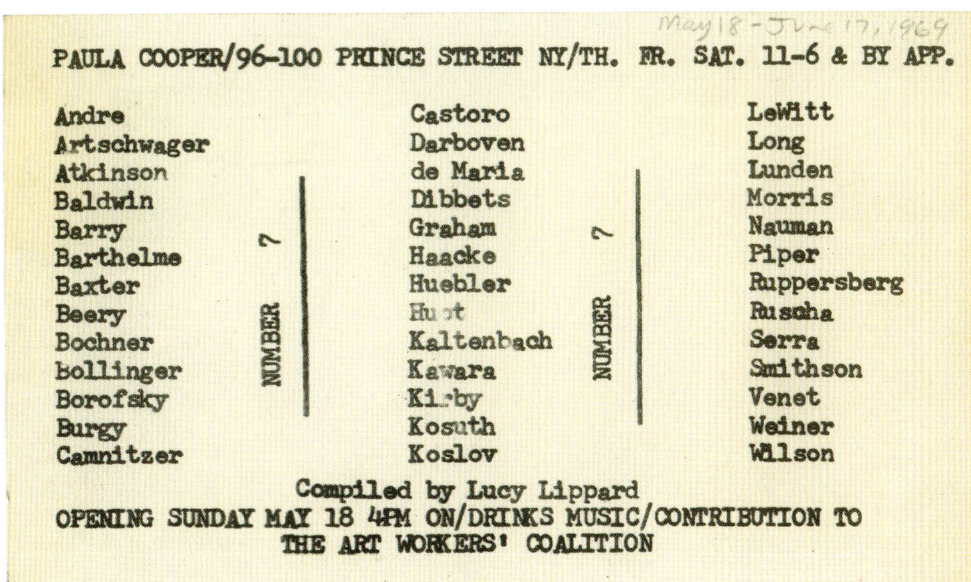

May 18 - June 17, 1969

PAULA COOPER/96-100 PRINCE STREET NY/TH. FR. SAT. 11-6 & BY APP.

Andre
Artschwager
Atkinson
Baldwin
Barry
Barthelme
Baxter
Beery
Bochner
Bollinger
Borofsky
Burgy
Camnitzer

NUMBER 7

Castoro
Darboven
de Maria
Dibbets
Graham
Haacke
Huebler
Huot
Kaltenbach
Kawara
Kirby
Kosuth
Koslov

NUMBER 7

LeWitt
Long
Lunden
Morris
Nauman
Piper
Ruppersberg
Ruscha
Serra
Smithson
Venet
Weiner
Wilson

Compiled by Lucy Lippard
OPENING SUNDAY MAY 18 4PM ON/DRINKS MUSIC/CONTRIBUTION TO
THE ART WORKERS' COALITION

FIGURE 102
Announcement card for *Number 7*, 1969. Printed card, 3¼ × 5½ in. (8.3 × 14 cm). © Paula Cooper Gallery, New York

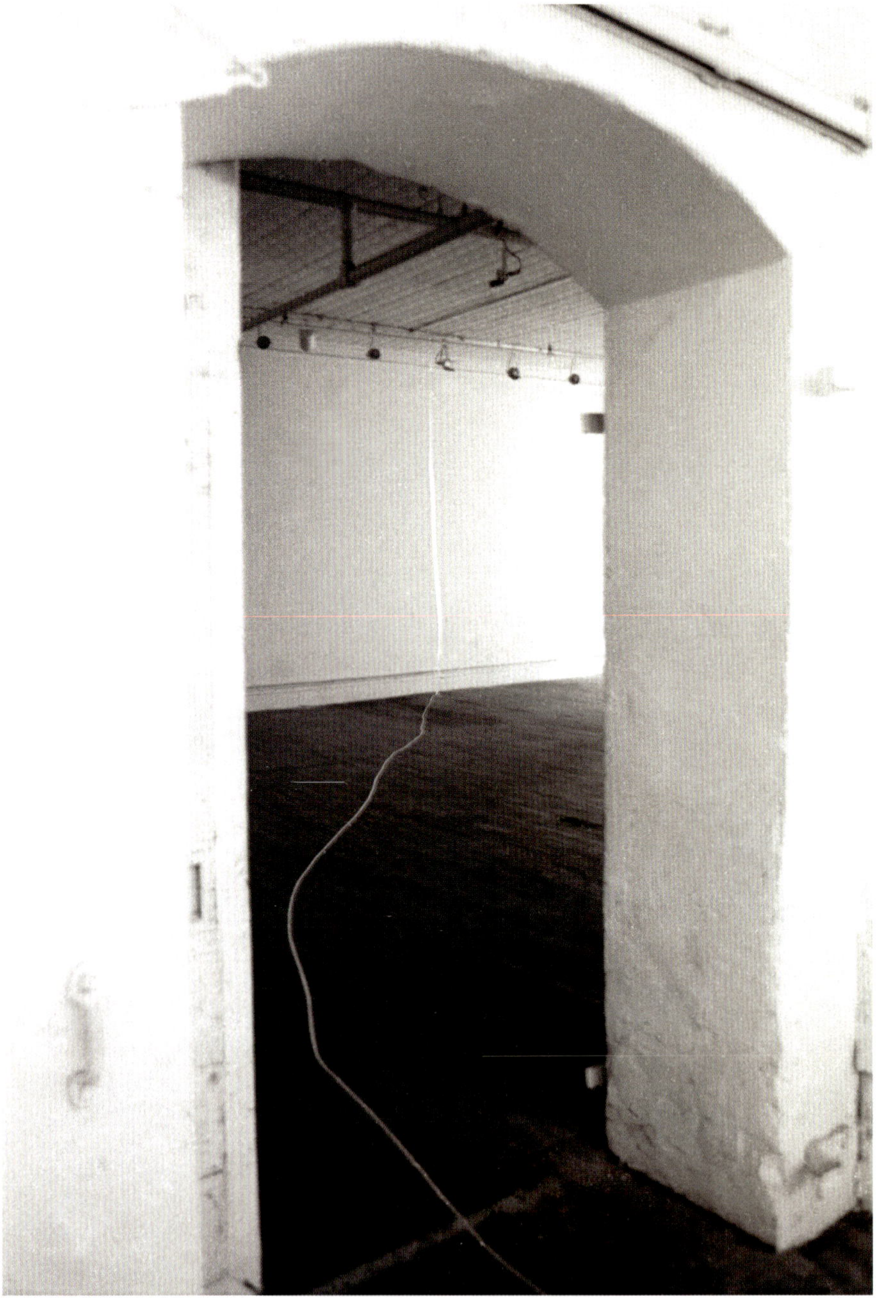

FIGURE 103

Rosemarie Castoro (American, b. 1939). *Room Cracking #7*, 1969. Installation piece for *Number 7* at Paula Cooper Gallery, New York. Collection of Rosemarie Castoro, courtesy Hal Bromm Gallery, New York. © Rosemarie Castoro. (Photo: Rosemarie Castoro)

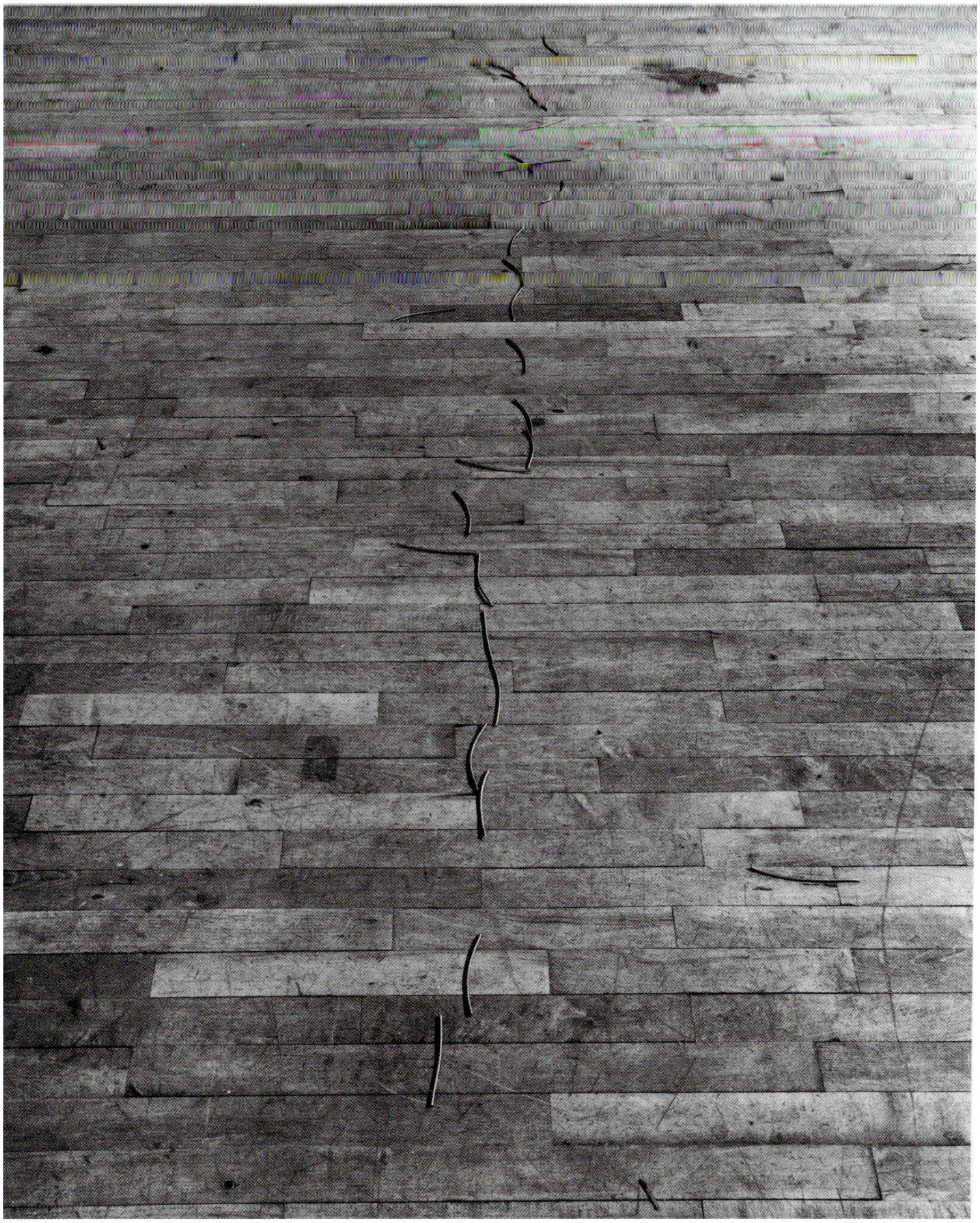

FIGURE 104

Carl Andre (American, b. 1935). *Portrait of Richard Long*, 1969. Cut wire, 24-unit line; approx. 6 in. (15.2 cm) each unit; approx. 144 in. (365.8 cm) overall. © Carl Andre/Licensed by VAGA, New York, NY. Courtesy Paula Cooper Gallery, New York

In this work, Andre, a leading Minimalist sculptor known for his repetitive use of machine-made building materials, pays tribute to the more idiosyncratic and ephemeral engagement with the environment explored by the British artist Richard Long, whose sculptures often consisted of the subtle displacement of grass or sticks as he walked, an impermanent impression that could be shared with an audience only through photographic documentation.

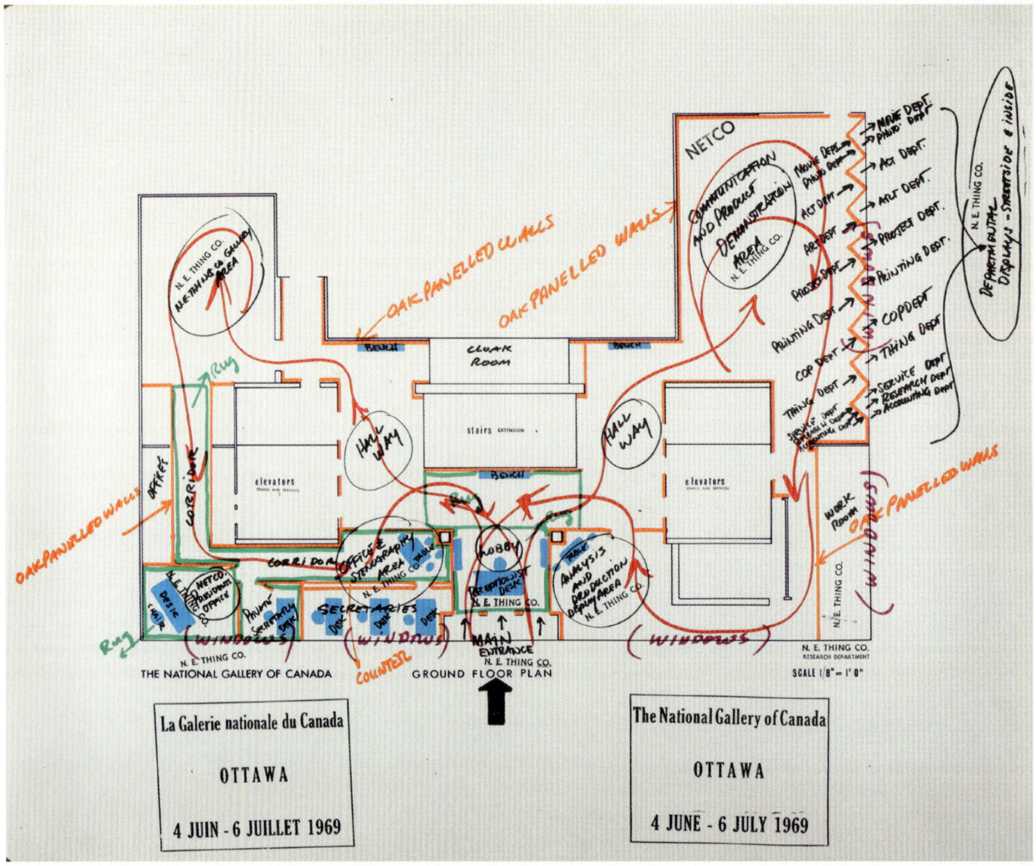

FIGURE 105

N. E. Thing Co. (Iain Baxter& [Canadian, b. England, 1936] and Ingrid Baxter [American, b. 1938]). Poster for *Look/Voyez*, 1969. Offset lithograph, 24 × 29 in. (60.7 × 73.7 cm). Collection of Alan Cravitz, Chicago

Founded in 1966 by Iain and Ingrid Baxter, the Vancouver-based N. E. Thing Co. used a variety of methods to investigate the permeation of technocratic, corporate, and consumer culture into all aspects of daily life, including art. For their exhibition at the National Gallery of Canada, they transformed the museum's first floor into a corporate environment complete with a "president's office" and "oak panelled walls," as noted on the floor plan that served as the exhibition poster.

FIGURES 106, 107

Gilbert & George (Gilbert, b. 1943; George, b. 1942). *Underneath the Arches*, 1969. A Living Sculpture. © Gilbert & George

After graduating from St. Martins School of Art, London, where they met, Gilbert & George presented themselves as "Living Sculptures," moving mechanically while singing the sentimental favorite "Underneath the Arches" at an International Jazz festival in the United Kingdom. This life-as-art performance model went on to structure much of their later work.

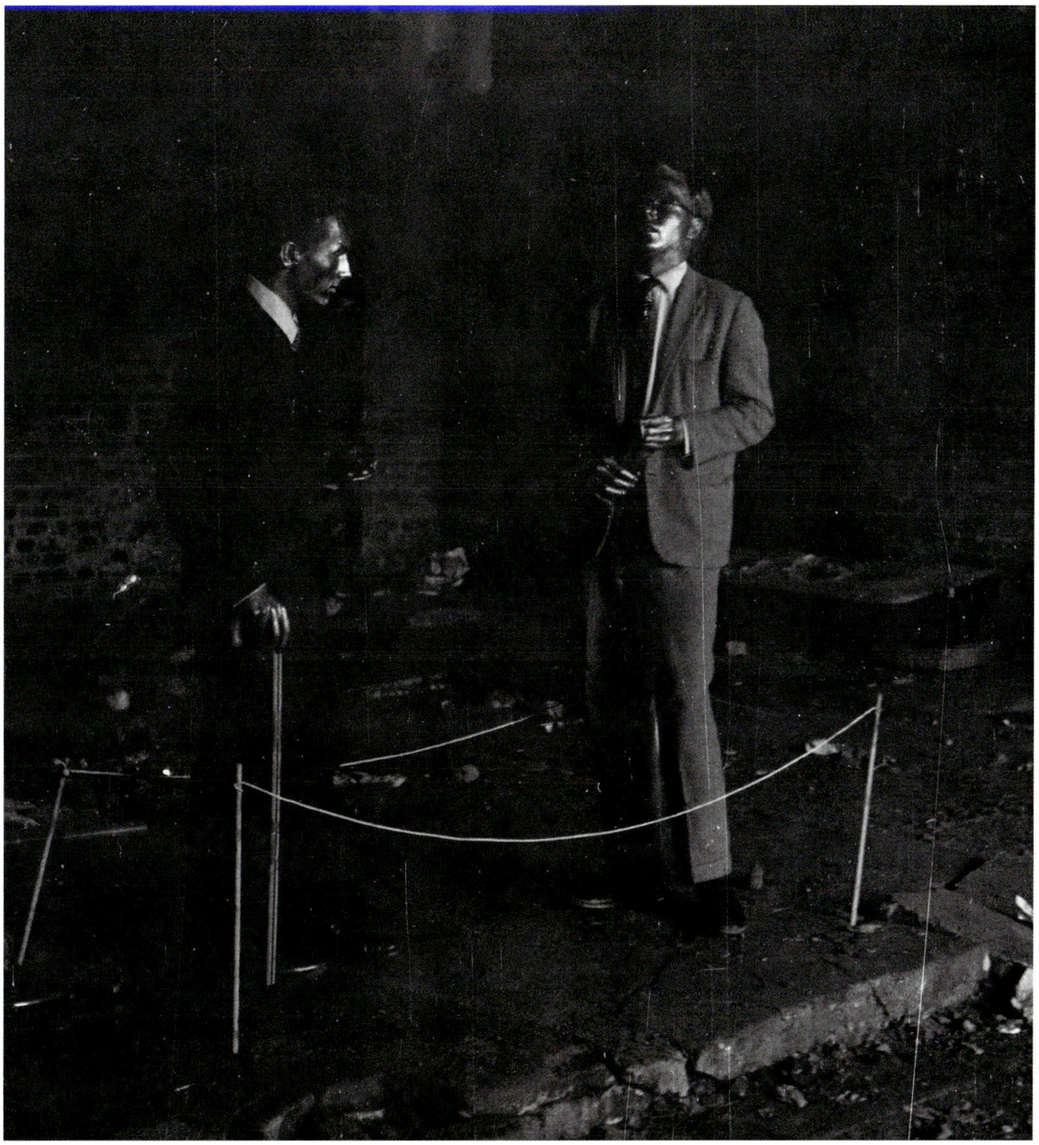

165

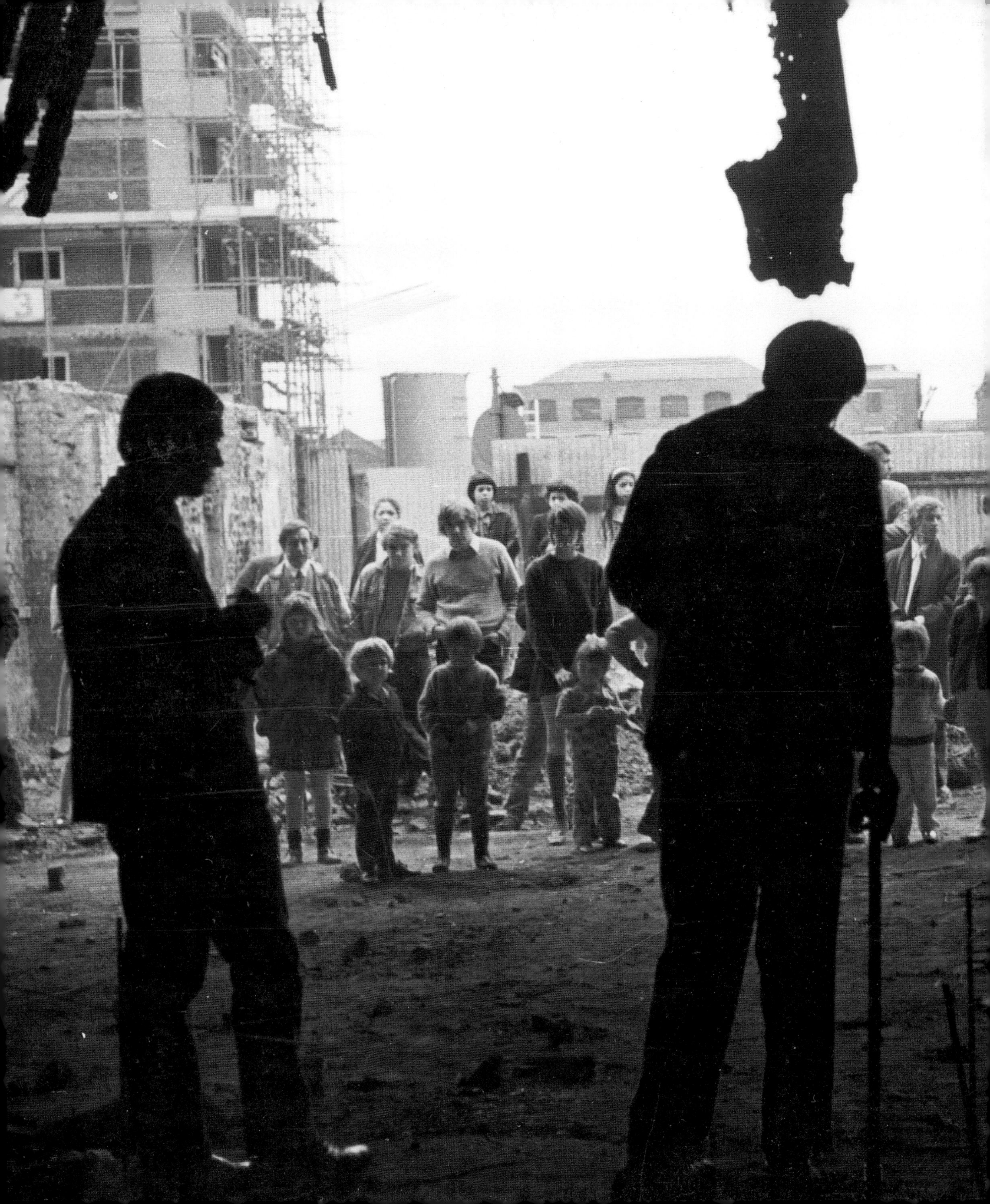

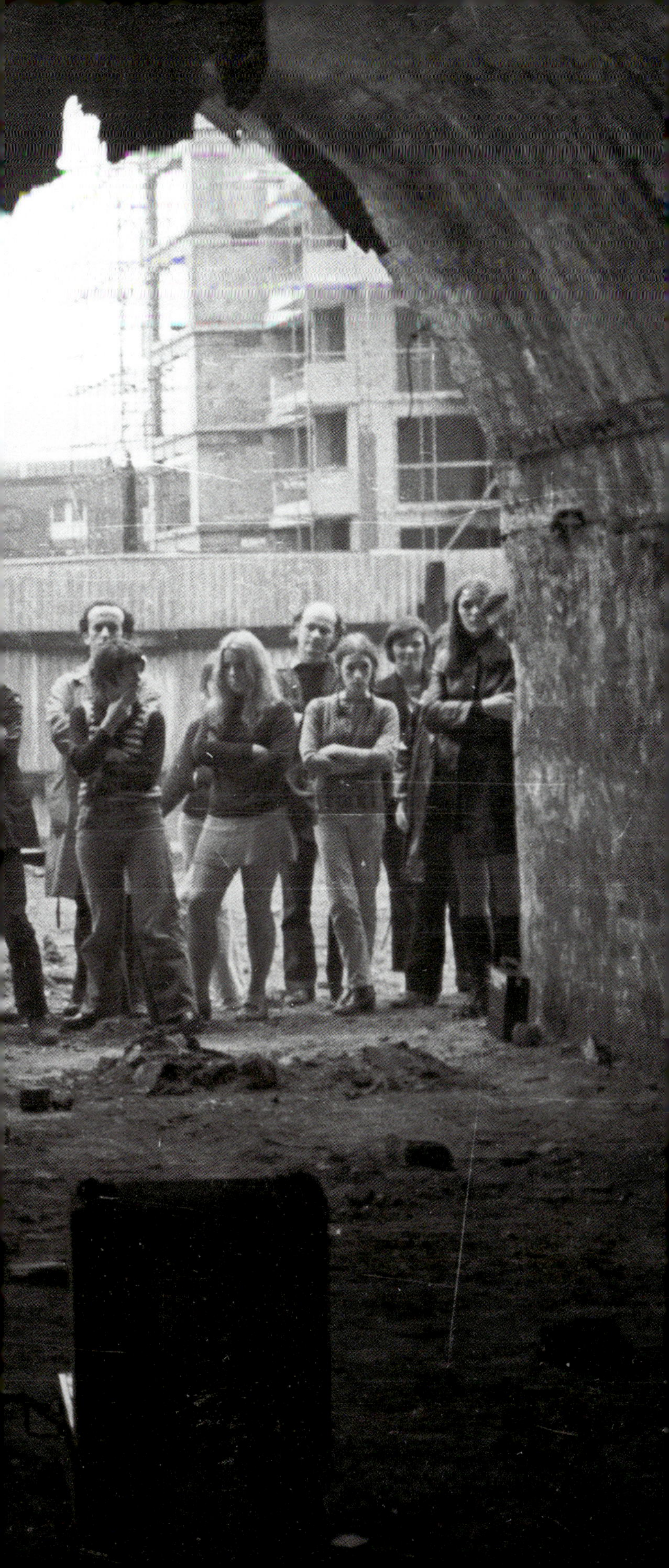

FIGURES 108, 109: Agnes Denes presents the ambition of her thinking in her extended visual exploration of the history of logic in *Exercises in Logic*, which includes *Dialectic Triangulation: A Visual Philosophy*, a component of which is detailed in *Dialectic Triangulation: A Visual Philosophy—The Human Argument*. Inside the triangle are listed all human logical arguments, which, according to the artist, "produce a so-called Truth Table and Lie Table."

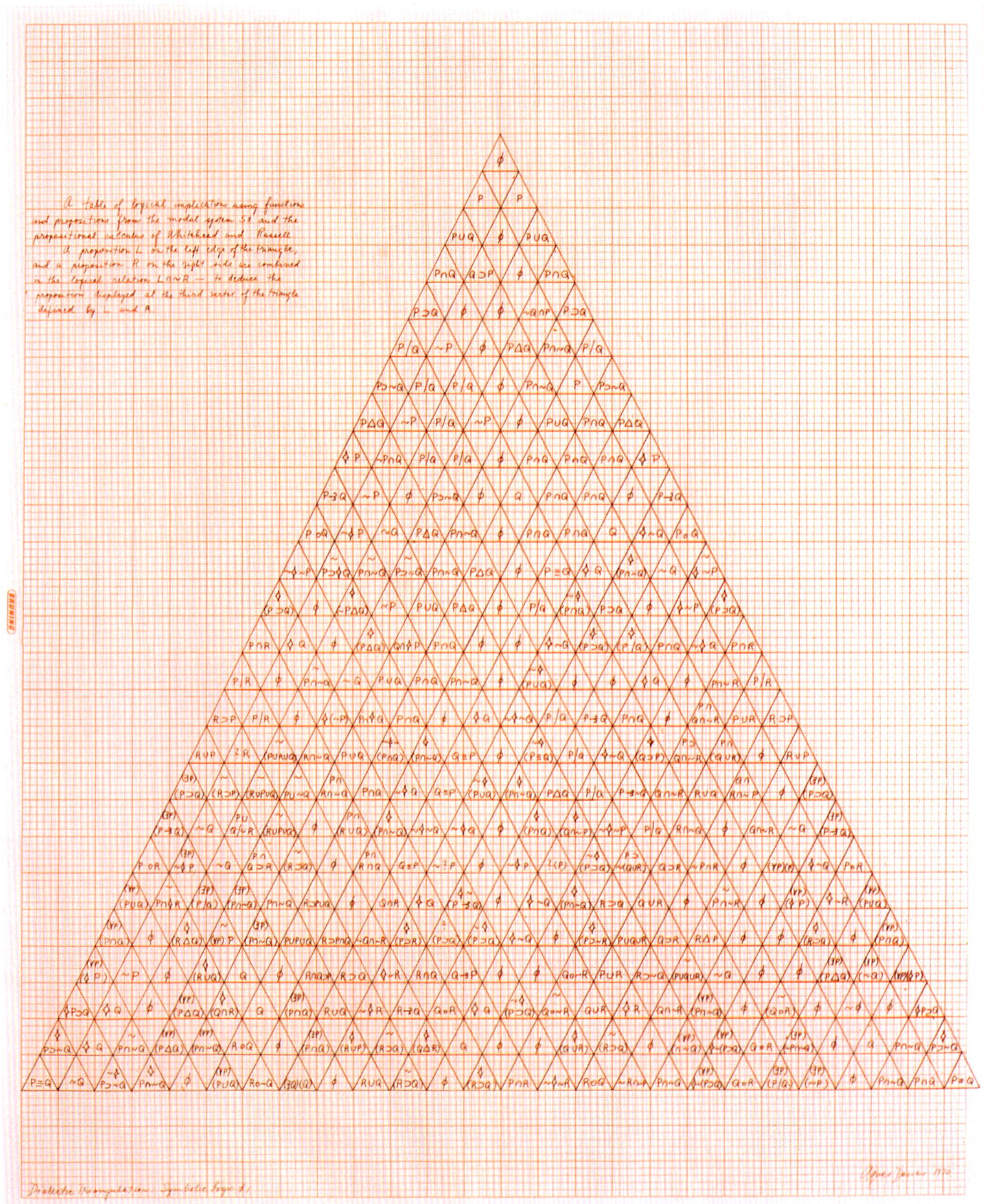

FIGURE 108

Agnes Denes (American, b. 1931). *Dialectic Triangulation: A Visual Philosophy—The Human Argument*, 1969. Drawing on graph paper, 22 × 18 in. (55.9 × 45.7 cm). Collection of Agnes Denes, New York. © Agnes Denes. (Photo: Agnes Denes)

170

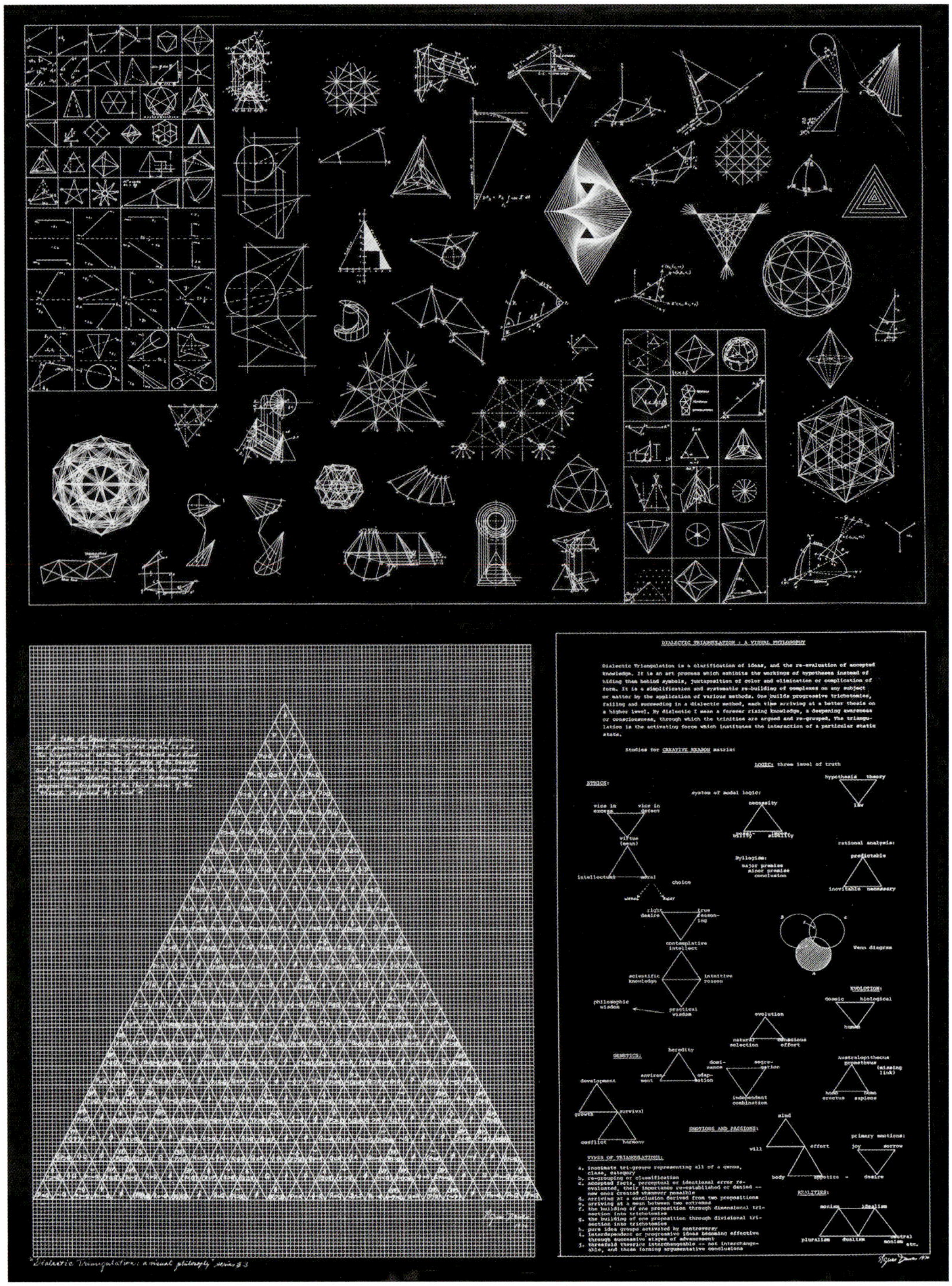
DIALECTIC TRIANGULATION : A VISUAL PHILOSOPHY
Dialectic Triangulation is a clarification of ideas, and the re-evaluation of accepted knowledge. It is an art process which exhibits the workings of hypotheses instead of hiding them behind symbols, juxtaposition of color and elimination or complication of form. It is a simplification and systematic re-building of complexes on any subject or matter by the application of various methods. One builds progressive trichotomies, failing and succeeding in a dialectic method, each time arriving at a better thesis on a higher level. By dialectic I mean a forever rising knowledge, a deepening awareness or consciousness, through which the trinities are argued and re-grouped. The triangulation is the activating force which institutes the interaction of a particular static state.
Studies for CREATIVE REASON matrix:
LOGIC: three level of truth
hypothesis
theory
law
ETHICS:
system of modal logic:
vice in excess
vice in defect
necessity
GENETICS:
heredity
environment
adaptation
development
growth
survival
conflict
harmony
dominance
segregation
independent combination
EMOTIONS AND PASSIONS:
will
body
TYPES OF TRIANGULATIONS:
a. inanimate tri-groups representing all of a genus, class, category
b. re-grouping or classification
c. accepted facts, perceptual or ideational error re-evaluated, their importance re-established or denied -- new ones created whenever possible
d. arriving at a conclusion derived from two propositions
e. arriving at a mean between two extremes
f. the building of one proposition through dimensional tri-section into trichotomies
g. the building of one proposition through divisional tri-section into trichotomies
h. pure idea groups activated by controversy
i. interdependent or progressive ideas becoming effective through successive stages of advancement
j. threefold theories interchangeable -- not interchangeable, and those forming argumentative conclusions

FIGURE 109

Agnes Denes (American, b. 1931). *Dialectic Triangulation: A Visual Philosophy*, 1969. Hand-pulled lithograph on hand-colored rice paper dusted with metallic powders in three colors, 31 × 25 in. (78.7 × 63.5 cm). Collection of Leslie Tonkonow, New York. © Agnes Denes. (Photo: Agnes Denes)

FIGURES 110–119: Lippard's curatorial and critical experiments expanded as she redefined her role, acting as mediator, collaborator, and producer, rather than connoisseur and gatekeeper. Most famously, this resulted in the almost impossibly ambitious multiyear curatorial adventure known as the "numbers" shows—the first presentation of which opened in Seattle in September 1969. Having gathered "conceptual" contributions using a standardized form letter, such as the one filled out by Sol LeWitt, the realization of the actual exhibition required others (Lippard, Seattle Art Museum staff, and volunteers) to create the physical manifestations of many of the works onsite. Buren's signature striped posters, for example, were to be installed throughout Seattle in a manner suggested by the photographs on his catalogue card, which shows the posters invading the streets of Paris.

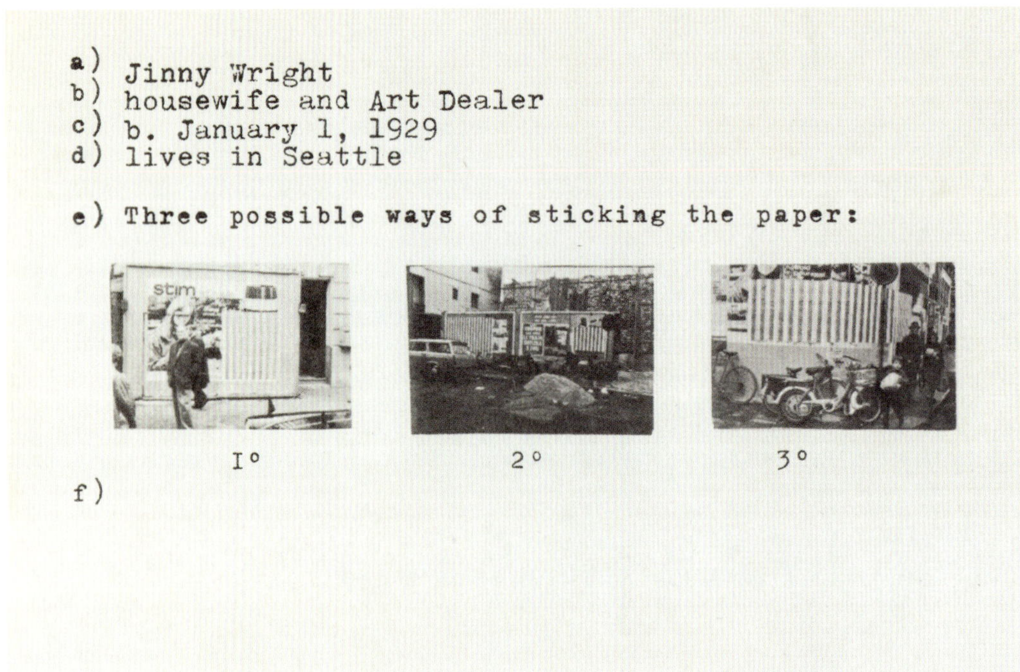

a) Jinny Wright
b) housewife and Art Dealer
c) b. January 1, 1929
d) lives in Seattle

e) Three possible ways of sticking the paper:

I° 2° 3°

f)

FIGURES 110, 111

Daniel Buren (French, b. 1938). *Photos-souvenirs: Affichages sauvages;* work in situ, Paris, April 1968. Contribution to the catalogues of *557,087*, 1969, and *955,000*, 1970. Double-sided index card, 4 × 6 in. (10.2 × 15.2 cm). Vancouver: Vancouver Art Gallery; Seattle: Seattle Art Museum, 1970. Photo-souvenir © D.B.-ADAGP Paris. (Photo: Brooklyn Museum)

a) Lucy R. Lippard
b) writer
c) b. April 14, 1937
d) lives in New York

e) Three possible ways of sticking the paper:

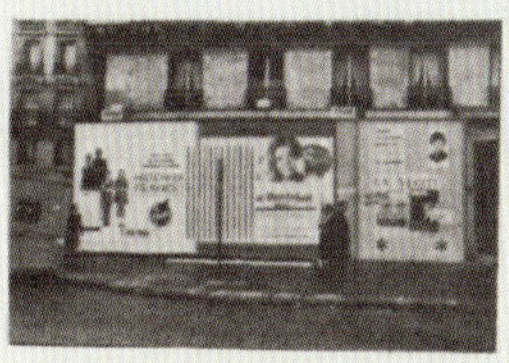

1°

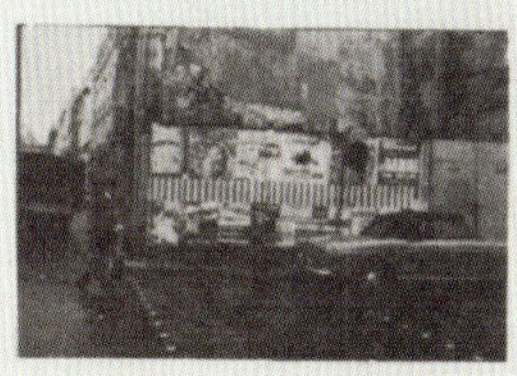

2°

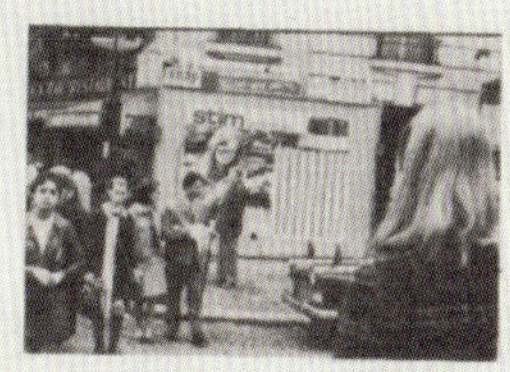

3°

f)

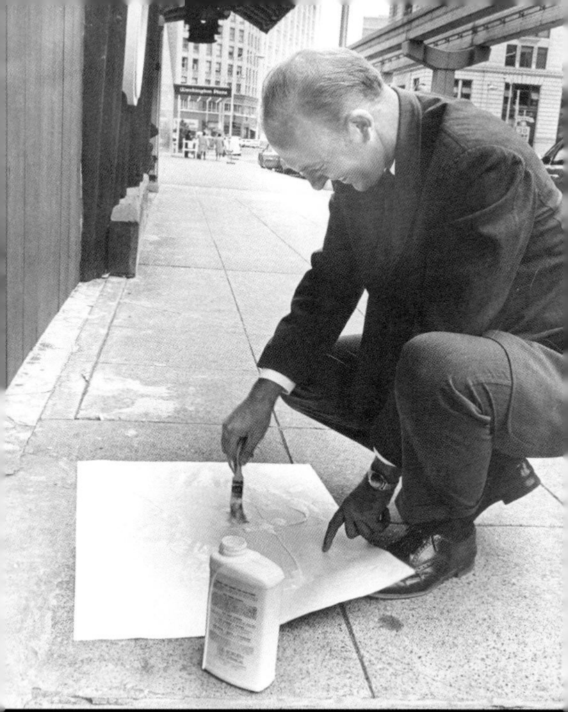

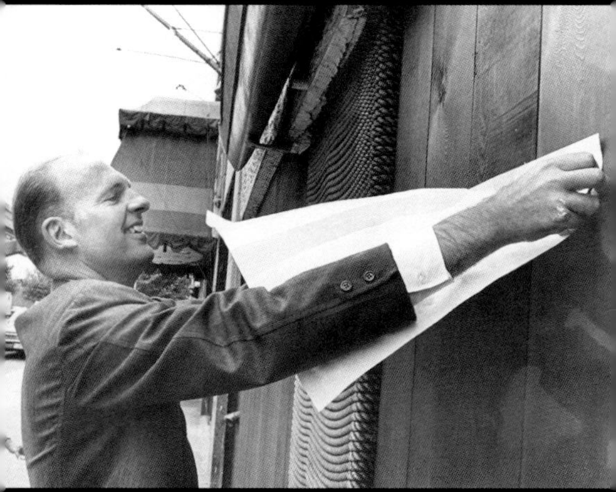

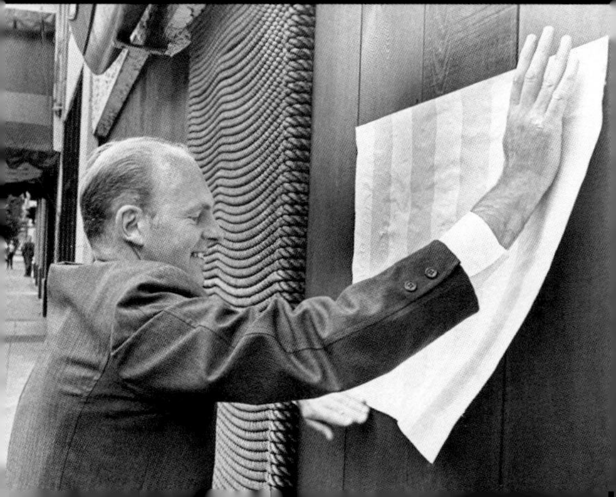

FIGURES 112–114

Seattle Art Museum Assistant Director Thomas Maytham installing Daniel Buren's contribution to *557,087*. Seattle Art Museum, September 5–October 5, 1969; organized by Lucy R. Lippard. (Photos: © Seattle Art Museum)

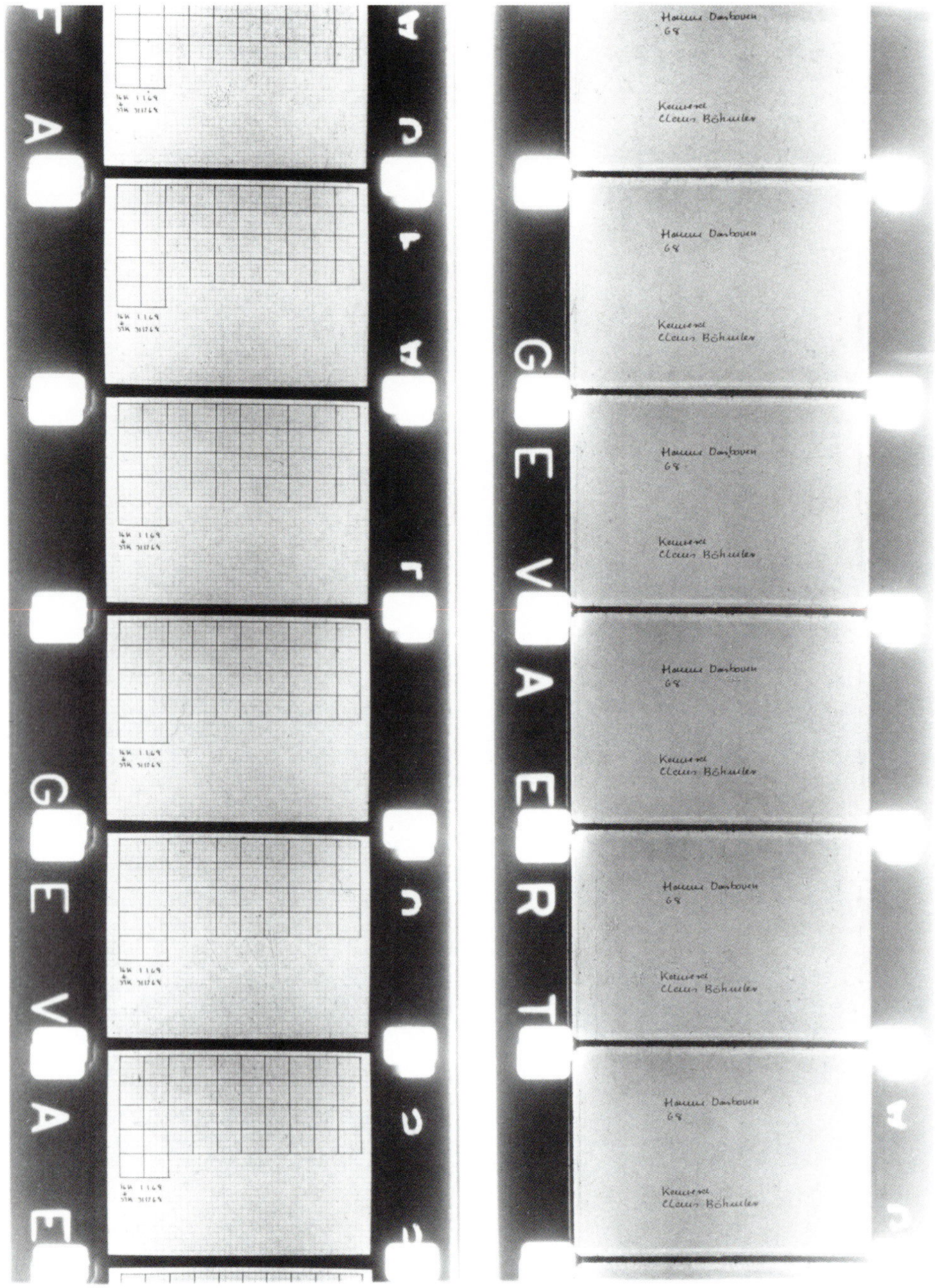

FIGURE 115

Hanne Darboven (German, 1941–2009). Filmstrip from *The Year 68 in 6 Books and 6 Films (6 Filmenach 6 Büchernüber 1968)*, 1969. 16mm black-and-white film, silent, 84 min. © 2011 Artists Rights Society (ARS), New York/VG BildKunst, Bonn. (Photo: Städtisches Museum Abteiberg, Mönchengladbach, Germany)

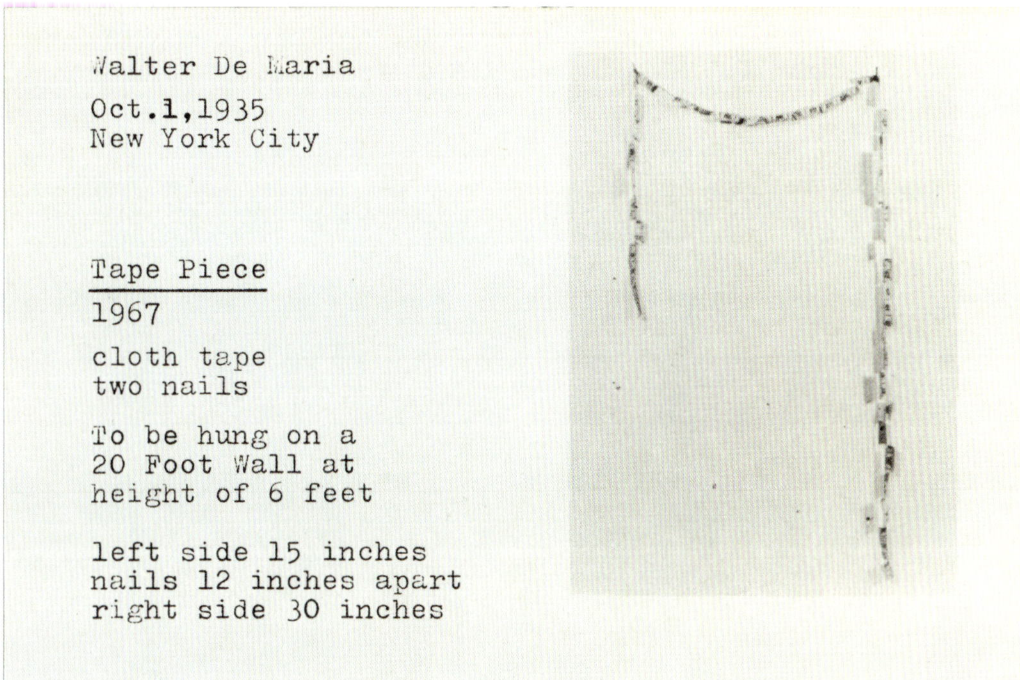

Walter De Maria

Oct.1,1935
New York City

Tape Piece

1967

cloth tape
two nails

To be hung on a
20 Foot Wall at
height of 6 feet

left side 15 inches
nails 12 inches apart
right side 30 inches

FIGURE 116

Walter De Maria (American, b. 1935). *Tape Piece*, 1967; contribution to the catalogues of *557,087*, 1969, and *955,000*, 1970. Index card, 4 × 6 in. (10.2 × 15.2 cm). Vancouver: Vancouver Art Gallery; Seattle: Seattle Art Museum, 1970. © Walter De Maria. (Photo: Brooklyn Museum)

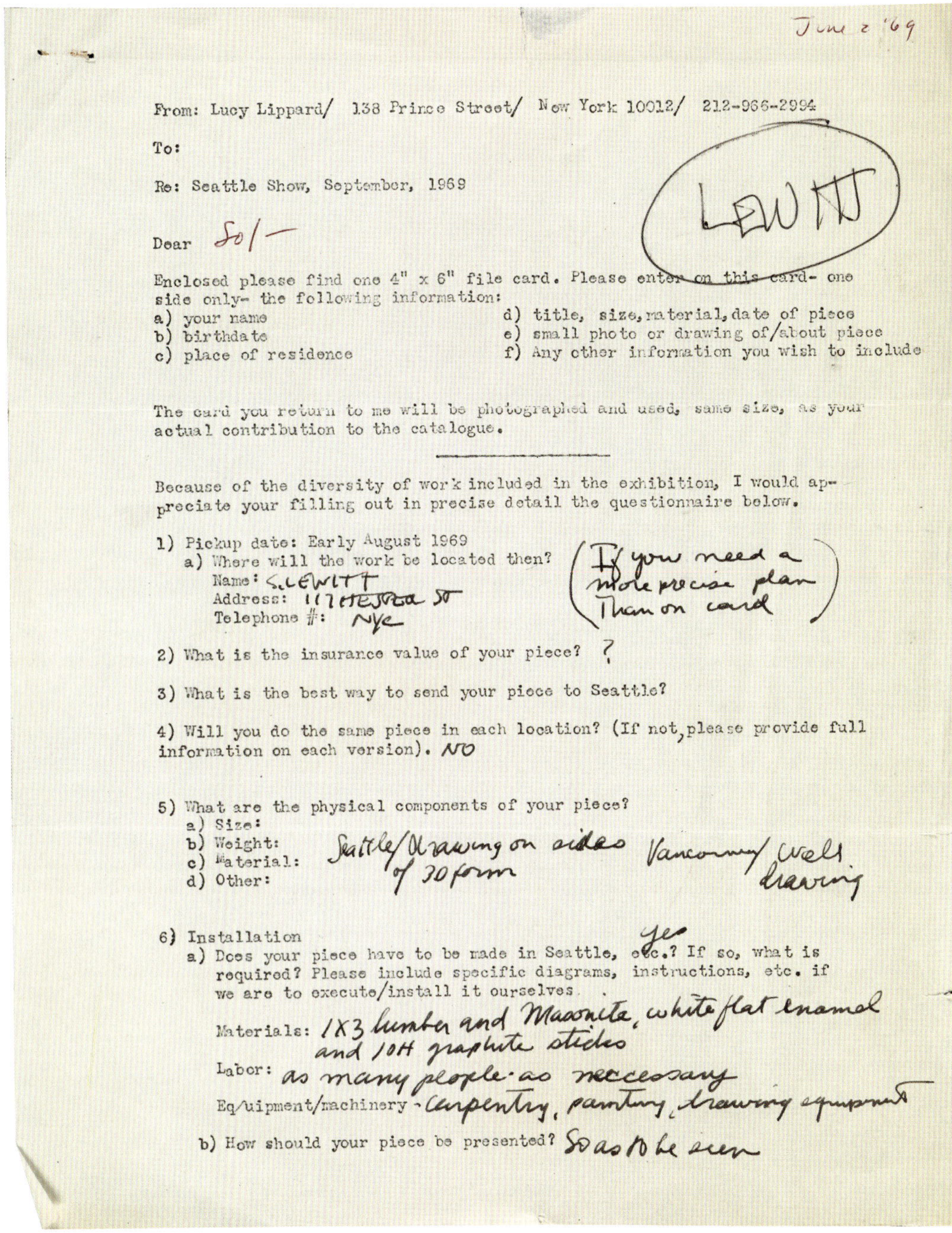

June 2 '69

From: Lucy Lippard/ 138 Prince Street/ New York 10012/ 212-966-2994

To:

Re: Seattle Show, September, 1969

LEWITT

Dear Sol –

Enclosed please find one 4" x 6" file card. Please enter on this card- one side only- the following information:

a) your name
b) birthdate
c) place of residence
d) title, size, material, date of piece
e) small photo or drawing of/about piece
f) Any other information you wish to include

The card you return to me will be photographed and used, same size, as your actual contribution to the catalogue.

Because of the diversity of work included in the exhibition, I would appreciate your filling out in precise detail the questionnaire below.

1) Pickup date: Early August 1969
   a) Where will the work be located then?
      Name: S. LEWITT
      Address: 117 HESTER ST
      Telephone #: NYC

(If you need a more precise plan than on card)

2) What is the insurance value of your piece? ?

3) What is the best way to send your piece to Seattle?

4) Will you do the same piece in each location? (If not, please provide full information on each version). NO

5) What are the physical components of your piece?
   a) Size:
   b) Weight:
   c) Material:
   d) Other:

Seattle/Drawing on sides of 3D form   Vancouver/Wall drawing

6) Installation
   a) Does your piece have to be made in Seattle, etc.? yes If so, what is required? Please include specific diagrams, instructions, etc. if we are to execute/install it ourselves.
      Materials: 1X3 lumber and Masonite, white flat enamel and 10H graphite sticks
      Labor: as many people as necessary
      Equipment/machinery - carpentry, painting, drawing equipment
   b) How should your piece be presented? So as to be seen

FIGURES 117, 118

Sol LeWitt (American, 1928–2007). Form sent by Lucy R. Lippard to LeWitt for the exhibition *557,087*, 1969. Printed form with handwritten responses: two pages, 11 × 8½ in. (27.9 × 21.6 cm) each. Lucy R. Lippard Papers, Archives of American Art, Smithsonian Institution, Washington, D.C. © 2011 The LeWitt Estate/Artists Rights Society (ARS), New York

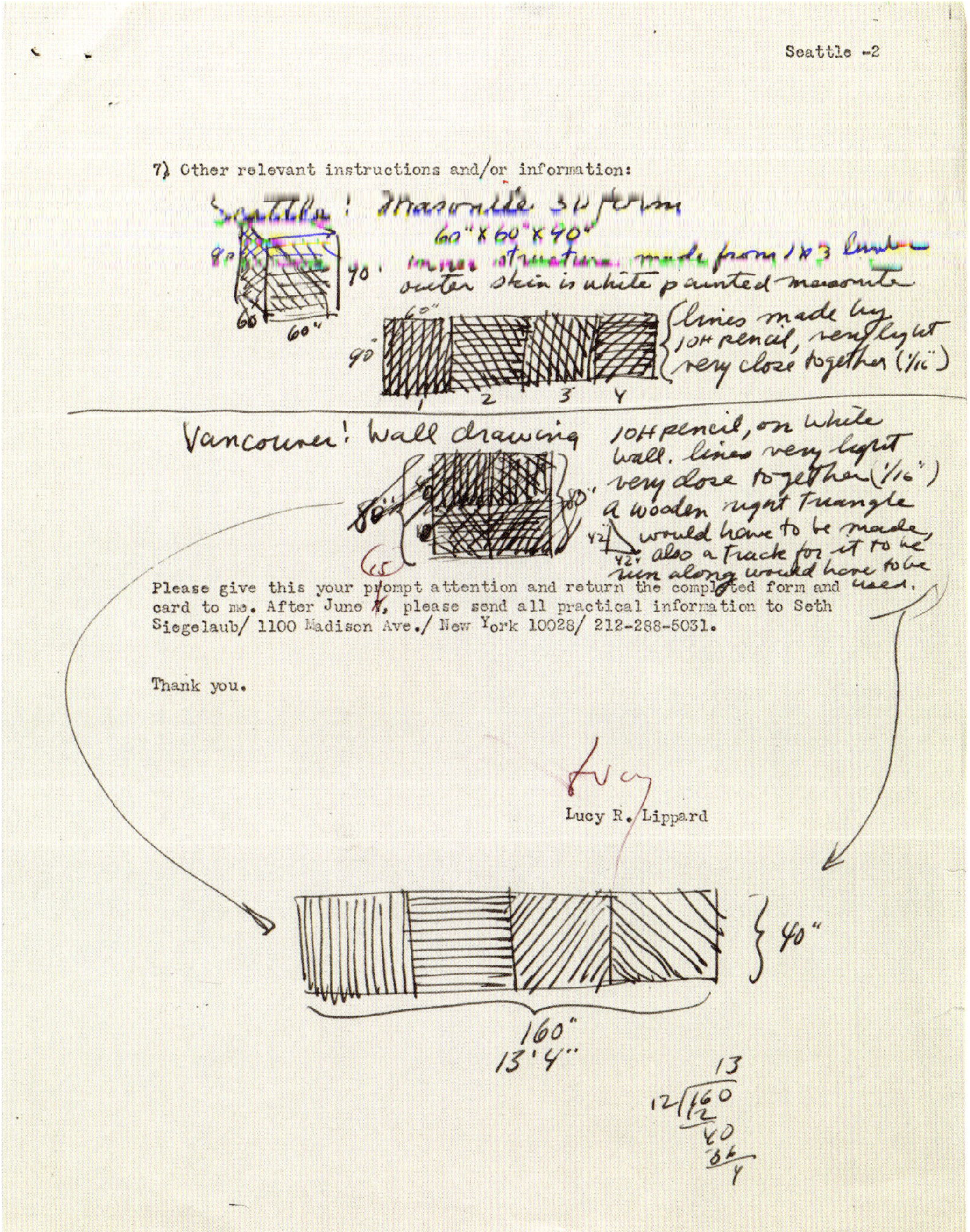

Seattle -2

7) Other relevant instructions and/or information:

Please give this your prompt attention and return the completed form and card to me. After June [illegible], please send all practical information to Seth Siegelaub/ 1100 Madison Ave./ New York 10028/ 212-288-5031.

Thank you.

Lucy

Lucy R. Lippard

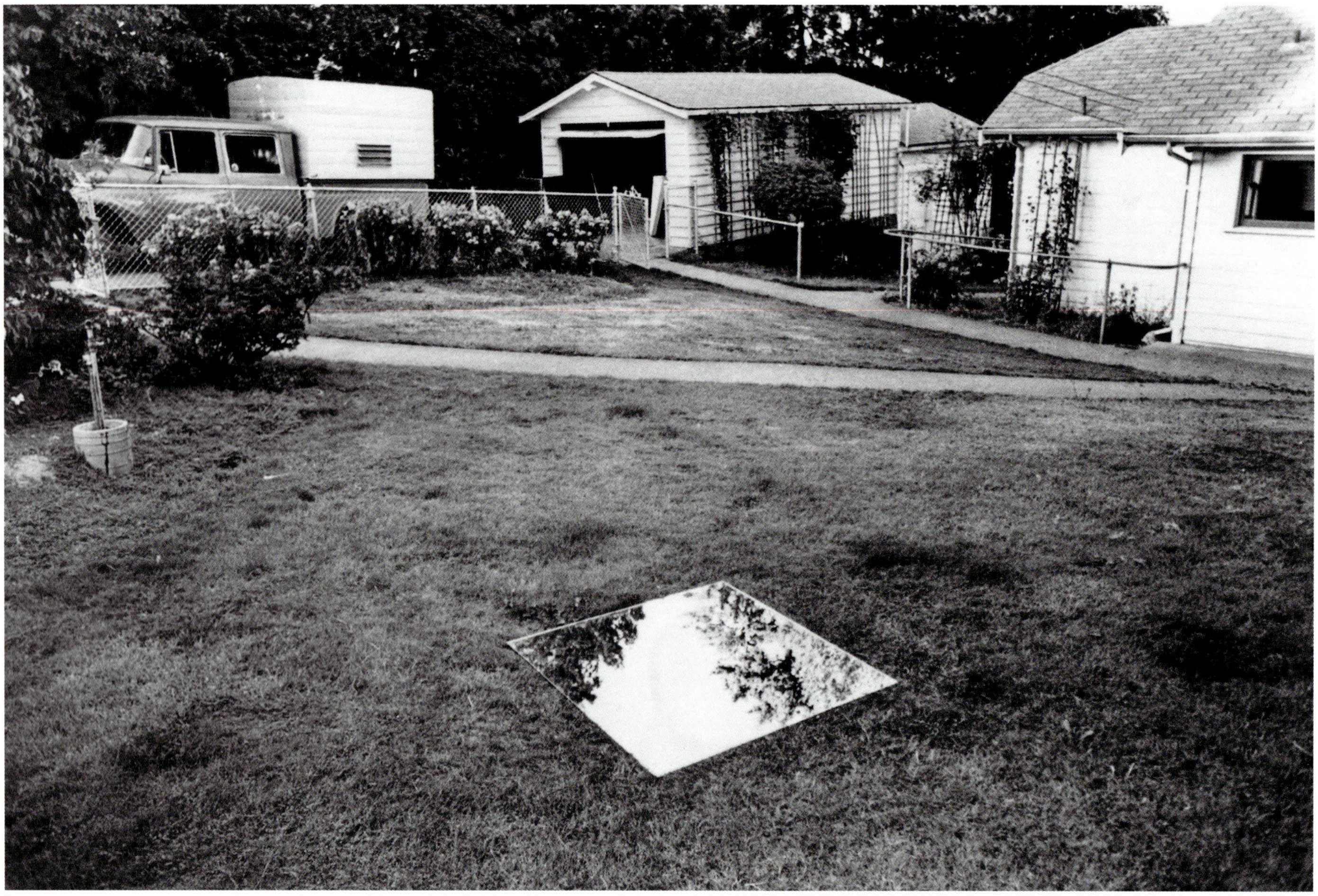

FIGURE 119

N. E. Thing Co. (Iain Baxter& [Canadian, b. England, 1936] and Ingrid Baxter [American, b. 1938]). Installation on view in *557,087*, Seattle Art Museum and offsite locations, September 5–October 5, 1969; organized by Lucy R. Lippard. (Photo: © Seattle Art Museum)

FIGURES 120–123: First performed as part of the exhibition *Street Works*, organized by the artist Marjorie Strider, which required artists to use New York City in the making of a work, *Following Piece* was an activity in which Acconci chose a random stranger to follow until their entry into a car or private space made it impossible for the stalking to continue. In *Private Piece for Lucy Lippard*, he reactivates this action, dedicating one day's worth of following to her.

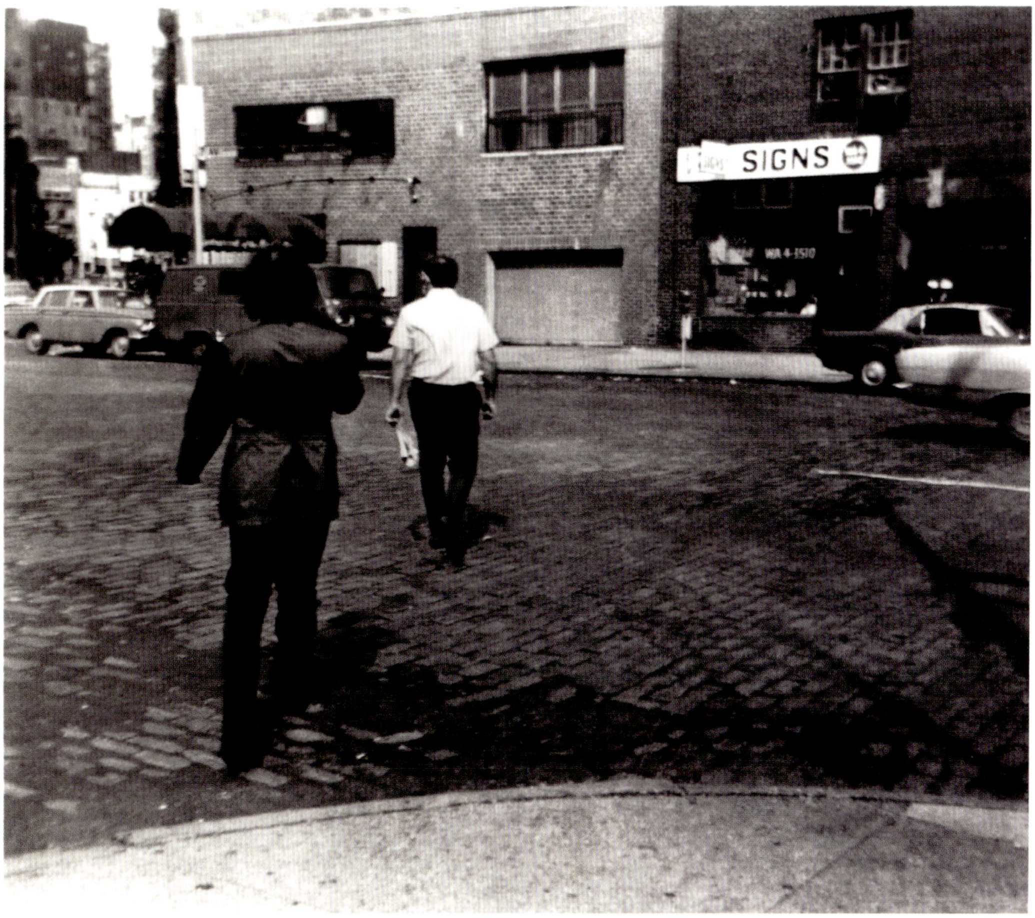

FIGURES 120–122

Vito Acconci (American, b. 1940). *Following Piece*, 1969. Activity, 23 days, varying times each day; typewritten statement, 11 × 8½ in. (27.9 × 21.6 cm). Photographic negatives: Acconci Studio; archival documents: Ilona Rich, Brooklyn. © Vito Acconci. (Photos: Betsy Jackson, courtesy Acconci Studio, New York)

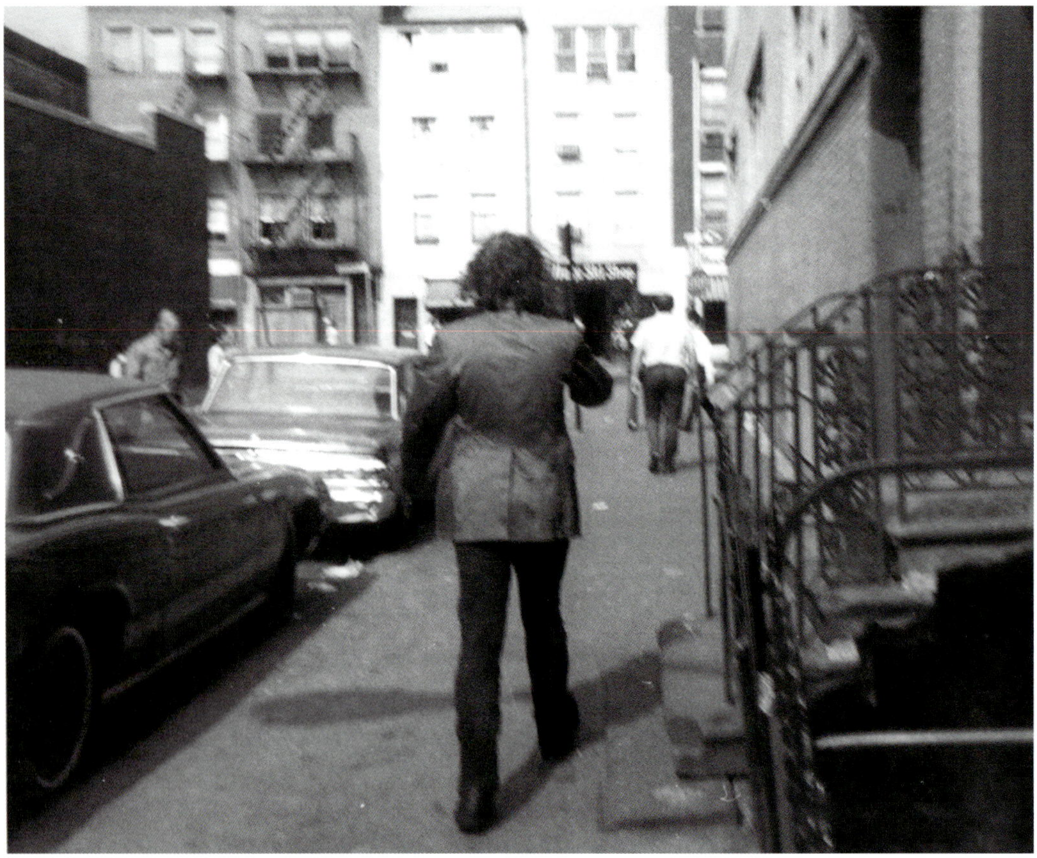

Vito Acconci
FOLLOWING PIECE
'Street Works IV,' sponsored by the Architectural League of New York.
October 3-25, 1969.
Activity.
New York City, various locations.
23 days, varying times each day.

Each day I pick out, at random, a person walking in the street.

I follow a different person everyday; I keep following until that person enters a private place (home, office, etc.) where I can't get in.

(The terms of the exhibition, 'Street Works IV,' were: to do a piece, sometime during the month, that used a street in New York City. FOLLOWING PIECE, potentially, could use all the time allotted and all the space available: I might be following people, all day long, everyday, through all the streets in New York City. In actuality, following episodes ranged from two or three minutes -- when someone got into a car and I couldn't grab a taxi, I couldn't follow -- to seven or eight hours -- when a person went to a restaurant, a movie...)

Private piece for Lucy Lippard (Nov. 16, 1969; city series): Follow-up to an activity situation using streets, travelling, following, changing location, "going wherever you go" (Street Works IV; New York City; October 3-25, 1969: "Each day, a person is chosen, at random, in the street, any location. I follow him wherever he goes, no matter how long or how far he travels. I stop following only when he enters a private place (home, his office, etc).")

October 16: I neglected to follow anyone.

November 16: The particular activity re-activated for Lucy Lippard.

– Vito Acconci

FIGURE 123

Vito Acconci (American, b. 1940). *Private Piece for Lucy Lippard ("City" Series)*, 1969. Typewritten statement, 11 × 8½ in. (27.9 × 21.6 cm). Lucy R. Lippard Papers, Archives of American Art, Smithsonian Institution, Washington, D.C. © Vito Acconci. (Photo: Acconci Studio, New York)

FIGURES 124, 125: *Projects Class*, organized by David Askevold at the pedagogically radical Nova Scotia College of Art and Design in Halifax, Canada, was one iteration of a multipart experiment in exhibition-making initiated by Lippard. The project began with her show *Groups*, at New York's School of Visual Arts (SVA), which asked approximately thirty artists to follow a series of instructions, the results of which were shown in the exhibition. Askevold then shared similar instructions with his students, who produced their own responses for *Projects Class*. The photo-text combinations from SVA were also turned into an exhibition-in-a-magazine when they were published in a special issue of *Studio International* (figures 20, 21).

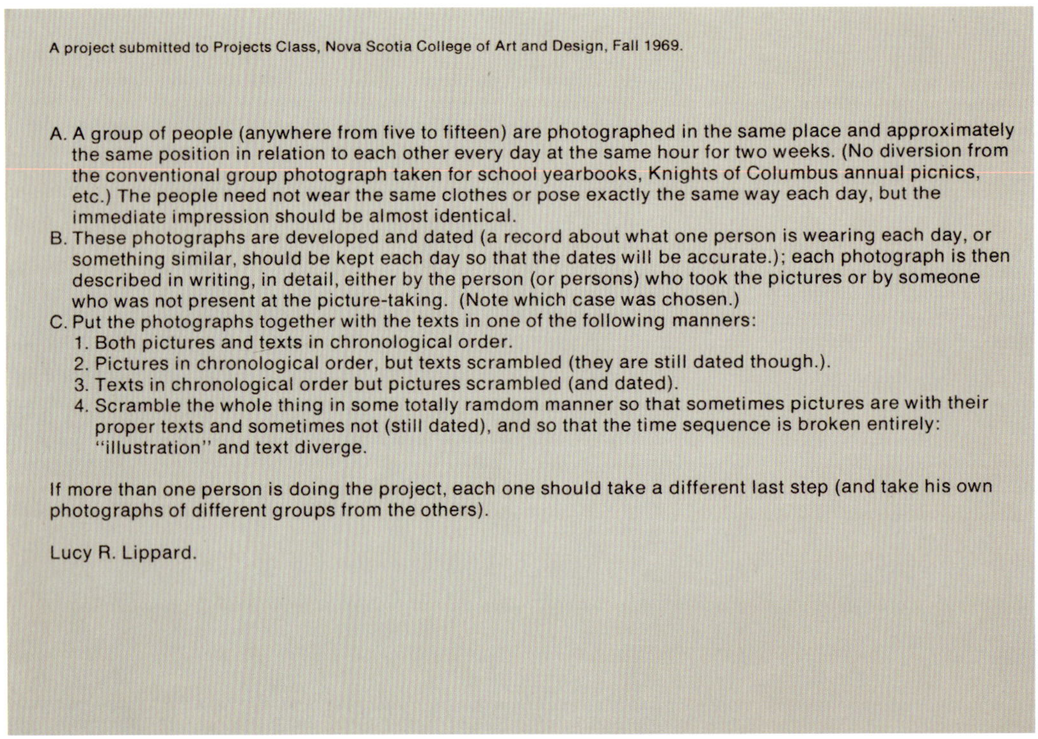

A project submitted to Projects Class, Nova Scotia College of Art and Design, Fall 1969.

A. A group of people (anywhere from five to fifteen) are photographed in the same place and approximately the same position in relation to each other every day at the same hour for two weeks. (No diversion from the conventional group photograph taken for school yearbooks, Knights of Columbus annual picnics, etc.) The people need not wear the same clothes or pose exactly the same way each day, but the immediate impression should be almost identical.
B. These photographs are developed and dated (a record about what one person is wearing each day, or something similar, should be kept each day so that the dates will be accurate.); each photograph is then described in writing, in detail, either by the person (or persons) who took the pictures or by someone who was not present at the picture-taking. (Note which case was chosen.)
C. Put the photographs together with the texts in one of the following manners:
   1. Both pictures and texts in chronological order.
   2. Pictures in chronological order, but texts scrambled (they are still dated though.).
   3. Texts in chronological order but pictures scrambled (and dated).
   4. Scramble the whole thing in some totally ramdom manner so that sometimes pictures are with their proper texts and sometimes not (still dated), and so that the time sequence is broken entirely: "illustration" and text diverge.

If more than one person is doing the project, each one should take a different last step (and take his own photographs of different groups from the others).

Lucy R. Lippard.

FIGURE 124

Lucy R. Lippard (American, b. 1937). *Groups Project for Projects Class, Halifax, Nova Scotia,* 1969. Printed card, 5½ × 7½ in. (14 × 19 cm). Collection of Alan Cravitz, Chicago. © Lucy R. Lippard. (Photo: Michael Tropea)

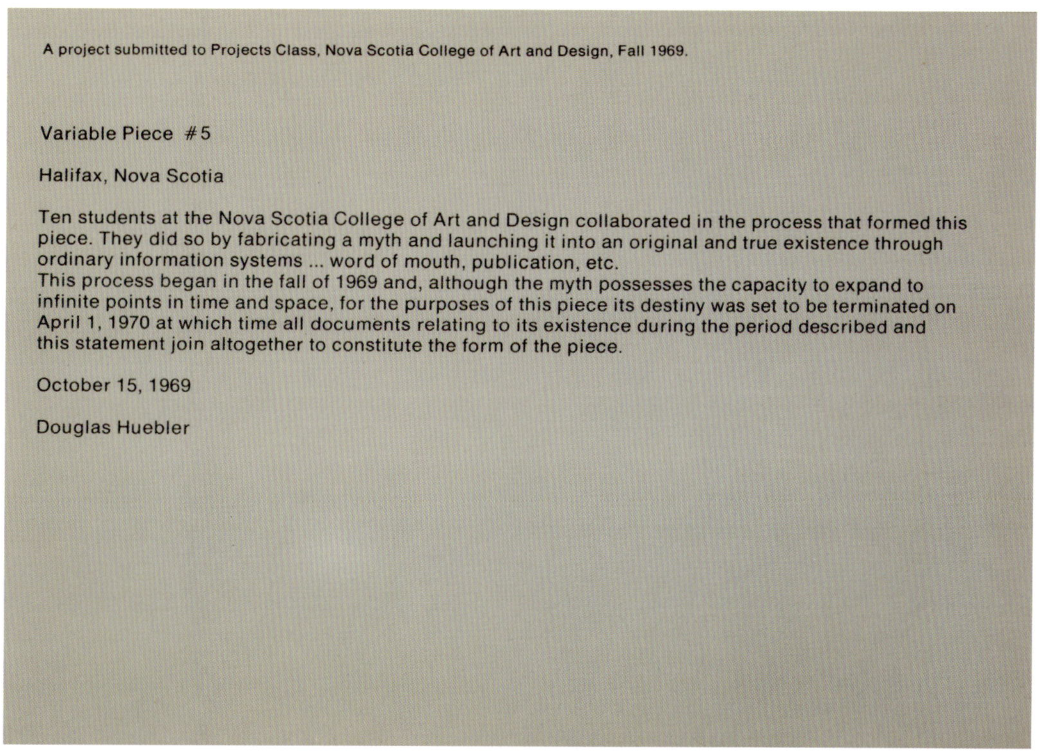

A project submitted to Projects Class, Nova Scotia College of Art and Design, Fall 1969.

Variable Piece #5

Halifax, Nova Scotia

Ten students at the Nova Scotia College of Art and Design collaborated in the process that formed this piece. They did so by fabricating a myth and launching it into an original and true existence through ordinary information systems ... word of mouth, publication, etc.
This process began in the fall of 1969 and, although the myth possesses the capacity to expand to infinite points in time and space, for the purposes of this piece its destiny was set to be terminated on April 1, 1970 at which time all documents relating to its existence during the period described and this statement join altogether to constitute the form of the piece.

October 15, 1969

Douglas Huebler

FIGURE 125

Douglas Huebler (American, 1924–1997). *Variable Piece #5; Halifax, Nova Scotia: A Project Submitted to Projects Class*, 1969. Printed card, 5½ × 7½ in. (14 × 19 cm). Collection of Alan Cravitz, Chicago. © Estate of Douglas Huebler/Artists Rights Society (ARS), New York. Courtesy Paula Cooper Gallery, New York. (Photo: Michael Tropea)

FIGURE 126

On Kawara. *I Got Up, November 1, 1969*, 1969. Postcard, 4 × 5 in. (10.2 × 12.7 cm). New Mexico Museum of Art, Santa Fe; Gift of Lucy R. Lippard. © On Kawara. Courtesy the artist and David Zwirner, New York. (Photo: New Mexico Museum of Art, Santa Fe)

On Kawara engaged Lippard directly in his highly personal and surprisingly moving project *I Got Up*, which uses postcards, sent to friends, to document and share the minimal facts of his continued existence. Over a four-month period, he sent Lippard one of his daily postcards, each simply recording the time he arose that day.

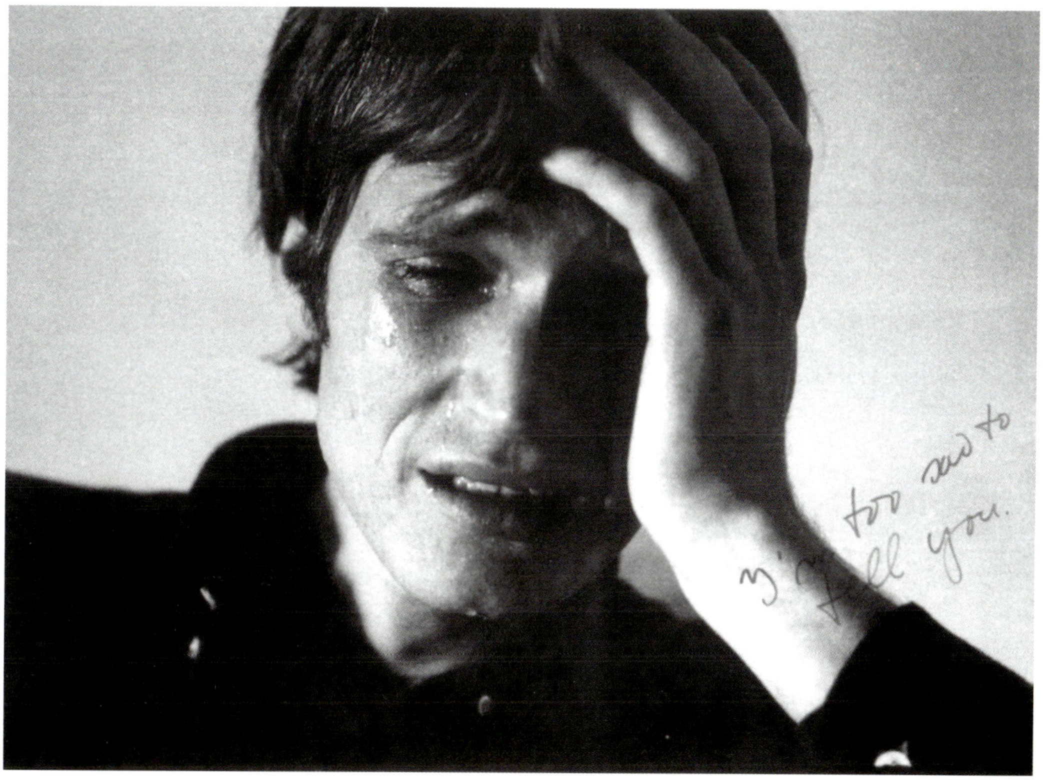

FIGURE 127

Bas Jan Ader (Dutch, 1942–1975). Still from *I'm too sad to tell you*, 1970. 16mm black-and-white film, silent, 3 min., 21 sec. © Bas Jan Ader/Courtesy Mary Sue Ader-Andersen, Bas Jan Ader Estate and Patrick Painter Editions. (Photo: Patrick Painter Editions)

In a poignantly minimal nod to existential angst, Bas Jan Ader's film *I'm too sad to tell you* simply presents a close-up clip of the artist crying after the title sequence plays.

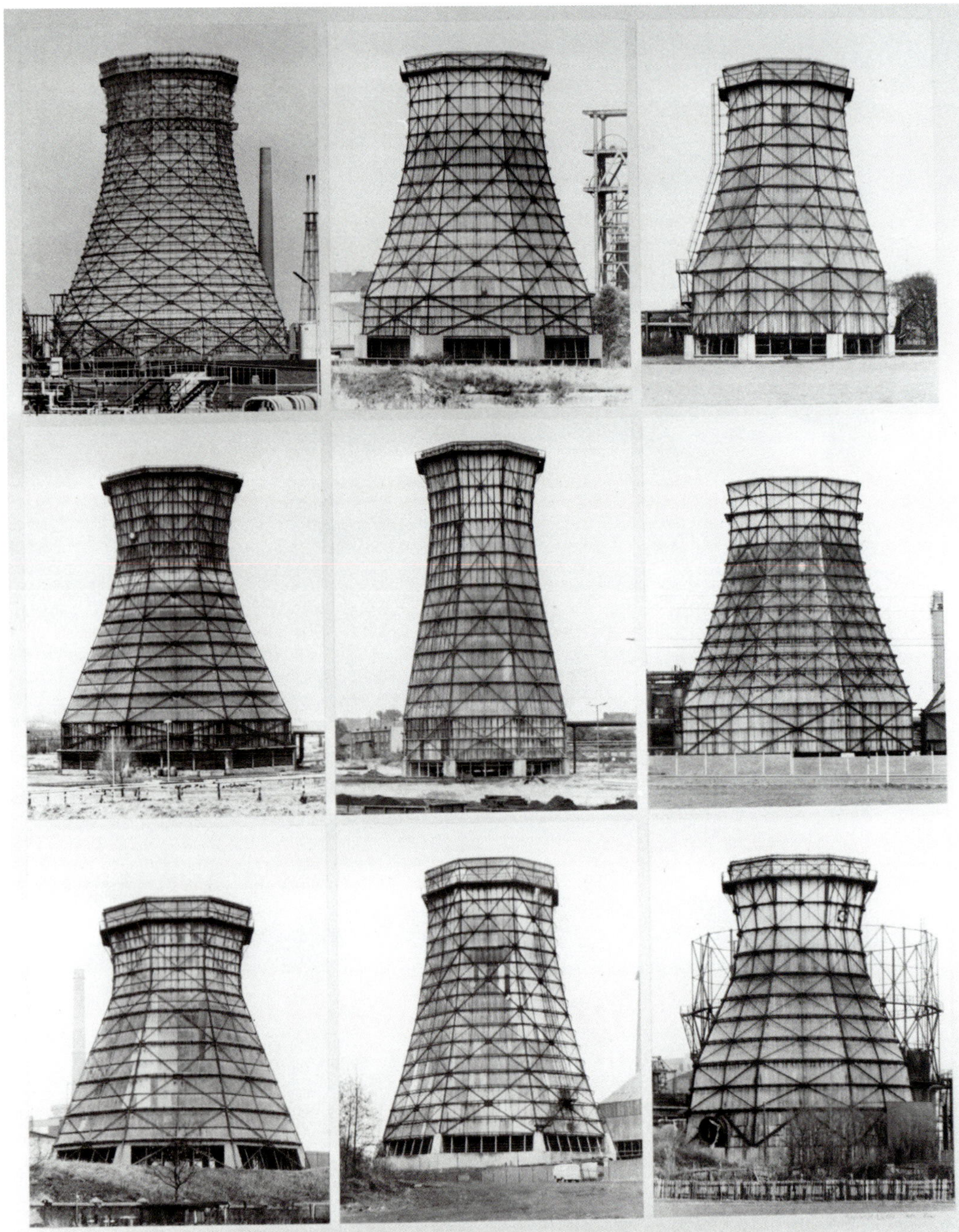

FIGURE 128

Bernd and Hilla Becher (German, 1931–2007; German, b. 1934). *Cooling Towers, Steel-Corrugated Concrete: Cologne, Ruhr District*, 1959–72. Black-and-white photographs, 60 × 40 in. (152.4 × 101.6 cm) overall. (Photo: Sonnabend Gallery, New York)

Bernd and Hilla Becher created their first photographic images of industrial structures, or typologies, in 1959, and in 1970 published their influential book *Anonyme Skulpturen: Eine Typologie technischer Bauten*, presenting their artistic production as a form of architectural taxonomy.

FIGURES 129–135: In 1970, Lippard brought her "numbers" exhibition to the Vancouver Art Gallery and the University of British Columbia Art Gallery, where, following the format she established in Seattle with *557,087*, the title changed to *955,000* in order to reflect the population of the Canadian city. The list of participants and the instructions were almost exactly the same, with only three artists added in Vancouver. One of these was Alex Hay, whose *Collection Bag* pieces are not complete until the canvas bag has been left out to collect dust, sand, and other "windblown" material for a period of time, integrating the detritus of a specific environment into the sculpture.

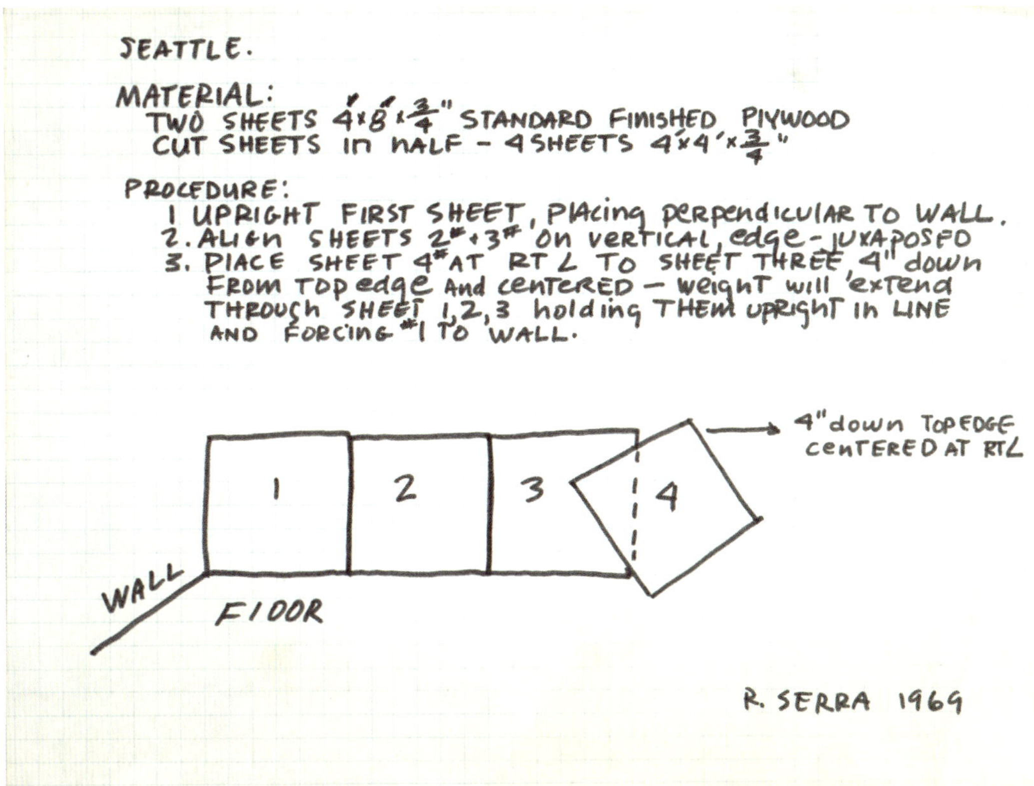

SEATTLE.

MATERIAL:
TWO SHEETS 4'x8'x¾" STANDARD FINISHED PLYWOOD
CUT SHEETS IN HALF – 4 SHEETS 4'x4'x¾"

PROCEDURE:
1 UPRIGHT FIRST SHEET, PLACING PERPENDICULAR TO WALL.
2. ALIGN SHEETS 2# + 3# ON VERTICAL, EDGE – JUXAPOSED
3. PLACE SHEET 4# AT RT ∠ TO SHEET THREE, 4" DOWN FROM TOP EDGE AND CENTERED – WEIGHT WILL EXTEND THROUGH SHEET 1,2,3 HOLDING THEM UPRIGHT IN LINE AND FORCING #1 TO WALL.

R. SERRA 1969

FIGURE 129

Richard Serra (American, b. 1938). Instructions and diagram for a sculpture installation; contribution to the exhibitions *557,087* and *955,000*, 1969. Ink on paper, 8½ × 11 in. (21.6 × 27.9 cm). Lucy R. Lippard Papers, Archives of American Art, Smithsonian Institution, Washington, D.C. © 2011 Richard Serra/ Artists Rights Society (ARS), New York

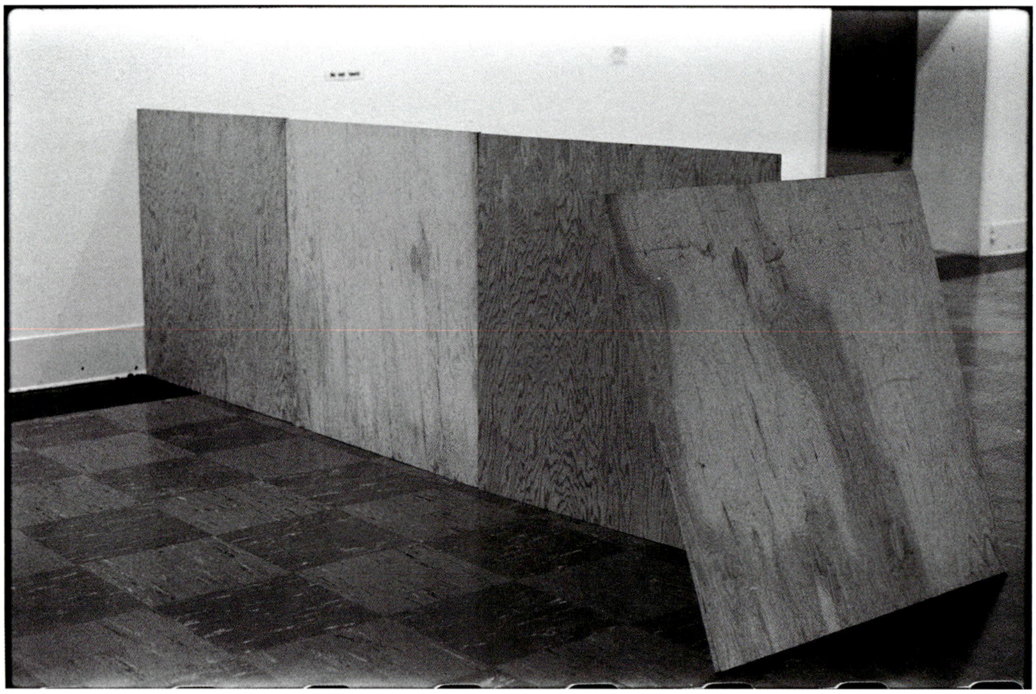

FIGURE 130

Installation view of the exhibition *955,000* including construction made following instructions provided by Richard Serra, Vancouver Art Gallery, January 13–February 8, 1970; organized by Lucy R. Lippard. Vancouver Art Gallery Archives. (Photo: Vancouver Art Gallery)

Alex Hay April 18 1930 New York City

Title; Collection of wind blown material

Description: Sail canvas 72"x54" coated inside with white flexible vinyl

Location positioning: Canvas positioned facing the prevailing wind direction 36" extends vertically 36" extends on ground surface

Contents: The predominate free surface material will represent the bulk collected along with incidental material Duration of process unspecified any amount of material acceptable

Collected material description: Weight in grams

FIGURE 131

Alex Hay (American, b. 1930). *Collection of Wind Blown Material,* 1970. Contribution to the catalogue of *955,000,* 1970. Index card, 4 × 6 in. (10.2 × 15.2 cm). Vancouver: Vancouver Art Gallery; Seattle: Seattle Art Museum, 1970. © Alex Hay. Courtesy Peter Freeman, Inc., New York (Photo: Brooklyn Museum)

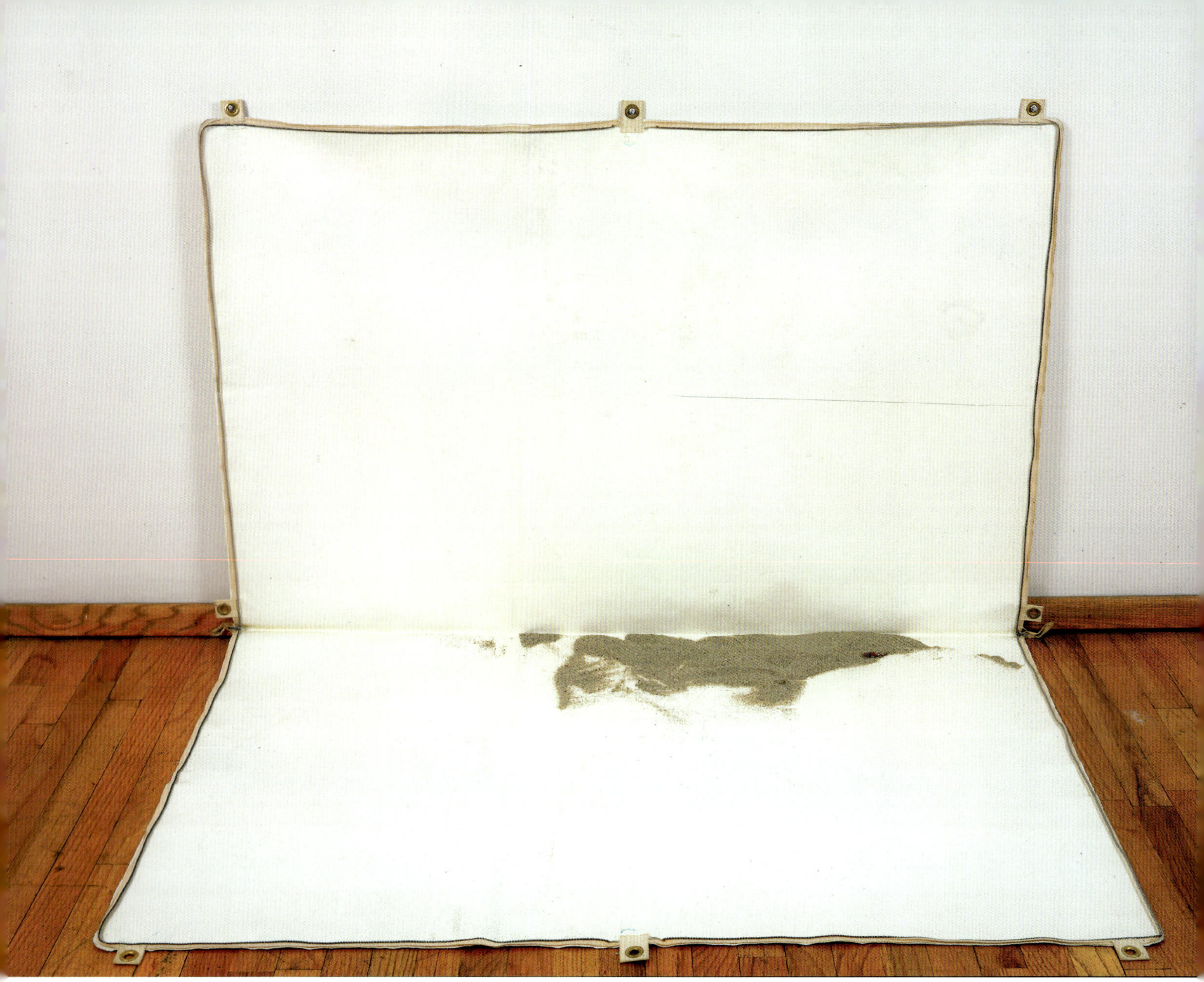

FIGURE 132

Alex Hay (American, b. 1930). *Collection Bag (Collection of Wind Blown Material)*, 1969. Sand and plant material within primed canvas with grommets and zipper: 35 × 53 in. (88.9 × 134.6 cm) closed; 35 × 53 × 35 in. (88.9 × 134.6 × 88.9 cm) opened as installed. Robert Rauschenberg, Inc., Archives, New York. © Alex Hay. (Photo: Bill Orcutt of Orcutt & Van Der Putten, courtesy Peter Freeman, Inc., New York)

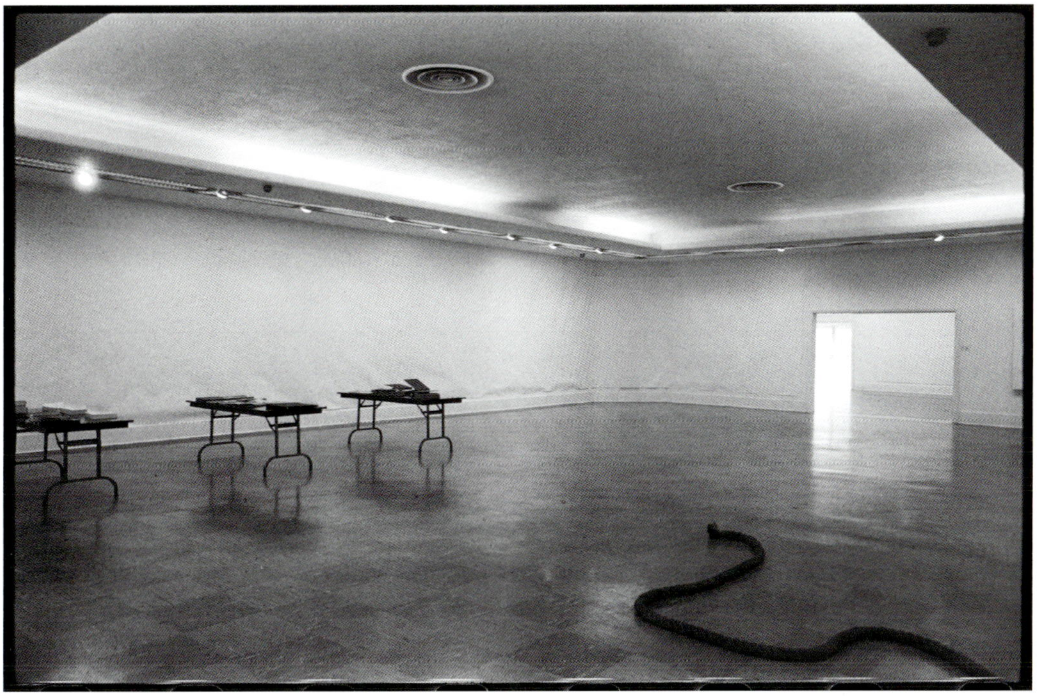

FIGURES 133–135

Installation views of the exhibition *955,000* including (figure 133) work by Barry Flanagan (lower right); (figure 134) work by N.E. Thing Co. (center); and (figure 135) various artists' contributions in binders; Vancouver Art Gallery, January 13–February 8, 1970; organized by Lucy R. Lippard. Vancouver Art Gallery Archives. (Photos: Vancouver Art Gallery)

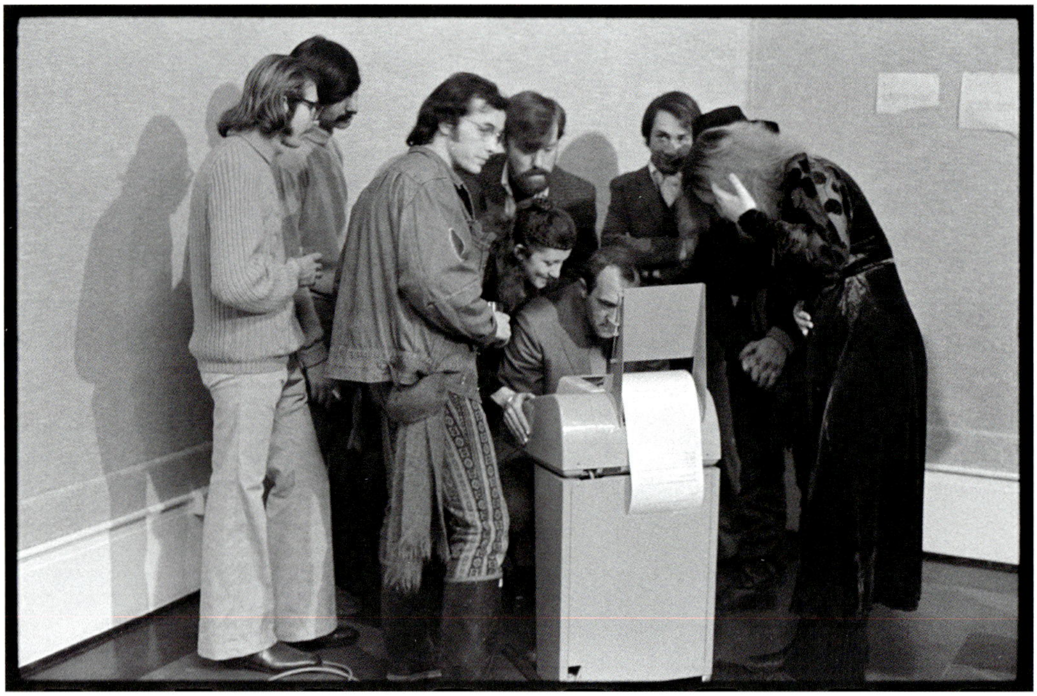

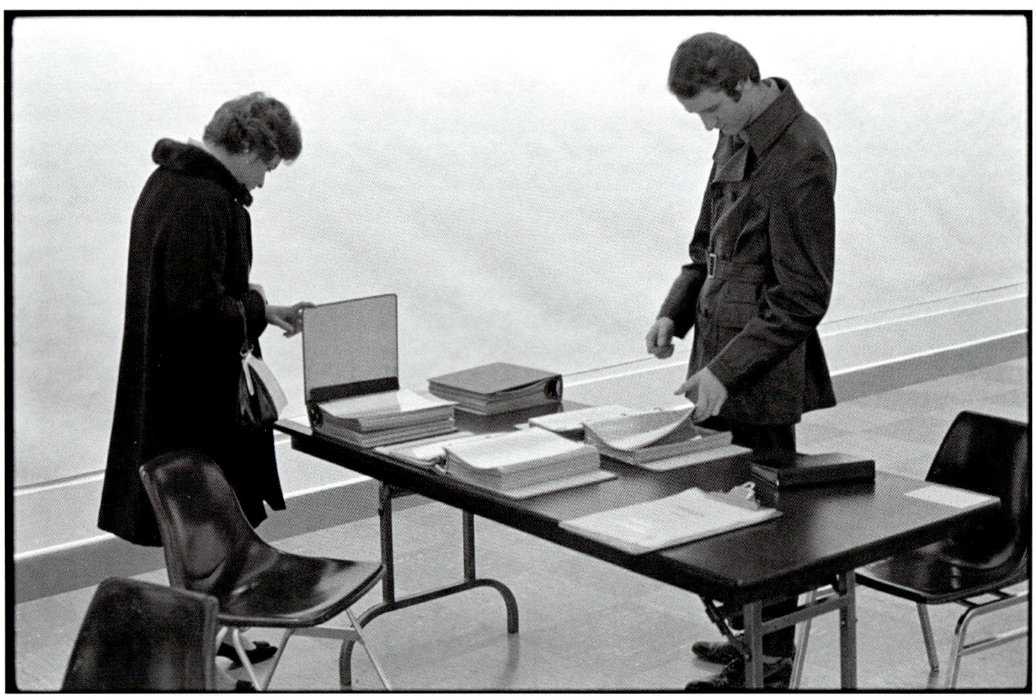

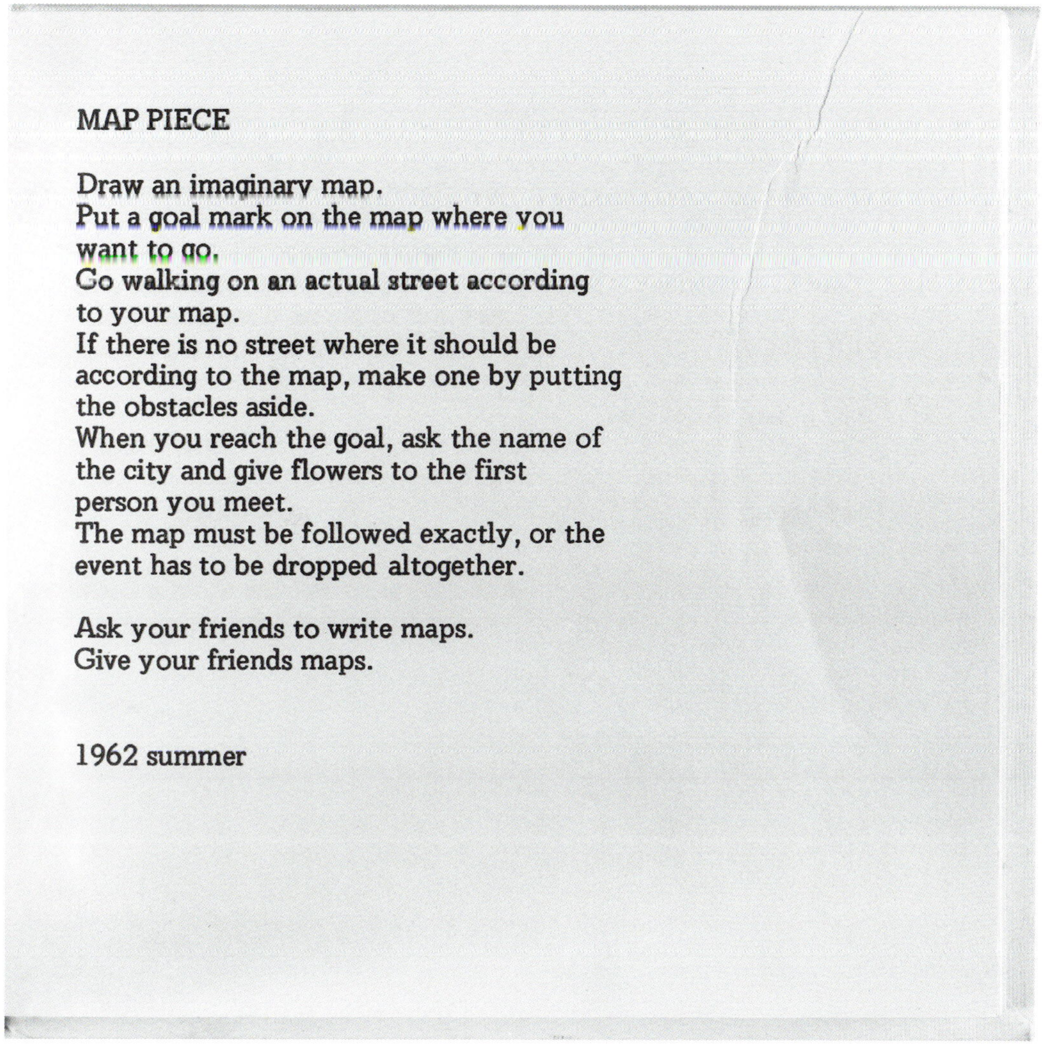

MAP PIECE

Draw an imaginary map.
Put a goal mark on the map where you want to go.
Go walking on an actual street according to your map.
If there is no street where it should be according to the map, make one by putting the obstacles aside.
When you reach the goal, ask the name of the city and give flowers to the first person you meet.
The map must be followed exactly, or the event has to be dropped altogether.

Ask your friends to write maps.
Give your friends maps.

1962 summer

FIGURE 136

Yoko Ono (Japanese, b. 1933). *Map Piece*, 1962. Offset and typewritten text, 5¼ × 5¼ in. (13.5 × 13.5 cm). © Yoko Ono. (Reproduced from Yoko Ono, *Grapefruit* [Tokyo: Wunternaum Press, 1964])

The parallel programs of critiquing the artistic status quo and attacking the socio-political-economic systems were given mainstream visibility and an institutional imprimatur when they converged in Kynaston McShine's exhibition *Information*, held at the Museum of Modern Art, July 2–September 20, 1970 (figure 34). Antecedents to the movement such as Yoko Ono's 1962 instruction work *Map Piece* were included along with new work such as David Askevold's relational diagram *Shoot/Shoot* (which reappeared as his contribution to Lippard's "numbers" exhibition *2,972,453* in Buenos Aires; figures 145–148). Pointedly political works were included, such as the Artists' Poster Committee of the Art Workers' Coalition's iconic poster *Q. And babies? A. And babies.* (figure 35), which overlaid a journalistic photograph with public testimony regarding civilian massacres in Vietnam.

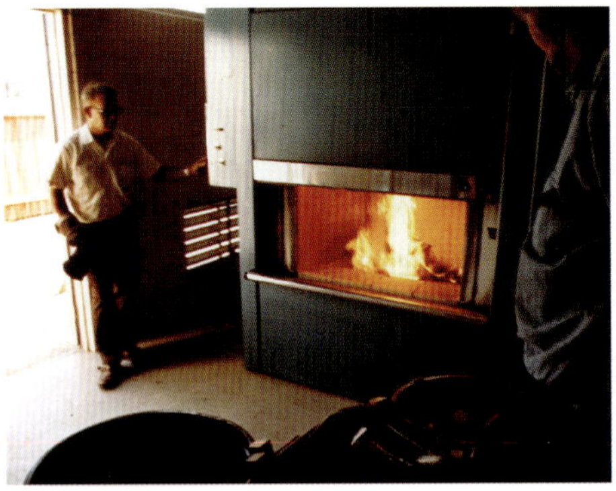

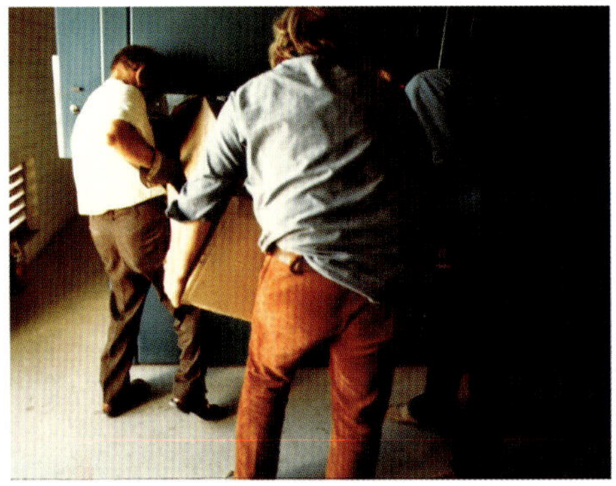

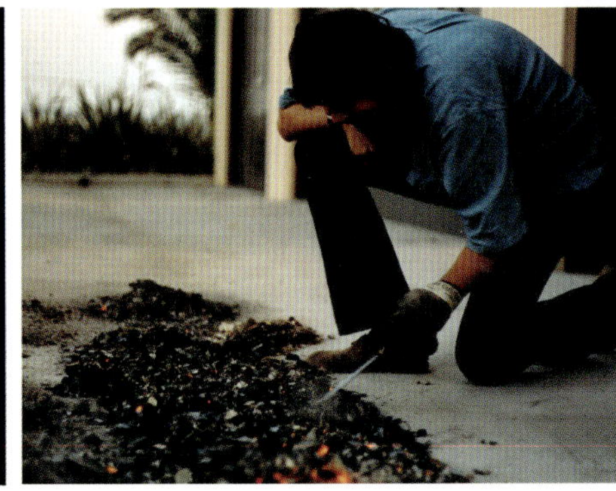

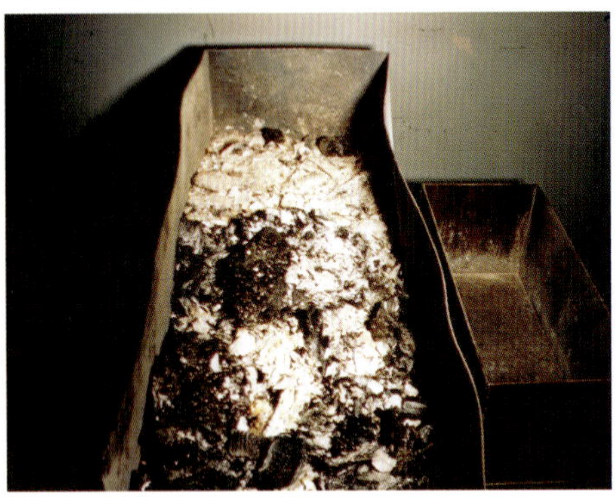

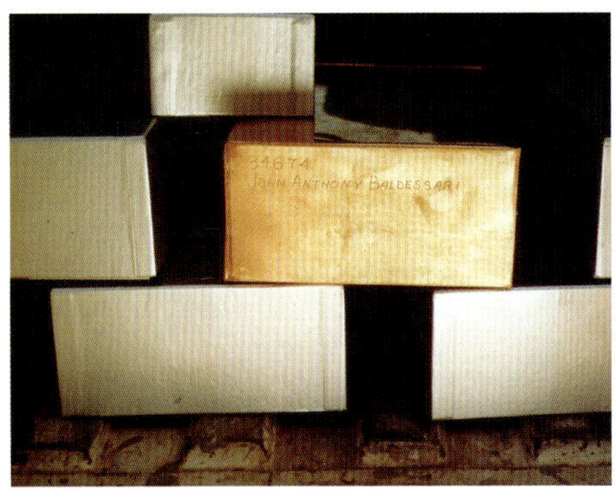

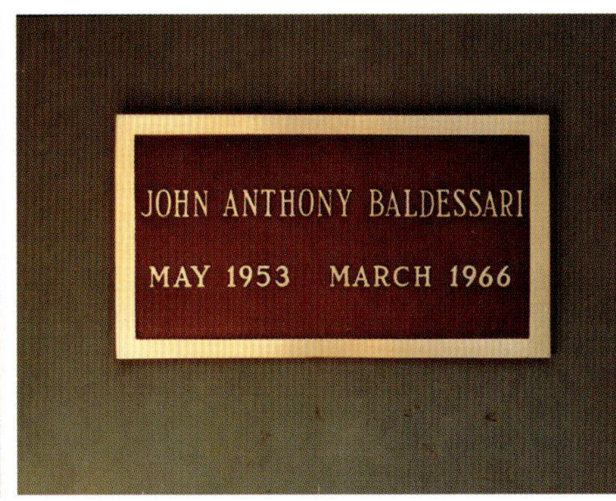

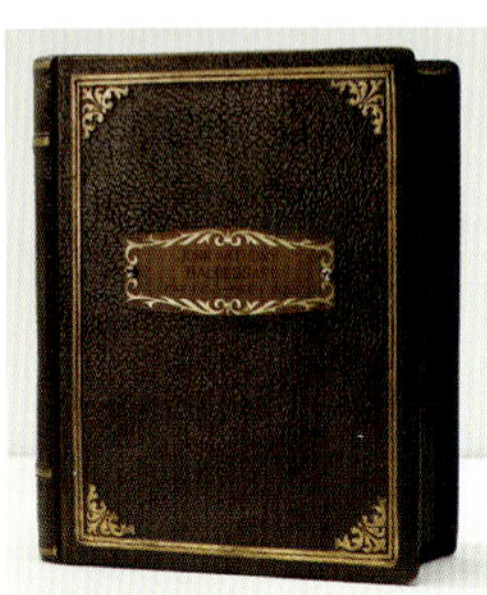

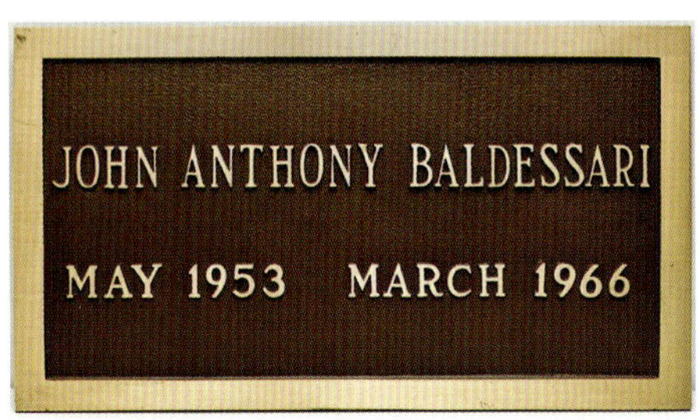

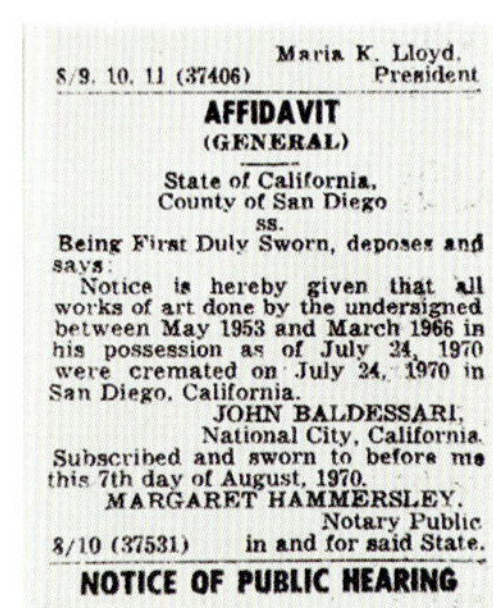

Maria K. Lloyd,
8/9, 10, 11 (37406) President

AFFIDAVIT
(GENERAL)

State of California,
County of San Diego
ss.

Being First Duly Sworn, deposes and says:

Notice is hereby given that all works of art done by the undersigned between May 1953 and March 1966 in his possession as of July 24, 1970 were cremated on July 24, 1970 in San Diego, California.

JOHN BALDESSARI,
National City, California.

Subscribed and sworn to before me this 7th day of August, 1970.

MARGARET HAMMERSLEY,
Notary Public
8/10 (37531) in and for said State.

NOTICE OF PUBLIC HEARING

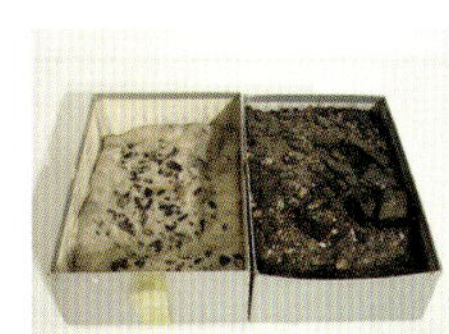

FIGURE 137

John Baldessari (American, b. 1931). *Cremation Project*, 1970. Six color photographs, bronze plaque, bronze urn in the shape of a book, mounted affidavit, extra box of ashes, overall dimensions variable. © John Baldessari. Courtesy John Baldessari and Marian Goodman Gallery, New York and Paris

In his *Cremation Project,* Baldessari performed his own radical act of aesthetic withdrawal, having all the paintings he had made prior to 1966 professionally cremated. This action was publicly promoted with a notice in the *San Diego Union* newspaper, legally confirmed with an affidavit, well documented in numerous photographs, and memorialized with the preservation of the resulting ashes, some of which were interred in a bronze urn, while others were baked into cookies.

FIGURES 138, 139: *Avalanche* magazine began its short but highly touted run as the diary of the downtown avant-garde with this first issue, featuring Joseph Beuys on the cover, effectively announcing the intellectual scope the editors Willoughby Sharp and Liza Béar set for themselves. They published a total of thirteen issues between 1970 and the magazine's dissolution in 1976. Sharp's essay for the first issue, "Body Works," featured a discussion of Oppenheim's *Arm & Wire,* a film shot by Bob Fiore, of the artist rolling a piece of wire across the same place on his arm, imprinting the image of the metal into his own flesh, which explored the artist's ongoing and often tongue-in-cheek interest in describing ways that information is transferred from one source to another. As Oppenheim states: "The body is seen as subject/object. Here the arm is receiving impressions of it's [*sic*] own energy. Material vs. tool looses [*sic*] distinction as the results of an action are fed back to the source."

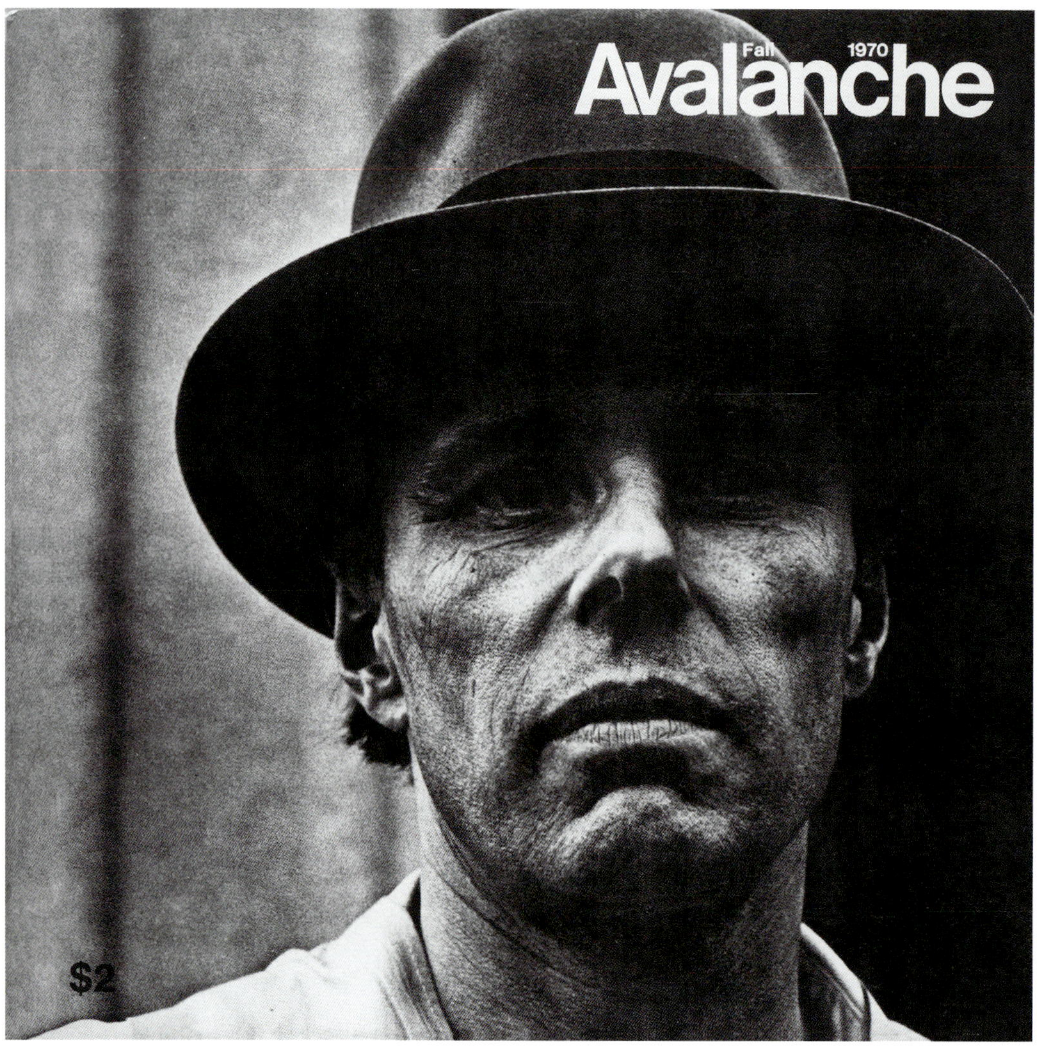

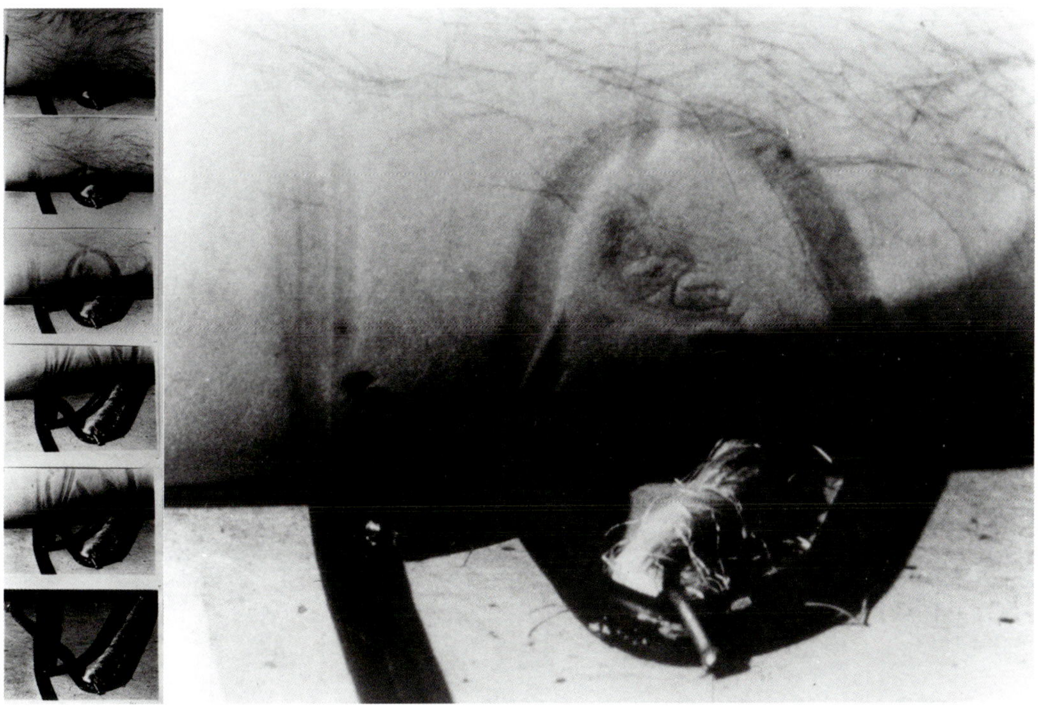

FIGURE 138

Cover of *Avalanche*, no. 1, fall 1970, with photograph of Joseph Beuys by Shunk-Kender. *Avalanche* published by Liza Béar and Willoughby Sharp. Printed magazine, 9⅜ × 9⅜ in. (23.8 × 23.8 cm). © Liza Béar and the Estate of Willoughby Sharp. (Photo: Brooklyn Museum)

FIGURE 139

Dennis Oppenheim (American, 1938–2011). Stills from *Arm & Wire*, 1969. 16mm black-and-white film, silent, 6 min. With Bob Fiore. © Dennis Oppenheim Estate

FIGURES 140–142

N. E. Thing Co. (Iain Baxter& [Canadian, b. England 1936] and Ingrid Baxter [American, b. 1938]). *North American Time Zone Photo–V.S.I. Simultaneity, October 18, 1970* (detail), 1970. Offset lithographs, 17½ × 17½ in. (44.5 × 44.5 cm) each. Morris and Helen Belkin Art Gallery, The University of British Columbia, Vancouver; Gift of Iain Baxter and Ingrid Baxter, 1995

In addition to strategically adopting the form of a corporation, N. E. Thing Company set out to systematically explore how the personal and quotidian can be broken down into quasi-scientific, seemingly neutral photographic data, in their project *North American Time Zone,* which documented sites of culture and everyday life, photographed at specific times, as a form of social topography.

INFORMATION

N.E.THING CO. LTD.
1419 Riverside Drive North Vancouver B.C. Canada tel. (604) 929-3002 Telex 04-507802 Cable Anything Vancouver B.C.

Project		Number
10.70.8	PHOTOGRAPHY & COMMUNICATIONS DEPARTMENTS NORTH AMERICAN TIME ZONE PHOTO - V.S.I. SIMULTANEITY OCTOBER 18, 1970	8

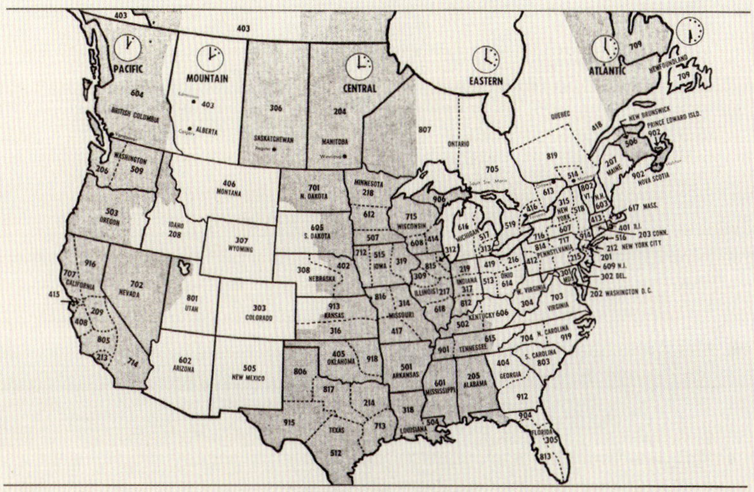

Description

PLEASE COMPLETE AND RETURN

N. E. THING COMPANY LIMITED

TRADEMARK ®

North American Time Zone Photo - V.S.I. Simultaneity was carried out by six photographers shooting the same subject matter in every time zone of North America at precisely the same moment in time on October 18, 1970.

Procedures: The N.E.THING CO. sent each photographer in the respective time zones of North America a shooting schedule with the times for his zone noted opposite the subject matter to be shot. On October 17 the photographers were contacted by phone to reconfirm procedures and to ask them to set watches by the C.B.C. (Canadian Broadcasting Corporation) time signals so as to ensure shooting synchronization. After the project was completed on October 18, the film from each of the photographers was mailed back to the N.E.THING CO., where it was processed. Work was then begun on the production of this folio.

In this project all negatives were given the same development and were printed full frame on the same grade of photographic paper. All cameras used were 35mm and in four cases the black and white film used was Ilford FP4, ASA 200, and in one case, Ilford HP4, ASA 400, and in the other case Kodak TRI-X, ASA 400. The Kodak film was developed in D-76 developer and the Ilford film was developed in Ilford Microphen. The prints were all printed on Ilford IB 1-3P.

Seal

PRINTED IN CANADA

FOR REPRODUCTION, REDUCE ENTIRE PRESENTATION INCLUDING THIS STATEMENT.

LAYOUT SHEET INFORMATION DEPARTMENT N.E.THING CO. LTD.

N.E.THING CO. LTD. Photography and Communications Departments. North American Time Zone Photo-V.S.I. Simultaneity. October 18, 1970

Location	**Vancouver, British Columbia**
Photographer	**N.E.THING CO. LTD.**
Time Zone	**Pacific Daylight Time**
Subject:	
1. Time.	8.00 a.m. P.D.T.
2. Nude.	8.15 a.m. P.D.T.
3. Still-life.	8.30 a.m. P.D.T.
4. Cityscape.	8.45 a.m. P.D.T.
5. Earth.	9.00 a.m. P.D.T.
6. Air.	9.15 a.m. P.D.T.
7. Fire.	9.30 a.m. P.D.T.
8. Water.	9.45 a.m. P.D.T.
9. North.	10.00 a.m. P.D.T.
10. South.	10.15 a.m. P.D.T.
11. East.	10.30 a.m. P.D.T.
12. West.	10.45 a.m. P.D.T.
13. Shadow.	11.00 a.m. P.D.T.
14. Self-portrait.	11.15 a.m. P.D.T.

Location	**Edmonton, Alberta**
Photographer	**Harry Savage**
Time Zone	**Mountain Daylight Time**
Subject:	
1. Time.	9.00 a.m. M.D.T.
2. Nude.	9.15 a.m. M.D.T.
3. Still-life.	9.30 a.m. M.D.T.
4. Cityscape.	9.45 a.m. M.D.T.
5. Earth.	10.00 a.m. M.D.T.
6. Air.	10.15 a.m. M.D.T.
7. Fire.	10.30 a.m. M.D.T.
8. Water.	10.45 a.m. M.D.T.
9. North.	11.00 a.m. M.D.T.
10. South.	11.15 a.m. M.D.T.
11. East.	11.30 a.m. M.D.T.
12. West.	11.45 a.m. M.D.T.
13. Shadow.	12.00 noon M.D.T.
14. Self-portrait.	12.15 p.m. M.D.T.

Location	**Winnipeg, Manitoba**
Photographer	**Ken Lochhead**
Time Zone	**Central Daylight Time**
Subject:	
1. Time.	10.00 a.m. C.D.T.
2. Nude.	10.15 a.m. C.D.T.
3. Still-life.	10.30 a.m. C.D.T.
4. Cityscape.	10.45 a.m. C.D.T.
5. Earth.	11.00 a.m. C.D.T.
6. Air.	11.15 a.m. C.D.T.
7. Fire.	11.30 a.m. C.D.T.
8. Water.	11.45 a.m. C.D.T.
9. North.	12.00 noon C.D.T.
10. South.	12.15 p.m. C.D.T.
11. East.	12.30 p.m. C.D.T.
12. West.	12.45 p.m. C.D.T.
13. Shadow.	1.00 p.m. C.D.T.
14. Self-portrait.	1.15 p.m. C.D.T.

Location	**London, Ontario**
Photographer	**Jack Chambers**
Time Zone	**Eastern Daylight Time**
Subject:	
1. Time.	11.00 a.m. E.D.T.
2. Nude.	11.15 a.m. E.D.T.
3. Still-life.	11.30 a.m. E.D.T.
4. Cityscape.	11.45 a.m. E.D.T.
5. Earth.	12.00 noon E.D.T.
6. Air.	12.15 p.m. E.D.T.
7. Fire.	12.30 p.m. E.D.T.
8. Water.	12.45 p.m. E.D.T.
9. North.	1.00 p.m. E.D.T.
10. South.	1.15 p.m. E.D.T.
11. East.	1.30 p.m. E.D.T.
12. West.	1.45 p.m. E.D.T.
13. Shadow.	2.00 p.m. E.D.T.
14. Self-portrait.	2.15 p.m. E.D.T.

Location	**Halifax, Nova Scotia**
Photographer	**Gerry Ferguson**
Time Zone	**Atlantic Daylight Time**
Subject:	
1. Time.	12.00 noon A.D.T.
2. Nude.	12.15 p.m. A.D.T.
3. Still-life.	12.30 p.m. A.D.T.
4. Cityscape.	12.45 p.m. A.D.T.
5. Earth.	1.00 p.m. A.D.T.
6. Air.	1.15 p.m. A.D.T.
7. Fire.	1.30 p.m. A.D.T.
8. Water.	1.45 p.m. A.D.T.
9. North.	2.00 p.m. A.D.T.
10. South.	2.15 p.m. A.D.T.
11. East.	2.30 p.m. A.D.T.
12. West.	2.45 p.m. A.D.T.
13. Shadow.	3.00 p.m. A.D.T.
14. Self-portrait.	3.15 p.m. A.D.T.

Location	**Mount Carmel, Newfoundland**
Photographer	**Chris Pratt**
Time Zone	**Newfoundland Daylight Time**
Subject:	
1. Time.	12.30 p.m. Nfld.D.T.
2. Nude.	12.45 p.m. Nfld.D.T.
3. Still-life.	1.00 p.m. Nfld.D.T.
4. Cityscape.	1.15 p.m. Nfld.D.T.
5. Earth.	1.30 p.m. Nfld.D.T.
6. Air.	1.45 p.m. Nfld.D.T.
7. Fire.	2.00 p.m. Nfld.D.T.
8. Water.	2.15 p.m. Nfld.D.T.
9. North.	2.30 p.m. Nfld.D.T.
10. South.	2.45 p.m. Nfld.D.T.
11. East.	3.00 p.m. Nfld.D.T.
12. West.	3.15 p.m. Nfld.D.T.
13. Shadow.	3.30 p.m. Nfld.D.T.
14. Self-portrait.	3.45 p.m. Nfld.D.T.

N.E.THING CO. LTD. Photography and Communications Departments. North American Time Zone Photo-V.S.I. Simultaneity. October 18, 1970 **1. TIME.**

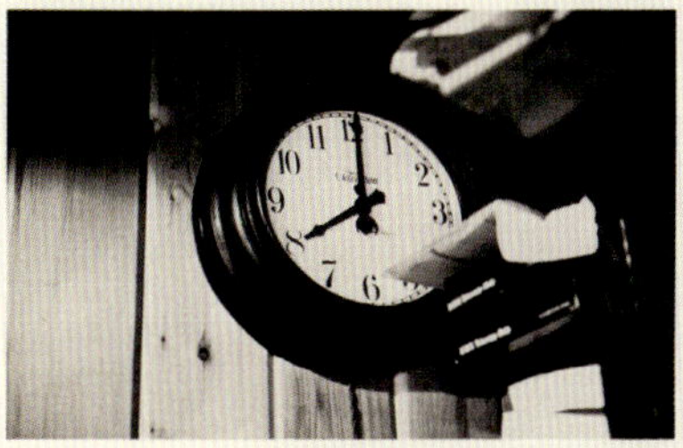

8.00 a.m. P.D.T.

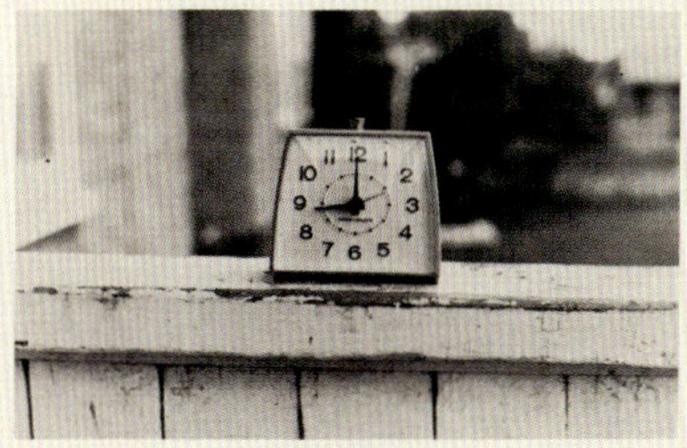

9.00 a.m. M.D.T.

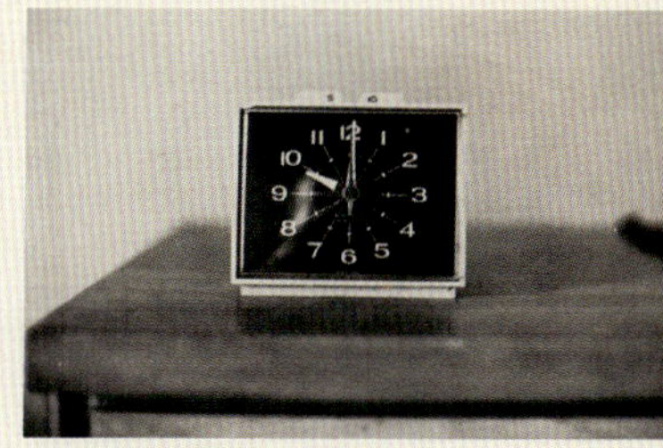

10.00 a.m. C.D.T.

11.00 a.m. E.D.T.

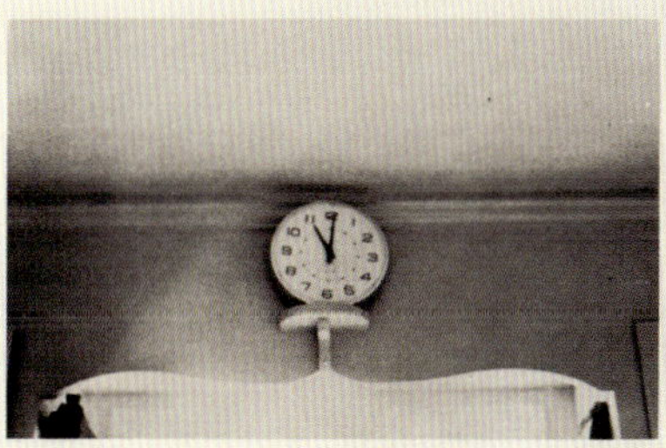

12.00 noon A.D.T.

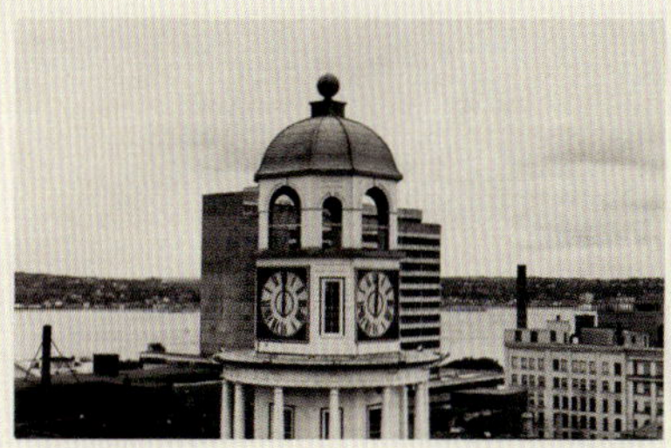

12.30 p.m. Nfld.D.T.

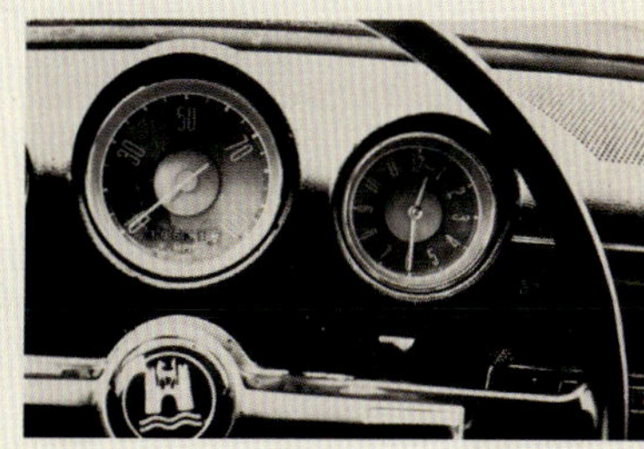

FIGURES 143–148: Following its presentation in Vancouver, Lippard tried to extend her portable exhibition-as-instructions model beyond North America, bringing it to Buenos Aires with the help of CAYC Director Jorge Glusberg. However, this time, the parameters for *2,972,453* were that none of the artists presented in Argentina were to have been in the previous numbers shows, making this a much smaller exhibition and catalogue. The distance proved difficult as, according to *Six Years*, the CAYC misprinted the index cards for the catalogue, "in defiance of the organizer's and artists' wishes."

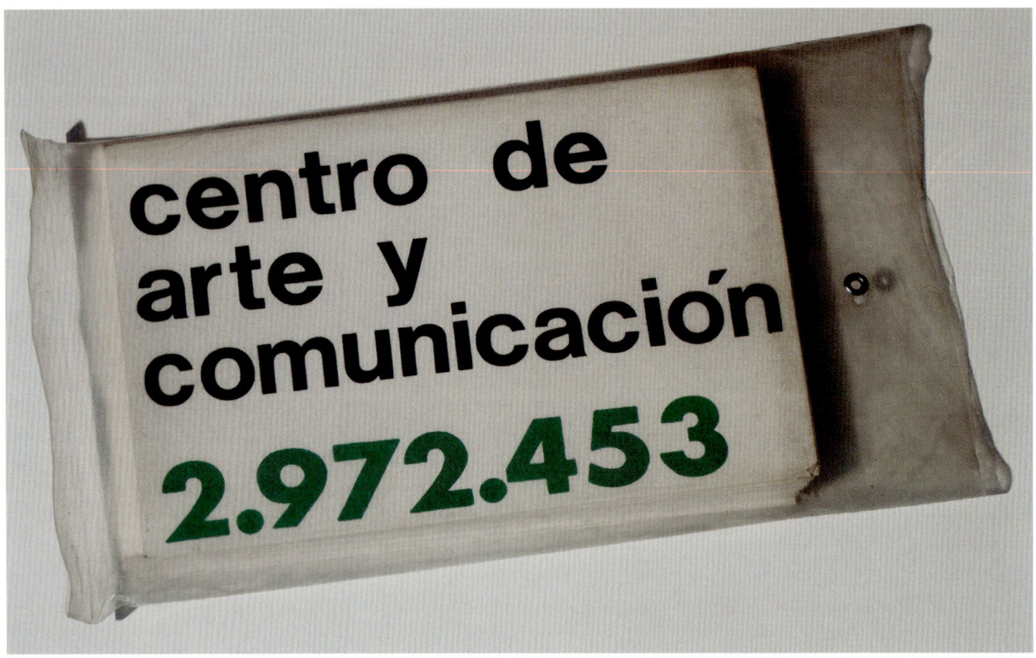

FIGURE 143

Cover of catalogue of *2,972,453,* 1970. Index cards, 4 × 6 in. (10.2 × 15.2 cm) each. Buenos Aires, Argentina: Centro de Arte y Comunicación [CAYC], 1970. © Centro de Arte y Comunicación, Buenos Aires, courtesy Jorge Glusberg. (Photo: Michael Tropea)

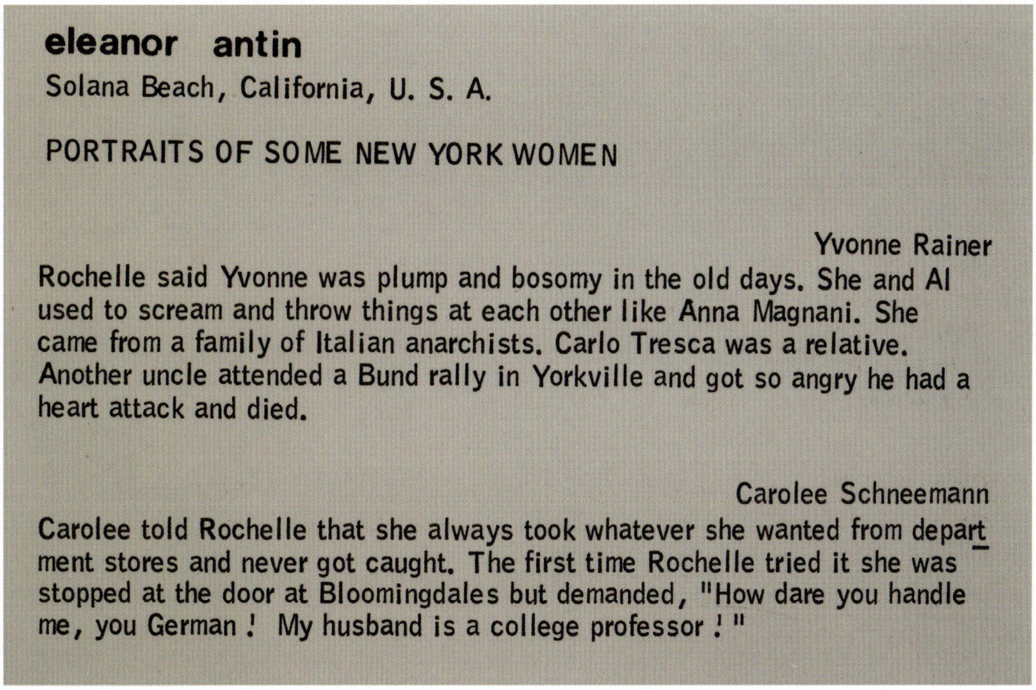

eleanor antin

Solana Beach, California, U. S. A.

PORTRAITS OF SOME NEW YORK WOMEN

Yvonne Rainer

Rochelle said Yvonne was plump and bosomy in the old days. She and Al used to scream and throw things at each other like Anna Magnani. She came from a family of Italian anarchists. Carlo Tresca was a relative. Another uncle attended a Bund rally in Yorkville and got so angry he had a heart attack and died.

Carolee Schneemann

Carolee told Rochelle that she always took whatever she wanted from depart-ment stores and never got caught. The first time Rochelle tried it she was stopped at the door at Bloomingdales but demanded, "How dare you handle me, you German! My husband is a college professor!"

FIGURE 144

Eleanor Antin (American, b. 1935). *Yvonne Rainer and Carolee Schneemann Texts* (from *Portraits of Some New York Women*), 1970. Contribution to the catalogue of *2,972,453,* 1970. Index card, 4 × 6 in. (10.2 × 15.2 cm). Buenos Aires, Argentina: Centro de Arte y Comunicación [CAYC], 1970. © Eleanor Antin. (Photo: Michael Tropea)

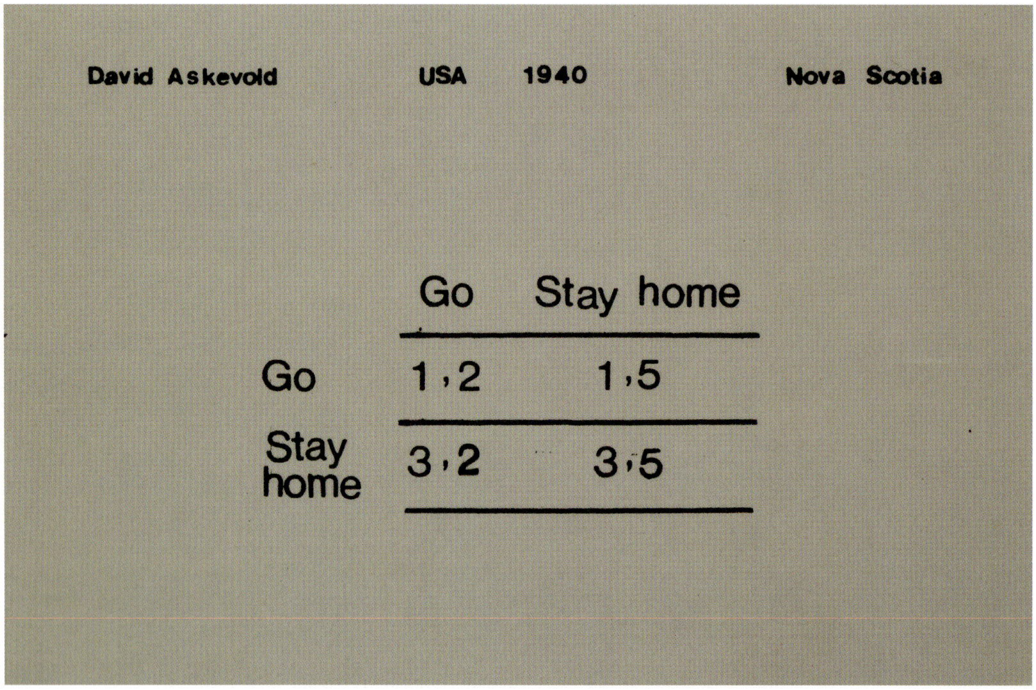

FIGURES 145–147

David Askevold (Canadian, 1940–2008). Contribution to the catalogue of *2,972,453,* 1970. Index cards, 4 × 6 in. (10.2 × 15.2 cm) each. Buenos Aires, Argentina: Centro de Arte y Comunicación [CAYC], 1970. (Photos: Michael Tropea)

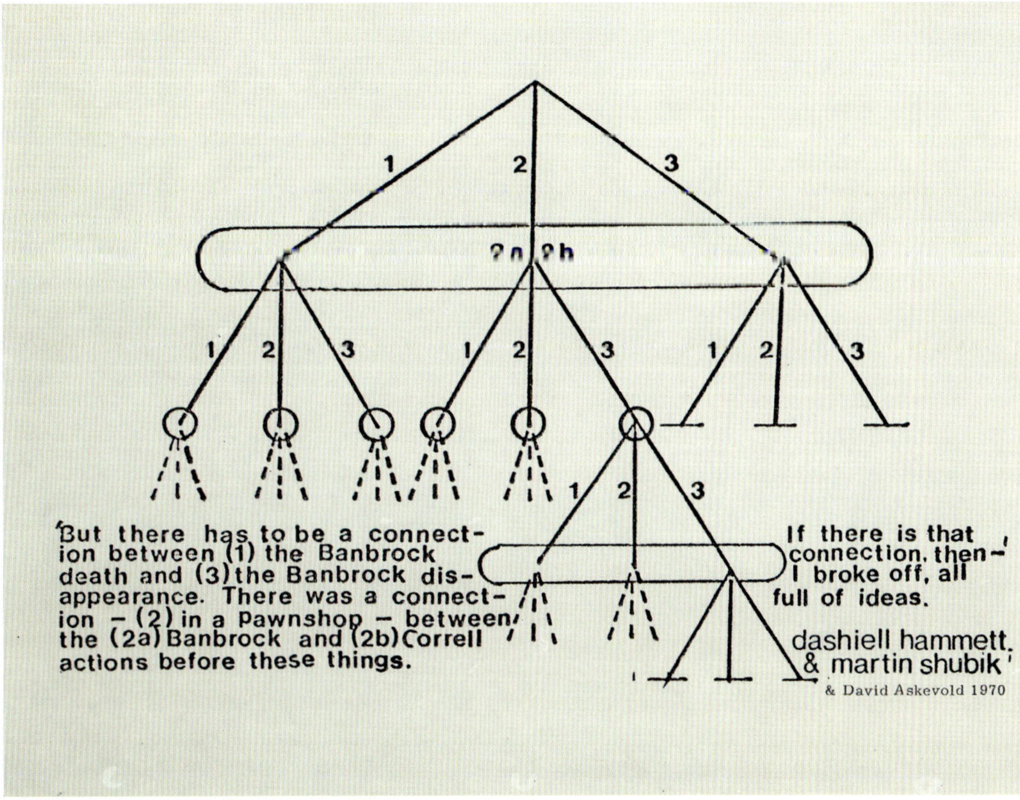

	Get	Dont Get
Get	Grab	Grab Let Go
Dont Get	Let Go Grab	Let Go

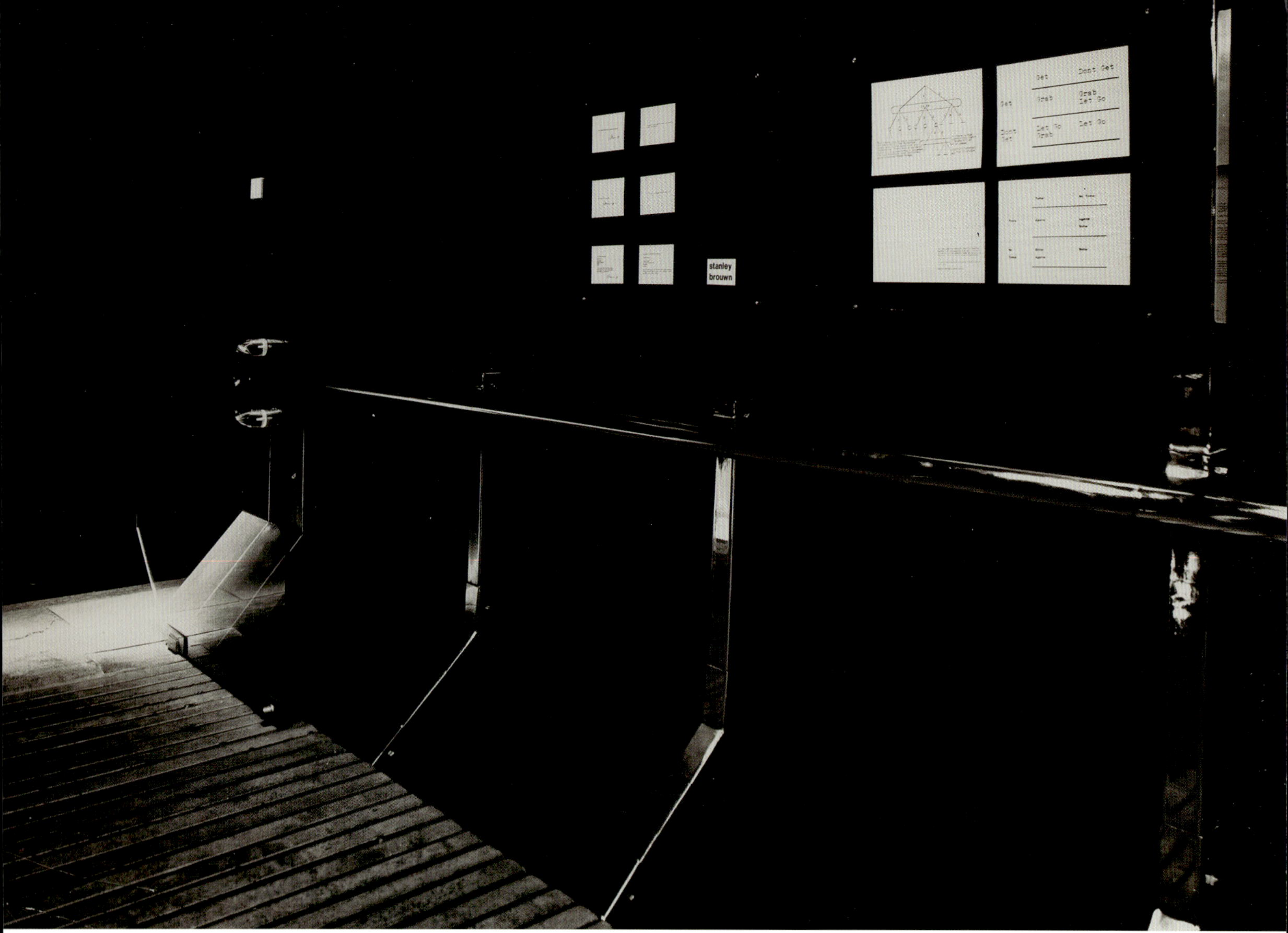

FIGURE 148

Installation view of *2,972,453* including works by David Askevold and Stanley Brouwn; Centro de Arte y Comunicación, Buenos Aires, opened December 4, 1970; organized by Lucy. R. Lippard. Collection of Alan Cravitz, Chicago. (Photographed for the Brooklyn Museum: Michael Tropea)

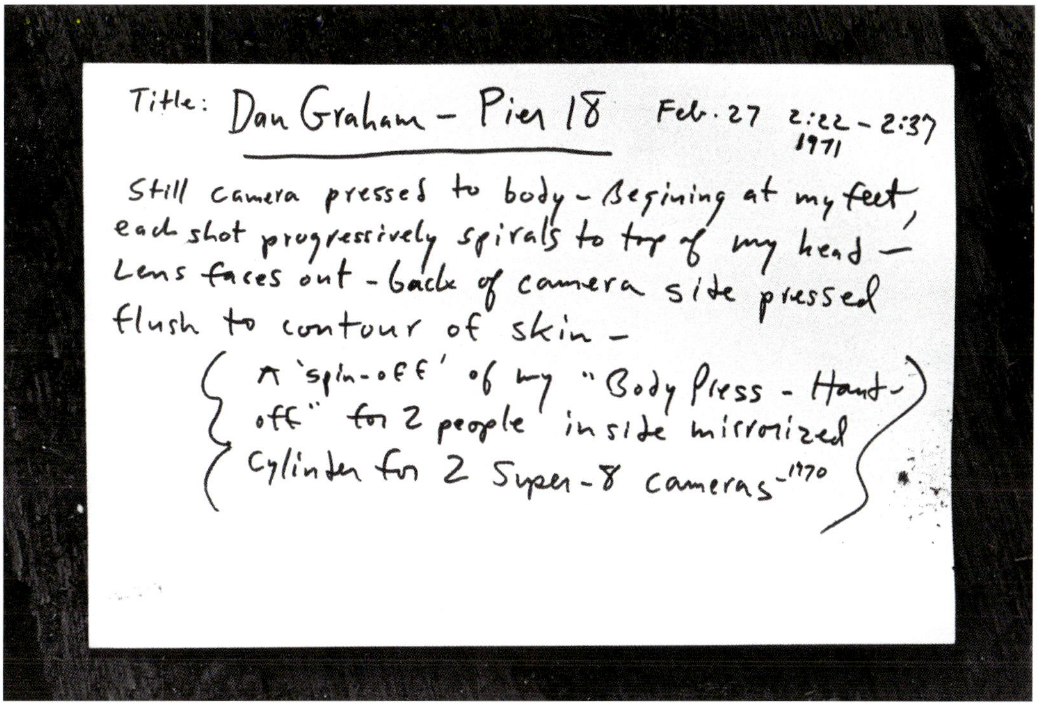

Title: Dan Graham – Pier 18 Feb. 27 2:22 – 2:37
1971

Still camera pressed to body – Begining at my feet, each shot progressively spirals to top of my head – Lens faces out – back of camera side pressed flush to contour of skin –

{ A 'spin-off' of my "Body Press – Hand-off" for 2 people inside mirrorized Cylinder for 2 Super-8 cameras –1970 }

FIGURES 149–177

Dan Graham (American, b. 1942). *Dan Graham—Pier 18*, 1971. Project for *Pier 18*, New York, February–March 1971; organized by Willoughby Sharp and photographed by Shunk-Kender. Gelatin silver prints, 8 × 10 in. (20.3 × 25.4 cm) each. Shunk-Kender (1959–1973) Photographic Archive, New York. (Photos: Shunk-Kender © Roy Lichtenstein Foundation, New York)

Pier 18 was a group show organized by the curator and *Avalanche* editor Willoughby Sharp. From February through March, projects were realized by almost thirty artists, including Dan Graham, John Baldessari, and Allen Ruppersberg, on and in an abandoned pier on the Hudson River. The pier, which was slated for demolition shortly after the exhibition, had to be the site for all the artists' projects, so the photo-documentation taken by the collaborative team of Shunk-Kender, and later exhibited at the Museum of Modern Art, became the only physical remnant of the works in the exhibition.

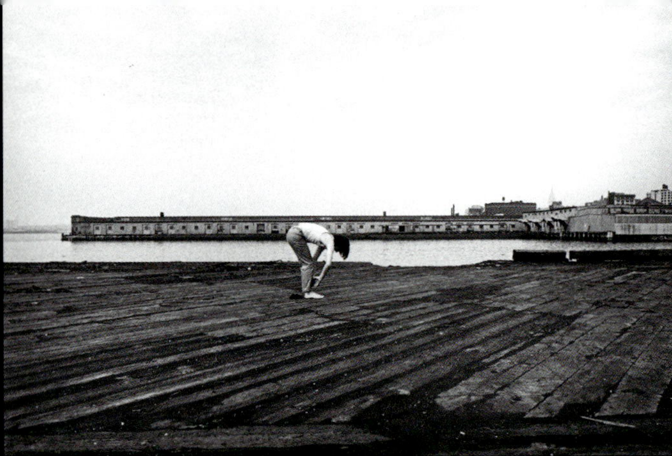
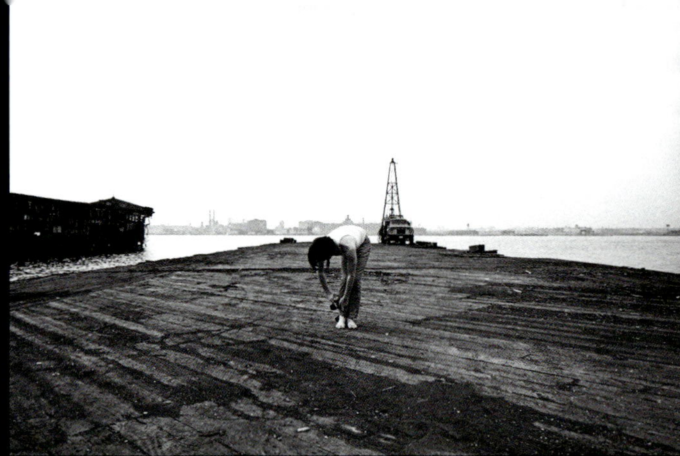
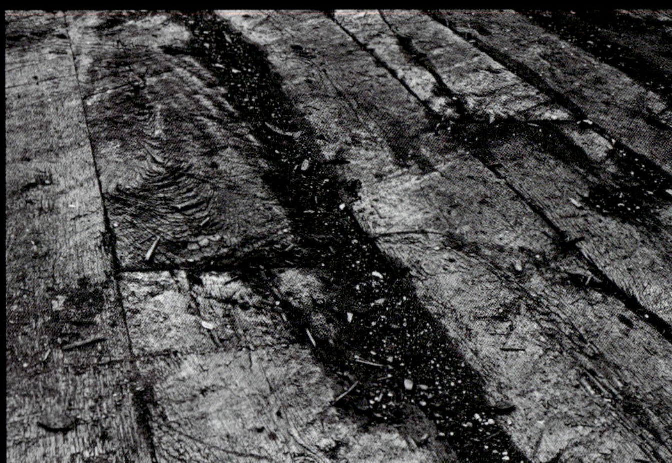
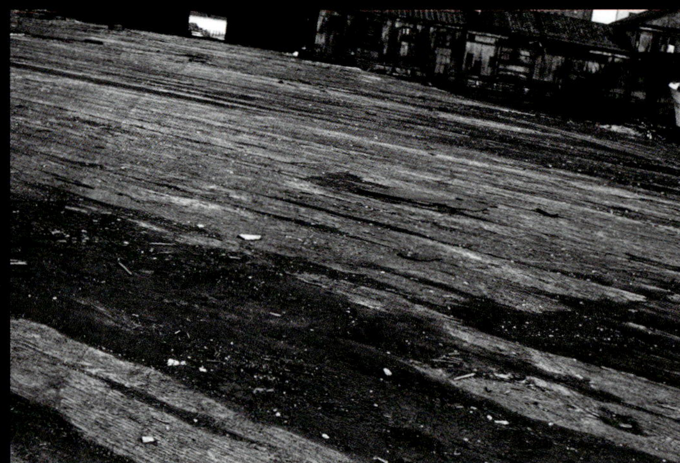

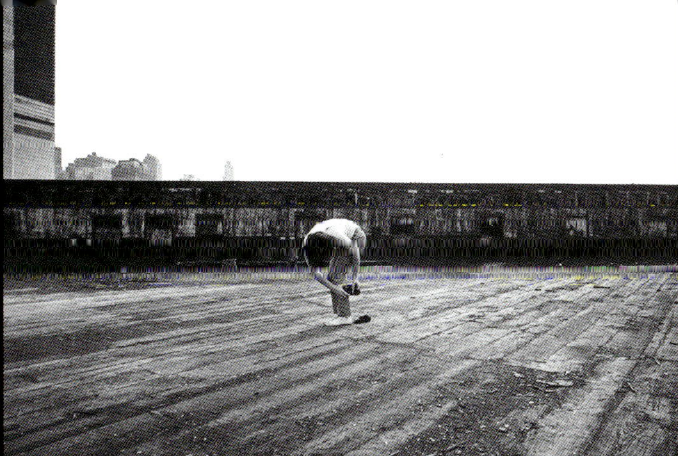

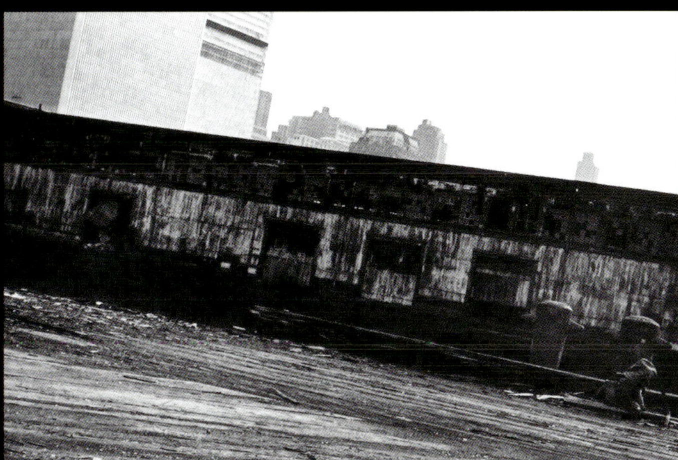

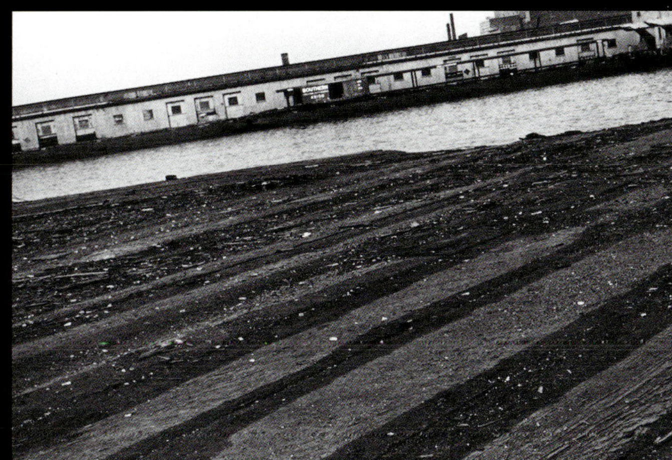

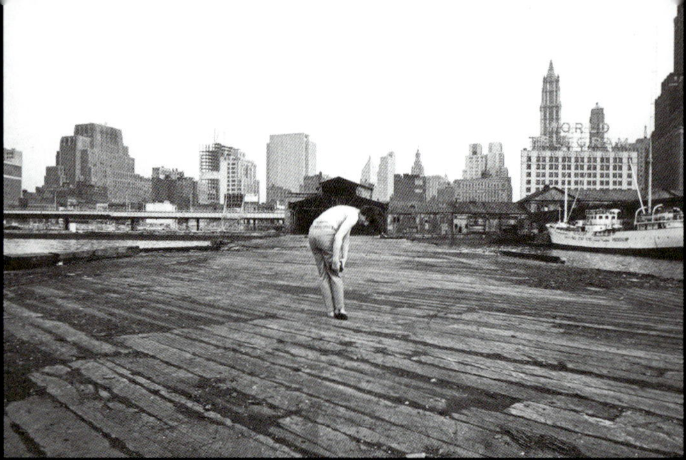

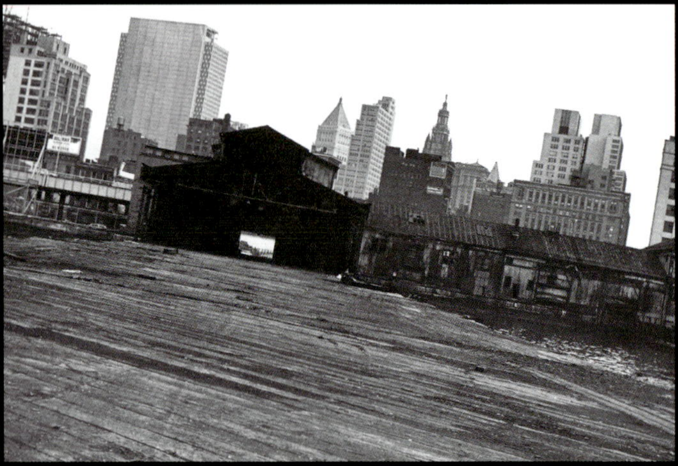

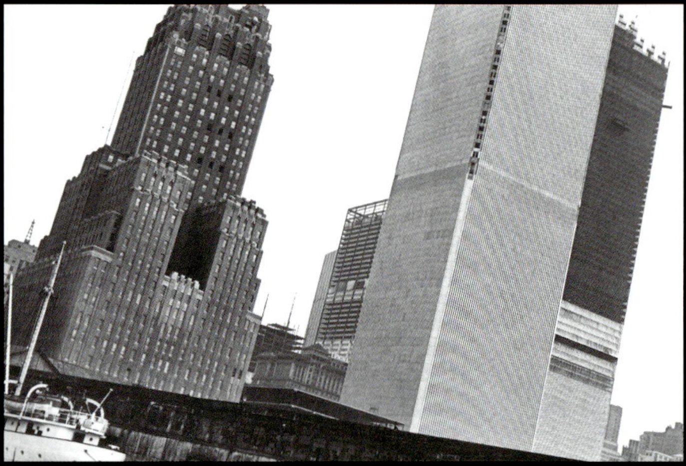

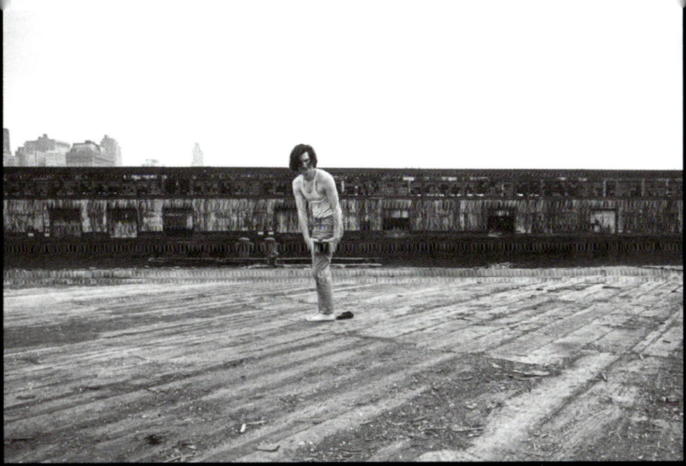

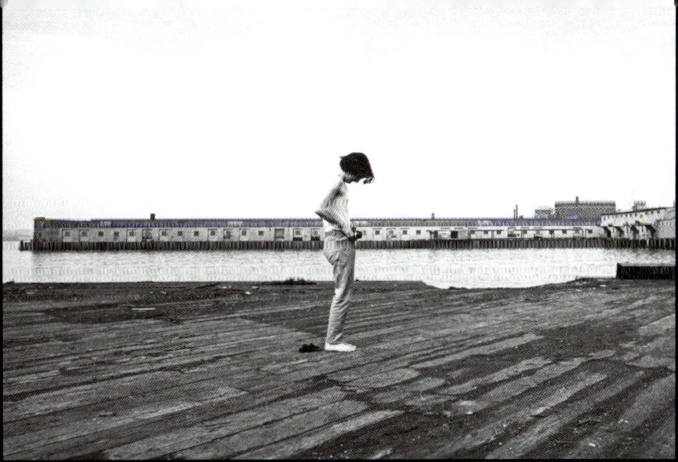

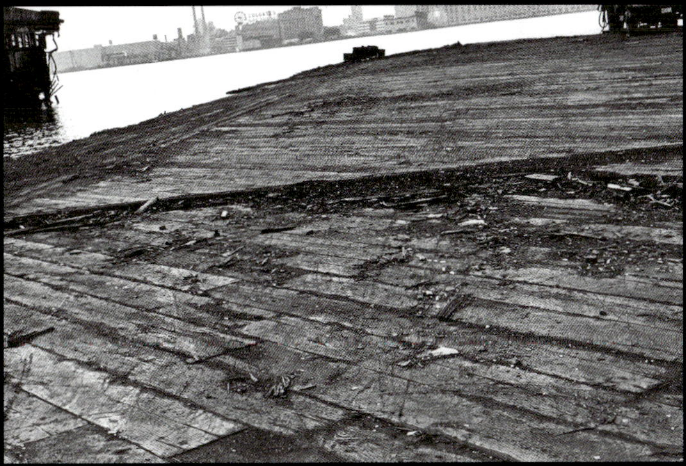

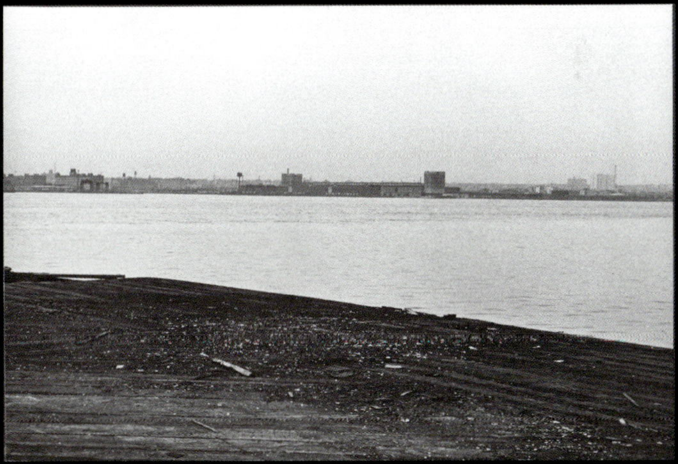

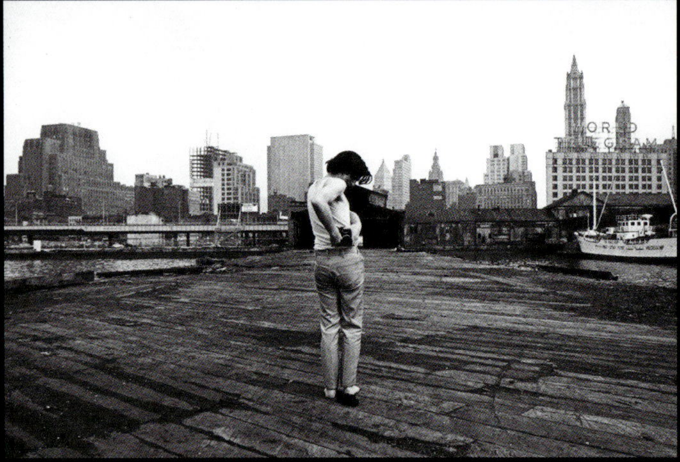
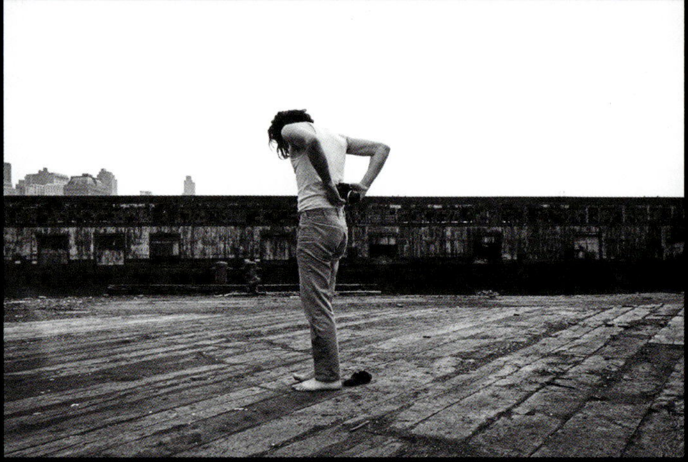
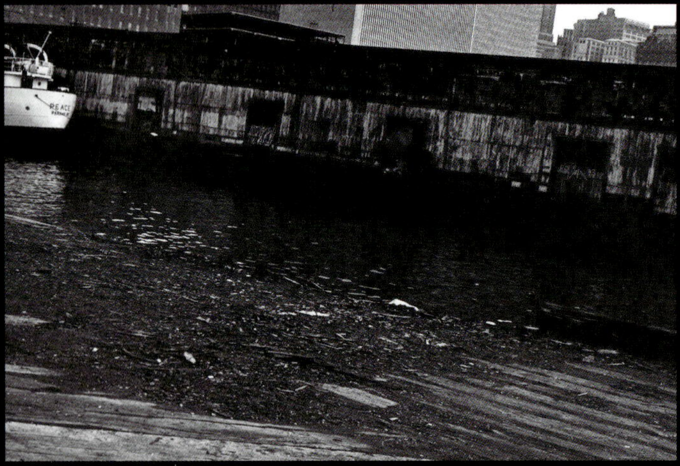
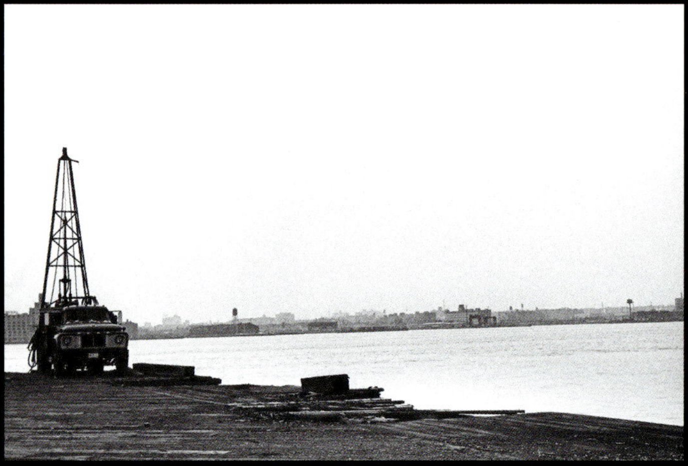

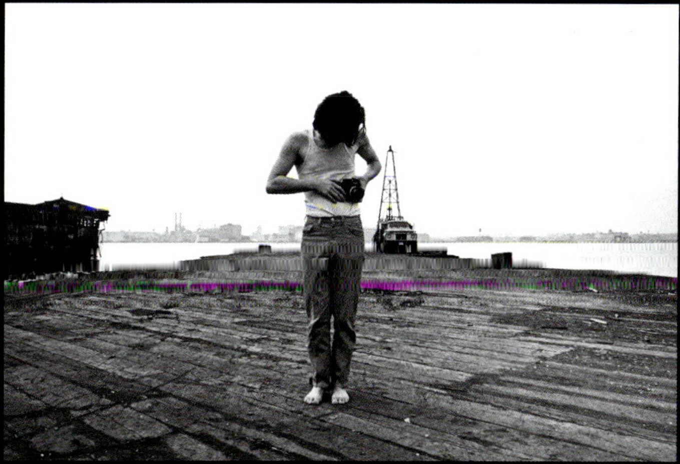

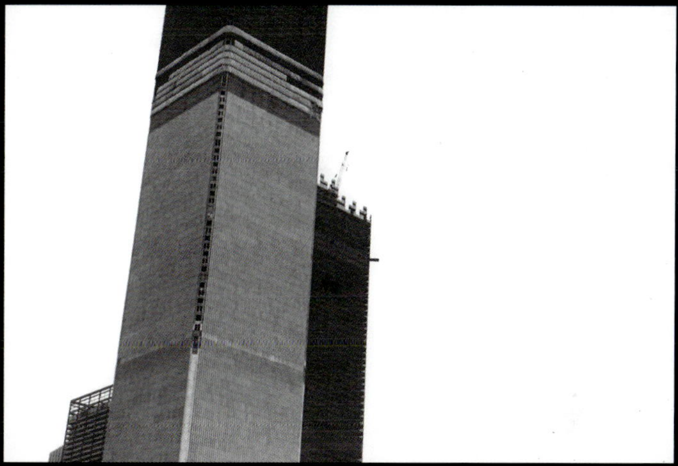

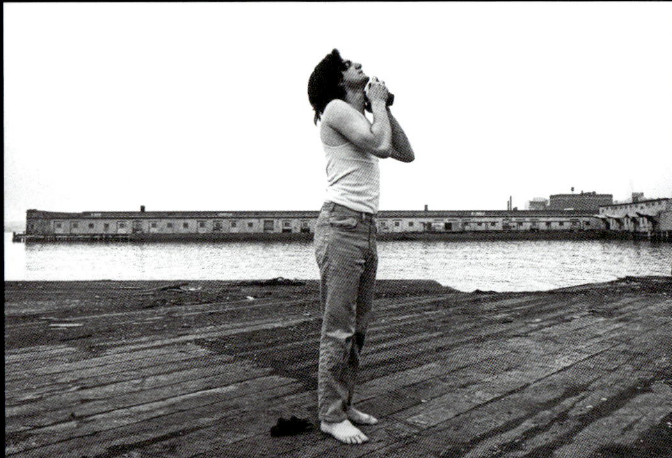

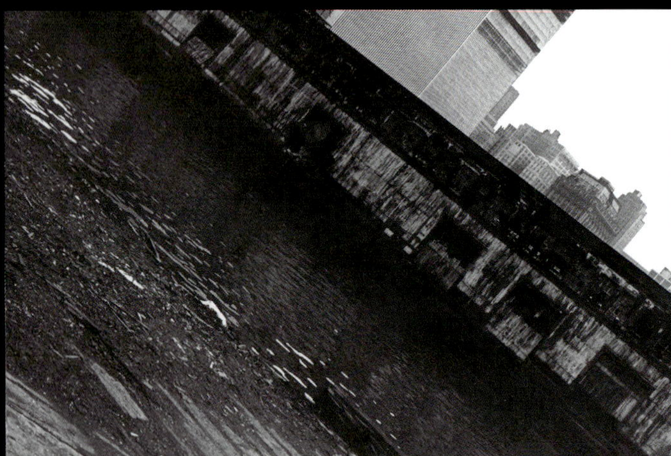

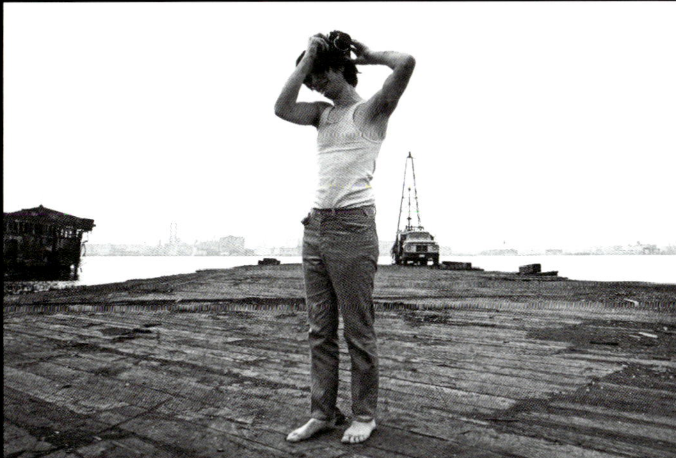

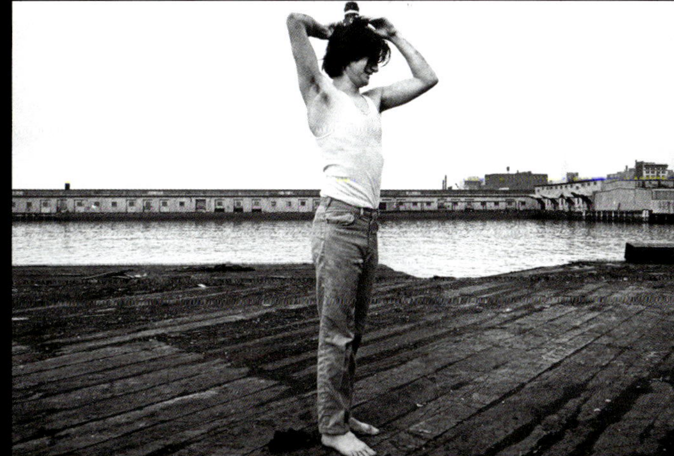

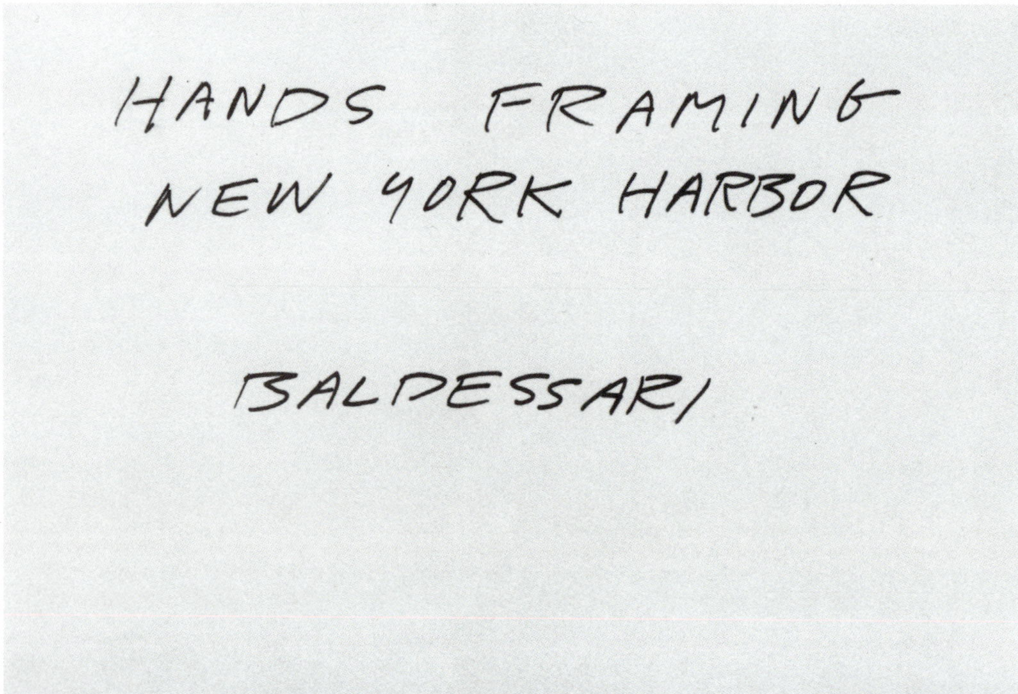
HANDS FRAMING
NEW YORK HARBOR
BALDESSARI

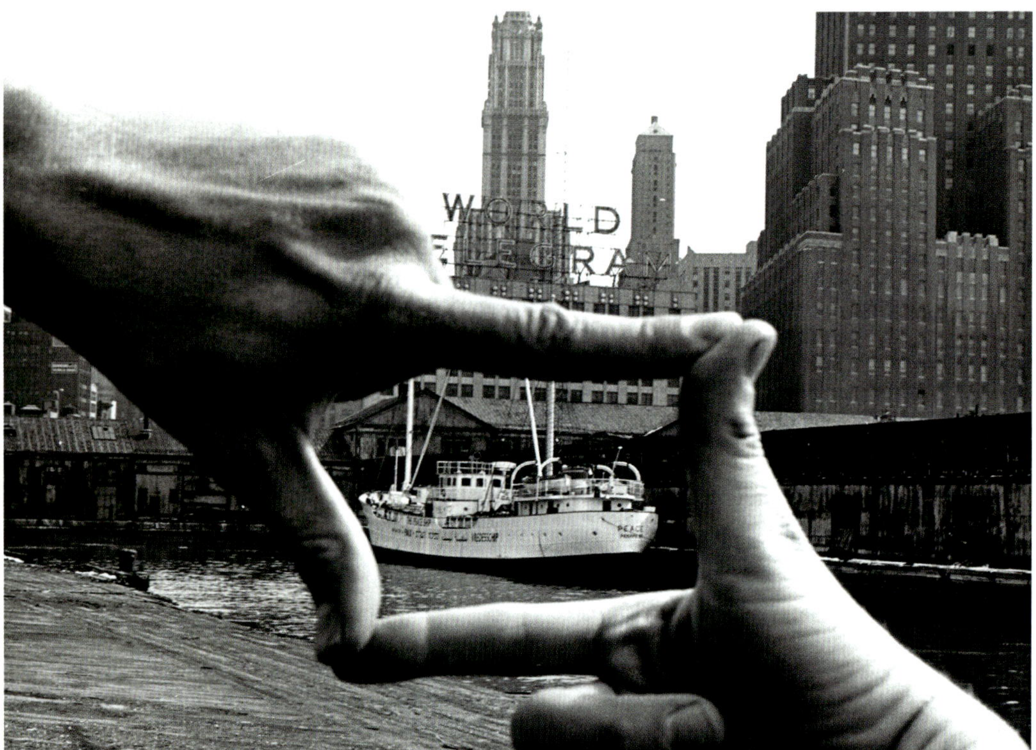

FIGURES 178, 179

John Baldessari (American, b. 1931). *Hands Framing New York Harbor*, 1971. Project for *Pier 18*, New York, February–March 1971; organized by Willoughby Sharp and photographed by Shunk-Kender. Gelatin silver prints, 8 × 10 in. (20.3 × 25.4 cm) each. Shunk-Kender (1959–1973) Photographic Archive, New York. (Photos: Shunk-Kender © Roy Lichtenstein Foundation, New York)

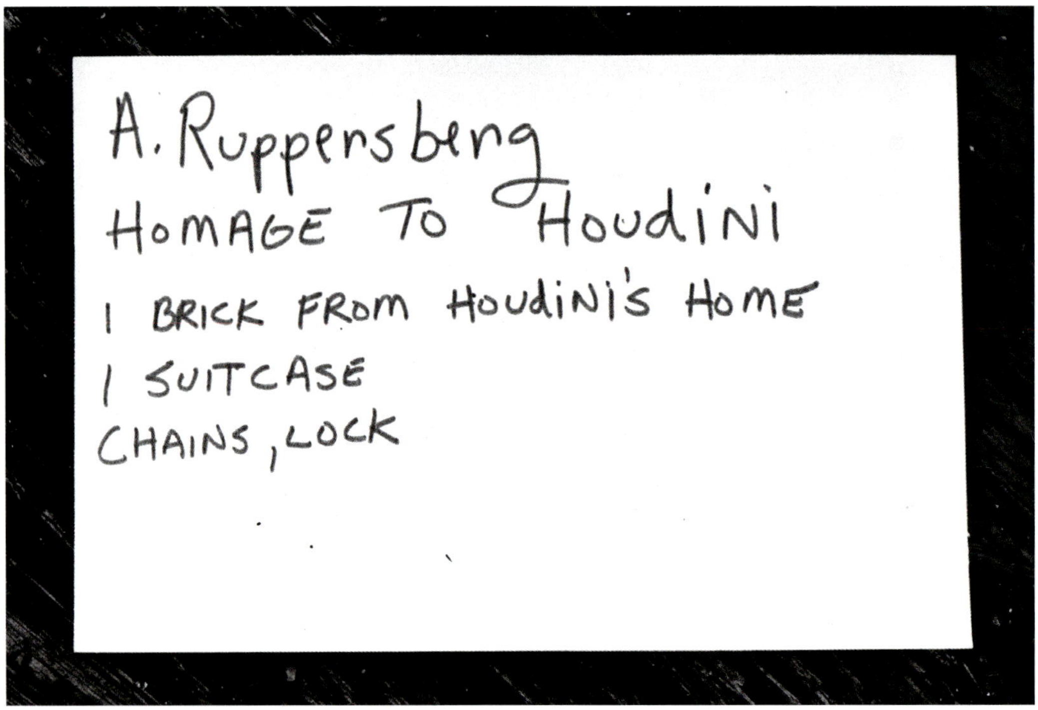

FIGURES 180–189

Allen Ruppersberg (American, b. 1944). *Homage to Houdini*, 1971. Project for *Pier 18*, New York, February–March 1971; organized by Willoughby Sharp and photographed by Shunk-Kender. Gelatin silver prints, 8 × 10 in. (20.3 × 25.4 cm) each. Shunk-Kender (1959–1973) Photographic Archive, New York. (Photos: Shunk-Kender © Roy Lichtenstein Foundation, New York)

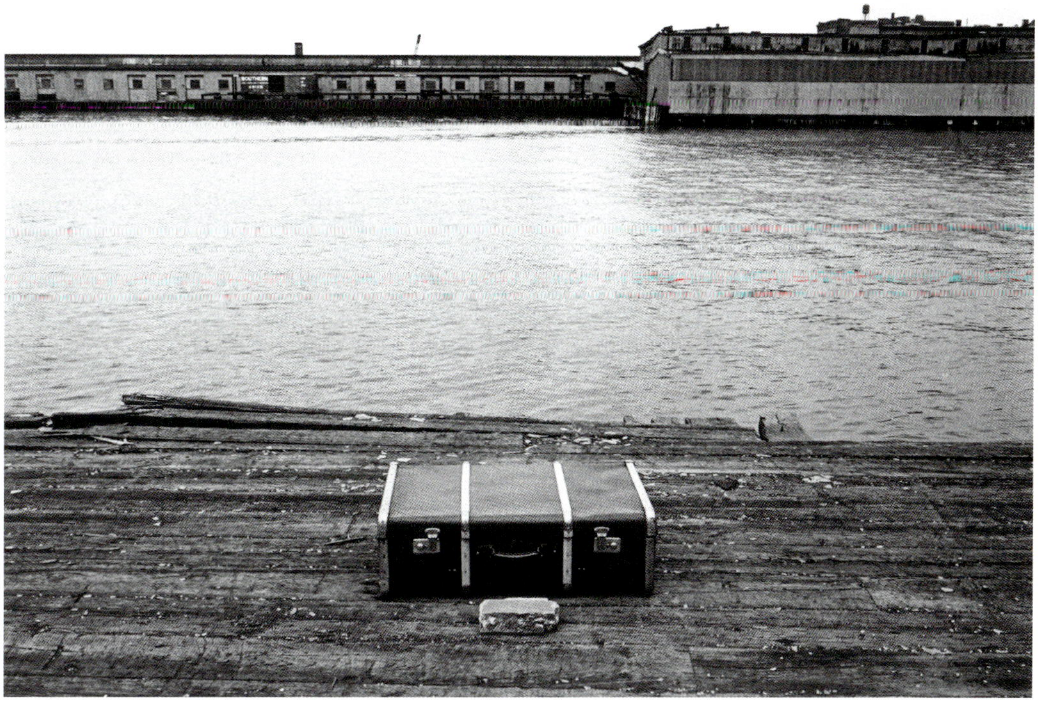

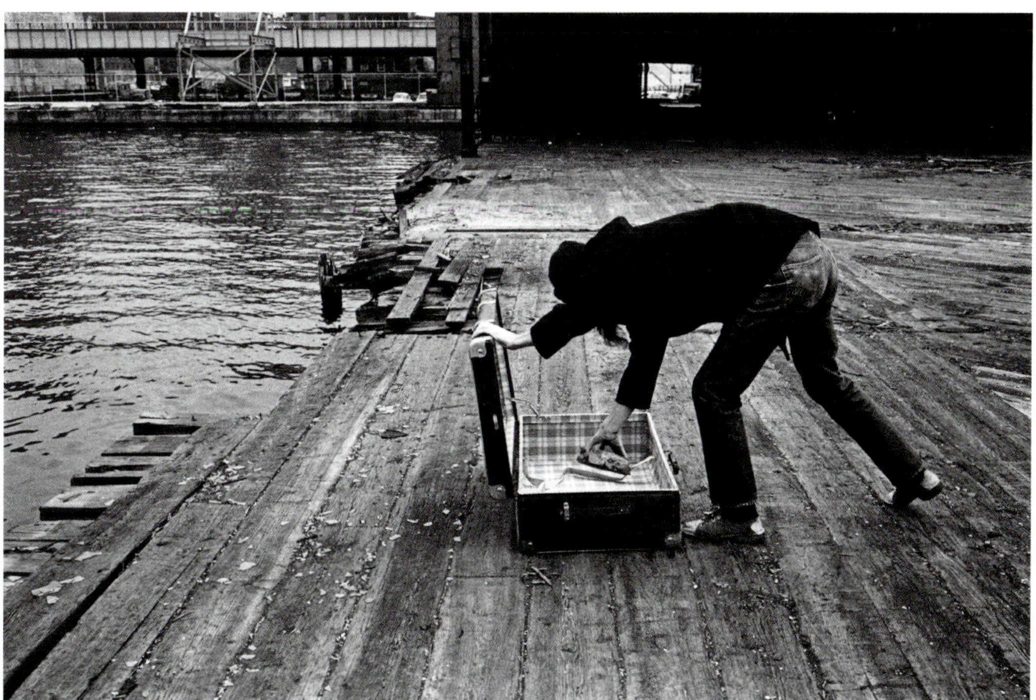

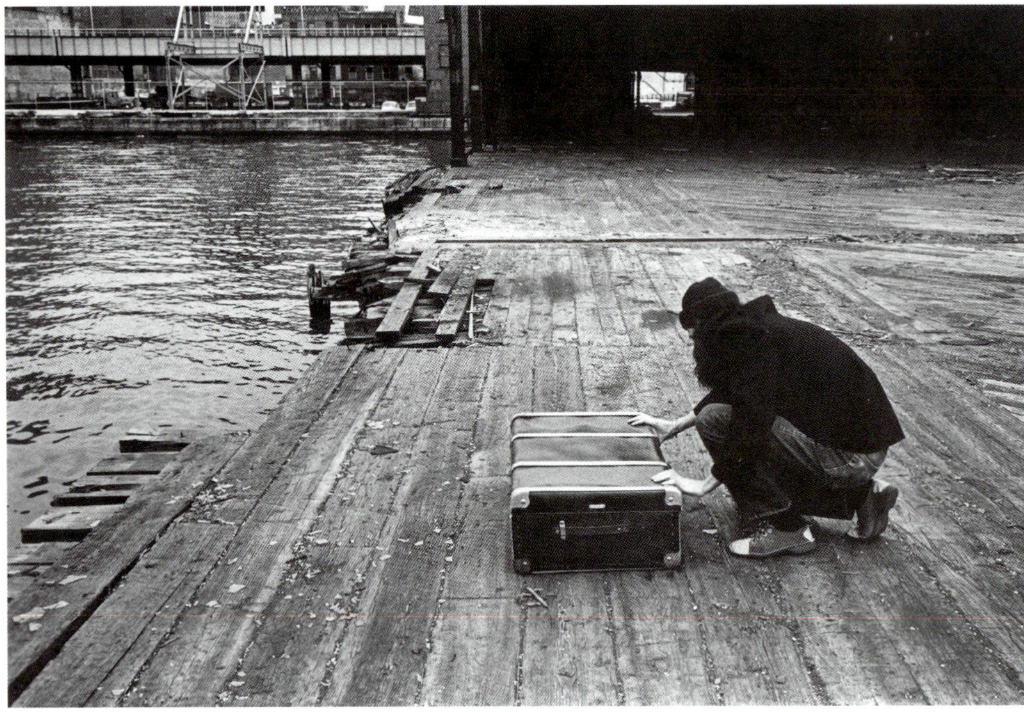

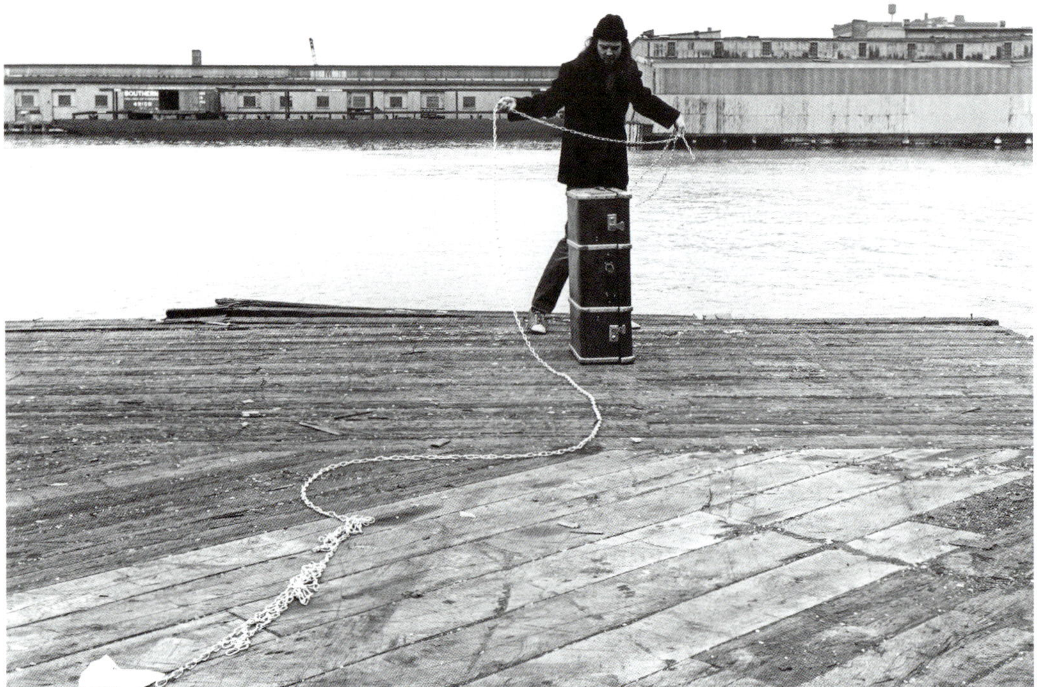

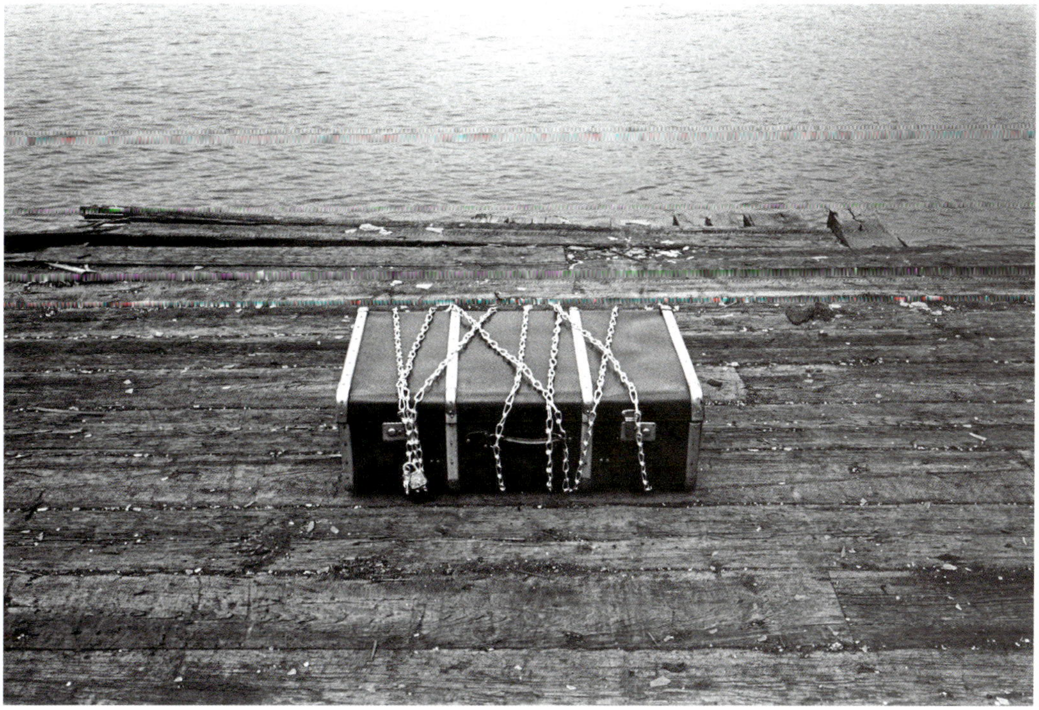

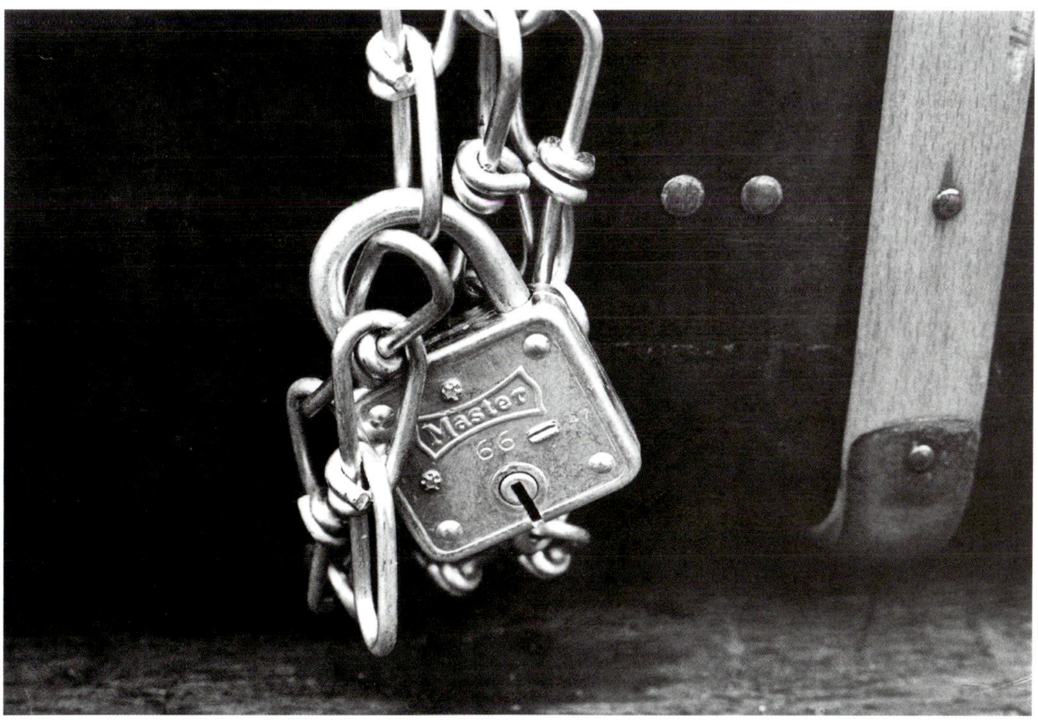
Master
66

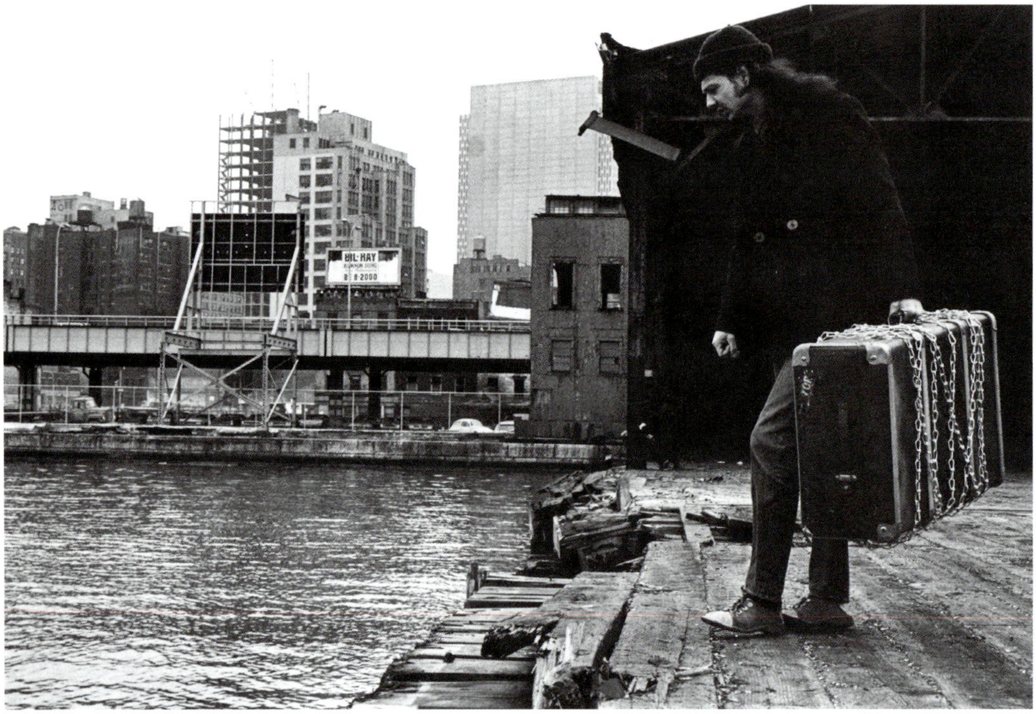

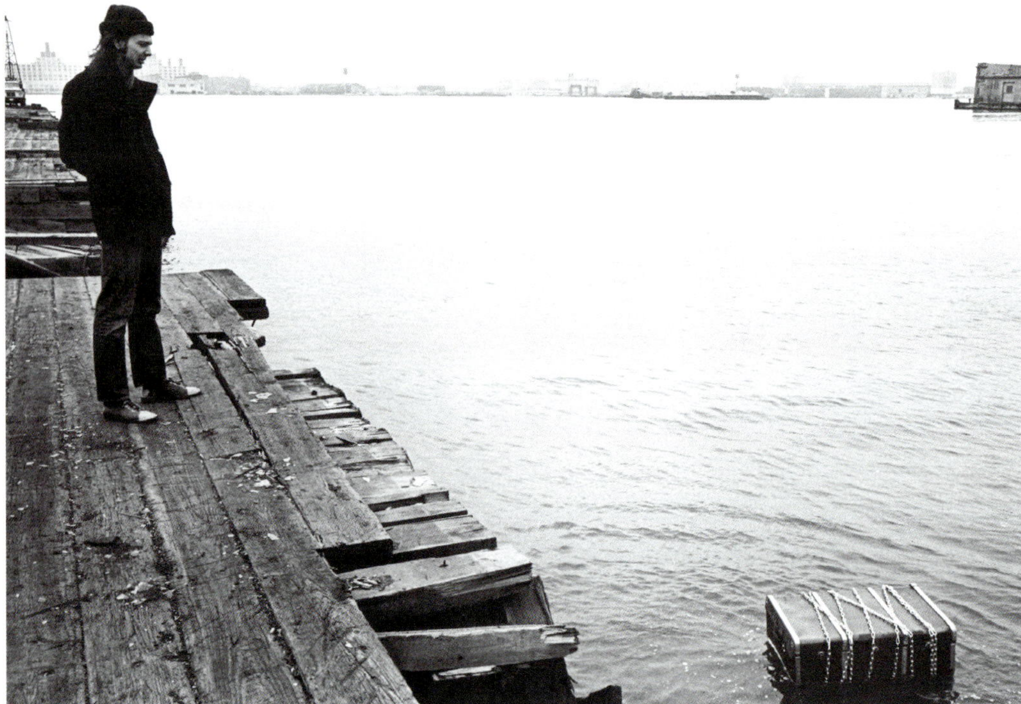

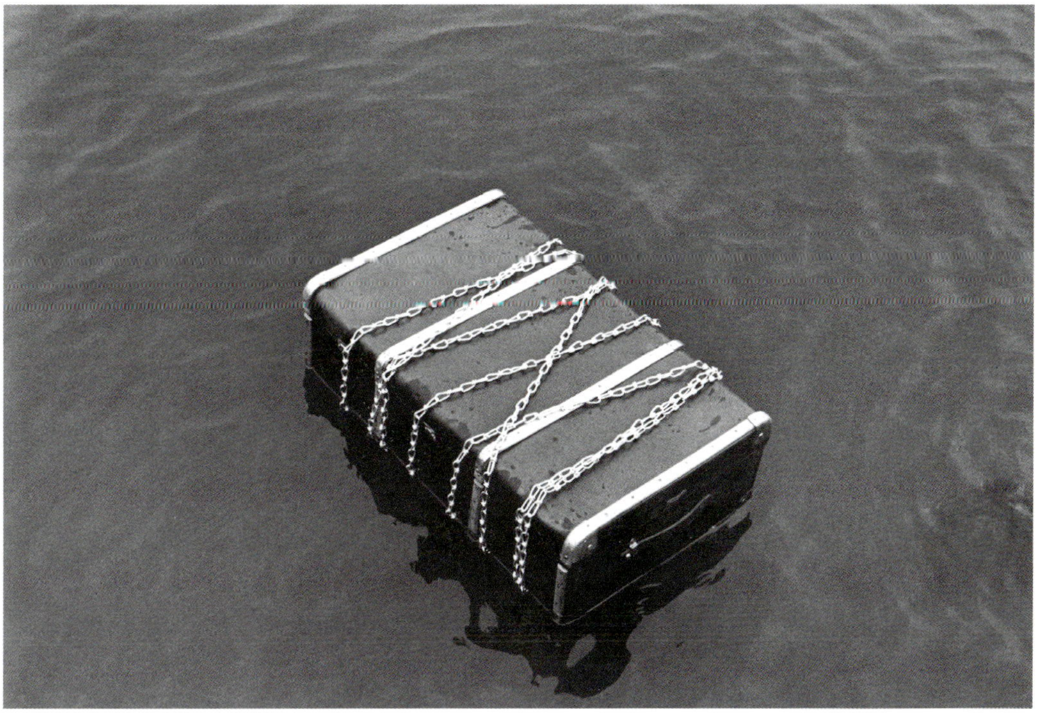

Braco & Nena Dimitrijević
Pantovčak 104 c
Zagreb
Y u g o s l a v i a

Dear Mr.__________________

The group show "AT THE MOMENT" is the first international show of conceptual art which will present our audience the works of several artists which they created in last two years.
The show will be open in March or April depending upon the printing of the cataloge-poster,and will take place in the hall of an apartment house in the center of the city,Zagreb Frankopanska 2a,which will together with the gallery audience allow as well the visit of the casual passers-by.In such specificconditions we have the possibilites to present the works by means of film,slides,photographs,texts and tape.In case you wish to participate please send the works at the latest February 5,1971.Address: Nena & Braco Dimitrijević
Pantovčak 104 c
41000 Zagreb
Y u g o s l a v i a

The materials will be returned by mail after the closing of the show.

The following artists are invited:

Carl Andre
Giovanni Anselmo
Robert Barry
Joseph Beuys
Aligihiero Boetti
Stanley Brouwn
Daniel Buren
Victor Burgin
Hanne Darboven
Jan Dibbets
Braco Dimitrijević
Ger Van Elk
ER Group
Luciano Fabro
Barry Flanagan
Douglas Huebler
Grupa Kôd
Alain Kirili
Joseph Kosuth
Jannis Kounellis
Richard Long
John Latham
Sol LeWitt
Roelof Louw
Mario Merz
OHO Group
Goran Trbuljak
Lawrence Weiner
Ian Wilson
Gilberto Zorio

Awaiting for your answer

Your sincerely,

Nena

"AT THE MOMENT"

HAUSTOR FRANK

ZAGREB 23·4·197

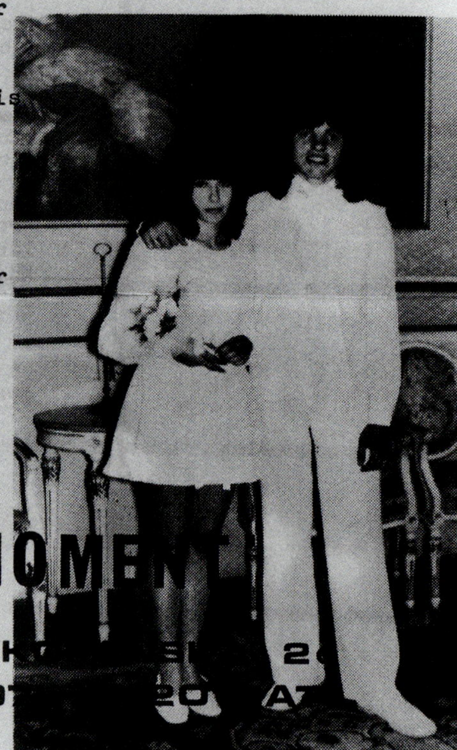

Our wedding photo,July 5,1969

FIGURE 190

Poster for the exhibition *At the Moment, March–April 1971*, 1971. Poster, 26 × 18½ in. (66 × 47 cm). © Braco Dimitrijević. Courtesy Galerie Torri, Paris. (Photo: Braco Dimitrijević Archive)

The possibilities that Conceptual art offered within various political contexts continued to be realized in cities around the world, with Eastern European artists, like their South American counterparts, responding to cultural repression with underground and ephemeral exhibitions. *At the Moment* was the first of two experimental exhibitions organized in 1971 by Braco and Nena Dimitrijević. The first was held for three hours in a randomly selected passageway to an apartment building in Zagreb. The second, held at a gallery in Belgrade, was called *In Another Moment* and proposed to show the same set of artworks in three different configurations, randomly rearranged every five days to undermine the expectation that a certain logic or taste guided the installation.

Unknown Piece

A woman is prevented from knowing the identity of her partner (sleeping pill, blindfold, total darkness) with certainty. On the evidence the child's features give her, she guesses who she slept with.

Unknown Piece

A woman under ether has a child in a large hospital. When she comes to, she is permitted to select the child she thinks is hers from among the babies in the nursery.

Astrological Piece

Couples with unexpected offspring are permitted to trade with couples whose children were born in a more sympathetic astrological sign to their own.

Color Piece

A dark-skinned couple and a light-skinned couple permutate. The resultant nine children are distributed in the most emotionally comfortable manner for the couples involved.

Determined Piece

A woman selects a couple for the genetic features she admires (good teeth, curly hair, green eyes, etc.) and raises their baby.

Determined Piece

A woman determines her child on the basis of some arbitrary system (a row of sperm-bottles marked with colors, the letters of the alphabet, numbers) according to what color, letter or number pleases her.

Determined Piece

A woman selects a couple on the basis of I. Q. test scores (high or low) and raises their baby.

Double Piece

Two couples agree to have babies and trade them. The real parents are in no way permitted to interfere with the upbringing of their child.

Cultural Piece

A WASP couple and a non-English-speaking ethnic couple have babies and trade them. The children may be told the identity of their parents if they ask.

Chauvinistic Piece

A man is injected with the hormone that produces symptoms of motherhood.

FIGURE 191

Martha Wilson (American, b. 1947). *Chauvinist Pieces*, September 1971. Typewritten texts, 17½ × 25¼ in. (44.5 × 64.1 cm). Collection of Martha Wilson, Brooklyn. © Martha Wilson

By 1971, the contributions of women Conceptual artists had become more prominent in *Six Years*, on the one hand illustrating Lippard's growing political commitment to redressing the unequal representation of women's work in the field and, on the other, prefiguring the next major movement with which she would be involved. Feminist art, often cast as less intellectual and more embodied than "pure" Conceptualism, can in fact be seen as extending its theoretical claims by foregrounding the conceptual nature of identity and asserting its investigation as an appropriate subject for advanced art. The preoccupations of feminist artists associated with postmodernism during the next decade are significantly prefigured in projects like Martha Wilson's *Chauvinist Pieces*, which proposes experimental manipulations of the factors that are assumed to determine identity. One of the more concise hypothetical scenarios listed in the piece suggests, "A man is injected with the hormone that produces symptoms of motherhood."

FIGURES 192, 193 (FOLLOWING PAGES)

Hans Haacke (American, b. Germany 1936). *Shapolsky et al. Manhattan Real Estate Holdings, a Real Time Social System, as of May 1, 1971* (details), 1971. Two maps (photo-enlargements); 142 black-and-white photographs; 142 typewritten sheets; six charts, an explanatory panel, dimensions variable. Edition no. 1 Collection Centre Georges Pompidou, Paris; Edition no. 2 jointly owned by Whitney Museum of American Art, New York, and Museu d'Art Contemporani, Barcelona. © Hans Haacke/Artist Rights Society (ARS), New York. (Photo: Hans Haacke)

In April 1971, the director of New York's Guggenheim Museum canceled Haacke's solo exhibition and fired its curator, Edward Fry. The controversial piece that caused this censorship was *Business Office of Shapolsky, et al., Manhattan Real Estate Holdings—A Real Time Social System as of Oct. 1, 1971*, which intricately documented the business practices of a notorious Manhattan landlord and had potentially compromising implications for the museum and its trustees.

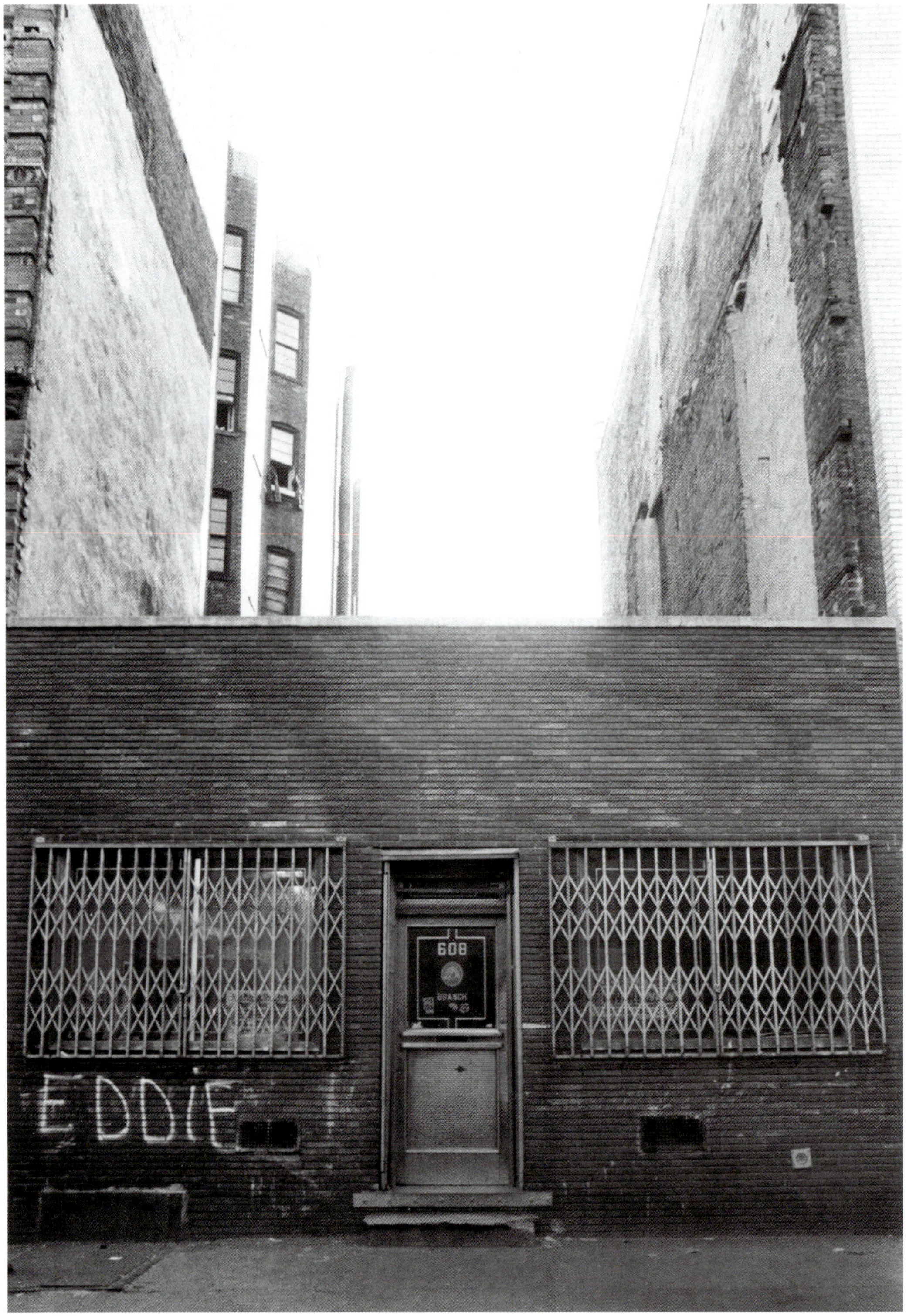
608
BRANCH
EDDIE

608 E 11 St.
Block 393 Lot 11
25 x 94' 1 story store bldg.

Business office of Shapolsky related corporations
Owned by 194 Ave. A Realty Corp., 608 E 11 St., NYC
Contracts signed by Sam Shapolsky, President('58)
Harry J. Shapolsky, Pres.('60)
Alfred Fayer, Vicepres. ('58)
Principal Harry J. Shapolsky(according to Real Estate Directory of Manhattan)

Acquired 3-27-1963 from Surenko Realties Inc,
608 E 11 St., NYC, Harry J. Shapolsky, President(63)

No mortgage(1971)

Assessed land value $8 500.- , total $24 000.- (1971)

FIGURES 194, 195: Produced for an exhibition devoted to women artists in San Diego and then Halifax, Eleanor Antin's *Library Science* collected "a piece of information" provided by each participating artist and an object that could represent them, items which were then indexed and classified according to the Library of Congress system, as if they were individual books. The same year, Antin began documenting the journey of one hundred boots, photographing their meandering, cross-country adventures from this beach in Southern California to their eventual arrival at the Museum of Modern Art in New York in May 1973. Each of the fifty-one photographs was reproduced as a postcard and mailed out to hundreds of people, who could follow the unfolding narrative of these anthropomorphized boots over the course of more than two years.

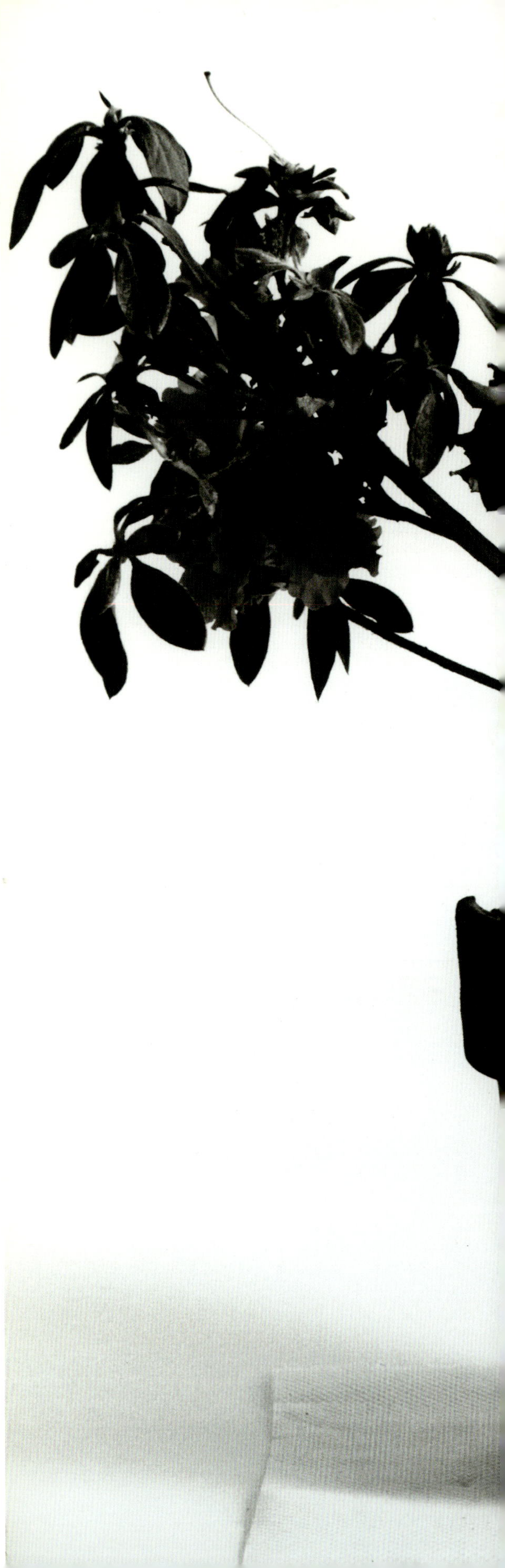

FIGURE 194

Eleanor Antin (American, b. 1935). *Library Science* (detail), 1971. Installation including library catalogue cards, mounted black-and-white photographs, original Xerox of artist's statement, and library pamphlet: 27 library catalogue cards, 2½ × 3½ in. (6.4 × 8.9 cm) each; 25 photographs, 8 × 10 in. (20.3 × 25.4 cm) each. © Eleanor Antin. (Photo: Ronald Feldman Fine Arts, New York/www.feldmangallery.com)

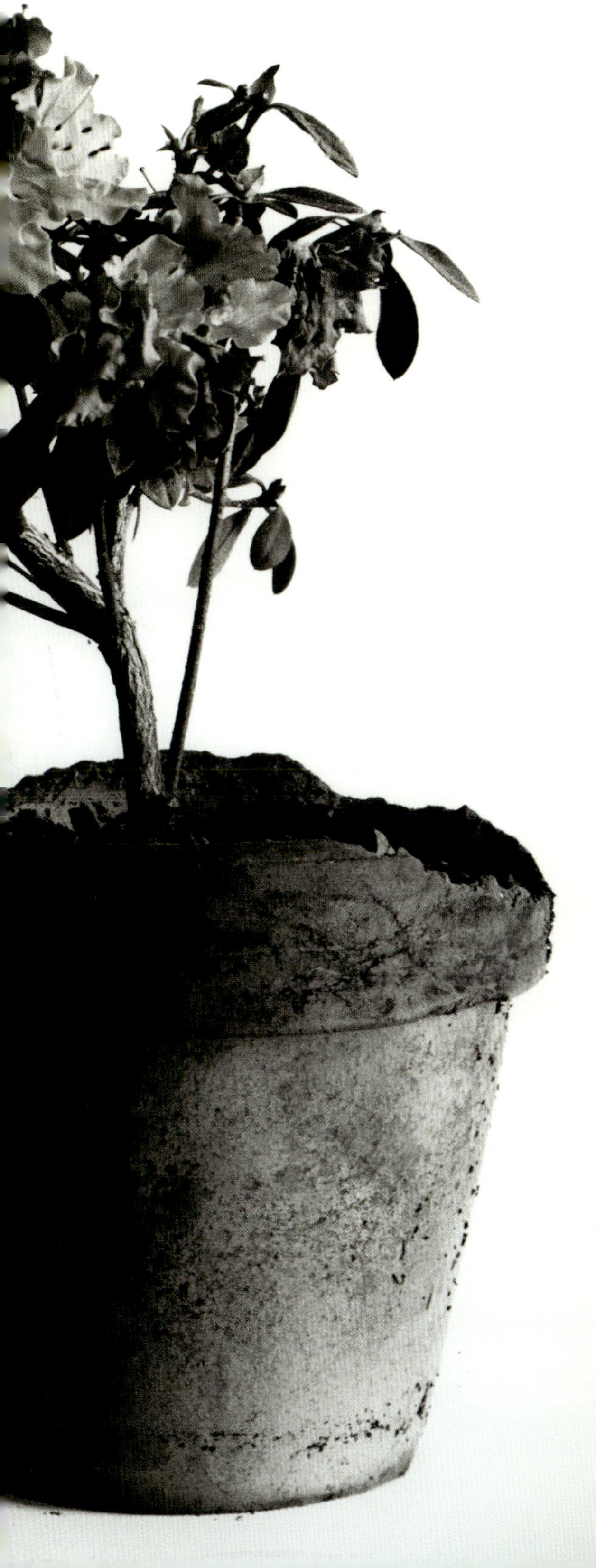

GUERILLA WARFARE

U Fredman, Faiya
240
F2

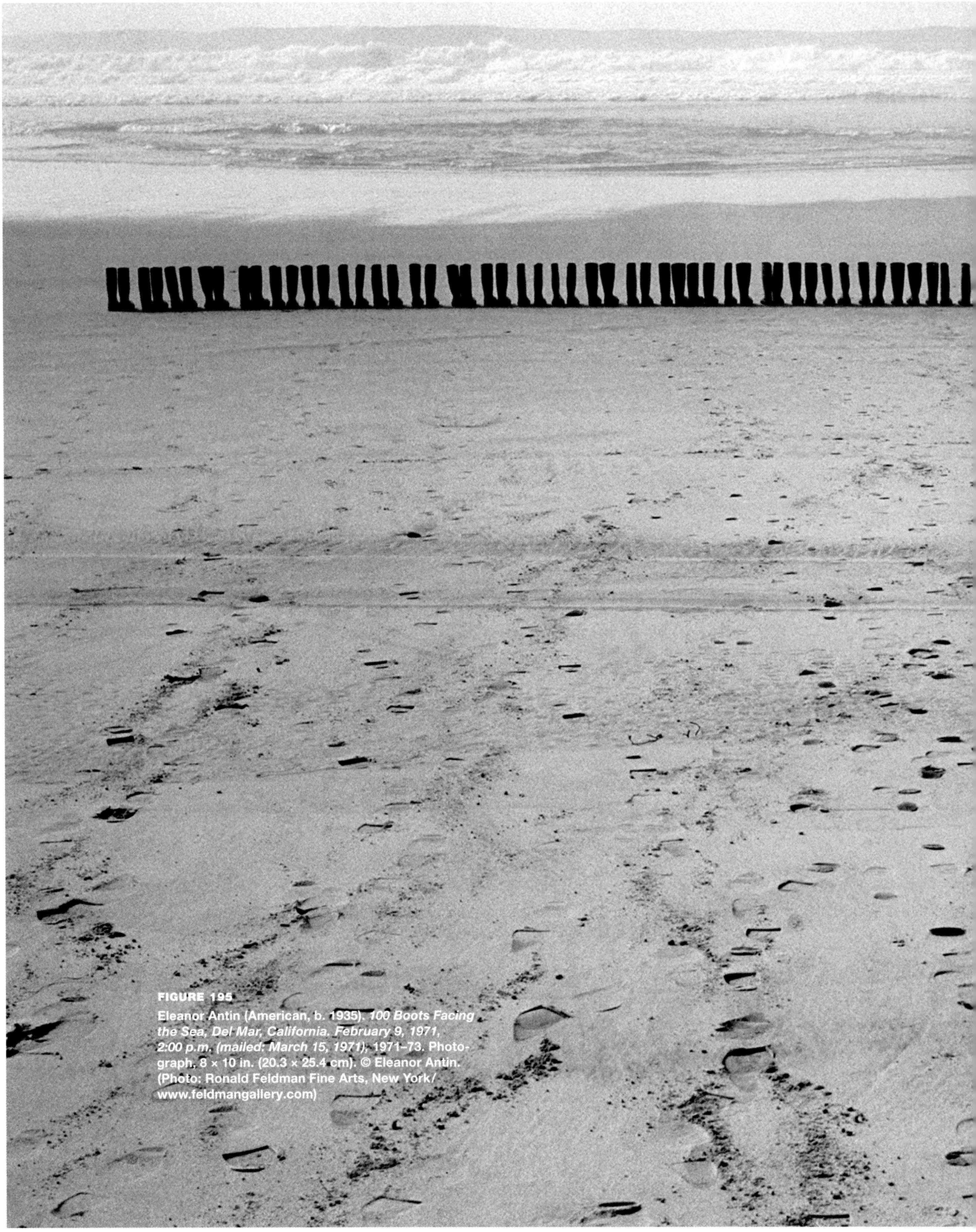

FIGURE 195

Eleanor Antin (American, b. 1935). *100 Boots Facing the Sea, Del Mar, California. February 9, 1971, 2:00 p.m. (mailed: March 15, 1971),* 1971–73. Photograph, 8 × 10 in. (20.3 × 25.4 cm). © Eleanor Antin. (Photo: Ronald Feldman Fine Arts, New York/ www.feldmangallery.com)

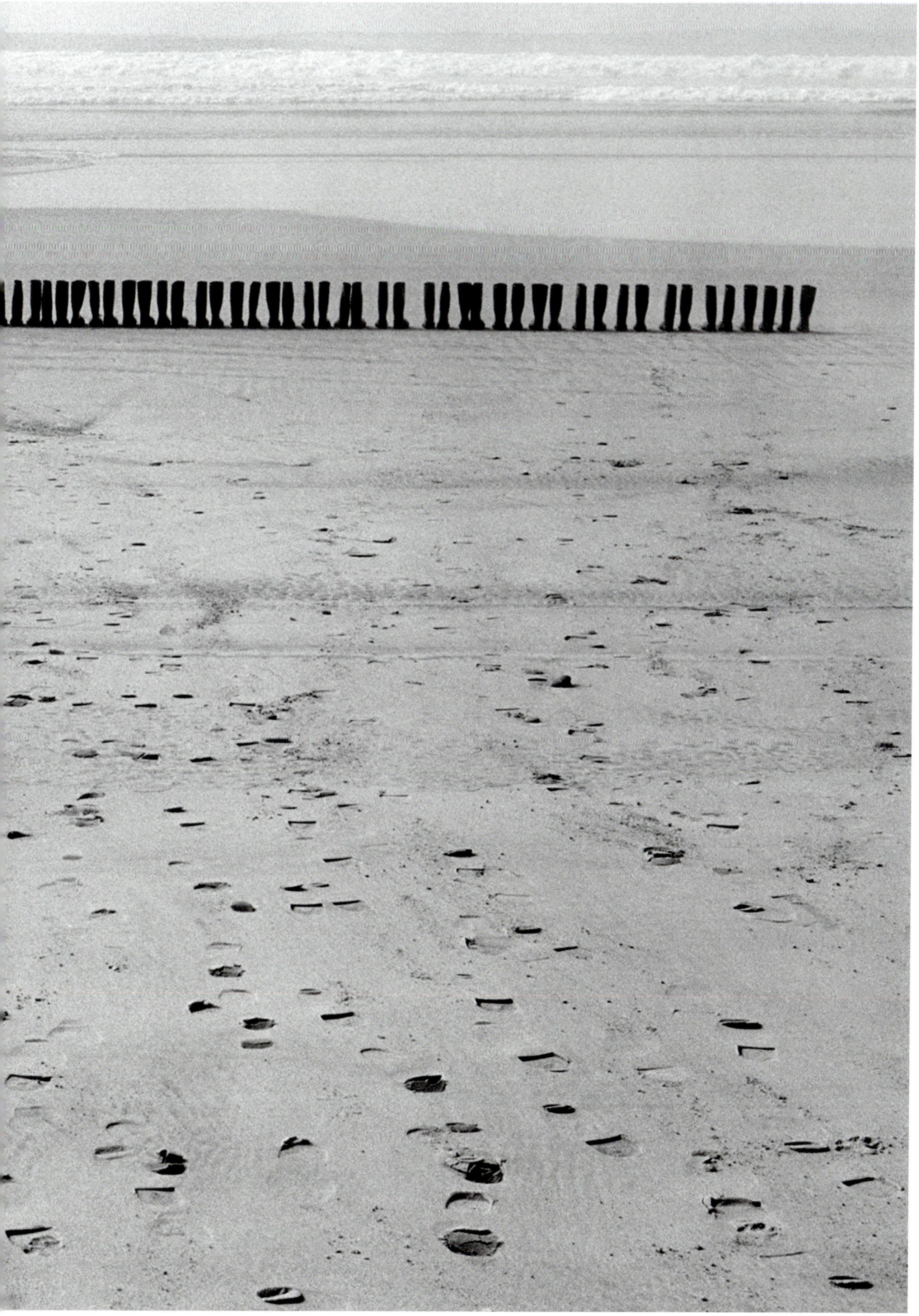

FIGURES 196–198: As the political and social idealism of the 1960s gave way to a greater pessimism in the 1970s, some artists dug in more fervently to an activist politics through art, exemplified by the Guerrilla Art Action Group (GAAG), which began a letter-writing campaign to high-profile figures involved in the Vietnam War. Each of these proposes actions that politicians should take, such as their suggestion that President Nixon should eat what he has killed, rotting meat in the fields of Vietnam.

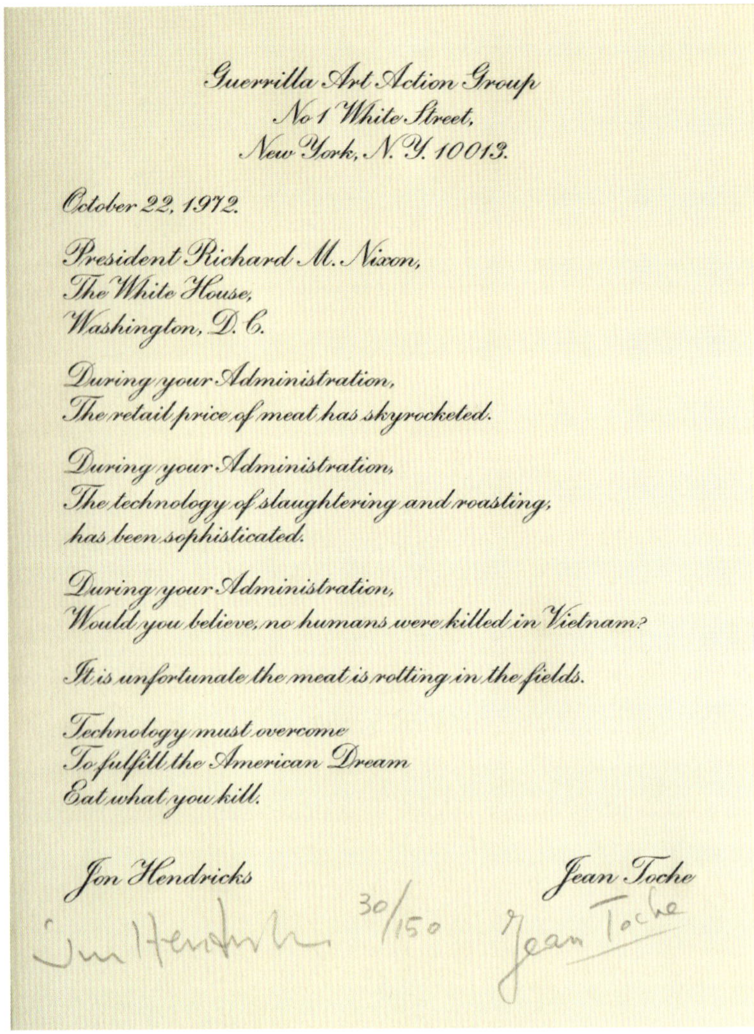

Guerrilla Art Action Group
No 1 White Street,
New York, N.Y. 10013.

October 22, 1972.

President Richard M. Nixon,
The White House,
Washington, D.C.

During your Administration,
The retail price of meat has skyrocketed.

During your Administration,
The technology of slaughtering and roasting,
has been sophisticated.

During your Administration,
Would you believe, no humans were killed in Vietnam?

It is unfortunate the meat is rotting in the fields.

Technology must overcome
To fulfill the American Dream
Eat what you kill.

Jon Hendricks — Jean Toche

30/150

FIGURE 196

Guerrilla Art Action Group (Jon Hendricks [American, b. 1939] and Jean Toche [American, b. Belgium 1932]). *Eat What You Kill*, 1971. Engraving, 7½ × 5½ in. (19 × 14 cm). Collection of Jon Hendricks. (Photo: Brooklyn Museum)

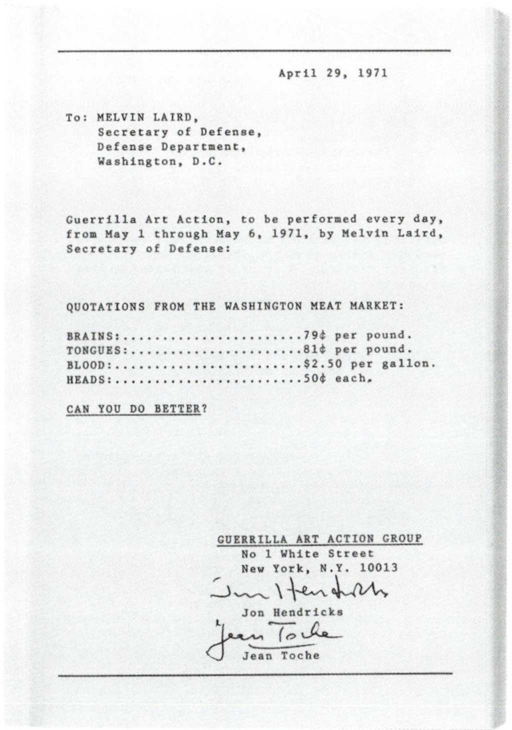

April 29, 1971

To: MELVIN LAIRD,
Secretary of Defense,
Defense Department,
Washington, D.C.

Guerrilla Art Action, to be performed every day, from May 1 through May 6, 1971, by Melvin Laird, Secretary of Defense:

QUOTATIONS FROM THE WASHINGTON MEAT MARKET:

BRAINS:.......................79¢ per pound.
TONGUES:......................81¢ per pound.
BLOOD:........................$2.50 per gallon.
HEADS:........................50¢ each.

CAN YOU DO BETTER?

GUERRILLA ART ACTION GROUP
No 1 White Street
New York, N.Y. 10013
Jon Hendricks
Jean Toche

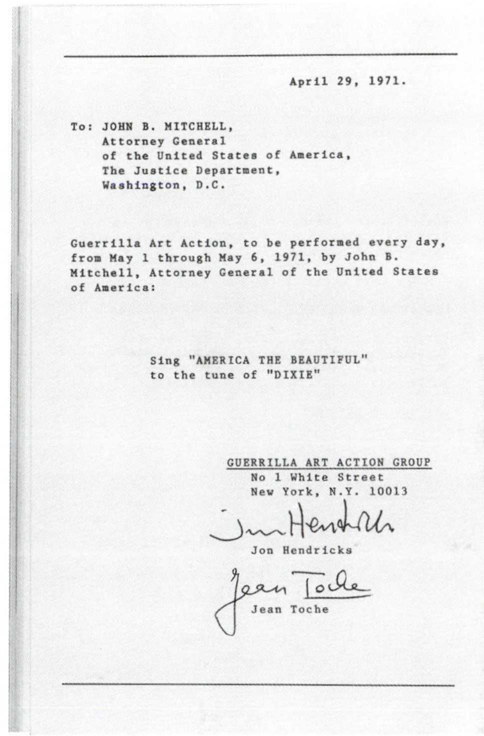

April 29, 1971.

To: JOHN B. MITCHELL,
Attorney General
of the United States of America,
The Justice Department,
Washington, D.C.

Guerrilla Art Action, to be performed every day, from May 1 through May 6, 1971, by John B. Mitchell, Attorney General of the United States of America:

Sing "AMERICA THE BEAUTIFUL"
to the tune of "DIXIE"

GUERRILLA ART ACTION GROUP
No 1 White Street
New York, N.Y. 10013
Jon Hendricks
Jean Toche

FIGURES 197, 198

Guerrilla Art Action Group (Jon Hendricks [American, b. 1939] and Jean Toche [American, b. Belgium 1932]). Two letters from *Send Letters to Nixon, Agnew, Hoover, Mitchell, Laird, Kissinger ... April 29, New York*, 1971. Typewritten letters, 11 × 8½ in. (27.9 × 21.6 cm) each. Collection of Alan Cravitz, Chicago. (Photo: Brooklyn Museum)

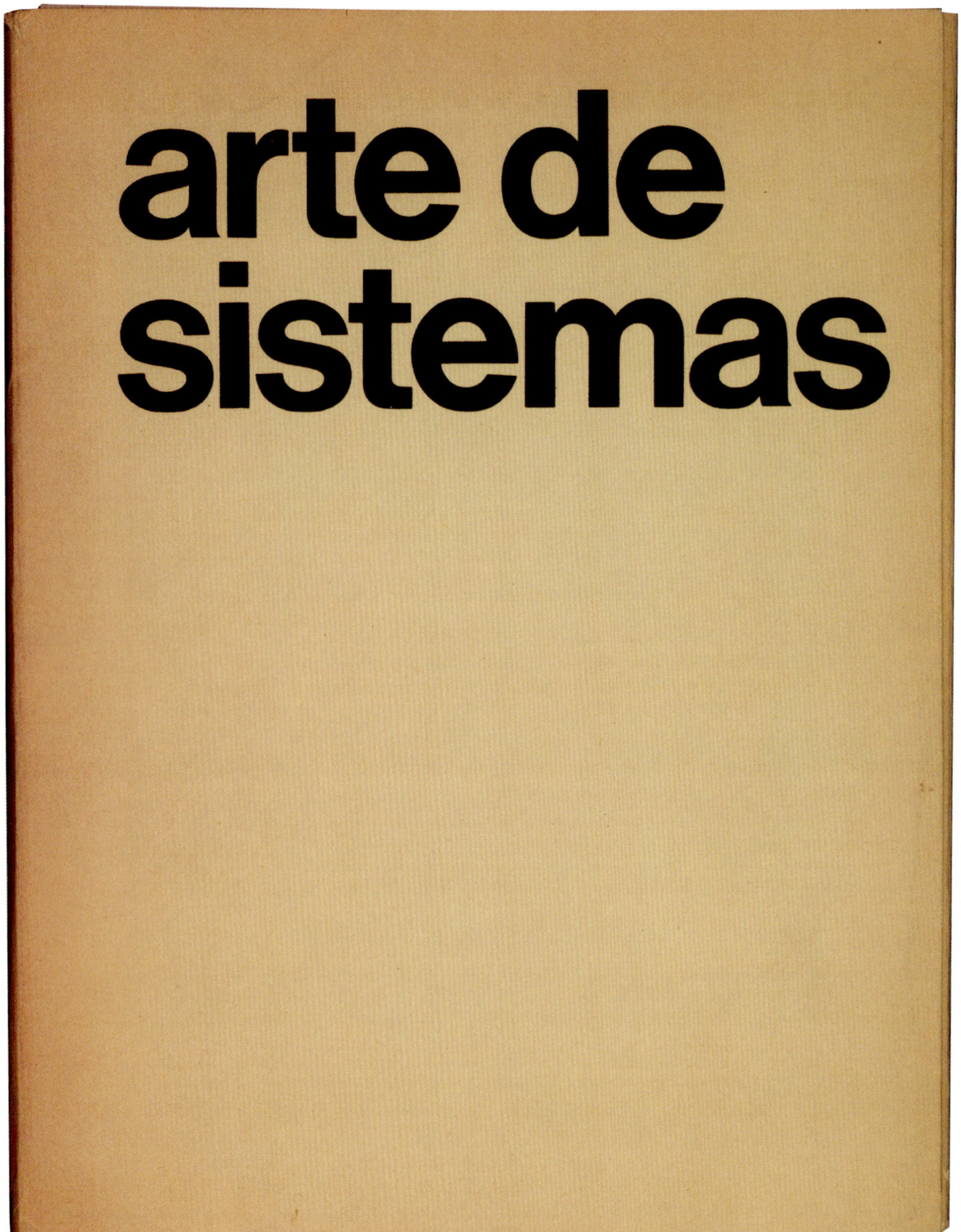
arte de
sistemas

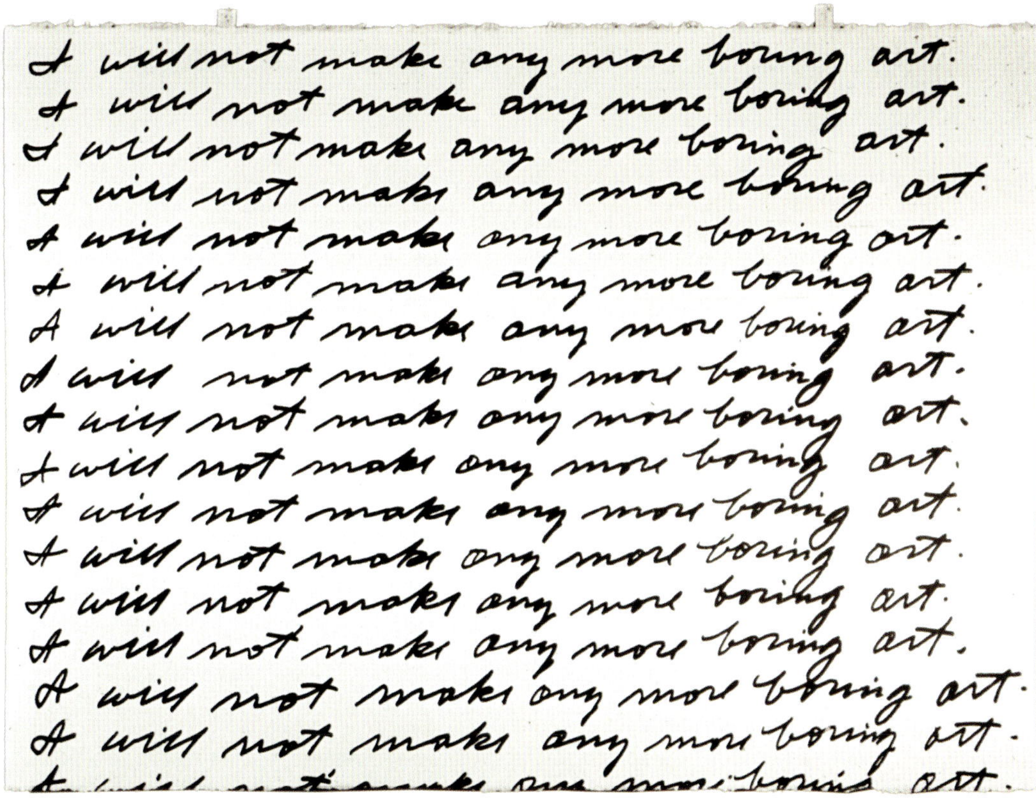

FIGURE 199

Catalogue of *Arte de sistemas (Art Systems)*. Printed sheets in cardboard box: sheets, 11 × 8 in. (27.9 × 20.3 cm) each. Buenos Aires, Argentina: Museo de Arte Moderno, Buenos Aires, 1971. (Photo: Michael Tropea)

Continuing to support avant-garde artists throughout South America and confirming Buenos Aires' role as a center for Conceptual art, Jorge Glusberg organized *Arte de sistemas (Art Systems)* at the Museo de Arte Moderno, Buenos Aires, as he believed that systems art allowed artists to analyze how political and economic systems determine social relations, particularly the endemic inequalities so pronounced in the Latin American context. This was a topic he continued to explore as director and curator at the Centro de Arte y Comunicación [CAYC].

FIGURE 200

John Baldessari (American, b. 1931). *I Will Not Make Any More Boring Art*, 1971. Lithograph on Arches paper, 22½ × 30 in. (57.2 × 76.2 cm). Published by The Press of the Nova Scotia College of Art and Design, Halifax, edition of 50. © John Baldessari. (Photo: John Baldessari)

Baldessari's piece *I Will Not Make Any More Boring Art* was enacted by a group of students, "whipping boys" for the artist, who wrote the phrase repeatedly on the walls of a gallery at the Nova Scotia College of Art and Design.

Orders & Co
P.O.B.33
N.Y.10013
U.S.A.

Sr. Jorge Pacheco Areco

Casa de Gobierno
Montevideo
Uruguay

Air Mail
Registered

Estimado Sr. Pacheco Areco: Hemos decidido ponerlo a Ud. bajo nuestras órdenes. Ud. recibirá las órdenes por correo a su debido tiempo. Elcumplimiento de nuestras órdenes no le ocuparán demasiado tiempo o energía. Dispondremos de ciertas zonas de su tiempo en el futuro porque consideramos que un individuo con la acumulación de poder que Ud. tiene, solamente puede humanizarse recibiendo órdenes.
En caso de negarse, en el momento de recibir cada órden, Ud. deberá comunicarlo así por la prensa. Copia de nuestras órdenes circularán entre segmentos de la población del Uruguay, quienes junto con nosotros asumirán que Ud. está cumpliendo estas órdenes salvo que Ud. públicamente exprese lo contrario.
Sin otro particular saludamos a Ud. muy atte.

Orders & Co.

REGISTERED NO.

Value		Special Delivery	$
Reg. Fee	$ 95	Return Receipt	$
Handling Charge	$	Restricted Delivery	$
Postage	$ 1.54	AIRMAIL	

POSTMASTER (By)

FROM

TO

POSTMARK OF
NEW YORK, NY G.P.O. USPO
SEP 18 1971
MAILING OFFICE

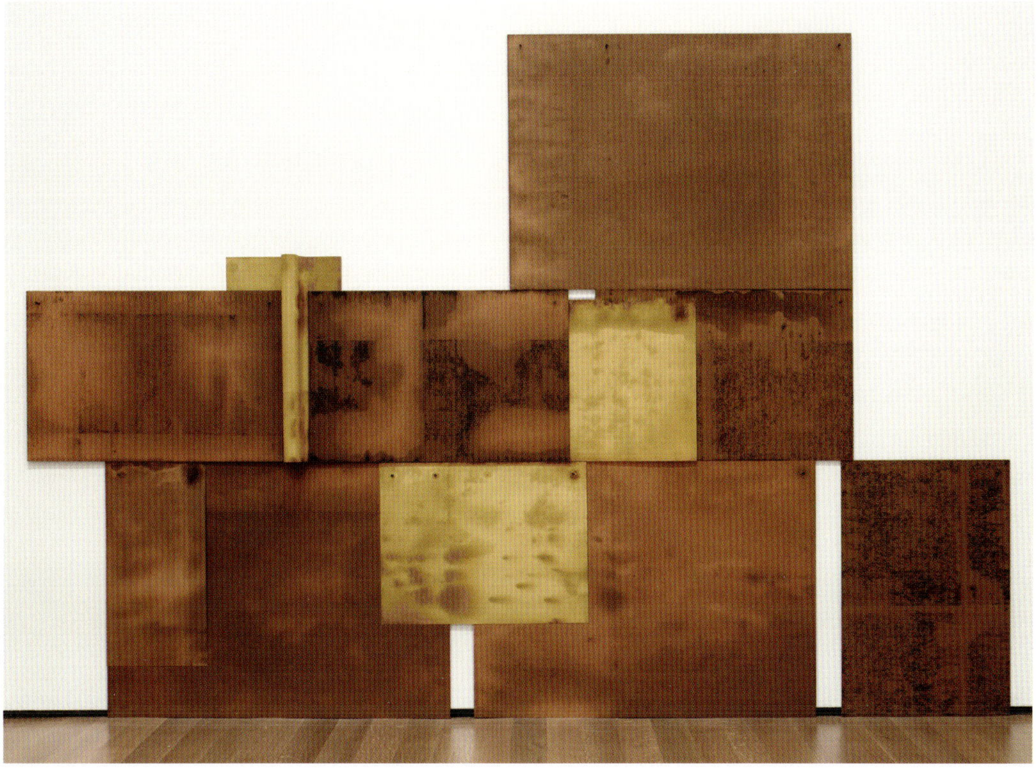

FIGURE 201

Orders & Co. *Letter to Uruguayan President Jorge Pacheco Areco, September 18, 1971*, 1971. Photocopy of a typewritten postcard, 11 × 8½ in. (27.9 × 21.6 cm). Lucy R. Lippard Papers, Archives of American Art, Smithsonian Institution, Washington, D.C.

In a gesture similar to the letter-writing campaign of the Guerrilla Art Action Group, the anonymous collective Orders & Co. sent instructions to Uruguayan President Jorge Pacheco Areco, telling him to do things he could not avoid doing, like making sure his fly was closed before leaving the house, thereby claiming a measure of control over a repressive leader. Their stated goal was, ultimately, to "invert the relationship between chief executives and subjects, breaking the vicious circle of power."

FIGURE 202

Dorothea Rockburne (Canadian, b. 1932). *Scalar*, 1971. Chipboard, crude oil, paper, and nails, 80 × 114½ × 3½ in. (203.2 × 289.5 × 8.9 cm) overall. The Museum of Modern Art, New York; Gift of Jo Carole and Ronald S. Lauder and Estée Lauder, Inc., in honor of J. Frederic Byers III. © 2011 Dorothea Rockburne/Artists Rights Society (ARS), New York. (Digital image: © The Museum of Modern Art/Licensed by SCALA/Art Resource, NY)

While Rockburne's sculpture *Scalar* appears materialized and pictorial, with structural interactions and textural modulations creating visual interest on its surface, Lippard noted in *Six Years* that Rockburne's process was conceptual, "based on the axioms of set theory, the surface sheets providing the 'givens,' the blots and stains the 'variables.' The arrangement follows an initially logical proposition."

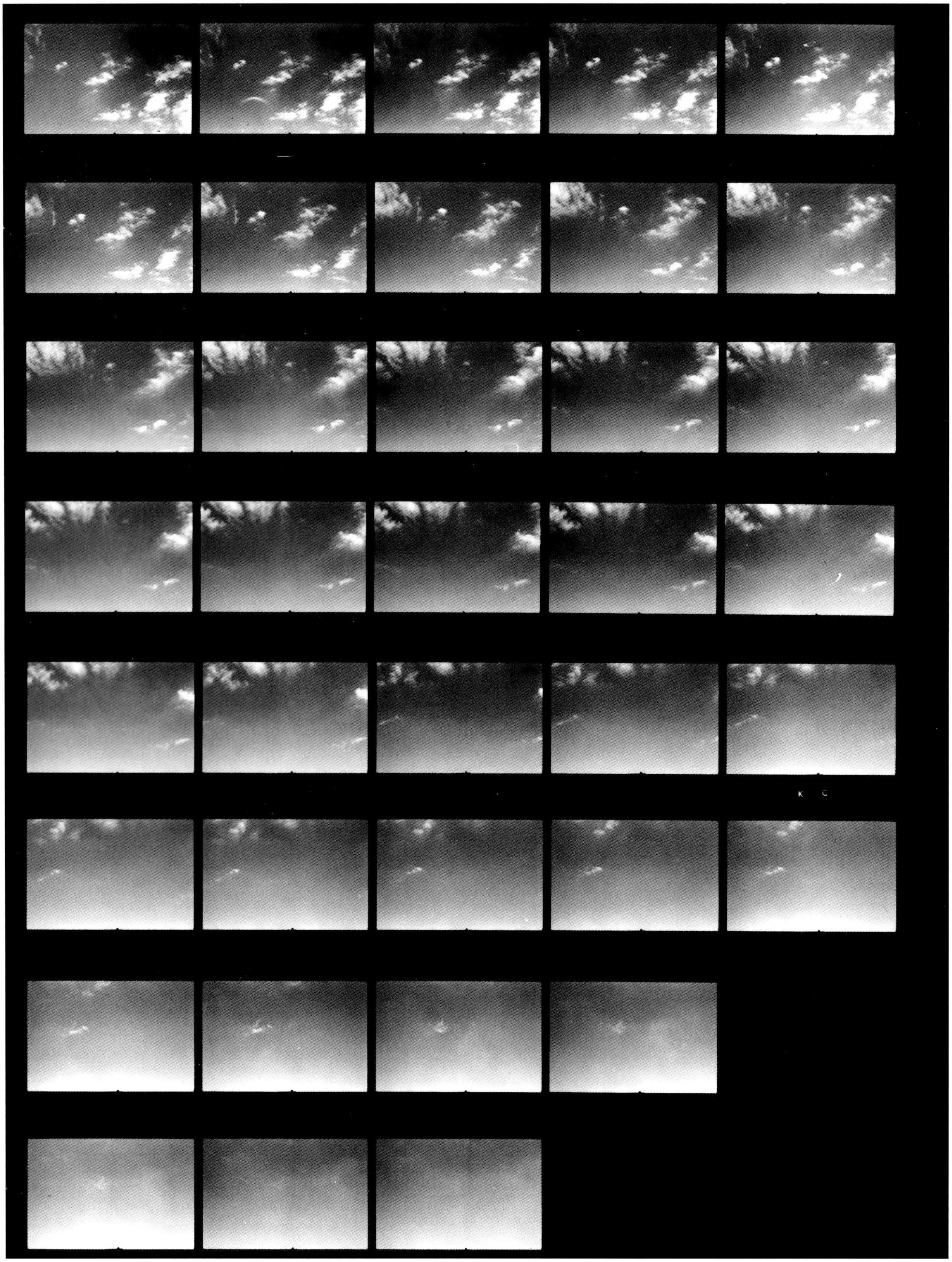

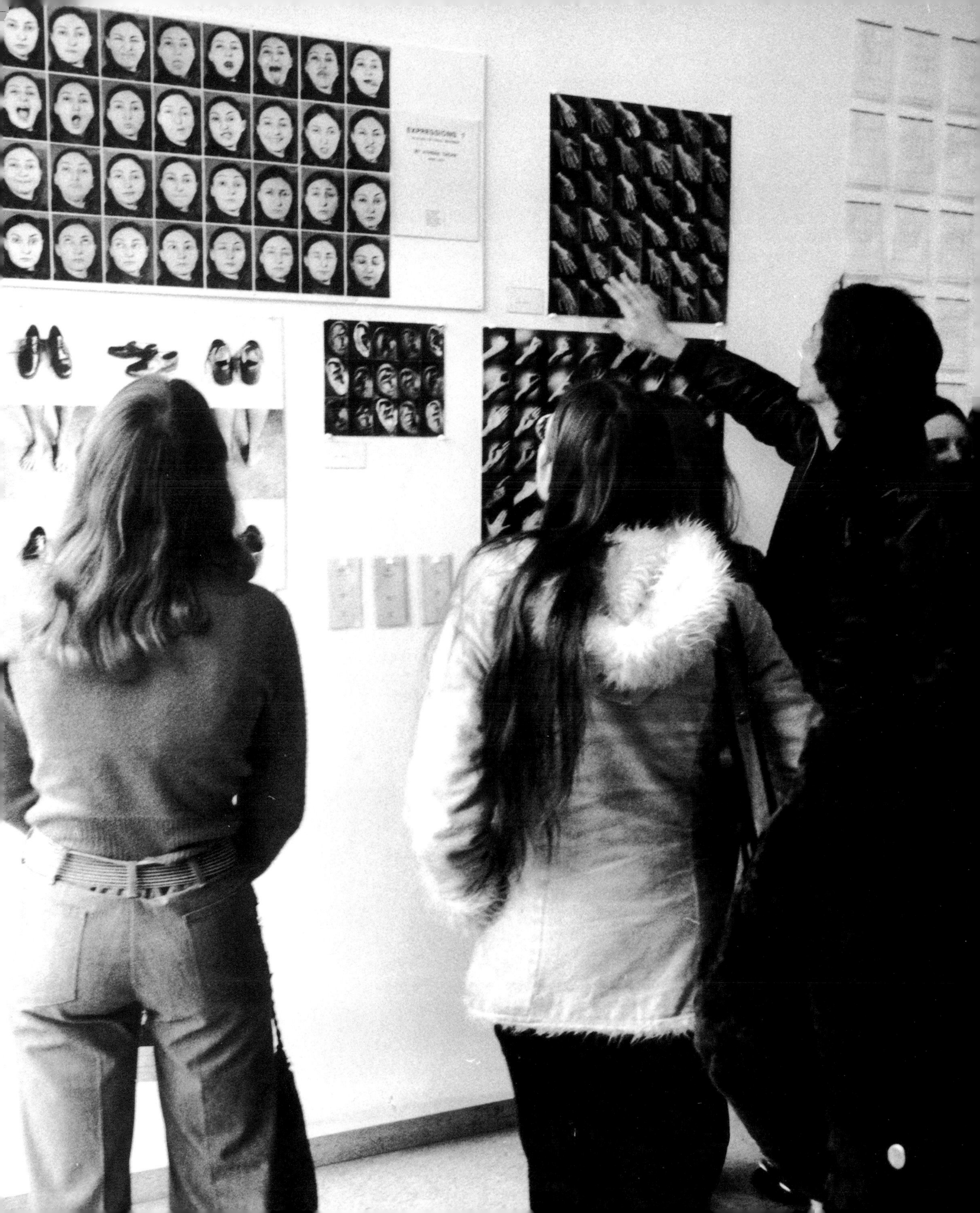

FIGURE 203

Alice Aycock (American, b. 1946). Segment of *Cloud Piece*, 1971. One of four black-and-white photo contact sheets, 21¾ × 15¾ in. (55 × 40 cm) each. © Alice Aycock. (Photo: Alice Aycock)

Describing her *Cloud Piece*, produced in Halifax, Alice Aycock wrote: "The following project is based on the fact that small, fair weather cumulus clouds dissipate within 5 to 15 minutes after formation. It consists of a series of four photographic black and white contact sheets. There are 36 to 38 exposures per contact sheet. Each contact sheet shows a cloud or clouds photographed from a stationary camera position for a 10 to 15 minute time period and until the roll of film was completed. Each contact sheet can be read from frame to frame in order to detect transition/change; cloud movement, dissipation, formation."

A copy of this Report and Offer for Sale has been presented to the Chairman, The Arts Council of Great Britain, together with a request that he forward it to the Minister responsible for the Environment, Her Majesty's Government, Documents specified will be open to inspection at the Hayward Gallery, London, during December.

Application has been made to the Arts Council of Great Britain as a subsidising body of the Artist Placement Group and as representing the many other departments of the United Kingdom concerned, for such financial provision as shall be compatible with the scale of the operations as are herein described.

apg research limited

The Individual and Organisation

artist placement group

on behalf of the trustees

Offer for Sale

of project specified by the above company

Required for execution of project :

£np: .000,000,5 per cent guaranteed unsecured reservation per annum 1972 – 1975 from United Kingdom Corporation to ensure adequate operation of the Group known as above for a period of 3 years after which a review of the situation to be made by both parties

£np measure of economic viability herein used shall in no way rank pari passu with the measure of viability of the activity described in terms of ▽ and units of attention so designated.

Capital / Assets

£np The company APG is a Charitable Trust and with its associate APG Research Limited is a non-profit making intermediary organisation charging only for services. There are no shares held in either organisation. Its capital value should be seen in terms of the experience of its administration over the six years and in the alternative measure of value represented by Delta.

▽ (Delta) Alternative system of measurement outlined in principle within. Fundamentally this refers to the unit of attention and to the level of attention induced or found within a group, society or population. Wealth in ▽ terms is measured in principle only but becomes evident as £np in retrospect

The capital value in Delta, available to APG, is a product of the capacity of the APG (noit) individuals in conjunction with their administrative body.

The concept as such is not part of this Offer for Sale, which is confined to its execution and financing only.

Neither the Group, nor the Company, have outstanding mortgages, charges, loan capital, bank overdraft or similar indebtedness, hire purchase agreements, guarantees or other material contingent liabilities.

FIGURE 204

Artist Placement Group (John Latham [British, b. South Africa, 1921–2006] and Barbara Steveni [British, b. 1928]). *APG Research Limited: The Individual and Organization; Prospectus and Offer for Sale of the Artist Placement Group.* Printed brochure, 11⅝ × 8 in. (29.5 × 20.2 cm). London: Artist Placement Group, 1971. The records of the Artist Placement Group (APG). © APG/courtesy Tate, London. (Photo: Michael Tropea)

In 1966 a strange combination of pragmatism and utopianism inspired the establishment of the Artist Placement Group, which sought to insinuate artist-advisors into major corporations or governmental agencies as a way to infuse alternative values and creative thinking into power structures that profoundly affect society. When a businessman suggested that they needed to pitch their services using the language of the business world, they produced this prospectus and offer of sale, modeled closely on documents drawn up by lawyers to sell shares in traditional public offerings.

FIGURES 205–216: The 1973 exhibition *c. 7,500*, while falling outside the span of *Six Years*, serves as an epilogue to Lippard's book because it concisely encapsulates the parameters of Conceptual art as it had developed since the mid-1960s, while simultaneously shifting toward a fully engaged social and political connection through feminism. After hearing repeatedly during the making of the numbers shows that there were no women Conceptual artists, Lippard set out to disabuse the art world of this groundless notion. In this sense, *c. 7,500* was about setting the record straight and marked a developmental leap, as many of these instruction-based projects reintroduced personal content, with significant socio-political implications for the artists, viewers, and society at large. This is perhaps best exemplified by Mierle Laderman Ukeles's proposals for *Maintenance Art Activities* to be conducted as part of *c. 7,500*, which would "wash the boundary between the world and the gallery" by literally making art out of the daily tasks of household cleaning that Ukeles, a wife and mother, had declared to be her creative milieu.

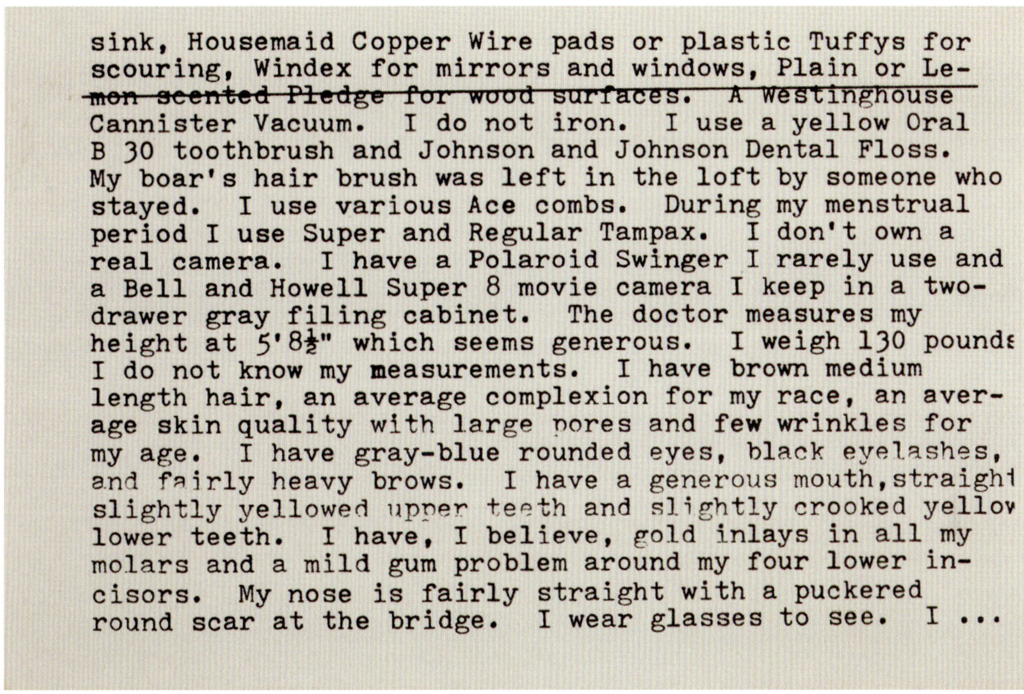

sink, Housemaid Copper Wire pads or plastic Tuffys for scouring, Windex for mirrors and windows, Plain or Le- ~~mon scented Pledge for wood surfaces.~~ A Westinghouse Cannister Vacuum. I do not iron. I use a yellow Oral B 30 toothbrush and Johnson and Johnson Dental Floss. My boar's hair brush was left in the loft by someone who stayed. I use various Ace combs. During my menstrual period I use Super and Regular Tampax. I don't own a real camera. I have a Polaroid Swinger I rarely use and a Bell and Howell Super 8 movie camera I keep in a two-drawer gray filing cabinet. The doctor measures my height at 5'8½" which seems generous. I weigh 130 pounds I do not know my measurements. I have brown medium length hair, an average complexion for my race, an average skin quality with large pores and few wrinkles for my age. I have gray-blue rounded eyes, black eyelashes, and fairly heavy brows. I have a generous mouth, straight slightly yellowed upper teeth and slightly crooked yellow lower teeth. I have, I believe, gold inlays in all my molars and a mild gum problem around my four lower incisors. My nose is fairly straight with a puckered round scar at the bridge. I wear glasses to see. I ...

FIGURE 205

Jennifer Bartlett (American, b. 1941). Contribution to the catalogue of *c. 7,500*. Index card, 4 × 6 in. (10.2 × 15.2 cm). Valencia, Calif.: California Institute of the Arts, 1974. © Jennifer Bartlett. (Photo: Michael Tropea)

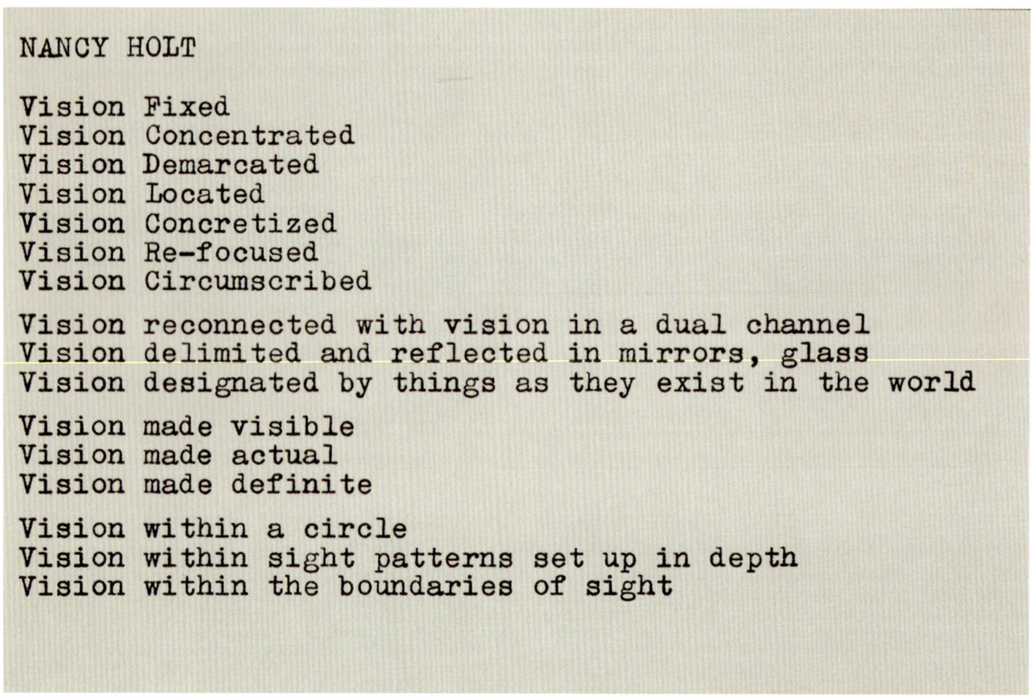

NANCY HOLT

Vision Fixed
Vision Concentrated
Vision Demarcated
Vision Located
Vision Concretized
Vision Re-focused
Vision Circumscribed

Vision reconnected with vision in a dual channel
Vision delimited and reflected in mirrors, glass
Vision designated by things as they exist in the world

Vision made visible
Vision made actual
Vision made definite

Vision within a circle
Vision within sight patterns set up in depth
Vision within the boundaries of sight

FIGURES 206, 207

Nancy Holt (American, b. 1938). Contribution to the catalogue of *c. 7,500* (front and [enlarged] back). Index card, 4 × 6 in. (10.2 × 15.2 cm). Valencia, Calif.: California Institute of the Arts, 1974. © Nancy Holt. (Photos: Michael Tropea)

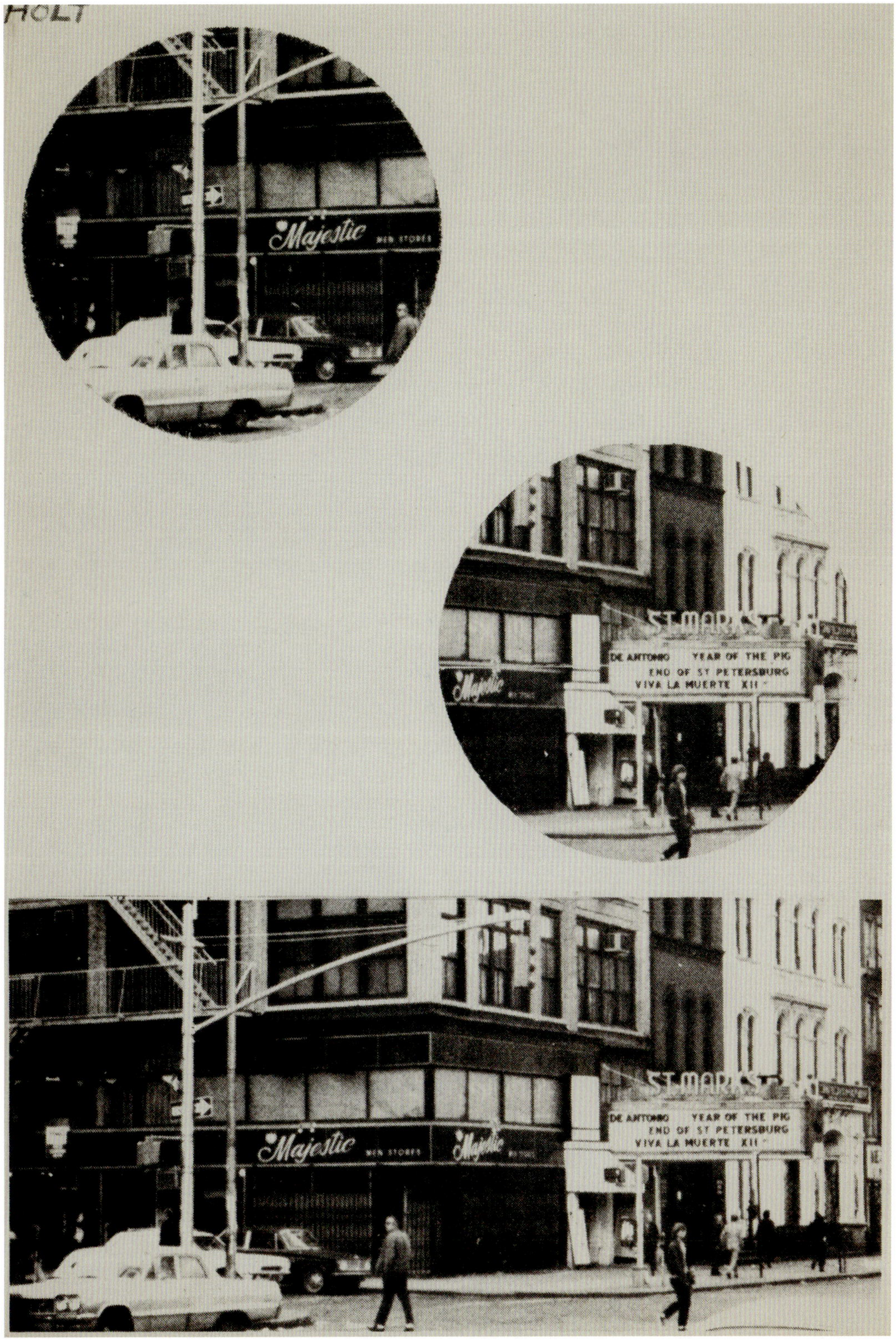
Majestic
MEN STORES
DE ANTONIO YEAR OF THE PIG
END OF ST PETERSBURG
VIVA LA MUERTE XII

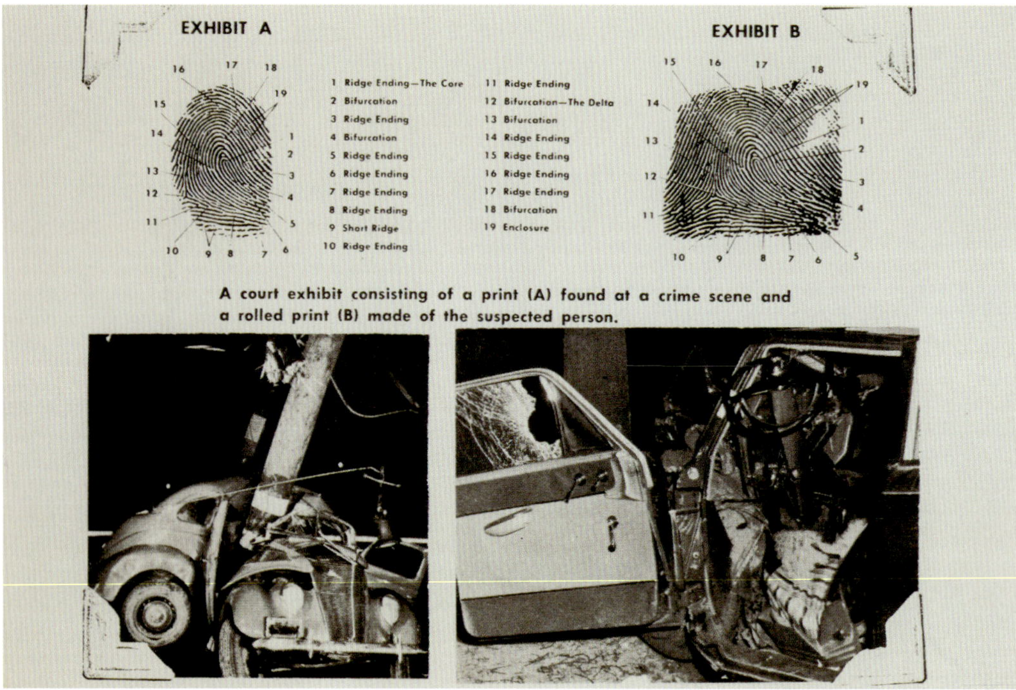

FIGURE 208

Ursula Meyer (German, 1915–2003). Contribution to the catalogue of *c. 7,500*. Index card, 4 × 6 in. (10.2 × 15.2 cm). Valencia, Calif.: California Institute of the Arts, 1974. © Ursula Meyer. (Photo: Michael Tropea)

Christiane Möbus, born 1947 Celle, W. Germany
lives in Essen, W. Germany

Title of work:
"Das unnötige Verlöbnis der Frau Holle mit dem Schamanen" (The Unnecessary Betrothal of Frau Holle with the Shaman), or, "A New Life". 1972.

About my work:
1. The Fata Morgana works are concerned with myself. They represent my struggle to get along in this world. Being a human being like everybody else, and being an individual in a world of total incompatibility, my work deals with the problems of other people insofar as I am like them and does not where I am different.

(Photo of winged Frau Holle: Renate Altenrath)

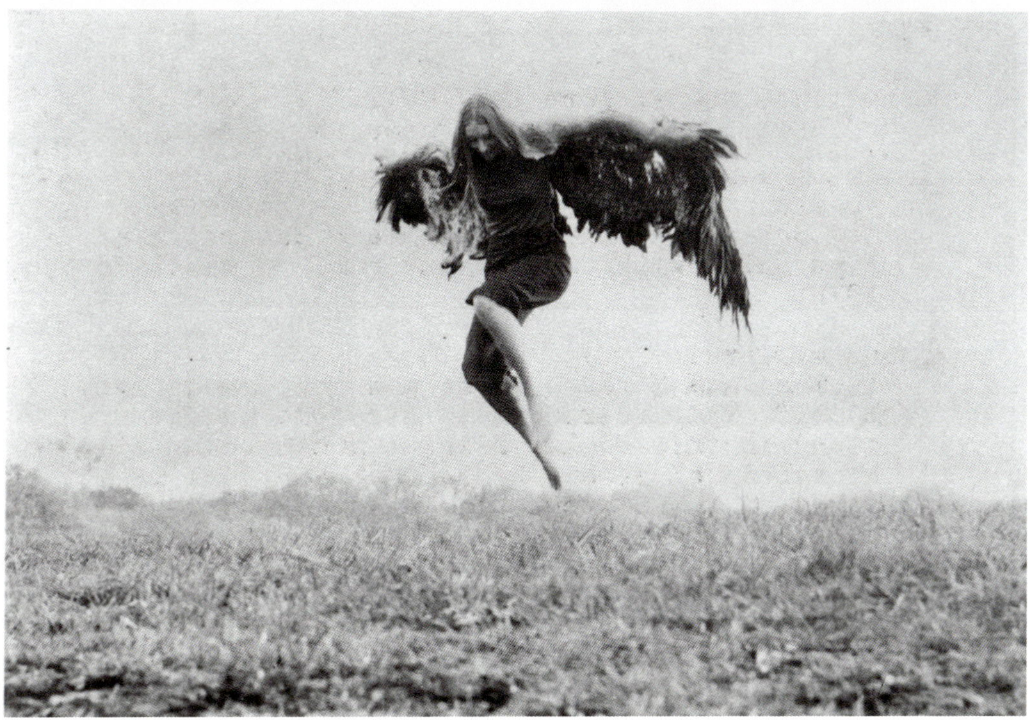

FIGURE 209

Christiane Möbus (German, b. 1947). *The Unnecessary Betrothal of Frau Holle with the Shaman (Das unnötige Verlöbnis der Frau Holle mit dem Schamanen), or, A New Life,* 1973. Contribution to the catalogue of *c. 7,500* (front and back). Index card, 4 × 6 in. (10.2 × 15.2 cm). Valencia, Calif.: California Institute of the Arts, 1974. Original photograph in card by Renate Altenrath. (Photography of card for reproduction: Michael Tropea)

Athena TACHA (Oberlin, Ohio)

Autobiography:

Born in 1936 in Larissa, Greece — a provincial town of a poor, underdeveloped country. Grew up during many years of wars. As a result, mentally retarded by at least ten years.

Wasted much time with various semi-useless degrees, including diplomas of musical theory and French literature (Larissa); a master's in sculpture (Athens); a master's in art history (Oberlin); and a doctorate in aesthetics (Paris).

For the last nine years have been wasting still more vital time and energy earning a living with a full-time job.

Gave a lot of myself to other people through deep emotional involvements (love or friendship).

Spent the rest of my life so far trying to understand what other people think is art.

Splintered myself by being acutely interested in numerous things, and may waste the rest of my life spreading myself thin in different directions.

Even a thousand lives might not be enough for all I want to do.

Works included in this exhibition:

Hands, 1970–72, thirty-six color photographs (two versions).

Ears, 1970–71, color photographs.

Feet and Shoes, 1970–72, nine black-and-white photographs.

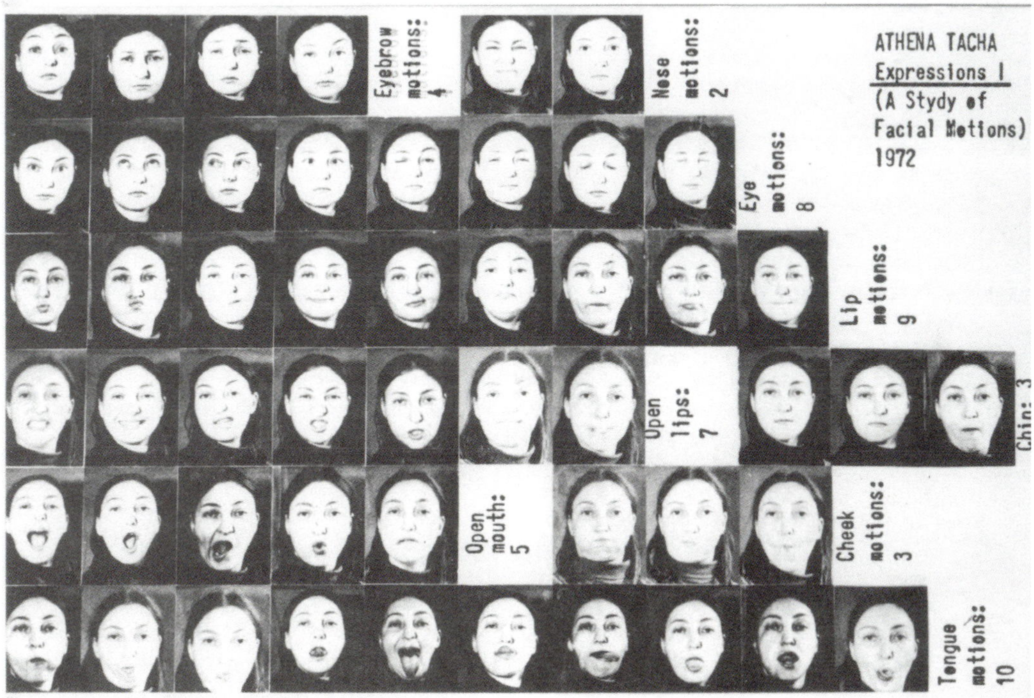

MIERLE LADERMAN UKELES. 2 Washington Square Village, NYC.

Born 100 years exactly after the birth of Cezanne, Denver, Colorado. BA Barnard College. Graduate studies: Pratt Institute, U of Colorado, U of Denver, NYU. Married Jack Ukeles, 1966. Trained Lamaze Method of Childbearing by Elizabeth Bing: 1968, 70, 72. Made Bindings and Air Art 1963-69.

1st Manifesto of MAINTENANCE ART, 1969. Excerpted in Artforum, Jack Burnham, "Problems of Criticism, IX." Jan. 1971. Also in Lucy R. Lippard. Six Years: The Dematerialization of the Art Object from 1966 to 1972. New York, Praeger, 1973. Two basic systems: Development and Maintenance. The sourball of every revolution: after the revolution, who's going to pick up the garbage on Monday morning? Development: pure individual creation; the new; change; progress, advance, excitement, flight or fleeing. Maintenance: keep the dust off the pure individual creation; preserve the new; sustain the change; protect progress; defend and prolong the advance; renew the excitement; repeat the flight.

FIGURE 210

Athena Tacha (Greek, b. 1936). *Expressions 1: A Study of Facial Motions,* 1972; contribution to the catalogue of *c. 7,500* (front and back). Index card, 4 × 6 in. (10.2 × 15.2 cm). Valencia, Calif.: California Institute of the Arts, 1974. Installation: fifty-one black-and-white photographs, 10 × 8 in. (25.4 × 20.3 cm) each. © 1973 Athena Tacha. Original photographs in card: Athena Tacha. (Photography of card for reproduction: Michael Tropea)

FIGURE 211

Mierle Laderman Ukeles (American, b. 1939). Contribution to the catalogue of *c. 7,500.* Index card, 4 × 6 in. (10.2 × 15.2 cm). Valencia, Calif.: California Institute of the Arts, 1974. © Mierle Laderman Ukeles. Courtesy Ronald Feldman Fine Arts, New York/ www.feldmangallery.com. (Photo: Michael Tropea)

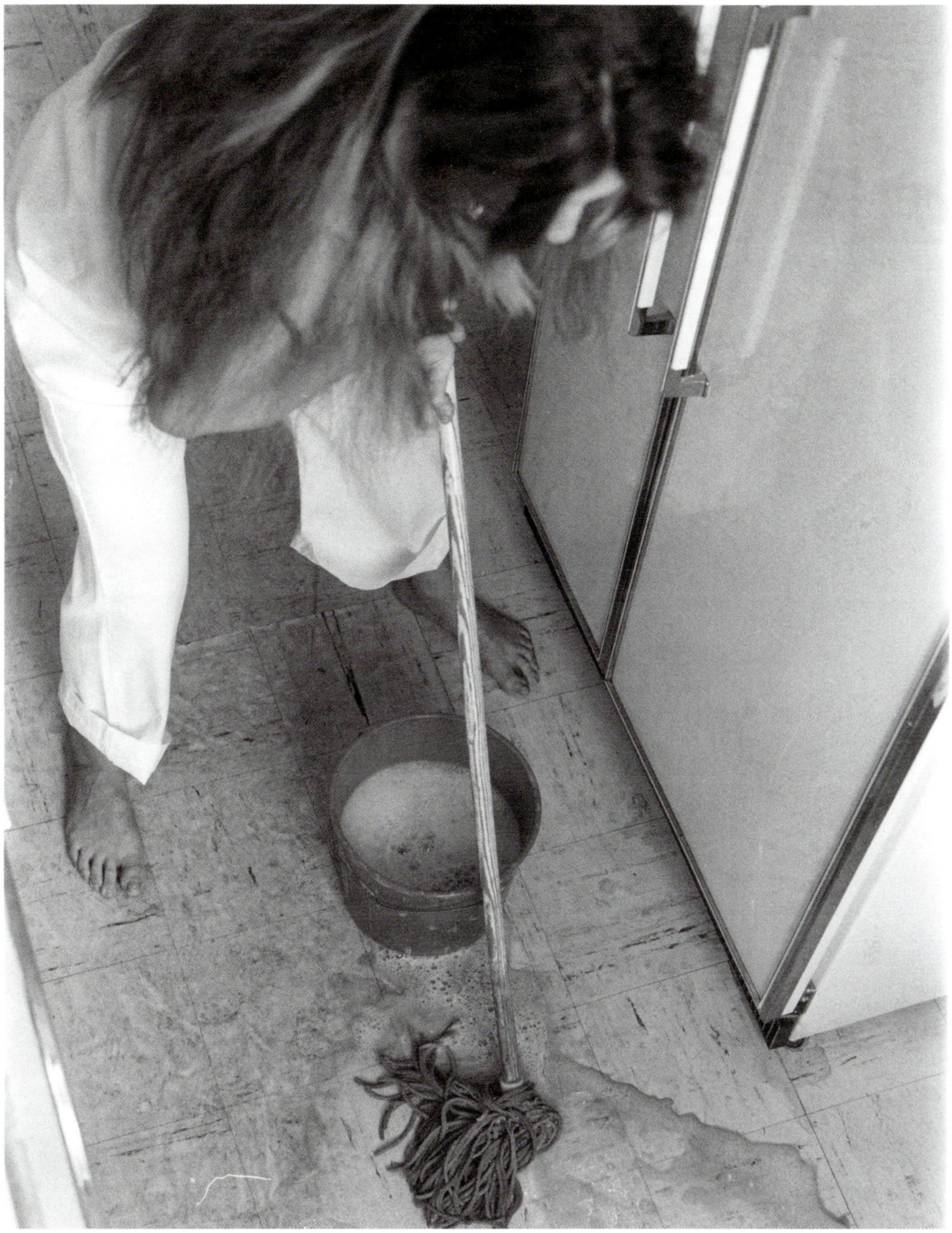

FIGURE 212

Mierle Laderman Ukeles (American, b. 1939). *Private Performances of Personal Maintenance as Art*, 1969. Black-and-white photograph, 10 × 8 in. (25.4 × 20.3 cm); later reproduced as contribution to the catalogue of *c. 7,500.* Index card, 4 × 6 in. (10.2 × 15.2 cm). Valencia, Calif.: California Institute of the Arts, 1974. © Mierle Laderman Ukeles. (Photo: Ronald Feldman Fine Arts, New York/www.feldmangallery.com)

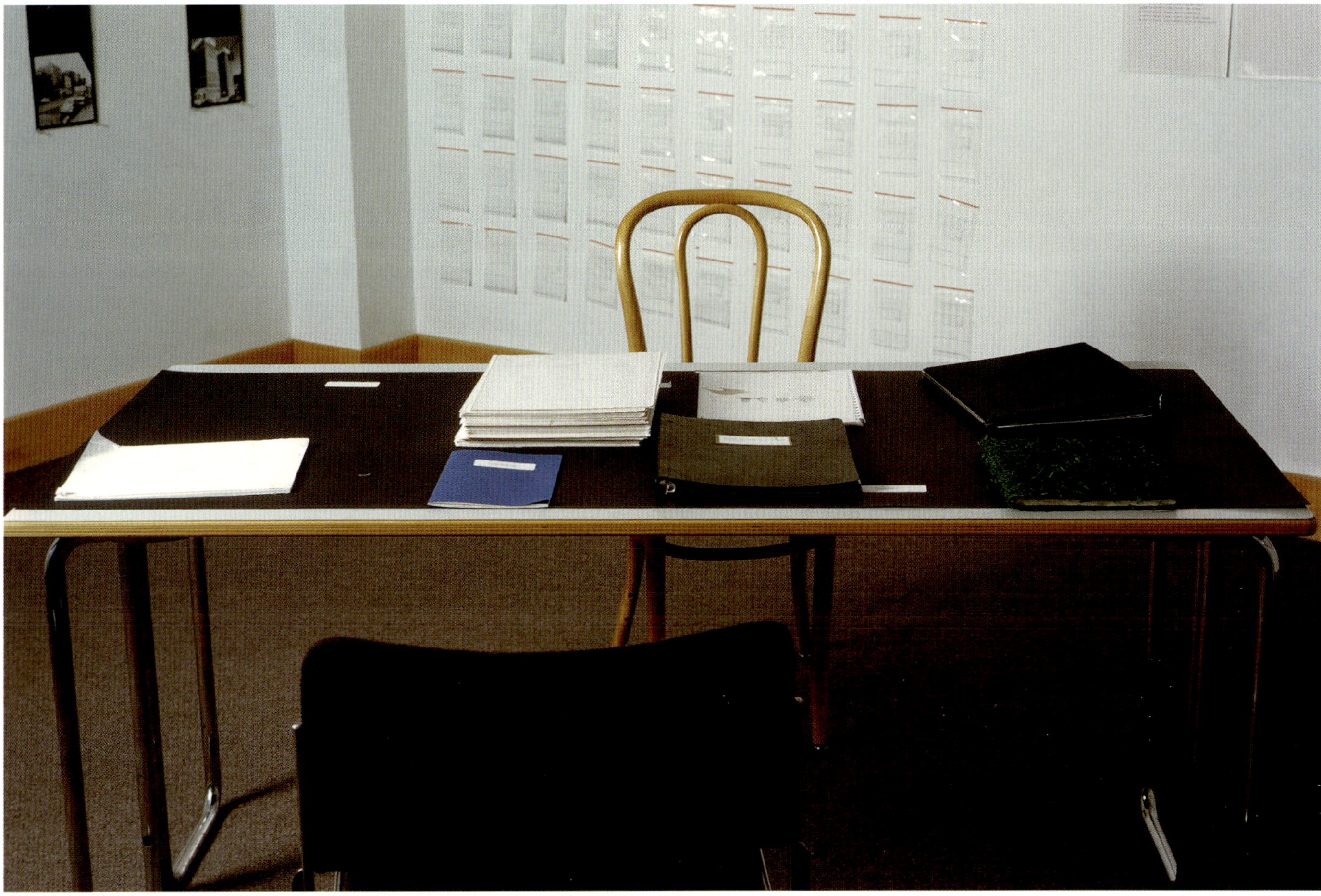

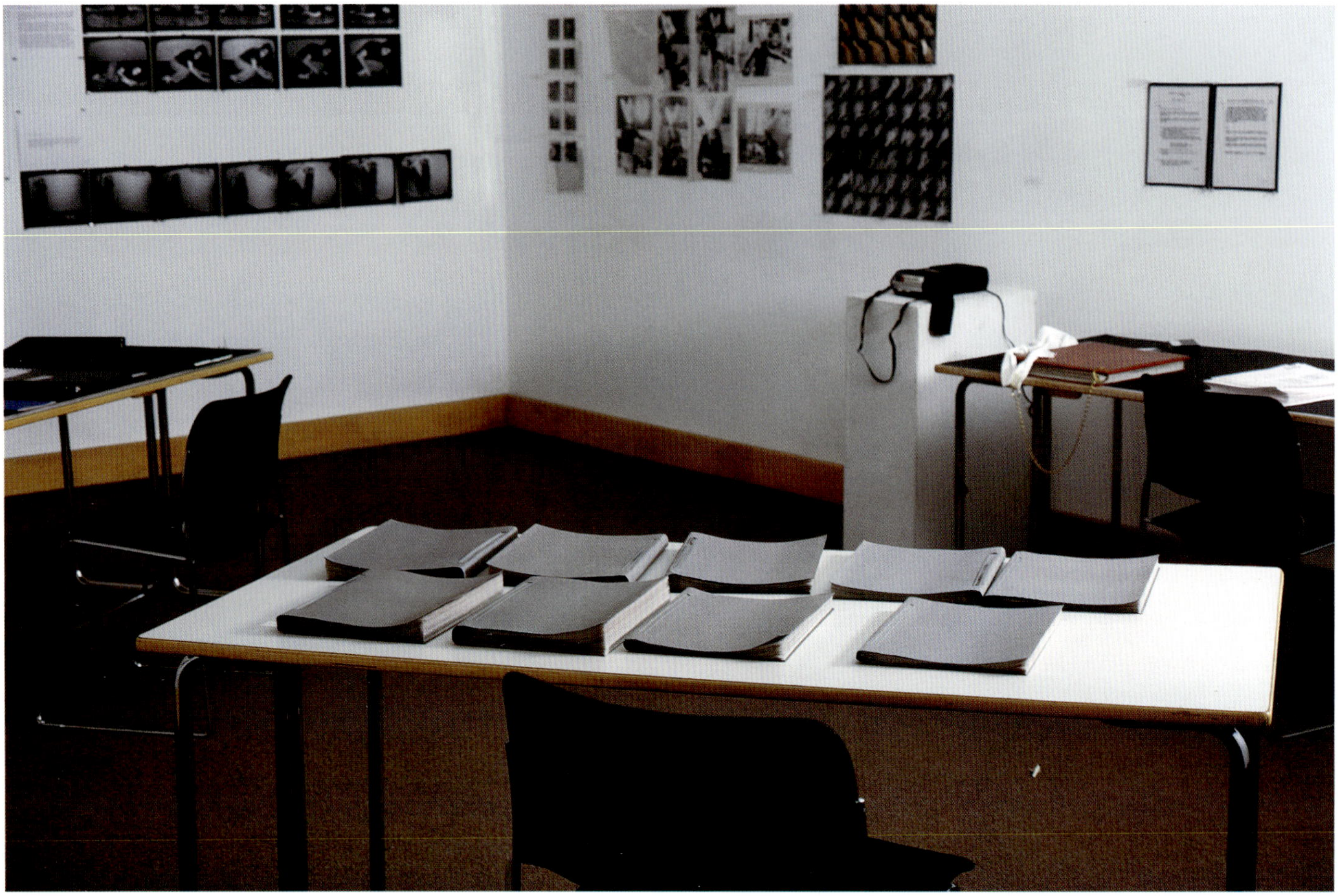

FIGURES 213, 214

Installation views of *c. 7,500*, California Institute of the Arts, Valencia, May 14–18, 1973; organized by Lucy R. Lippard. California Institute of the Arts Library Visual Resource Collection, Valencia. (Photo: California Institute of the Arts)

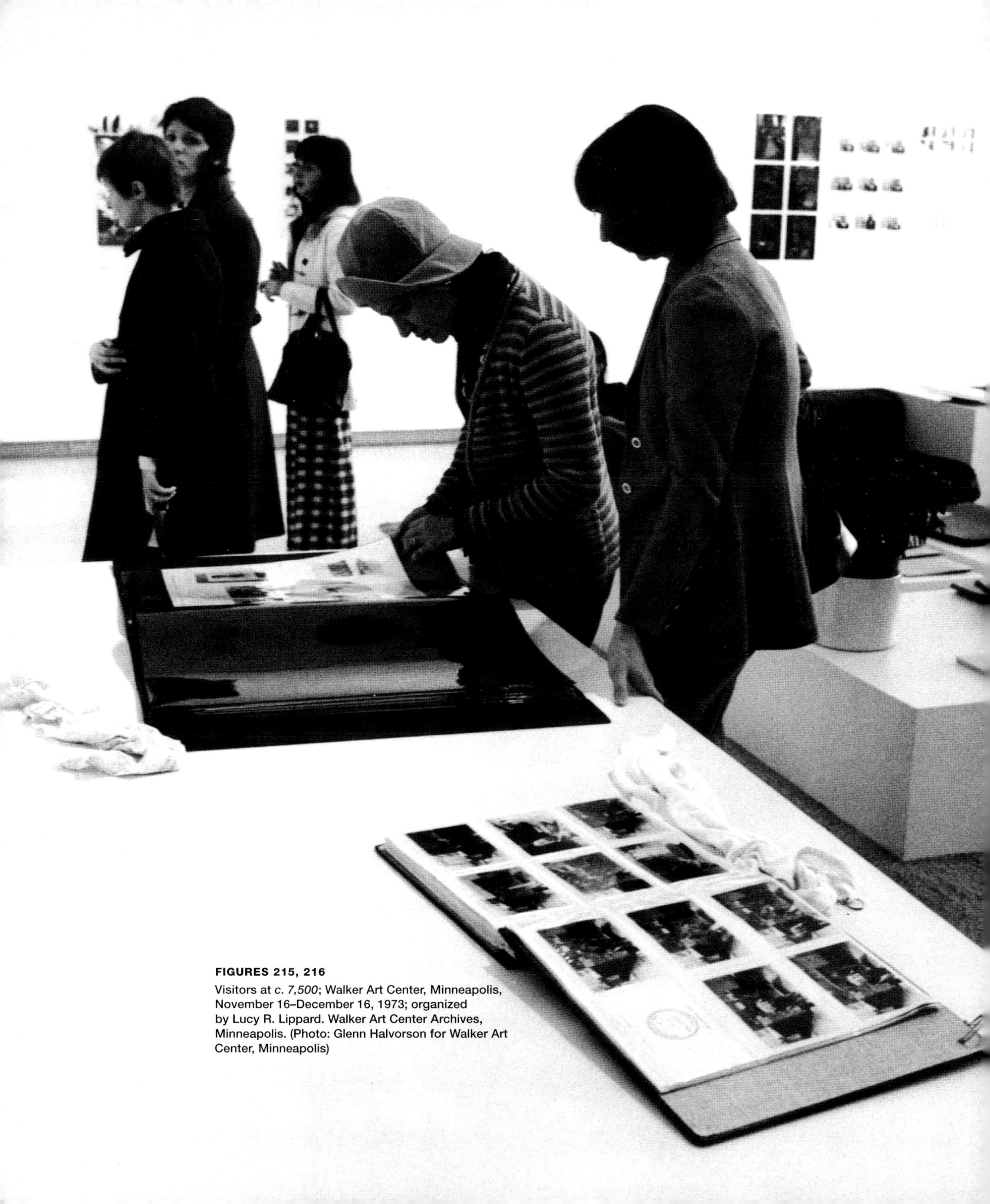

FIGURES 215, 216

Visitors at *c. 7,500*; Walker Art Center, Minneapolis, November 16–December 16, 1973; organized by Lucy R. Lippard. Walker Art Center Archives, Minneapolis. (Photo: Glenn Halvorson for Walker Art Center, Minneapolis)

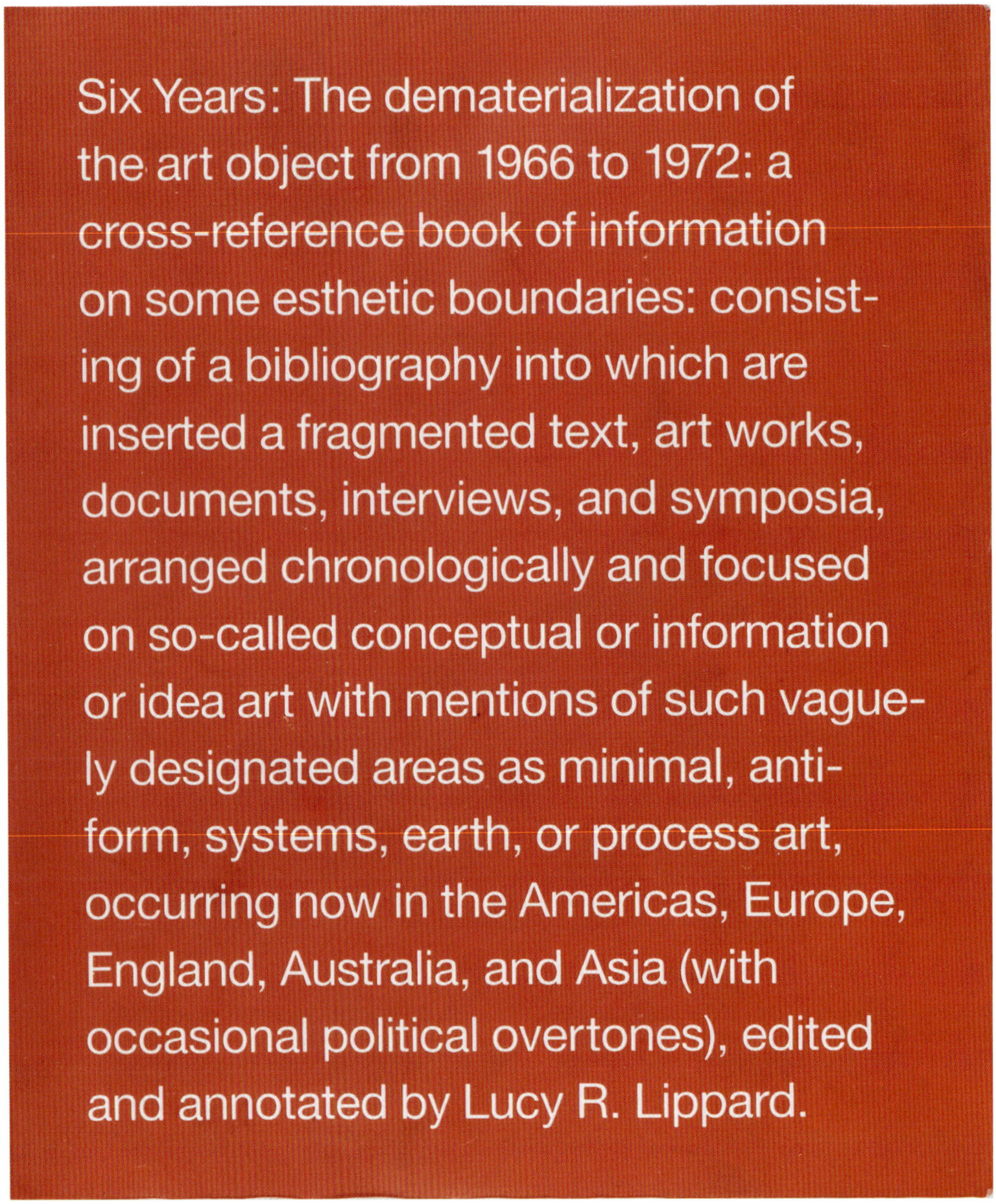

Six Years: The dematerialization of the art object from 1966 to 1972: a cross-reference book of information on some esthetic boundaries: consisting of a bibliography into which are inserted a fragmented text, art works, documents, interviews, and symposia, arranged chronologically and focused on so-called conceptual or information or idea art with mentions of such vaguely designated areas as minimal, anti-form, systems, earth, or process art, occurring now in the Americas, Europe, England, Australia, and Asia (with occasional political overtones), edited and annotated by Lucy R. Lippard.

Front cover of *Six Years*, 1973. See page x.

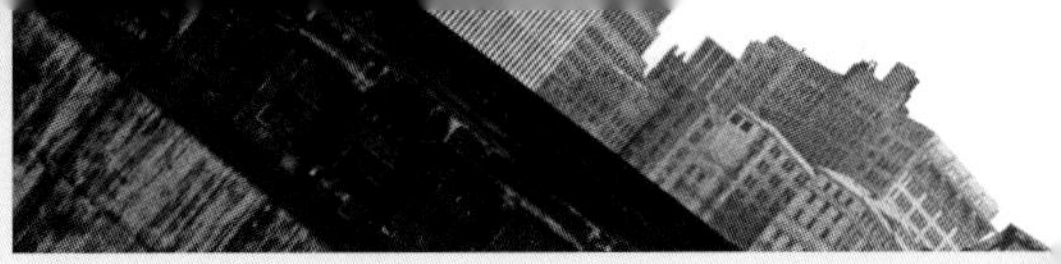

Acknowledgments

Like the book from which we drew our inspiration, this exhibition and publication are indebted to a remarkable number of people who have contributed in numerous ways: Arnold Lehman, Director of the Brooklyn Museum, and Elizabeth A. Sackler immediately saw the pertinence of this exhibition to the larger program of the Elizabeth A. Sackler Center for Feminist Art at the Brooklyn Museum. The Trustees of the Elizabeth A. Sackler Foundation, Janet Bajan and Janet McCay, along with Dr. Sackler, have made this catalogue and the exhibition possible, as they have made the Center possible since its opening in 2007.

Lucy R. Lippard has generously supported our idea to take her brilliant book and use it as an armature for a project that in many ways inverts her original intention. And while it may seem to be stating the obvious to say this project couldn't have happened without her because it certainly couldn't have happened without *Six Years*, it also wouldn't have happened without her acknowledging the value of the enterprise, and for that we are extremely grateful. Lucy's Preface to this volume offers a unique rounding up of how she has seen critical understanding of the material she collected develop and change as a growing number of scholars have spent time addressing its impact.

We thank all the artists represented in our show, and we are indebted to all those who were included in *Six Years*, even when we were unable to present their work in this exhibition. We would like to acknowledge the following artists and their studio staff, who helped to make the exhibition possible: Chris Dierks of the Acconci Studio, Shannon Haskett of the Bas Jan Ader Estate, Graciela Carnevale of the Archivo Tucumán Arde, Ann Artschwager of the Richard Artschwager Studio, Jerry Gorovoy and Wendy Williams of the Louise Bourgeois Studio, Jane Crawford and Bob Fiore, the Hanne Darboven Foundation, Yu Yigang of the Gilbert & George Studio, Jane Perry of the Nancy Holt Studio, Cindy Smith of the Joseph Kosuth Studio, Veronica Roberts of the LeWitt Foundation, Amy Plumb Oppenheim of the Dennis Oppenheim Estate, Fee Altmann at the Adrian Piper Foundation, David White of the Rauschenberg Foundation, Trina McKeever of the Richard Serra Studio, the Shunk-Kender Photographic Archive at the Roy Lichtenstein Foundation, Jon Hendricks of Studio One, and Jacki Mansfield of the Bernar Venet Studio.

Sharing our deep and abiding respect for *Six Years,* many private collectors have graciously supported this exhibition. First among them is Alan Cravitz, who was an important early supporter and intellectual sounding board on the exhibition. Time spent with him and with his collection in Chicago helped solidify our ideas on how to structure this often unwieldy material. Works from his unique collection are a key component of this exhibition. We are also grateful to the following private collectors who have helped us realize this project: David Diao, Pamela and Richard Kramlich of the Kramlich Collection, Marilyn Thompson, the Daros Collection, and Thea Westreich and Ethan Wagner.

Institutional colleagues have helped with loans from their collections and additional forms of support. Cornelia H. Butler, The Robert Lehman Foundation Chief Curator of Drawings at the Museum of Modern Art, graciously shared her own research into Lippard's "numbers" shows. Research conducted in the Lucy R. Lippard Papers at the Archives of American Art in Washington, D.C., was vitally important to our work, and we thank Marisa Bourgoin for her assistance and patience. Likewise, the website and archives of Specific Object/David Platzker were a key resource for this project. Peter Eleey and Peter Murphy offered generous assistance with some of the obstacles that arise from trying to work with cross-generational technologies. We are also thankful for the generosity of the many institutional lenders, including Allen Memorial Art Museum, Oberlin College, Oberlin, Ohio; Archives of American Art, Smithsonian Institution, Washington, D.C.; Art Gallery of New South Wales, Sydney; Art Gallery of Ontario, Toronto; The Morris and Helen Belkin Art Gallery, Vancouver; California Institute of the Arts, Valencia; Corcoran Gallery of Art, Washington, D.C.; Electronic Arts Intermix, New York; Solomon R. Guggenheim Museum, New York; Hamburger Kunsthalle, Hamburg; The Museum of Contemporary Art, Los Angeles; The Museum of Modern Art, New York; New Mexico Museum of Art, Santa Fe; Seattle Art Museum; Tate Britain, London; Vancouver Art Gallery; Wadsworth Atheneum Museum of Art, Hartford; and Walker Art Center, Minneapolis. Numerous galleries have shepherded loans, facilitated conversations with artists, and offered thoughtful research suggestions. We particularly thank Angela Westwater for her insight and firsthand experience with much of this work. Other gallery support was provided by Alexander and Bonin Gallery, New York; Hal Bromm Gallery, New York; Elyse Goldberg at James Cohan Gallery, New York; Kristoffer Haynes at Paula Cooper Gallery, New York; Elizabeth Dee Gallery, New York; Marco Nocella and Eleanore Hopper at Ronald Feldman Fine Arts, New York; Blair Asbury Brooks at Peter Freeman, Inc., New York; Jillian Murphy at Gagosian Gallery, New York; Mary Sabbatino at Galerie LeLong, New York; Lissa McClure at Marian Goodman Gallery, New York; Hauser & Wirth, New York, Zurich, and London; Sean Kelly Gallery, New York; Stephanie Smith at Lehman Maupin Gallery, New York; Olivier Belot at Yvon Lambert, Paris; Joanna Thornberry at Lisson Gallery, London; Jan Mot Gallery, Brussels; P.P.O.W. Gallery, New York; Pace Gallery, New York; Patrick Painter Editions, Los Angeles; Thomas Solomon Gallery, London; Queenie Wong at Sonnabend Gallery, New York; and Meghan Hill at David Zwirner Gallery, New York.

We thank Julia Bryan-Wilson for her contribution to this catalogue. Julia's innovative work on the Art Workers' Coalition made her our first choice as a collaborator, and we are gratified to add her perspective to this discussion.

A constituency of Canadians played a role in realizing this project. The Canadian Council for the Arts provided funds for Vincent Bonin to pursue research for the exhibition and to write the essay in the publication. Michelle Thériault, Director of the Leonard & Bina Ellen Art Gallery at Concordia University in Montreal, provided early support for the development of this exhibition. Vincent would also like to thank Simon Brown for translating his essay from the French.

We have been very lucky to have a talented and dedicated team of colleagues at the Brooklyn Museum to help realize this complex and challenging project. We thank Kevin Stayton, Chief Curator, for his guidance and support; Judith Frankfurt, Deputy Director for Administration; Paul Johnson, Deputy Director for Development; and Cynthia Mayeda, Deputy Director for Institutional Advancement; along with Charles Desmarais, formerly Deputy Director for Art, all contributed to realizing this project. Sharon Matt Atkins, Managing Curator for Exhibitions, and

Lisa Small, Curator for Exhibitions, along with Dolores Pukki, Jessica Palmieri, and Danny Tuss have all helped facilitate numerous details for the show and catalogue, as have John Carini, Kevin Cooper, and Melanie McNair. Eugenie Tsai, John and Barbara Vogelstein Curator of Contemporary Art, offered much collegial advice.

The logistical complexities of the loans for the exhibition were expertly handled by Liz Reynolds, Chief Registrar, while Ken Moser, Vice Director for Collections; Toni Owen, Senior Paper Conservator; Lisa Bruno, Objects Conservator; and Chrisy Tselentakis, Records Manager, have advised and assisted on innumerable aspects of individual loans. Matthew Yokobosky, Chief Designer; Walter Andersons, Collections Manager; Filippo Gentile, and the entire Collections and installation staff, have once again made what sometimes seemed like an impossible dream into a stunning reality.

James Leggio, Head of Publications and Editorial Services, guided this publication steadily through sometimes choppy waters. Sallie Stutz, Vice Director for Merchandising, and Deborah Wythe, Head of Digital Collections and Services, made important contributions to realizing this catalogue. Alice Cork, our indefatigable photo researcher, did a remarkable job researching, acquiring, and organizing images for this publication. With her expertise in printed matter from this period, Deirdre Lawrence, Principal Librarian, and the staff of the Museum's Libraries and Archives helped enormously on a show that is largely devoted to ephemera and books.

Each dedicated and talented staff member of the Sackler Center for Feminist Art is owed well-deserved recognition for their help in making this project a reality. Special thanks go to Saisha Grayson, Assistant Curator, who bravely stepped into this project in mid-stream and contributed enormously to its final execution. Her clarity and enthusiasm have been as invaluable as her thoughtful research and writing. Sarah Giovanniello, Research Assistant, has seen this project grow from the inception of our idea, handling innumerable details, while Jess Wilcox, Adult Programs Coordinator, has creatively engaged with the Museum's Education Division, notably Radiah Harper, Vice Director for Education, and her able staff, to develop intelligent and wide-ranging public programs. A large group of interns has pitched in at various points over the past several years, each of them making a significant dent in the workload. They included Laura Castagnini, Michelle Donnelly, Maya Harakawa, Kelly Johnson, Elizabeth Reilly-Brown, and the ace Rebecca Shaykin.

Vincent Bonin would also like to thank Lorna Bauer and Jon Knowles, friends who participated in numerous conversations about the project. Catherine Morris would like to recognize in print the patience of her daughter, Elizabeth MacGregor, who always helped keep things in perspective.

Finally, we would like to dedicate this volume to Lucy R. Lippard and Elizabeth A. Sackler, two inspiring women who have taught many of us to believe we can change the world.

C. M. and V. B.

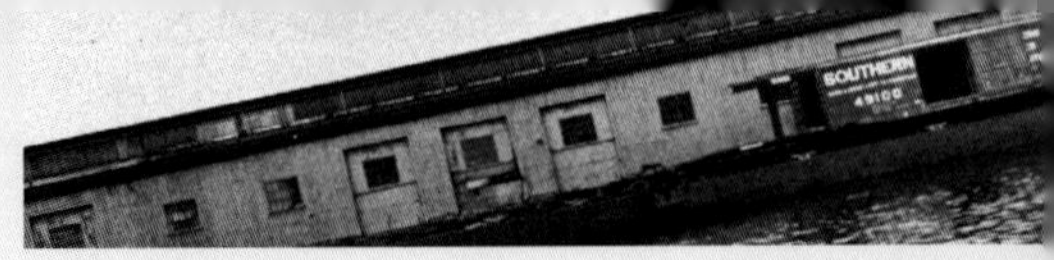
SOUTHERN

Selected Bibliography

Alberro, Alexander. *Conceptual Art and the Politics of Publicity*. Cambridge, Mass.: The MIT Press, 2003.

Alberro, Alexander, and Sabeth Buchmann, eds. *Art After Conceptual Art*. Cambridge, Mass.: The MIT Press; Vienna: Generali Foundation, 2006.

Alberro, Alexander, and Blake Stimson, eds. *Conceptual Art: A Critical Anthology*. Cambridge, Mass.: The MIT Press, 1999.

Allen, Gwen. *Artists' Magazines: An Alternative Space for Art.* Cambridge, Mass.: The MIT Press, 2011.

Altshuler, Bruce J. *The Avant-Garde in Exhibition: New Art in the Twentieth Century*. New York: Harry N. Abrams, 1994.

Arnold, Grant, ed. *Traffic: Conceptual Art in Canada, 1965–1981/Trafic: l'art conceptuel au Canada, 1965–1981*. Exh. cat. Vancouver: Vancouver Art Gallery; Douglas & McIntyre, forthcoming in 2012.

Barber, Bruce, ed. *Conceptual Art: The NSCAD Connection, 1967–1973*. Exh. cat. Halifax: Anna Leonowens Gallery, Nova Scotia College of Art and Design, 2001.

Battcock, Gregory. *Idea Art: A Critical Anthology*. New York: E. P. Dutton, 1973.

Beeren, Wim, ed. *Op Loose Schroeven: Situaties en Kryptostructuren*. Exh. cat. Amsterdam: Stedelijk Museum, 1969.

Buchloh, Benjamin H. D. "Conceptual Art, 1962–1969: From the Aesthetics of Administration to the Critique of Institutions." *October*, no. 55 (Winter 1990), pp. 105–43.

Burgin, Victor. "Situational Aesthetics." *Studio International*, vol. 178, no. 915 (October 1969), pp. 118–21.

Burnham, Jack. "Real-Time Systems." *Artforum*, vol. 8, no. 1 (September 1969), pp. 49–55.

———. "Alice's Head: Reflections on Conceptual Art." *Artforum,* vol. 8, no. 6 (February 1970), pp. 37–43.

———, ed. *Software*. Exh. cat. New York: The Jewish Museum, 1970.

Bryan-Wilson, Julia. *Art Workers: Radical Practice in the Vietnam War Era*. Berkeley, Los Angeles, and London: University of California Press, 2009.

Camnitzer, Luis. *Conceptualism in Latin American Art: Didactics of Liberation*. Austin: University of Texas Press, 2007.

Camnitzer, Luis, Jane Farver, and Rachel Weiss, eds. *Global Conceptualism: Points of Origin, 1950s–1980s*. Exh. cat. Queens, N.Y.: Queens Museum of Art, 1999.

Celant, Germano. *Arte Povera: Conceptual, Actual or Impossible Art?* Milan: Mazzotta; London: Studio Vista; New York: Praeger Publishers; and Tübingen: Studio Wasmuth, 1969.

Cherix, Christophe, ed. *In and Out of Amsterdam: Travels in Conceptual Art, 1960–1976*. Exh. cat. New York: The Museum of Modern Art, 2009.

Chris, Hans D., and Iris Dressler. *Subversive Practices: Art Under Conditions of Political Repression, 60s–80s*. Exh. cat. Ostfildern: Hatje Cantz Verlag, 2010.

Claura, Michel, ed. *Yvon Lambert: Actualité d'un bilan*. Exh. cat. Paris: Yvon Lambert, 1972.

Clay, Jean. "Art Tamed and Wild." *Studio International*, vol. 177, no. 912 (June 1969), pp. 262–65.

Corris, Michael, ed. *Conceptual Art: Theory, Myth, and Practice*. Cambridge: Cambridge University Press, 2004.

De Salvo, Donna, ed. *Open Systems: Rethinking Art, c. 1970*. Exh. cat. London: Tate, 2005.

De Vries, Gerd, ed. *On Art: Artists' Writings on the Changed Notion of Art after 1965*. Cologne: Verlag DuMont Schauberg, 1974.

Eleey, Peter. *The Quick and the Dead*. Exh. cat. Minneapolis: Walker Art Center, 2009.

Fischer, Konrad, and Rolf Wederer, eds. *Konzeption/Conception*. Exh. cat. Cologne: Westdeutscher Verlage; Stadtische Museum, 1969.

Fogle, Douglas. *The Last Picture Show: Artists Using Photography, 1960–1982.* Exh. cat. Minneapolis: Walker Art Center, 2003.

Gintz, Claude, ed. *L'art conceptuel, une perspective*. Exh. cat. Paris: Musée d'Art Moderne de la Ville de Paris, 1990.

Glusberg, Jorge, ed. *Arte de sistemas*. Exh. cat. Buenos Aires: Museo de Arte Moderno, Centro de Arte y Comunicación, 1971.

Godfrey, Tony. *Conceptual Art.* Art & Ideas series. London: Phaidon, 1998.

Goldstein, Ann, and Anne Rorimer, eds. *Reconsidering the Object of Art, 1965–1975.* Exh. cat. Los Angeles: The Museum of Contemporary Art; Cambridge, Mass.: The MIT Press, 1995.

Harrison, Charles. "Notes Toward Art Work." *Studio International*, vol. 179, no. 919 (February 1970), pp. 42–43.

——, ed. *Idea Structures*. Exh. cat. London: Borough of Camden [Camden Arts Center], 1970.

——. *Essays on Art and Language*. Cambridge, Mass.: The MIT Press, 1991.

Honnef, Klaus. *Concept Art*. Cologne: Phaidon, 1971.

Karshan, Donald, ed. *Conceptual Art and Conceptual Aspects.* Exh. cat. New York: New York Cultural Center, 1970.

Katzenstein, Inès, and Andrea Giunta, eds. *Listen Here Now!: Argentine Art of the 1960s; Writings on the Avant-Garde*. New York: The Museum of Modern Art, 2004.

Kelly, Mary. "Re-viewing Modernist Criticism." *Screen,* vol. 22, no. 3 (1981), pp. 41–52.

Kosuth, Joseph. "Art After Philosophy." *Studio International*, vol. 178, no. 915 (October 1969), pp. 134–37; no. 916 (November 1969), pp. 160–61; no. 917 (December 1969), pp. 212–13.

——, ed. *Non-Anthropomorphic Art by Four Young Artists: Joseph Kosuth, Christine Kozlov, Michael Rinaldi, Ernest Rossi*. Exh. cat. New York: Lannis Gallery, 1967.

Kosuth, Joseph, and Christine Kozlov. "Ad Reinhardt: Evolution into Darkness; The Art of an Informal Formalist—Negativity, Purity and the Clearness of Ambiguity." Unpublished paper, School of Visual Arts, New York, May 1966.

Kotz, Liz. *Words to Be Looked At: Language in 1960s Art*. Cambridge, Mass.: The MIT Press, 2007.

Lamelas, David. *Publication*. London: Nigel Greenwood, 1970.

LeWitt, Sol. "Paragraphs on Conceptual Art." *Artforum*, vol. 5, no. 10 (Summer 1967), pp. 79–84.

Maenz, Paul, ed. *19:45–21:55, 1967*. Exh. cat. Frankfurt: Paul Maenz, 1967.

McShine, Kynaston L., ed. *Information*. Exh. cat. New York: The Museum of Modern Art, 1970.

Meyer, Ursula. "De-Objectification of the Object." *Arts Magazine*, vol. 43, no. 8 (Summer 1969), pp. 20–22.

——— . *Conceptual Art*. New York: E. P. Dutton, 1972.

Millet, Catherine. “L’art conceptuel.” *VH 101: revue trimestrielle*, no. 3 (Fall 1970), pp. 1–53.

Molesworth, Helen, ed. *Work Ethic.* Exh. cat. Baltimore: The Baltimore Museum of Art; University Park, Pa.: Pennsylvania State University Press, 2003.

Morgan, Robert C. “The Situation of Conceptual Art: The January Show and After.” *Arts Magazine,* vol. 63, no. 6 (February 1989), pp. 40–43.

——— . *Conceptual Art: An American Perspective*. Jefferson, N.C.: McFarland & Co., 1994.

Morris, Robert. “Notes on Sculpture, Part IV: Beyond Object.” *Artforum*, vol. 7, no. 8 (April 1969), pp. 50–54.

Moseley, Catherine, ed. *Conception: Conceptual Documents, 1968 to 1972*. Exh. cat. Norwich: Norwich Gallery, Norwich School of Art and Design, 2001.

Moure, Gloria, ed. *Behind the Facts: Interfunktionen 1968–1975*. Exh. cat. Barcelona: Poligrafa, 2004.

Newman, Michael, and Jon Bird, eds. *Rewriting Conceptual Art*. Critical Views series. London: Reaktion Books, 1999.

Norvell, Patricia, and Alexander Alberro, eds. *Recording Conceptual Art: Early Interviews with Barry, Huebler, Kaltenbach, LeWitt, Morris, Oppenheim, Siegelaub, Smithson, Weiner*. Berkeley: University of California Press, 2001.

Obrist, Hans Ulrich. *A Brief History of Curating*. Zurich: JRP/Ringier, 2008.

Osborne, Peter, ed. *Conceptual Art*. London: Phaidon, 2002.

Phillpot, Clive, and Andrea Tarisia, eds. *Live in Your Head: Concept and Experiment in Britain, 1965–75*. Exh. cat. London: Whitechapel Art Gallery, 2000.

Rattemeyer, Christian, ed. *Exhibiting the New Art: “Op Losse Schroeven” and “When Attitudes Become Form,” 1969*. London: Afterall Books, 2010.

Richard, Sophie. *Unconcealed: The International Network of Conceptual Artists, 1967–1977: Dealers, Exhibitions and Public Collections*. London: Ridinghouse, 2009.

Roberts, John, ed. *The Impossible Document: Photography and Conceptual Art in Britain, 1966–1976.* London: Cameraworks, 1997.

——— . *The Intangibilities of Form: Skill and Deskilling in Art After the Readymade*. London and New York: Verso, 2007.

Rorimer, Anne. *New Art of the 60s and 70s: Redefining Reality*. New York: Thames & Hudson, 2001.

Rose, Barbara. “The Value of Didactic Art.” *Artforum*, vol. 5, no. 8 (April 1967), pp. 32–36.

Rosenberg, Harold. *The De-definition of Art: Action Art to Pop to Earthworks*. New York: Horizon Press, 1973.

“Round Table: The Present Conditions of Art Criticism” (George Baker, Rosalind Krauss, Benjamin H. D. Buchloh, Andrea Fraser, David Joselit, James Meyer, Robert Storr, Hal Foster, John Miller, Helen Molesworth). *October*, no. 100 (Spring 2002), pp. 200–28.

Schimmel, Paul, ed. *Out of Actions: Between Performance and the Object, 1949–1979.* Los Angeles: The Museum of Contemporary Art; New York: Thames & Hudson, 1998.

Schmidt Burkhardt, Astrid, ed. *Maciunas’ Learning Machines: From Art History to a Chronology of Fluxus*. Detroit: The Gilbert and Silverman Fluxus Collection; Berlin: Vice Versa Verlag, 2003.

Shirey, David L. “Impossible Art—What Is It?” *Art in America*, vol. 57, no. 3 (May–June 1969), pp. 32–47.

Siegelaub, Seth, ed. *January 5–31, 1969*. Exh. cat. New York: Seth Siegelaub, 1969.

——. *July–August–September 1969*. Exh. cat. New York: Seth Siegelaub, 1969.

——. "July–August." *Studio International*, vol. 180, no. 924 (July–August 1970), pp. 1–48.

——. *18 Paris IV. 70.* Exh. cat. Paris: Seth Siegelaub, 1970.

Siegelaub, Seth, and John W. Wendler, eds. *Xerox Book: Carl Andre, Robert Barry, Douglas Huebler, Joseph Kosuth, Sol LeWitt, Robert Morris, Lawrence Weiner*. Exh. cat. New York: Seth Siegelaub, John W. Wendler, 1968.

Sixth Guggenheim International Exhibition. Exh. cat. New York: Solomon R. Guggenheim Museum, 1970.

Sperlinger, Mike, ed. *Afterthoughts: New Writings on Conceptual Art.* [London]: Rachmaninoff's, [2005].

Steinberg, Leo. *Other Criteria: Confrontations with Twentieth-Century Art*. New York: Oxford University Press, 1972.

Szeemann, Harald, ed. *Live in Your Head: When Attitudes Become Form; Works, Concepts, Processes, Situations, Information*. Exh. cat. Bern: Kunsthalle Bern, 1969.

Tacha, Athena Spear, ed. *Art in the Mind.* Exh. cat. Oberlin, Ohio: Allen Art Museum, Oberlin College, 1971.

Vanderlip, Diane, ed. *Recorded Activities*. Philadelphia: Moore College of Art, 1970.

Wevers, Ursula, Barbara Hess, and Ulrike Groos, eds. *Ready to Shoot: Fernsehgalerie Gerry Schum*. Exh. cat. Düsseldorf: Kunsthalle Düsseldorf, 2003.

By Lucy R. Lippard

Pop Art. With contributions by Lawrence Alloway, Nancy Marmer, and Nicolas Calas. New York: Praeger Publishers, c. 1966.

Eccentric Abstraction: Alice Adams, Louise Bourgeois, Eva Hesse, Gary Kuehn, Bruce Nauman, Don Potts, Keith Sonnier, Frank Lincoln Viner. Exh. brochure. New York: Fischbach Gallery, 1966.

"Eccentric Abstraction." *Art International*, vol. 10, no. 9 (November 1966), pp. 28, 34–40.

"Sol LeWitt: Non-Visual Structures." *Artforum*, vol. 5, no. 8 (April 1967), pp. 42–46.

With John Chandler. "Visible Art and the Invisible World." *Art International*, vol. 11, no. 5 (May 1967), pp. 27–30.

With John Chandler. "The Dematerialization of Art." *Art International*, vol. 12, no. 2 (February 1968), pp. 31–36.

Ed., "Time: A Panel Discussion." *Art International,* vol. 13, no. 9 (November 1969), pp. 20–23.

Ed., *557,087: An Exhibition*. Exh. cat. Seattle: The Contemporary Art Council of the Seattle Art Museum, 1969.

"Art within the Arctic Circle." *The Hudson Review*, vol. 22, no. 4 (Winter 1969–1970), pp. 665–74.

"Groups." *Studio International,* vol. 179, no. 920 (March 1970), pp. 93–100.

"The Art Workers' Coalition: Not a History." *Studio International*, vol. 180, no. 927 (November 1970), pp. 171–74.

Ed., *955,000: An Exhibition*. Exh. cat. Vancouver: Vancouver Art Gallery, 1970.

"Absentee Information and or Criticism." In Kynaston L. McShine, ed., *Information*. Exh. cat. New York: The Museum of Modern Art, 1970.

Ed., *2,972,453*. Exh. cat. Buenos Aires: Centro de Arte y Comunicación, 1970.

Ed., *Surrealists on Art*. Englewood Cliffs, N.J.: Prentice-Hall, 1970.

Ed., *Twenty-Six Contemporary Women Artists*. Exh. cat. Ridgefield, Conn.: The Aldrich Museum of Contemporary Art, [1971].

Changing: Essays in Art Criticism. New York: E. P. Dutton, 1971.

Ed., *Dadas on Art*. Englewood Cliffs, N.J.: Prentice-Hall, 1971.

"Douglas Huebler: Everything About Everything." *Art News*, vol. 71, no. 8 (December 1972), pp. 29–32.

Grids grids grids grids grids grids grids grids. Exh. cat. Philadelphia: Institute of Contemporary Art, University of Pennsylvania, 1972.

"Deep in Numbers." *Artforum*, vol. 12, no. 1 (October 1973), pp. 35–39.

Six Years: The dematerialization of the art object from 1966 to 1972: a cross-reference book of information on some esthetic boundaries: consisting of a bibliography into which are inserted a fragmented text, art works, documents, interviews, and symposia, arranged chronologically and focused on so-called conceptual or information or idea art with mentions of such vaguely designated areas as minimal, anti-form, systems, earth, or process art, occurring now in the Americas, Europe, England, Australia, and Asia (with occasional political overtones), edited and annotated by Lucy R. Lippard. New York and London: Praeger Publishers, 1973. Reprinted, with a new introduction, Berkeley and Los Angeles: University of California Press, 1997.

Ed., *c. 7,500.* Exh. cat. Valencia, Calif.: California Institute of the Arts, 1973.

"Projecting a Feminist Criticism." *Art Journal,* vol. 35, no. 4 (Summer 1976), pp. 337–39.

From the Center: Feminist Essays on Women's Art. New York: E. P. Dutton, 1976.

Eva Hesse. Exh. cat. New York: New York University Press, 1976.

Ed., *Strata: Nancy Graves, Eva Hesse, Michelle Stuart, Jackie Winsor*. Exh. cat. Vancouver: Vancouver Art Gallery, 1977.

I See/You Mean. Los Angeles: Chrysalis Books, 1979.

With Charles Simonds. *Cracking*. Cologne: Buchhandlung Walther König, 1979.

Ad Reinhardt. New York: Harry N. Abrams, 1981.

Overlay: Contemporary Art and the Art of Prehistory. New York: Pantheon Books, 1983.

Get the Message? A Decade of Art for Social Change. New York: E. P. Dutton, 1984.

Mixed Blessings: New Art in a Multicultural America. New York: Pantheon Books, c. 1990.

Ed., *A Different War: Vietnam in Art*. Bellingham, Wash.: Whatcom Museum of History and Art; Seattle: Real Comet Press, 1990.

"Escape Attempts." In Ann Goldstein and Anne Rorimer, eds., *Reconsidering the Object of Art, 1965–1975*. Exh. cat. Los Angeles: The Museum of Contemporary Art; Cambridge, Mass.: The MIT Press, 1995. Also published in the reprint edition of *Six Years*. Berkeley and Los Angeles: University of California Press, 1997.

The Pink Glass Swan: Selected Essays on Feminist Art. New York: New Press, 1995.

The Lure of the Local: Senses of Place in a Multicentered Society. New York: New Press, 1997.

Florence Pierce: In Touch with Light. Sante Fe: Smith Book Fund, 1998.

On the Beaten Track: Tourism, Art, and Place. New York: New Press, 1999.

"Biting the Hand: Artists and Museums in New York since 1969." In Julie Ault, ed., *Alternative New York, 1965–1985*. Minneapolis: University of Minnesota Press, 2002.

Down Country: The Tano of the Galisteo Basin, 1250–1782. Photographs by Edward Rannay. Santa Fe: Museum of New Mexico Press, 2010.

With Iris Müller-Westerman and Jo Applin. *Lee Lozano*. Ostfildern, Germany: Hatje Cantz, 2010.

On Lucy R. Lippard and Her Work

Antin, David. “Another Category: ‘Eccentric Abstraction.’” *Artforum,* vol. 5, no. 3 (November 1966), pp. 56–57.

Bochner, Mel. “In the Galleries.” *Arts Magazine,* vol. 41, no. 1 (November 1966), pp. 57–58.

——. “Six Years: The Dematerialization of the Art Object from 1966 to 1972.” *Artforum*, vol. 11, no. 10 (June 1973); republished in Mel Bochner, *Solar System and Rest Rooms: Writings and Interviews, 1965–2007*. Cambridge, Mass.: The MIT Press, 2008.

Cash, Stephanie. “The Art Criticism and Politics of Lucy Lippard.” *Art Criticism*, vol. 9, no. 1 (1999), pp. 32–40.

Frankel, David, ed. *Sniper's Nest: Art That Has Lived with Lucy Lippard*. Exh. cat. Annandale-on-Hudson, N.Y.: Center for Curatorial Studies, Bard College, 1996.

Gillick, Liam. “Twenty-five Years: The Rematerialization of the Art World.” *Art Monthly*, no. 223 (February 1999), pp. 43–44.

Kauffman, John A. “Lucy Lippard: Becoming Feminist.” Doctoral dissertation, City University of New York, 1998.

Kramer, Hilton. “And Now ‘Eccentric Abstraction’: It's Art, But Does It Matter?; New Materials.” *New York Times,* September 25, 1966, p. 135.

Lafuente, Pablo, ed. *From Conceptualism to Feminism: Lucy Lippard's Numbers Shows, 1969–74*. London: Afterall Books, forthcoming in 2012.

Lauritis, Beth Anne. “Lucy Lippard and the Provisional Exhibition: Intersections of Conceptual Art and Feminism, 1970–1980.” Doctoral dissertation, University of California, Los Angeles, 2009.

Phillpot, Clive. “Six Years: The Dematerialization of the Art Object from 1966 to 1972 (…).” *Leonardo,* vol. 8, no. 3 (Summer 1975), p. 261.

Plagens, Peter. “557,087.” *Artforum*, vol. 8, no. 3 (November 1969), pp. 64–67.